Chris Masters PSM is a powerful force in Australian journalism. In 1985, he won Australia's most prestigious award in journalism, the Gold Walkley, for his *Four Corners* report on the sinking of the *Rainbow Warrior*. His reports 'The Big League' and 'The Moonlight State' both led to royal commissions that helped transform the nation. The winner of several other Walkley and Logie awards for his journalism over five decades, he is known for his fearless pursuit of the truth. Masters spent extended periods embedded with Australian forces, including special forces, during Australia's longest war in Afghanistan, and he is respected for the depth of his knowledge of the Australian Army. He is the author of the bestselling *Jonestown*, *Uncommon Soldier* and *No Front Line*.

What the reviewers said about Chris Ma
special forces at war in Afghanistan

'In this remarkable book about the intense combat environment experienced by our soldiers in Afghanistan, Chris Masters captures the highs, the lows, the courage and the sacrifice of Australian warriors and their loved ones in our longest war.'—**Air Chief Marshal Sir Angus Houston AK, AFC (Ret'd)**

'This book tells a story that many of us had not told our loved ones and will no doubt help to articulate and heal all those who sacrificed much in and out of uniform.' —**Commando Warrant Officer**

'I was impressed by [*No Front Line*'s] detail, quality and objectivity ... I wanted to reassure you that most Regiment members understand this and are speaking positively about the book.'—**Former SASR Patrol Sergeant**

'Thank you, Chris Masters, for your dedication and attention to detail in documenting this most comprehensive story of Australian special forces in Afghanistan.'—**Former Commando Corporal**

‘I have always felt that 90 per cent of the blokes in the unit would be supportive of the book . . .’—**SASR Troop Sergeant**

‘Brilliant. There’s seriously no one else in Australia with the knowledge that Chris Masters has in relation to Australian Special Forces in Afghanistan. Lots of lessons learned and examples of heroism that if not for Chris Masters would be lost forever.’—**Former Commando Major**

‘Thanks for your professionalism and intellectual honesty. It is much needed in this space.’—**Former SASR Trooper**

‘I think you captured the feelings of many of us at the end of that deployment perfectly.’—**Former Special Forces Major**

FLAWED HERO

TRUTH, LIES AND WAR CRIMES

CHRIS MASTERS

ALLEN&UNWIN
SYDNEY • MELBOURNE • AUCKLAND • LONDON

First published in 2023

Allen & Unwin
Cammeraygal Country
83 Alexander Street
Crows Nest NSW 2065
Australia
Phone: (61 2) 8425 0100
Email: info@allenandunwin.com
Web: www.allenandunwin.com

Allen & Unwin acknowledges the Traditional Owners of the Country on which we live and work. We pay our respects to all Aboriginal and Torres Strait Islander Elders, past and present.

NATIONAL LIBRARY OF AUSTRALIA

A catalogue record for this book is available from the National Library of Australia

ISBN 978 1 76106 981 9

Map by Guy Holt
Set in 10.5/16 pt Minion Pro by Midland Typesetters, Australia
Printed and bound in Australia by the Opus Group

10 9 8 7 6 5 4 3 2 1

MIX
Paper | Supporting responsible forestry
FSC www.fsc.org
FSC® C001695

The paper in this book is FSC® certified. FSC® promotes environmentally responsible, socially beneficial and economically viable management of the world's forests.

To my grandchildren

Truth is not what you want it to be; it is what it is.
And you must bend to its power or live a lie.

Warrior philosopher Miyamoto Musashi

CONTENTS

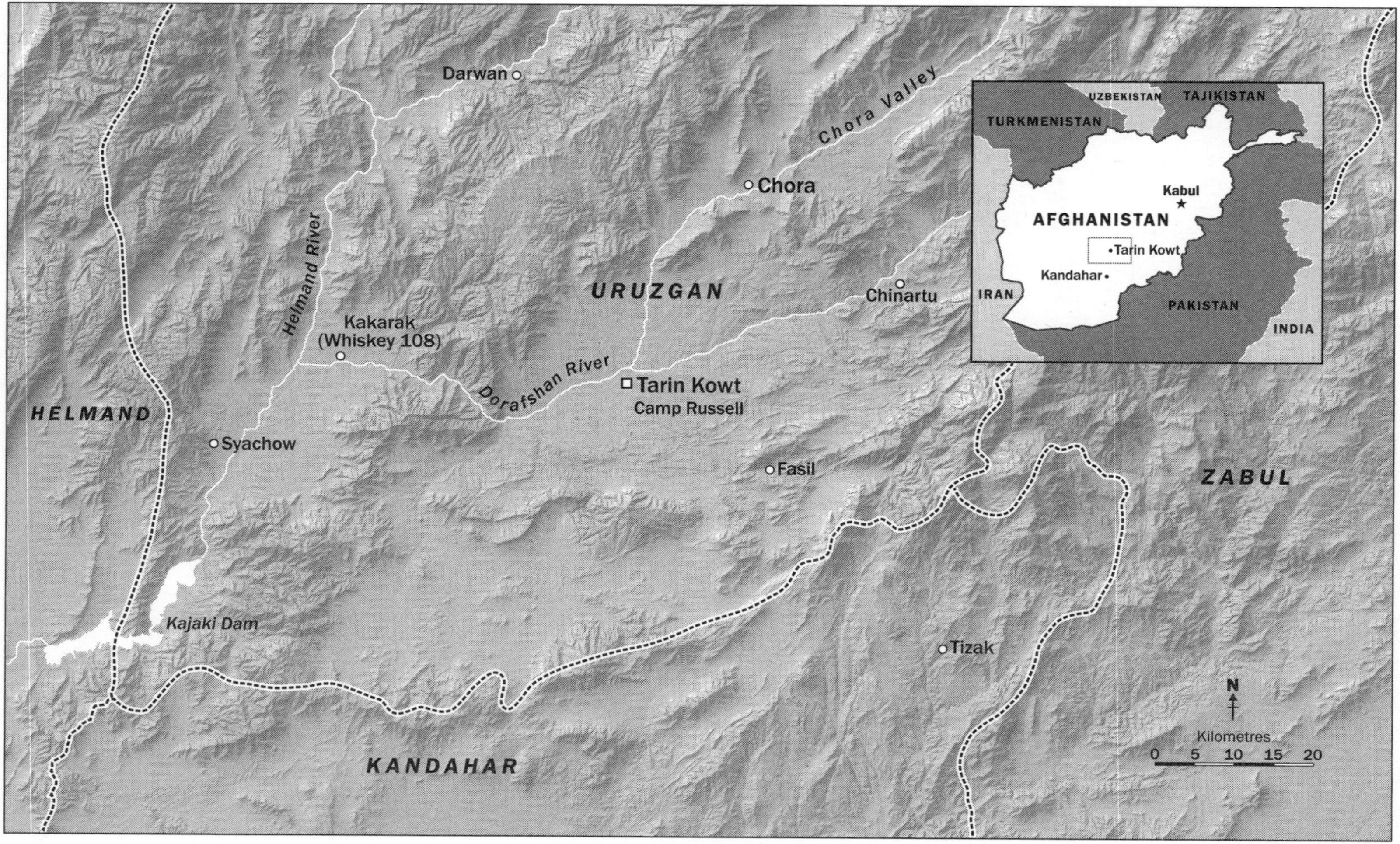
Darwan
Chora Valley
Chora
Helmand River
URUZGAN
Chinartu
Kakarak
(Whiskey 108)
Dorafshan River
Tarin Kowt
Camp Russell
HELMAND
Syachow
Fasil
ZABUL
Kajaki Dam
Tizak
KANDAHAR
N
Kilometres
0 5 10 15 20
UZBEKISTAN
TAJIKISTAN
TURKMENISTAN
Kabul
AFGHANISTAN
Tarin Kowt
Kandahar
IRAN
PAKISTAN
INDIA

PSEUDONYMS

Australian Special Forces personnel have protected identity status. As such, the Federal Court identified witnesses by numerals, Persons 1 to 100 plus. In addition, a civilian witness, via a suppression order, came to be identified as Person 17. In this manuscript, to help readers follow the story and add a hint of personality, **the numbered soldiers have been given pseudonyms, even in court transcripts and other quoted materials**. The pseudonyms do not represent a precise definition of the witness.

The following is a glossary of brief descriptions of each of the witnesses who feature, sometimes extensively, sometimes in brief.

Person 8 Not called. Fought at Tizak with Roberts-Smith in 2010.

Person 17 Called by the respondents. She alleged she was struck by Roberts-Smith when they were in an extra-marital relationship in 2017–18.

Person 23 Was to be called by the applicant but did not give evidence. He was the US radio operator for the Koran Ghar mission in 2006.

Person 33 Was to be called by the applicant but did not give evidence. He was the British patrol commander at Koran Ghar in 2006.

Person 55 Not called. He was a key figure in the Chora Valley 'blue-on-blue' incident in 2012.

Person 57 Not called. He was wounded by a stray bullet when a dog was shot by an Afghan partner force member in 2012.

The 2IC **Person 40.** Called by the respondents. A witness at Whiskey 108.

The Analyst **Person 69.** Called by the respondents, he deployed with Roberts-Smith for Rotation III in 2006.

The Bodyguard **Person 38.** Called by the applicant, he was a witness at Whiskey 108.

The Captain **Person 81.** Called by the applicant, he was the ground force commander at Whiskey 108 in 2009.

The Corporal **Person 32.** Called by the applicant, he fought with Roberts-Smith at Tizak in 2010 and was at Darwan in 2012. He was another witness to contend The Lieutenant had been removed.

The Cyclist **Person 41.** Called by the respondents, he gave evidence of witnessing two alleged executions at Whiskey 108.

The Dog Handler **Person 9.** Was to be called by the applicant but did not give evidence. He played the role of the alleged victim at the pre-deployment mock-execution training exercise at Lancelin in 2012.

The Driver **Person 42.** Called by the respondents, he was a witness at Whiskey 108.

The Freefaller **Person 29.** Called by the applicant, he was at Whiskey 108 in 2009 and fought at Tizak in 2010.

The Gunner **Person 24.** Called by the respondents, he allegedly witnessed an execution at Whiskey 108 in 2009.

The Gunsmith **Person 4.** Called by the respondents, he was the alleged 'blooded' rookie at Whiskey 108 in 2009 and fought alongside Roberts-Smith at Tizak in 2010. Also a witness at Darwan in 2012.

The Hunter **Person 35.** Called by the applicant, he was at Whiskey 108 in 2009, at Tizak in 2010 and at Darwan in 2012. He was another to allege The Lieutenant had been removed.

The Lieutenant **Person 12.** Not called. He was a leader of the Afghan partner forces. He was present for the alleged execution of a detainee at Chinartu in 2012. However, this was contentious given a case proposed by the applicant that he was earlier removed from operations following an incident in which a dog was shot.

The Mechanic Person 19. Called by the respondents. He witnessed the alleged pre-deployment mock-execution as a new member of Roberts-Smith's patrol in 2012.

The Medic Person 16. Called by the respondents, he gave evidence of Roberts-Smith confessing to shooting a detainee at Fasil in 2012.

The Mentor Person 31. Called by the respondents, he was a witness at Lancelin in 2012 and deployed for the subsequent Rotation XVIII.

The Peacekeeper Person 21. Called by the respondents. After The Redhead was removed from Roberts-Smith's patrol in 2006, he became that junior soldier's patrol commander.

The Reader Person 43. Called by the respondents, he was a witness at Whiskey 108 and fought at Tizak in 2010.

The Redhead Person 1. Called by the respondents, he fought at Koran Ghar with Roberts-Smith in 2006 and was allegedly subjected thereafter to a campaign of bullying.

The Replacement Person 56. Called by the respondents, he was at Darwan in 2012.

The Rifleman Person 22. Called by the applicant, he was a member of Roberts-Smith's patrol at Chora in 2012.

The Ring-In Person 66. Called by the respondents, he was at Syachow in 2012.

The RSM Person 100. Called by the applicant, he officiated in two meetings at Campbell Barracks in 2013 when complaints were made about Roberts-Smith.

The Scientist Person 27. Called by the applicant, he was at Whiskey 108 in 2009 and deployed with Roberts-Smith in 2012. He gave conflicted evidence that The Lieutenant was removed after the dog-shooting incident.

The Scot Person 5. Called by the applicant, he was Roberts-Smith's patrol commander at Whiskey 108 in 2009 and at Tizak in 2010.

The Scout Person 14. Called by the respondents, he gave evidence of witnessing an execution at Whiskey 108 in 2009 and at Chinartu in 2012.

The Sergeant **Person 7.** Called by the respondents, he fought at Tizak in 2010 and was Roberts-Smith's troop sergeant for Rotation XVIII in 2012.

The Sig **Person 2.** Called by the respondents, he fought at Koran Ghar with Roberts-Smith in 2006.

The Sniper **Person 11.** Called by the applicant, he fought with Roberts-Smith on Rotation XVIII in 2012. He was accused of executing Ali Jan, who had been allegedly kicked off a cliff by Roberts-Smith.

The Specialist **Person 36.** Called by the applicant, he deployed with Roberts-Smith for Rotation III in 2006.

The SSE **Person 18.** Called by the respondents, he was at Whiskey 108 in 2009 and fought with Roberts-Smith at Tizak in 2010. In 2018, he received a threatening letter, allegedly authored by Roberts-Smith.

The Terp **Person 13.** Not called. He was an interpreter present at Chinartu and Darwan in 2012.

The Trooper **Person 10.** Called by the respondents, he was allegedly instructed to shoot the 'prisoner' at the Lancelin exercise in 2012. Later, after being punched by Roberts-Smith, he was removed from Roberts-Smith's patrol and soon after left the Army.

The Veteran **Person 6.** Not called. Fought at Whiskey 108 in 2009 and was deployed with Roberts-Smith on Rotation XVIII in 2012.

The XO **Person 39.** Called by the applicant, he deployed with Roberts-Smith in 2012 and was one of the witnesses to contend The Lieutenant had been removed.

ABBREVIATIONS AND ACRONYMS

1RAR	1st Battalion of the Royal Australian Regiment
2IC	second-in-command
3RAR	3rd Battalion of the Royal Australian Regiment
ACLEI	Australian Commission for Law Enforcement Integrity
ACM	anti-Coalition militia
ADF	Australian Defence Force
ANA	Afghan National Army
AWM	Australian War Memorial
CDF	Chief of the Defence Force
CDS	Commendation for Distinguished Service
COI	compound of interest
EKIA	enemy killed in action
FAM	fighting-age male
HAZ	high-activity zone
IGADF	Inspector-General of the Australian Defence Force
ISR	intelligence surveillance reconnaissance (drone)
JTAC	joint terminal attack controller
LUP	lying-up position
MBITR	multiband inter/intra team radio
MNBTK	Multi-National Base Tarin Kowt
MUC	Meritorious Unit Citation

NCO	non-commissioned officer
NDS	National Directorate of Security (Afghanistan), aka Wakunish
NPO	non-publication order
NTPs	notices to produce
OP	observation post
OpSums	operational summaries
PAP(s)	potentially affected person(s) notice
PTSD	post-traumatic stress disorder
PUC	person under control
RoE	rules of engagement
RPG	rocket-propelled grenade
RSM	regimental sergeant major
RV	rendezvous
SAS or SASR	Special Air Service Regiment
SBS	Special Boat Service
SITREP	situation report
SOCAUST	Special Operations Commander Australia
SOCOMD	Special Operations Command
SOP	standard operating procedure
SSE	sensitive site exploitation
TQ	tactical questioning
VC	Victoria Cross
VRI	very reliable intelligence

FLAWED HERO

A RUMOUR OF WAR CRIMES

The common representation of investigative journalists at work involves sneaky meetings with Deep Throats in underground car parks. People telling us stuff, which is then converted into breathless revelations.

It is sometimes like that. But more often interactions are abstract, and the discovery process is internal. Lots of engagement with truth-tellers and liars, and lots of reading between the lines. The investigative journalist's beat is quicksand and shadowland.

Mostly it is about figuring something out. And that is how this one went.

It was 11 September 2011, the tenth anniversary of the terrorist attacks in the United States that triggered Australia's longest war. I was finding my feet in the Australian Special Forces compound, Camp Russell, having arrived a few days earlier. It was my third embed with Australian soldiers in Afghanistan.

To the soldiers, my presence was unthinkable—that a journalist would have the code to the keypad entry at their uber-secret enclave. At many stages up to this point, it was unthinkable even to me. But there I was: the first and, as it happens, the last journalist to be granted access.

The simple explanation is trust.

My reporting over the preceding decade had been supportive of the soldiers and their mission. I never thought we were on the wrong side in Afghanistan. I believed that, back at home, our country's humanitarian objectives and complex challenges were poorly understood. I admired the selfless bravery of Australian soldiers stepping out, with their fingers off the trigger and yet at great risk of being blown to bits, so as to provide a protective screen for a blighted people.

I had seen Australians at war (or, more precisely, engaged in peace-keeping missions) many times before. In Timor, a villager had enthused to me his heartfelt astonishment that soldiers were there to shield them from danger. 'We hide our daughters when men in uniform appear,' he said. 'We think of them as bandits.'

In Rwanda, the Australian Special Air Service Regiment (SASR, but commonly known as the SAS) had faced off against genocidal mobs, risking their lives to dampen rather than inflame violence. In Somalia, young soldiers of the 1st Battalion of the Royal Australian Regiment (1RAR) had patrolled aid posts and raced in to fight thugs who were bashing starving women and children out of the way so they could steal and resell lifesaving provisions.

For me, Australia's reputation for civilised soldiering, for toughness and fairness, held up. I was inspired—somewhat romantically, I admit—by a belief that Australian major general John Cantwell had expressed in an interview with me: 'There is something about the Australian character that is suited to the things soldiers are asked to do.'[1]

The soldiers saw my belief in what they were doing. So, to some degree, I was trusted. Of course, I would remind them that I would report bad behaviour if I ever saw it—but nobody took much notice of that, because nobody expected it to occur, especially in front of a camera.

The goodwill I enjoyed among the soldiers was probably equal in strength to the misgivings about me within the ranks of my fellow journalists. There were plenty in the news business who were convinced I'd been 'captured' by the Australian Army. Some saw me as a flake, a flunky—Major Masters of Defence Public Relations. The great Dr Johnson believed that 'every man thinks meanly of himself for not having been a soldier'; perhaps I was an example.

During my embed, I saw only a little of what would later initiate some searching questions. It was mainly that quick glimpse of hatred in the eyes of Afghans before they were blindfolded and brought back for questioning. Yes, I was admiring, but not to the degree of suspending scepticism, a critical attribute in the armoury of any journalist.

What really counted was that the soldiers' trust in me led some of them to share their concerns—not all at once, but over time. The irony is unmissable. While plenty of reporters had set out to uncover war crimes, the first team to do so was not so narrowly focused.

This is another feature of investigative journalism. Revelation rarely comes in a blinding flash. It is usually a graduated light of truth that steers you along an unanticipated path.

When my first book covering Australian operations in Afghanistan, *Uncommon Soldier*, was published in 2012, it included references to the famous soldier Ben Roberts-Smith. At the time I checked my text with him and he asked for some amendments. The action in 2006 that had earned him a Medal for Gallantry I described in my book as follows:

> On 2 June, Ben Roberts-Smith was forced to fight for his life when his observation post came under attack from two flanks. He split and manoeuvred from his team, catching sixteen approaching enemy in the open. Roberts-Smith took them on with his sniper rifle, attracting accurate return fire but holding the enemy off for the forty minutes it took for air support to arrive.[2]

What I wrote fell short of a more complete truth.

I had not depicted it as a war crime, but this incident atop a barren mountain range in southern Afghanistan would trigger the largest war crimes inquiry in Australian history.

CHAPTER 1

2 JUNE 2006

The observation post (OP) folded them seamlessly into the dry dirt. Two Australian soldiers were concealed behind rocks, wearing desert camouflage and bush hats. The mission was classic SAS.

Part of a six-man patrol, they were on a mountain called Koran Ghar, watching the Chora Valley below and reporting enemy movements. They were to avoid 'going loud' and maintain concealment. The troopers were well trained; they could endure this for days. Piss in a bottle, chew dry rations, and concentrate, concentrate, concentrate.

This was their second day. Their muscles were still strained from lugging 70-kilogram packs up the steep slope in what was a ten-hour haul the night they arrived. Many years later, throughout the marathon defamation court battle, they would be anonymised as Person 1 and Person 2. We will refer to them as The Redhead and The Sig. Both were new to the regiment, the latter a qualified signaller, specialising in radio communications.

Behind them, occupying a lying-up position (LUP), or defensive fighting post, were the four other members of the patrol: a British sergeant from the Special Boat Service (SBS), an American special forces radio operator (specialising in providing aerial combat support), and Australian SAS members Sergeant Matthew Locke and Lance Corporal Ben Roberts-Smith, the latter close friends.

Just after 0900 hours, through binoculars The Sig saw a young Afghan male approaching. A laser range finder placed him at 75 to 80 metres away. Whispered into the radio: 'All call signs, one male, front of the OP, moving from right to left.'

The Afghan disappeared behind rocks, but within a minute he was sighted again, this time carrying a small bag. 'All call signs, one male reappeared, now moving from left to right away from the OP.'

In the acronym-rich military vocabulary, the Afghan was clocked as a FAM (fighting-age male) and a likely spotter for the ACM (anti-Coalition militia, as the Taliban were described at that time).

After hearing the second call, Sergeant Locke and Lance Corporal Roberts-Smith moved to the OP. Locke queried why the spotter had not been engaged. The soldiers replied that they understood they were there to observe and not get into a gunfight. They had noted no 'dinner-plate eyes', the look of shock on the Afghan's face that would have revealed to them that they had been detected.

The Sig would later further explain: 'I did not join the regiment to shoot an unarmed teenager in the back.' But Locke and Roberts-Smith were of another view. They took off after the Afghan and an echo of rifle fire was heard. According to Roberts-Smith, 'Matt shot him.'

Roberts-Smith and Locke would later claim that one of their bullet strikes had triggered smoke from a device hidden in the Afghan's chest webbing. But The Redhead and The Sig saw no webbing or smoke; nor, for that matter, had they sighted a weapon. Yet the patrol transmitted a situation report (SITREP) describing an 'armed ACM with AK variant weapon, aggressively patrolling, both hands on weapon, ready to fire'.

Taliban forces later began to swarm the mountain, with the six Coalition men soon fighting for their lives. The Redhead aimed his Minimi machine gun in the direction of the approaching Taliban and fired a short burst. But his weapon quickly jammed. The Sig moved forward to support Roberts-Smith. *Click!* His weapon also failed.

Roberts-Smith, with an identical SR-25 sniper rifle, fired when he glimpsed fleeting targets in front of him, after Sergeant Locke had slung his M4 assault rifle and climbed a rock face to attack a fighter trying to outflank them. Calm and assured, he killed the man after a 'persistent one on one fight', according to a later patrol report.

The Taliban continued to advance. The Sig rectified his stoppage and moved to support Roberts-Smith. The Redhead, still struggling with his Minimi machine gun, searched for targets. Recognising an imminent risk of being overrun, the patrol's American radio operator called for air support.

A shriek of jet engines and the ripping-canvas sound of 30mm chain gun cannon fire announced that air support had arrived. The ground erupted, rock splinters stung, dust swirled. Through strained eyes, the patrol spotted two A-10 Warthogs streaking past, flying below and away.

More terrifying hours followed. Finally, under the cover of darkness, the patrol was extracted to safety.

That was pretty much when the internal war started. For the next decade and beyond, bitterness and recrimination dogged the Koran Ghar mission.

The failure of The Redhead's weapon was all the proof needed to drum him out of the patrol. The young trooper, raw by his own admission, had failed to pack gun oil. Roberts-Smith complained that the reduced firepower almost got them killed.

He saw The Sig as similarly to blame. His weapon failure had put him out of action for 'a crucial twenty minutes'. The Sig acknowledged having to 'strip a bolt and put it back', but he contended this was done 'within a minute', after which he was able to join Roberts-Smith in holding off the Taliban.

But even before the haul up the hill to the OP, there had been trouble. Roberts-Smith and Locke had not taken to The Redhead, who was new to the regiment. He came from the derided 'choco' ranks—the 'chocolate soldier' reservists. Short of stature, from Sydney's North Shore, no tattoos, didn't talk shit. He later told of being bullied from the day he joined the SASR; his face had been slammed against the steering wheel during vehicle training.

The SAS's sabre squadron consists of land, air and water operators, depending on their insertion skills—land (vehicles), air (parachute) or water (diving). The last of these, the 'wateries', are considered, at least by the wateries themselves, as an elite within an elite. Like their US counterparts, the Navy SEALs, their unquestionable ability can be tinged with arrogance. The Redhead's qualification as a watery may have provoked some of this hostility.

On the patrol's return to base, the bullying increased. Roberts-Smith threatened to shoot The Redhead in the back of the head. The animosity and vilification was unceasing. Already a polarising figure, Big Ben's treatment of the little redhead further divided SAS ranks. At least one of Roberts-Smith's former friends turned away: 'I was opposed to his bullying and supported The Redhead. There was so much vindictiveness, scapegoats and stuff-ups. A bit of a pattern developed of destroying soldiers' careers. Both The Sig and The Redhead were hounded after 2006. The Redhead became a hollow shell.'[1]

The Koran Ghar mission was telling, but not because there was clear-cut evidence of a war crime. The shooting of the unarmed teenager was ugly but, under the rules of engagement (RoE), arguably justifiable. The young Afghan was likely a spotter. If he succeeded in reporting their presence, the patrol might have been overwhelmed. In a similar circumstance, twelve months earlier, a US special forces patrol was all but wiped out after an unarmed Afghan was released and alerted a small army of Taliban.[2]

More at question was the honesty of the patrol's reporting. The shooting of the unarmed male meant a covert surveillance operation had been compromised. The mission's objective had to be aborted and an exposed patrol had been imperilled. Lies were told, then and later, about what really happened. Through succeeding missions, the Roberts-Smith refrain—that The Redhead was an incompetent coward—increasingly lost credibility as the young soldier proved his capacity and courage.

Could it have been that Roberts-Smith's enduring denigration of these two junior soldiers was driven more by his concern that The Redhead and The Sig knew the truth?

Four months after the Koran Ghar mission, Sergeant Matthew Locke and Lance Corporal Ben Roberts-Smith were each awarded the Medal for Gallantry. The latter's citation noted that the soldiers 'moved out of their relatively secure Observation Post', when 'the Militia attempted to outflank' them. It went on: 'Lance Corporal Roberts-Smith's actions on the 2nd of June 2006, whilst under heavy Anti Coalition Militia fire and in a precarious position, threatened by a numerically superior force, are testament to his courage, tenacity and sense of duty to his patrol.'[3]

CHAPTER 2

2 JUNE 2015

Was it by cosmic design, human intervention or just chance?

Exactly nine years after the Koran Ghar action, by coincidence, the Royal Military College, Duntroon, staged a dining-in night. I had accepted a speaking invitation, generated by the publication of *Uncommon Soldier*, which had poked its nose inside the parade grounds and panoply of Australia's officer training school.

That evening, as I sat among the dress whites and gleaming silver, I felt a little awkward. Perhaps I felt overweight, aged and unkempt in a room brimming with bracingly fit, fresh-faced and immaculately attired officer cadets. But when the soldier to my left introduced himself, I began to feel more at home. We had never met. It was The Sig.

He was affable, thoughtful and good-natured. Conversation came easily. He was deep into officer training after moving on from the SASR. Just short of graduating as a lieutenant, The Sig told me a great deal about how the special forces experience had helped him grow as a soldier and a person; yet, for all that, he had always felt like 'a square peg in a round hole'. 'They are unique individuals,' he explained. 'It is dog eat dog, and you are socially and professionally ostracised if you don't fit in. There was bullying. It was not enjoyable.'

Roast chicken was served. I contemplated the wishbone and the fabled lucky break it might offer me. Luck is an important component of journalism, and I was more than usually in need. I was working on a new book on the special forces. But my hunt for interviewees was a struggle because they were all conditioned to silence—and to suspicion, particularly of media. My phone calls were not answered; appointments were cancelled. I spent many a frustrated hour fretting in hotel rooms. So I was keen to follow up with The Sig, and we had further conversations.

The former SAS trooper spoke widely of his experiences, including the Koran Ghar action in 2006. He told me how the perilous gunfight had been triggered after a single unarmed adolescent Afghan had been pursued and shot. In addition, he confirmed the subsequent and relentless bullying of The Redhead.

By chance, I had also heard of this from a different source. When *Uncommon Soldier* was published in 2012 a reference to Ben Roberts-Smith's Medal for Gallantry action prompted a comment from a Sydney neighbour who suggested that not all on the official record was necessarily gospel. That neighbour happened to be the father of The Redhead.

When reporters pounce on a lead, they follow it. In this case to the Australian War Memorial, which was actually my sometime workplace. The research library is well known to military authors, and I had been employed as a part-time co-curator since 2013. The director, Dr Brendan Nelson, had recruited me to assist with the Afghanistan galleries. We got on well, sharing a view that Australians knew more about the wars fought by their grandparents than those fought by their sons and daughters.

Knowing that the Australian War Memorial had published an account in its magazine, *Wartime*, of Ben Roberts-Smith's actions, I requested copies of the original interview tapes. Listening to them, I heard Roberts-Smith tell the interviewer, Dr Peter Pedersen, that the Koran Ghar battle was triggered after 'a couple of blokes just walked up literally, probably about two hours before dark, walked straight up to the front of the OP'.[1]

In an interview with *The Australian*'s Brendan Nicholson a few months later, Roberts-Smith's account had been significantly different.

He had spoken then of the intrusion of a single gun-toting enemy: 'an armed insurgent walked to within 30 metres of their position'.[2]

Reports of combat commonly differ. In the blaze of battle, the fog of war settles, and personal attention is acutely focused. In many interviews, I have heard vivid accounts by soldiers of what was in front of them, even as they acknowledge their complete unawareness of an equally intense conflict just metres away.

Nonetheless, these inconsistencies needed reconciliation. I would have to schedule an interview with Ben Roberts-Smith.

CHAPTER 3
LIFTING THE TIN

The meeting did not go well, or so it seemed at the time.

It was August 2015 and I had found my way to Special Operations Command (SOCOMD) at Russell Offices in Canberra. As was the routine, I surrendered all my electronic devices and notebooks, entered the gullet of an X-ray chamber and then was transported downwards into a windowless sub-basement. The experience always seemed like the opening scenes of a *Get Smart* episode.

SOCOMD oversees Australia's select and premium strike force. At the tip of the spear are the SASR in Perth; the 2nd Commando Regiment (2 Commando) at Holsworthy Barracks, New South Wales; the 1st Commando Regiment (1 Commando) located in both Sydney and Melbourne; and the Special Operations Engineer Regiment, also in Sydney. With a range of support units, staffing runs to around 3000. The annual budget of approximately $80 million is much envied across the deep green of 'Big Army'.

It was not my first visit. There had been meetings in 2011, before I was embedded with the special forces in Afghanistan, and again between 2013 and 2014, when I sought cooperation for my book *No Front Line*. For a rounded account, I needed contact with serving personnel who knew their stuff. And I needed to keep them out of trouble. So, in December 2014, after a year of negotiation, a deed of agreement was signed, permitting soldiers to have contact with me for the sake of the book, which would be vetted by Defence. The arrangement was neither new nor particularly troubling. The vetting would apply only to matters of operational security and personal identity. I was not losing editorial control and, by virtue of the fact-checking, I was gaining a more accurate comprehension.

It took me a while to secure an appointment with the latest Special Operations Commander Australia (SOCAUST). Major General Jeff Sengelman had been appointed in December 2014, only days after the preceding administration signed the deed of agreement.

Jeff Sengelman is scary smart. In his spare moments he writes poetry. The grandson of a garbo, and a graduate of Ipswich State High, he joined the Army straight out of school and earned the coveted SASR sandy beret at the age of 25. He would later serve in Iraq and, perhaps significantly, miss Afghanistan. He is a classic old-school special forces man, a thinker as well as a fighter. In a rare piece of public commentary, he told an interviewer: 'Killing is an aspect of war, not the purpose of it.'[1]

Seated opposite him in his modest office, I felt like the new boy in for a dressing-down. He told me my deed of agreement should not have been supported. He said his people needed no publicity as they were already revered. Secrecy, a core strength of the command, was non-negotiable.

There was much unsaid. I did not know him well enough to share all I knew, and clearly he felt the same, so this first meeting was a study of mutual caution. Sengelman knew I had been poking around. We had both picked up the low-frequency murmur from chaplains, psychologists and intelligence personnel that suggested trouble was brewing. By 2015, it was a talking point all through senior command. Drunks gobbing off at parties in the special forces diaspora would occasionally let word slip of secret soldiers' business. But then silence.

There was something I did not know as I sat talking to Sengelman that day, but which I learned about later. He was also poking around. Earlier in the year, soon after he came into the job and had sniffed the wind, the major general had written to SAS members. While he saw secrecy as a key strength of the special forces, he knew it was worthless if trust was lost. He had suspicions of his own, about the prospect of war crimes and cultural degeneration within the SASR. As he would later explain, 'Working on intuition, I brought in the bulk of the regiment in a single room and I asked them to tell me their stories, but in a way that encouraged them to believe in me.'[2]

What resulted was a sheaf of letters from soldiers, the contents of which Sengelman had promised them he would not reveal. The most he would say was that 'in the end perhaps the greatest stories will never be told. I know I have many that I need to take to the grave.'

Obviously, though, there was enough that was concerning for him to press the emergency button. 'I did for a fleeting moment think that we were the metaphoric equivalent of the *Titanic* just about to hit an iceberg,' he explained. 'So, I grabbed a wheel and pulled a hard right.'[3]

Two days after my meeting with Sengelman, I received a letter from the Chief of Army, Lieutenant General Angus Campbell, requesting I cooperate with a scoping study, 'Special Operations Command Culture and Interactions: Perceptions, Reputation and Risk', to be conducted by a sociologist, Dr Samantha Crompvoets. The executive director of a Canberra firm, Rapid Context, Sam Crompvoets had already undertaken a range of cultural reform programs for the Australian Defence Force.

This new work would put a target on her—for two reasons. Having been commissioned by Defence to conduct her study, she would be attacked for daring to suggest that Australians might commit war crimes, and she would be attacked because she was a woman.

Addressing the dismal levels of female participation in the Australian Defence Force means confronting ingrained misogyny. So it was no surprise that a young, assured and unafraid female sociologist would become a target of culture warrior grievance about alleged Defence prioritisation of gender equity over battlefield success. As one anonymous blogosphere veteran put it, 'I look back now on my time and know I just could not do it again with the current leaders in Canberra. They are going to get people killed in the name of diversity and political correctness.'

Ultimately, the academic researcher held her nerve. Her report was delivered to the Chief of Army in January 2016. Again, anonymity was promised. The report, *Special Operations Command (SOCOMD) Culture and Interactions: Insights and Reflection*, identified no whistleblower, nor any war criminal.

There was detailed feedback in her report, such as the following:

> Someone who deployed a number of times with SF (Special Forces) remarked 2012 was by far the worst year he had ever seen. He mentioned that the Afghan interpreter they worked with kept reporting that Australian SF were executing farmers, but no one ever followed anything up.

Additional concerning comments included:

> You need to conform to survive. If you do not conform you aren't trusted. Soldiers would do 'bad stuff' to fit in. It becomes a part of the banter.
>
> Guys just had this blood lust. Psychos. Absolute psychos. And we bred them.
>
> Patrol Commander level is the worst. They are responsible for the worst of it. Core group of people who wield so much influence that officers find it very difficult to manage, especially if the patrol commander has been awarded medals for gallantry for example. They are hero worshipped and unstoppable.

The Crompvoets report precipitated yet another inquiry, this one directed to reach even further. In May 2016, the Inspector-General of the Australian

Defence Force (IGADF) was requested by the Chief of Army, Lieutenant General Angus Campbell, to investigate 'rumours of possible breaches of the Laws of Armed Conflict by members of the Australian Defence Force'.

Anyone with deep experience of formal inquiries into the nation's dirty secrets will show caution. Perhaps like a soldier approaching a choke point laced with improvised explosive devices (IEDs), I knew I needed to be wary of trust and engagement.

If the cynics were correct and Defence was only doing the right thing after trying everything else, there was clear need for caution. The cynics also held to the view that governments never called on anything unless they were already assured of the outcome.

I well recalled my own experience of former Queensland premier Sir Joh Bjelke-Petersen when he opposed a probe into police corruption back in 1987. His attorney-general, Paul Clauson, later told me Joh's view was that 'if you lift up a piece of tin, you'll find one of two things, a snake or a dead cat'.

Critics immediately attacked what seemed to be an inquiry into mere rumour. This bothered me too. The special forces community is well stocked with aggressive high achievers. There is toxic rivalry. The proposition that some allegations might be driven by fear and loathing, rather than fact and logic, couldn't be discounted.

Despite our frosty beginning, over time the major general, Jeff Sengelman, and I, the journalist, became unlikely allies. Both of us were intent on lifting the tin, and both were conscious of having to endure either the stink or a retaliatory strike.

Up to this point, to my knowledge the name of Ben Roberts-Smith had not been connected to any clear allegation of a war crime. Listening around the edges, the most I heard was that Big Ben was seen as a 'morale vampire'.

CHAPTER 4

ACHILLES

It's curious that there is no Tizak Day.

On the anniversary of big battles, soldiers often get together to raise a glass. It happens on 22 September, when veterans remember Bagh Khoshack, the SAS's first serious gunfight in Afghanistan from 2005, where two Medals for Gallantry were earned. It happens on 2 September, in honour of the 2008 action at Ana Kalay, where Trooper Mark Donaldson earned Australia's first Victoria Cross since the Vietnam War. But not so much for 11 June, the biggest battle of all, when in 2010 Lance Corporal Ben Roberts-Smith earned his Victoria Cross at Tizak.

As a feat of arms, it was remarkable. A searing hot day. A squadron helicoptered into a narrow valley and a terrifying ambush. Trapped and surrounded by an enemy that had dug in and outnumbered them. It was classic SAS 'who dares wins', 'up the guts' combat.

Five patrols, each of them with five or six men, fought forward. In the dappled light of a terraced fig orchard, through dry creek beds, they closed on the insurgents. They traded rounds, sometimes face to face.

Three machine guns, positioned above and behind a wall in front of a mosque, had Roberts-Smith's patrol hugging the earth. Accurate fire tore the rocks and tree cover all around them. His patrol commander, desperate, seized the moment. 'It got to the stage I was sick of getting shot at. Nothing was happening and there was the potential we were going to get flanked,' he later recalled.[1]

So the commander split his patrol into two teams of three. On one flank they lobbed a hand grenade over a building, towards the unseen enemy, while Roberts-Smith and two comrades on the other flank stood upright before withering fire, straining forward. In the end, all three enemy gunners were killed.

According to Roberts-Smith, in his interview with Dr Pedersen:

> The centre gun, as I remember it, was on the wall and all I could see was his head and the gun . . . and he was holding and traversing it . . . he's trying to turn, and I've got there to a gap in the wall and was faster than him.[2]

It would take a while before the questioning and resentment built. There is a drab but common pattern to griping over honours and awards. For all its checks and balances, the process of determining who was most brave remains inexact. It can often be said that another soldier was more deserving. And it is often said (as was the case with Ben Roberts-Smith) that the individual receives the award on behalf of the group.

A regiment already divided over Roberts-Smith became more so. Even before the conferral of Roberts-Smith's high honour, the acrimony was seeping beyond Campbell Barracks, the home of the SASR. On Boxing Day in 2010, reporter Alex Mitchell wrote: 'A top-brass proposal to award the Victoria Cross to an Australian soldier who has been investigated for bullying in Afghanistan is mired in politics and recriminations.'[3]

Within Roberts-Smith's own patrol there was discord about the merit of the VC, but at this stage the broader disquiet seemed to be more about whether the character matched the honour. As public adulation for the newly minted war hero grew, so did private grievance among his detractors. As a close observer put it, 'There was an overwhelming contrast between his public persona and reality.' To Roberts-Smith and his supporters, the griping was simply jealousy and envy.

In 2012, now a corporal, Ben Roberts-Smith returned to Afghanistan. It was this deployment that would generate the most controversy. Some of his peers would blame the Victoria Cross. Long regarded as entitled, BRS VC MG became untouchable.

It was after this deployment, when he was further awarded a Commendation for Distinguished Service (CDS), that challenges were formalised, if only tentatively.

The first was just before Anzac Day in 2013, when the bullying, harassment and threats to kill The Redhead, dating back to 2006, were reported to the SAS's regimental sergeant major (Person 100, The RSM). The Redhead, having heard that Roberts-Smith was continuing to undermine his career, had had enough. Mediation followed, ending in a handshake. But, as I can personally attest, that did not stop Roberts-Smith from continuing to malign his comrade.

Another challenge came the following year, soon after the award of the CDS. Five sergeants delivered a written protest. In their view, on that rotation Roberts-Smith had been the least deserving patrol commander.

At the end of 2013, Ben Roberts-Smith announced his retirement from the Army. He was 35 years old.

He had started at Kapooka on Remembrance Day in 1996, having spent the last two years of his secondary education at Perth's most prestigious private school, Hale. Among a regal line-up of Old Haleians were Christian Porter, the federal attorney-general when the war crimes scandal broke, and David Irvine, a former ASIO director who would oversee a consequent special forces reform process.

'RS', as he became known, was from the start conspicuous for more than his 2.02-metre stature. The son of Major General Len Roberts-Smith, a former justice of the Supreme Court of Western Australia, he came from privilege. An officer who served with him told me, 'RS intimidated other soldiers because of his size, and the rest of us because of his connections.'

His first regiment, the 3rd Battalion of the Royal Australian Regiment (3RAR), would have done little to restrain the anger—or was it insecurity?—that appeared to boil within him. Bullying and soldiering have long marched in concert, and by this time 3RAR, a parachute regiment, had institutionalised rough justice. According to *Time* magazine: 'Back in 1997, at 3RAR's Holsworthy barracks the rules were simple: step out of line and the consequences would be swift and violent. This policy was actively condoned by key superiors and widely employed.'[4]

A Military Police inquiry in 1990 uncovered numerous examples of bullying, bastardisation and bashings, the three pillars of barrack-room justice. It is ironic that a broad reform process—in part driven by the inquiry into 3RAR, which became known as the 'Rough Justice Inquiry'—led to the creation of an independent office of the IGADF.[5]

Many young diggers enlisted with the aim of going bush with mates, blowing stuff up, maybe travelling a bit and then getting out after four years. But Roberts-Smith was different: he took soldiering seriously. By 2001, following deployments to East Timor and Malaysia, he was promoted to corporal.

By then he was renting a room in Sydney, close to 3RAR's Holsworthy base, which he shared with Emma Groom. Four years older than him and working in marketing at Murdoch Magazines, Emma had met her man at 3RAR's Kapyong Ball, held each year to commemorate the regiment's feats at Kapyong, during the Korean War.

But Ben Roberts-Smith wanted to be in Perth and in the SASR, so he took three months' leave and set about shedding weight. In his first years of service life, his weight and fitness levels had fluctuated. Self-image seems to have been important to him, but there had been periods when he had stacked on the kilos. Now, however, was not the time to be out of condition. It was during this time, he recalled many years later, that he did 'the hardest training I had done in my life': it was even 'harder than [SASR] selection.'[6]

Following the three-week SAS selection trial in February 2003, Roberts-Smith was one of 30 (out of 150) to finish, and one of only fifteen to be awarded the coveted sandy beret. Starting again in the SAS meant surrendering his two stripes and assuming the base rank of trooper.

Later that year, Ben and Emma married. Over the subsequent decade, she would stick by him through multiple, lengthy and dangerous deployments. However, it was not until 2010, after IVF intervention, that they became parents to twin girls, Eve and Liz.

During his years of military service, the walking controversy that was Ben Roberts-Smith had numerous defenders. He was seen by many as a serious soldier who did not suffer fools, 'a massive unit', 'a killing machine'. But to others, for all his achievements, he was more of an outline, a plan of a man. A sergeant who worked alongside him for years saw 'a massive façade, a little boy inside a big body, not too bright and hard to get close to'.

On his final deployment, Roberts-Smith attracted a nickname, 'Achilles'. Its use was confined to a few of the non-believers, who mocked the warrior self-image, seeing it as a façade masking serious character flaws.

In seventeen years of service within the Australian regular Army, the most decorated soldier in the Commonwealth did not rise above the rank of corporal. But bigger things were to come.

CHAPTER 5

THE ANZAC AVATAR

When Ben Roberts-Smith left the Army, the legend came alive. The myth of the classic Anzac, seven-foot-tall and bulletproof, found human form. Gallantry medals were a big part of the transfusion, but so too was a further array of honours, obligations and privileges in civilian life.

On Father's Day in 2013, he was named Father of the Year. This award is partly in the hands of the Shepherd Centre, whose 'vice-patron' was Brendan Nelson, the director of the Australian War Memorial and a Roberts-Smith enthusiast. Past winners included former Chief of the Defence Force Sir Angus Houston and famed obstetrician Dr William McBride.[1] To friends, Ben Roberts-Smith confessed that it was more his wife, Emma, who deserved the credit for raising the girls.

In 2014, Roberts-Smith became deputy chair of Prime Minister Tony Abbott's advisory committee on mental health and a spokesperson for a range of mental health charities. Among his former comrades, this sparked some derision. A group of soldiers, watching him being interviewed on Channel Seven's breakfast program, hooted. One SAS operator was heard loudly proclaiming that 'RS gave The Redhead depression. Now he is going to help him fight it.'

There were many more appointments, including chair of the National Australia Day Council and a seat on the Queensland Veterans' Advisory Council.

At the Australian War Memorial, he had become a centrepiece. Two portraits of him hung in the galleries. His medals were on show; the uniform he had worn for the VC action at Tizak in 2010 was encased in a glass cabinet.

Queensland was now his home. He started a Master of Business Administration (MBA) degree at The University of Queensland. In the same month that he and Emma bought a $1.6-million property at Wooloowin, in Brisbane, he commenced employment at Channel Seven.

The chair of the Australian War Memorial and the owner of Channel Seven, Kerry Stokes, was both a friend and mentor to Roberts-Smith. Stokes helped elevate him from being an Army corporal on around $120,000 per annum to a management role in an industry with which he was not familiar, with a salary that rose to $700,000.

Roberts-Smith's baby steps were in regional television, as deputy general manager at a Seven affiliate at Maroochydore, north of Brisbane. There, some staff regarded him as clearly out of his depth; he once asked why iPhones could not be used to collect news. He is remembered there for having introduced bonding exercises such as skydiving. He bought fruit hampers for staff and took them out on the town. One of the administrative staff told me, 'He likes a drink, but it felt like he was trying to buy respect.'

The job prompted another house move. In 2015, Ben and Emma sold their Wooloowin house to buy a ten-acre property at Ilkley, on the Sunshine Coast, which became a kind of compound. The address meant a lengthy commute, and there were more nights away when, the following year, he was appointed to the big job: general manager of Seven Queensland, back in Brisbane.

By this time, stories of an epic mismatch were taking on elements of tragedy. We might guess at the logic. In the Stokes portfolio, Seven Media was an underperforming asset, struggling to pay down its debt, but it was valuable—perhaps for its capacity to project political influence.

Television is often a shallow bloat of ego and self-importance. Perhaps, it could be argued, a straight-talking sergeant major type would inject a little discipline. Or maybe his appointment was simply an expression of both men's derision for the media. Roberts-Smith told confidants he was reluctant to take on the job, but had done so on the understanding he would be personally mentored by Stokes.

According to a number of colleagues, Roberts-Smith was brought in 'to straighten the culture' and help build integrity: 'His early motivational speeches were full of military analogies.' But he was also 'given the brutal assignment of sacking people—head counts becoming kill counts.'

Roberts-Smith appointed a few hand-picked friends, but they added little comfort. 'He's totally incompetent,' said one insider. 'He's supposed to have an MBA. You learn in business school that it is better to reward than punish. But to BRS it is better to punish than reward.'[2]

According to another staff member, at an alcohol-fuelled conference, the new GM reverted to an old Army trick of ritual humiliation. 'He openly belittled staff he didn't like. He didn't like the venue and he stood up and said, "Who organised this fucking shithole?" And he made him go around and take everyone's drinks orders.'

Roberts-Smith's insecurity and paranoia ultimately saw him recruit a personal spy—but not a fellow ex-digger. Indeed, it was not someone he had known well or for long at all.

John McLeod and the VC recipient had crossed paths in 2011, at the hotel where McLeod worked as security and safety manager. Soon after, when the Roberts-Smiths moved to Queensland, McLeod helped the family settle in. He would later explain this involved 'mundane stuff' such as finding plumbers, gardeners and electricians, as well as 'picking up stuff', such as suits and 'Ben's medals.'

Of stocky frame, taciturn manner and ruddy complexion, the former police officer is what might be called a colourful Queensland identity. As a private inquiry agent, he specialised in helping secure the release of Australians imprisoned overseas. When Schapelle Corby was released from her Bali jail, McLeod successfully sneaked her past a massive scrum of the reptiles of the press, whom he openly despised.

Now Roberts-Smith, perhaps to address his own lack of corporate experience, found a use for McLeod's fixing skills. One of his tasks was to act as a waiter at functions the general manager hosted, and to report back anything he overheard from guests as he poured drinks and offered canapes.

Cracks in the façade of the public Ben Roberts-Smith persona were beginning to appear. While outside the ADF his reputation continued to grow, within the organisation it was in further retreat. In special forces, a veteran who cashes in on his fame can quickly become persona non grata. From SF drinking holes the world over, there are stories of transgressors being shunned and even physically ejected. Extracting profit from sworn duty is a no-no. The profession of arms is supposed to be humble, and the bragging confined to Anzac Day. While Roberts-Smith was hardly the first operator to monetise his reputation, he was more conspicuous than most. Brand BRS VC MG became a talking point.

Roberts-Smith's celebrity attracted invitations to all manner of functions. And from some events, word began to filter back of a well-lubricated BRS mouthing off: 'What do I know about fucking television? I shoot cunts in the face.' At the Australian War Memorial, I picked up a concern that inviting him to speak at an event presented some risk. As the soldiers used to say, when Ben arrives, it can be like a black cloud entering the room.

When you look at this period of his life, it is not hard to feel a little sorry for him, despite all the fame and fortune. His fast track to the top of civic honours and an industry he neither understood nor admired was willingly embraced. But was it also wished upon him by a cheer squad of myth makers and an idol-hungry nation?

CHAPTER 6

A SPECTATOR TO A TROUBLED SOUL

There is a stretch of water near the mouth of the Hawkesbury River where I like to paddle my kayak. More for therapy than exercise. Long-form investigative journalism is nerve-racking. While daily journalism is high-energy and offers quick relief, by contrast the long form means the burden stays with you, often well beyond publication.

As 2017 dawned, my stresses were mounting. There was the deadline for my book on the special forces, begun four years earlier. There was a great deal of static coming from the SAS—it was as if I had become a spectator to the troubled soul of that place. And there was the unknown of the IGADF war crimes inquiry. I remember similar misgivings when the Fitzgerald inquiry was initiated in Queensland in 1987. If the investigation does not succeed, life for all those who called for it becomes worse—and so too does the corruption. All this meant many sleepless nights.

When you take a tributary of the Hawkesbury up into the wilds of the surrounding national park, the burdens ease. Sea eagles peer down from overhead branches. Stingrays move politely aside. The kayak glides through blessed water and the mind begins to clear.

I was often paddling with a friend I'd met during the research for my book. We will call him The Mechanic, but he was known later as Person 19 during the defamation proceedings. He was trained as a mechanic when he first joined the Army, but there was a fighting soldier inside him.

He ultimately qualified as a commando, deploying to Afghanistan several times. Once, in the middle of a protracted gunfight, he coolly replaced the gearbox of a patrol vehicle to help his company extract to safety. His peers referred to him as a 'soldier's soldier'.

When he moved on from the Commandos to the SASR, The Mechanic topped his selection trial and was hand-picked into Ben Roberts-Smith's patrol for the projected 2012 tour. As it turned out, he stayed behind. After all the blood, sweat and treasure expended in perfecting his specialist skills, his career was paralysed by a perfect storm of bad luck.

After a shoot at a firing range, a fellow soldier asked him to return to stores some ammunition that had not been used. He left this on the back seat of his car and promptly forgot about it. But his car was stolen and became involved in a fatal accident. He attempted to explain his failure to return this ammunition, which was recovered by the police from the crash site, but his explanation was not accepted. Some of his friends thought his patrol commander, Corporal Ben Roberts-Smith, could have done more to protect him.

When I asked, The Mechanic insisted that Roberts-Smith was not to blame. He served 31 days in a Defence Force Correctional Facility and was discharged from the Army. This brutal consequence, the loss of a cherished vocation, he ruefully accepted.

One paddle across the Hawkesbury takes you to Refuge Bay, which for the special forces community is rich in history. When you climb above the waterfall you can find the old foundations of a World War II training camp. It is where Z Special Unit was based in preparation for Operation Jaywick, their famous raid on Singapore in 1943, using the MV *Krait* and then kayaks.

While paddling, we talked, mostly simply about soldiering at first, for the sake of the book. Scandalous secrets were not at the front of my mind, as with the many other soldiers I was then interviewing. Only occasionally something that was said might raise an eyebrow—or provoke a follow-up question.

I was not the only one curious about a number of official accounts of Afghans being shot after they had surrendered. The usual explanation was that, while manacled, they had attempted to overwhelm a heavily armed soldier—but this did not pass the pub test. There were whispers about 'the magic Makarov', an enemy pistol that kept turning up on the corpses of dead Afghans. The term 'throwdown' was bandied about—an item, such as a radio or a weapon, was planted to justify a kill as legitimate. In my earlier days, when reporting on crime and corruption, I'd heard much the same thing, although it was then called 'loading'.

'Blooding' was also mentioned. Getting a first kill is a thing with soldiers. It's brutal but understandable, given that a core objective of soldiering is to kill. For normal human beings, imbued with the preciousness of life, we can understand hesitation, indeed acute reluctance. But a soldier is not always meant to act like a normal human being. For them, hesitation could have a personal and fatal consequence.

But you did wonder, from some of the stories told, whether some of the kills might have occurred more in cold blood than battle heat. The 'Big Boys' Rules' phenomenon—said to have emanated during the Troubles in Northern Ireland—refers to British special forces taking the law into their own hands and executing, rather than prosecuting, suspected members of the Irish Republican Army.[3]

Ben Roberts-Smith's patrol commander in 2009 and 2010 (Person 5, The Scot) had transferred from Britain's Special Boat Service and had served in Northern Ireland. He allegedly spoke openly of the need to 'blood rookies'. An unspoken logic that had apparently developed in Northern Ireland—that it was unwise to leave an enemy alive to fight another day—also gained currency in Afghanistan.

The Mechanic, as a recruit to Ben Roberts-Smith's patrol in 2012, had inside knowledge of the culture that had developed. In the beginning, he hinted at it rather than divulging it to me openly. He became animated when telling me how not deploying in 2012 had become a stroke of fortune. 'When that sort of shit happens, and someone is standing over you, what can you do?'

As I got to know The Mechanic and other SAS operators better, I sensed their anger that there was not more duty of care extended to their own. One hardened sergeant, when discussing the killing of captured

Taliban, was blunt: 'I have no problem dropping the hammer. But do it yourself. Don't order some kid to push a dirt farmer to his knees and do something they can't live with.'

I told The Mechanic that, for the sake of his own peace of mind, he should not keep this stuff to himself. This was, in fact, advice appropriate to many veterans. The ADF was already getting in front of something that no lid could effectively seal. It was only a matter of time before a soldier somewhere—because of a marriage broken, or the dispersal of his mates, or his inability to close his eyes on the image of a panicked last breath—spoke up and screamed for the truth to be told.

When The Mechanic was approached to give evidence to the IGADF Brereton inquiry, as with others, I encouraged cooperation. Major General Paul Brereton was a respected judge of the Supreme Court of New South Wales and member of the Army Reserve. You could say he was made for the job. His father, Russell Brereton, had also trained in the law and begun World War II as a private; he ended it as an investigator of Japanese war crimes, and as prosecutor at the Sandakan Death Marches trial.

While Justice Brereton would bring a century of skilful contemplation to the task, it was still an Everest-like challenge. His first battle would be against popular opinion. In the tabloid media in particular, the sacred digger can do no wrong. Their chant was already ringing out: 'We need rough men to keep us safe.' 'You can't judge decisions taken in the heat of battle from the comfort of home.' 'Do we really need to know?' 'War is messy, mistakes are made.'

What soon became clear, however, was that Justice Brereton and his team were not second-guessing split-second decisions. It was well understood that battle heat and human error are common companions. The focus was on clear evidence of breaches of the laws of armed conflict. There was concern that ignoring the truth brought deep moral pain to all the ranks. It meant the ADF did not know itself. It left Australia open to prosecution by international actors. It amounted to a descent to the depravity we fight against. As the judge would later say, 'Fundamentally laws are useless if they are not enforced.'[4]

The practical challenges were perhaps even more daunting. As a sitting judge, later promoted to the NSW Court of Appeal, Brereton was not able to devote all his time to the investigation. And, from what I could see, there was no army of investigators to back him up. Compared to other public inquiries, this one seemed poorly resourced.

But Justice Brereton would later say otherwise; he reported to the Office of the Inspector-General that he was given all the resources he requested, and did not believe more would have helped.[5] Perhaps a compact team was better suited to maintaining oversight of an inquiry that would scale those Everest-like heights of the complex and sensitive.

The special forces world is loath to give up its secrets. Its operators are trained to withstand interrogation. Soldiers were formally encouraged to do the right thing. But that other voice was just as loud: 'Head down! Trap shut!' A constant fear prevailed that in the real world—rather than in the ethics class's fantasyland—recrimination from bosses, from family and from mates would rain down on them without relent.

But the IGADF's inquiry team persisted. In the end they uncovered much more than the investigative journalists.

CHAPTER 7

THE ROSE GARDEN

In the fading afternoon light of 12 April 2017, Australia's most decorated soldier was unmistakeable as he surged through the front door of Canberra's Hyatt Hotel, not only because of his conspicuous height and tailored business suit. The awarding of the Victoria Cross six years earlier had turned Ben Roberts-Smith into a towering public figure.

Work on my book on the Australian special forces' thirteen-year tour of Afghanistan was in its final stages. The interview I had at last arranged with Roberts-Smith would plug a few gaps. It was later claimed that I was on a mission to 'tear down a hero', but that was a long way from true. Any challenge to Roberts-Smith's reputation would have required a lot of evidence, which had not materialised up to this time. Any negative commentary from his detractors was countered by praise from his supporters.

I shook hands with him and, to avoid turned heads, we settled in the empty rose garden. Under thinning tree cover, there was no mistaking an autumn chill in the air—and a degree of tension. The former SAS corporal had been hearing for some time that I was aware of negative commentary from some of his former brothers-in-arms, and that I had been asking questions.

We'd already met a few times and, after the obligatory small talk, got down to business, tracking through his Afghanistan rotations, the

Victoria Cross action, his ideas about junior leadership and the loss of comrades.

When I broached the subject of bullying, he bristled: 'I am hard. I get that, but there is no one I beat up harder than myself. You are supposed to be better; if not, you should not be there. Because if you make a mistake, someone is going to die.'

A waiter appeared. Ben ordered red wine and I settled on a mineral water.

'I love battle,' he went on. 'I have a pure passion for soldiering and that is why I have this trouble.'

This mirrored something one of his officers had said to me: 'Ben is one of the bravest, dedicated, hardworking soldiers out there. The whingeing about him happened only after he got the VC.'

While I was obliged to asked difficult questions, which is the job of a journalist, I was in a mood to mediate. As to a prime minister or president, respect has to be accorded to a recipient of the pre-eminent award for valour, the Victoria Cross, irrespective of personality.

And there was much to impress in the early stages of this interview. Shining through an overcast demeanour were moments when Roberts-Smith revealed himself as articulate, measured and persuasive. But the more we spoke, the more his guard appeared to slip. I later noted: 'For the first hour he reasoned, for the second hour he ranted.'[1]

I also came to glimpse what one of his detractors described as the 'frill-necked lizard'. What unsettled Roberts-Smith most was any mention of those he saw as 'rats in the ranks', as happened when I began to ask the questions I needed to ask about the action that had earned Lance Corporal Ben Roberts-Smith and Sergeant Matt Locke Medals for Gallantry in June 2006.

As he had done back at Koran Ghar, Roberts-Smith went on the attack. He condemned The Redhead as a coward, and both him and The Sig as incompetent, telling me they had not properly prepared their weapons. Roberts-Smith and Locke were forced into action, because 'on that actual patrol those two guys failed . . . when the enemy walked into our position, they failed to fire their weapons . . . I got the MG because they did not do their job.'

I will confess to disappointment. Being drawn into a dispute with a national icon was not on my wish list, but I was also far from convinced. The stories from the two troopers were consistent and plausible. Roberts-Smith's account of one (or was it two?) insurgents entering the perimeter, and a gunfight being triggered when a chest rig detonated, did not so readily stack up.

Still, there was no clear evidence of a war crime. In the overall narrative, the action was revealing for the moral dilemma it posed, which was emblematic of the Afghanistan conflict. The decision to hunt the Afghan down and to kill him was callous, but war is callous. The soldiers had a moral duty to apply vigilance in the use of lethal force, but they also shared an ethical responsibility to defend themselves.

I saw no value in the dominant narrative becoming an unedifying blame game, and I faced additional concern about the legacy of Matt Locke. Roberts-Smith told me it was Locke who shot the teenager, and Sergeant Locke was no longer able to speak for himself, having been killed the following year on his next deployment to Afghanistan.

But the rose garden interview soon degenerated. Roberts-Smith was equally vicious towards other soldiers he suspected had spoken to me. His troop sergeant from 2012 (Person 7, The Sergeant), by now a known opponent, was, Roberts-Smith claimed, inexperienced and jealous.

A patrol sergeant from the rotation, who had written a formal complaint about Roberts-Smith being awarded a Commendation for Distinguished Service (Person 6, The Veteran), was 'toxic'.

Another soldier from Roberts-Smith's own patrol (Person 10, The Trooper), 'should have been sent home'. 'I love the SAS, but it is full of people with grievances,' he railed. 'That is why I got out. I left because of those individuals.'

It was nearing 7 pm and Roberts-Smith was running late for a dinner appointment. I offered to drive him to the Ottoman restaurant, but the ex-soldier said he would get a taxi. He told me I was the first person to 'ask me about this stuff'. He offered to show me patrol reports and to take me through the detail of the Koran Ghar action if I came to Brisbane. His phone rang. He had to go. In the crisp Canberra air, his anger was like steam.

The staff, the guests and I watched him leave. My overwhelming impression, reinforced in the coming months, was that Ben Roberts-Smith VC, MG was not behaving like a man with nothing to hide.

CHAPTER 8
THE CLIFF

'He kicked this bloke off a cliff. As his face spun down, it smashed against the wall and his teeth sprayed out. The bloke who saw it can't get the image out of his mind. He said he had to get away from Roberts-Smith. It was not the first time he said this stuff happened. RS is a bloody psychopath.'

The phone call left me shaken. My mobile had buzzed sometime through the night, a few days after the meeting in the rose garden. An anonymous source on an encrypted line.

Shocking but unreportable, the information rated less than second-hand. The cliff kick was being talked about by a small group of SAS operators in Perth who were concerned for the firsthand witness, who was not coping.

Journalists need primary evidence and more—an additional source, further corroboration. But it was a strong lead; the vivid detail enhanced its credibility.

After the phone call, I pumped as hard as I could for further details, but the scale of the task and the seriousness of the allegation meant it was unlikely the cliff kick story would feature in my book.

Eventually, after I made various inquiries of sources, the outline of a story emerged, cruel to the point of abomination, and wantonly banal.

The SAS had had blood in their eyes. They were pursuing a rogue Afghan soldier who had murdered three of their Australian allies: Lance Corporal Stjepan Milosevic, Private Robert Poate and Sapper James Martin.

On 28 August 2012, a composite team—made up of Afghan soldiers and some Australians, drawn mainly from Roberts-Smith's old regiment, 3RAR—had been manning Patrol Base Wahib. A nineteen-year-old Afghan National Army (ANA) sergeant, Hekmatullah, had suddenly turned his M16 on the Australians and fled.

Hekmatullah was instantly deemed by Australia to be a National Priority Target, tagged Objective Jungle Effect. In the following weeks there was a fervent and ruthless pursuit of the fugitive. But the Australians were frustrated by the actions of many locals, also supposed to be our allies, who provided refuge along a rat line out of Uruzgan Province for him.

This was the background for a helicopter descent into the village of Darwan on 11 September—a fateful day, exactly eleven years on from the attacks in New York and elsewhere that had triggered this relentless violence. After a fifteen-minute flight, 42 Australian soldiers and eighteen ANA soldiers surrounded the village.

Ben Roberts-Smith's patrol immediately went on the attack. Spotting a 'squirter'—Army slang for someone who takes off as soldiers approach—whom they thought might be Hekmatullah, Roberts-Smith waded alone across the Helmand River, then hunted and killed him. While armed and later identified as a Taliban fighter, the man was not their primary target.

During the next hours a routine played out. The fighting-age males captured in the village were separated for questioning. Hekmatullah was not among them. The Afghan soldiers, with a sharp eye for who belonged here and who didn't, isolated a man, Ali Jan, who was not from Darwan. Some suspects were to be transported to the main base at Tarin Kowt for questioning. Others were released.

Later in the day, with the soldiers preparing to leave, Ben Roberts-Smith is said to have been standing on the edge of a so-called cliff, with the manacled Ali Jan.

Ali Jan's donkey was tethered a small distance away, stacked with firewood to sell and wheat to mill for his family. A father of three, he had travelled here from the village of Baag. While it was often difficult to tell, there were strong indications he was not Taliban.

Of course, he would have been frightened to have such a tall soldier facing him. He is said to have laughed. Some thought this was through fear and bewilderment, but perhaps the tall soldier saw insolence and contempt. It is claimed that the Australian then took a few steps backwards and lunged at Ali Jan, kicking him in the chest, sending him ten metres down the slope, his face striking the rocks, teeth erupting in a splash of blood and pain.

It is said that the tall soldier and two others went down and dragged the unconscious farmer under some tree cover. There, gaining consciousness, Ali Jan had tried to stand. Then, still manacled, it is claimed, he was shot dead.

There were Afghan witnesses, but that was unlikely to cause much bother. The Australians would soon be half a world away, and who would believe the Afghans? There were Australian witnesses too, but only a few; all of them had their own reasons to keep quiet.

For all that, back at base, whispers began to creep about Roberts-Smith '300-ing' an Afghan. This was a reference to a Hollywood movie, *300*, in which a Spartan warrior character, Leonidas, kicked an enemy off an edge and into oblivion.

A shocking story. But how believable?

It was not the only tale doing the rounds. I had also heard there was supposed to be video footage of an SAS operator using a massive knife to behead a man. Another was of a soldier shooting a farmer in the head with his pistol when the Afghan dared to complain about crop damage. Even in Samantha Crompvoets' report, there was an unlikely report of Australian soldiers allegedly slitting the throats of two fourteen-year-olds and throwing their bodies into a river.

Celebrities attract gossip—and, especially after many a round in the pub, many a tale becomes twisted. Yet the story of the cliff kick called for greater scrutiny.

CHAPTER 9

SHOOTING BAMBI

After watching Ben Roberts-Smith depart after our meeting in the rose garden, and hearing for the first time the cliff kick story, I sensed that the anticipated path for the months and years ahead might have dramatically deviated from its course—for me, Ben, the ADF and the nation.

Truth has a gravitational pull of its own. You can imagine many corners within the ADF and government resisting full and frank disclosure of what was coming to light. A large swathe of the media and the public, too, was not ready to hear the truth. When I discussed with a senior colleague the prospect of me challenging the reputation of this eminent Victoria Cross recipient, he told me it would be like 'shooting Bambi'.

And there was no doubt about it—a big part of me did not want the grievance or the distraction. While he was a towering figure, Ben Roberts-Smith played only a small part in my large book on the special forces. I needed to deal with the controversy about what really happened at Koran Ghar in 2006, but the cliff kick stuff was already deep in my too-hard basket.

I wondered whether I should share some of my concerns with Brendan Nelson. We had worked together on the Afghanistan galleries and I was comfortable talking to him. But, nonetheless, my words would need to be carefully chosen. Much of the griping about Roberts-Smith was unproven, and Brendan's chairman, Kerry Stokes, who was Roberts-Smith's employer, was not so well known to me, even though a documentary I had produced in 2016—*Afghanistan: The Australian Story*—had been screened on his Seven Network.

The IGADF's inquiry was now underway. Given that it was likely to produce some confronting findings, I took the opportunity to raise this at a morning meeting with Brendan soon after Anzac Day in 2017. I made the point that Charles Bean, who had founded the Australian War Memorial, had never shied away from the ugly face of war: his official history of World War I, while commonly criticised for romanticising the Anzacs, had referenced widespread misconduct, including war crimes. I wondered out loud whether it was time to frame a new debate about war bringing out the worst in us, as well as the best.

The director was immediately animated—not about war crimes, but about the damage he had seen to veterans and their families, as they struggled to reconcile trauma. To my surprise, he cited Ben Roberts-Smith as an example. 'I am worried that Ben might be self-destructing,' he said.

His comment showed concern more than criticism. He mentioned Ben being at odds with his own parents, who had been banned from seeing their grandchildren. Brendan thought this was wrong, and said he would look for an opportunity to counsel Ben. In further conversation, he told me that Roberts-Smith had revealed having killed 84 men, which Brendan thought might account for his personal demons, which were now making occasional public appearances.

We moved on and talked about an upcoming exhibit. A little later, Brendan Nelson would be again dragged into this saga, but not in a way I might have anticipated.

One promise I had made to Ben Roberts-Smith at the rose garden meeting was that, once the manuscript for my book was complete, I would send him all text that related to him, so he could review it and amend it if it was erroneous.

Ben had in turn recommended I speak to his Brisbane-based lawyer. This I did. The lawyer advised me that inconsistencies at Koran Ghar could be reconciled if I trusted the contemporaneous after-action report. But treating official records as gospel, particularly in the face of contrary evidence, is not what reporters are supposed to do.

Having finalised the chapters, I emailed the relevant extracts to Ben on 5 July 2017. In my email I referred to the alleged cliff kick.

'Ben. The attachment contains quotes and references to yourself in my book, due for publication October/November. This is a draft, so I am open to all opportunity to amend and correct for the sake of fairness and accuracy. Some allegations/assertions might make difficult reading and for that I apologise. A more serious accusation pertaining to yourself, the alleged execution of a PUC [person under control] during the pursuit of OBJ Jungle Effect on Rot XVIII is not dealt with in this manuscript. But if you wish to discuss this, I am again open to do so . . .'[1]

The response was a flurry of legal letters, not from Roberts-Smith but from Mark O'Brien Legal. The former counsel for the Nine Network, Mark O'Brien is a heavyweight defamation lawyer with a well-established practice in Sydney, a city grimly regarded by many in the media as the defamation capital of the world.

On 11 July, O'Brien wrote to my publisher, Allen & Unwin, claiming that I was clearly doing 'a complete "hatchet job" on my client'.[2] On behalf of his client, he challenged the accuracy of the content in my extracts, but he did not address the factual inconsistencies that I had highlighted.

On the same day, Ben Roberts-Smith wrote to Dr Brendan Nelson. He began:

> It has been brought to my attention by Mr Chris Masters that an interview conducted by Dr Peter Pederson [*sic*] with myself on the 22 February 2011 around my experiences contains some inaccuracies. Given the important role of the Australian War Memorial in documenting our war history, I feel it only right to offer to correct the record. I am detailing this formally to ensure any changes are transparent.[3]

He went on to explain that his many engagements and deployments may have contributed to the confusion, and he was happy to re-record the interview.

A week later, The Redhead received a letter demanding that he align his account of the Koran Ghar battle with that of Roberts-Smith and the official report, otherwise 'my client has instructed me to commence defamation proceedings against you, separate from any proceedings which he may commence against Mr Masters and the publisher'.[4]

The next day, The Sig received similar correspondence. 'My letter requests you immediately contact Mr Masters to confirm that you do not dispute the sequence of battle in June 2006 as outlined by my client and set out in the after-action report . . . if necessary, this will be relied upon in any defamation proceedings.'[5] Another letter followed, repeating the threat, and further accusing The Sig of conspiring with The Redhead.[6]

So, in one breath Ben Roberts-Smith was admitting that his version of what happened at Koran Ghar was wrong. And in another, he threatened two former comrades with legal action if they did not surrender to his account.

It was now lawyers at ten paces. From here on, differences would not be mediated via public relations channels or face to face. And so it came to pass that the key players in this matter set out on a legal blood trail that only fools and billionaires would contemplate.

CHAPTER 10

SCOOP

I needed an ally.

Nick McKenzie was the obvious choice. We had first met in 2002. In his first year in journalism, Nick had been awarded an Andrew Olle Scholarship.

I don't think I took to him immediately. A force of nature, commanding and with confidence way outstripping his experience, the brash cadet was not what you might expect of a 21-year-old.

Some of my colleagues at *Four Corners* later took to calling him 'Scoop'. Well deserved, considering the stories he has broken over the years. I know of no one more prolific. Hard to fully get a grip on, even now. '*Sui generis*,' I would reply, when asked. One of a kind.

Despite a 30-year age difference, we became close friends. I liked talking stories with Nick. And here is a key. Of all the qualifications that matter—researching, writing, interviewing, scholarship, endurance and more—passion is what most counts. A reporter's enthusiasm for a story, big or small, fuels an engine room of effort. You can have a dozen degrees, proficiency in ten languages and the charisma of a matinee idol, but if you're not interested in the story, it is not going to work.

When I was in Afghanistan I would write to Nick, and in Australia—though he was based in Victoria and me in New South Wales—we often caught up. Over the years, we collaborated on a range of projects.

Here was something else you don't often see in the scribbler's playbook. Journalists tend to be possessive. The last thing we want is to be gazumped by a competitor who has put in half the effort. Time and time again I saw Nick work in a range of partnerships. He liked to share.

Through 2017, there was many a long conversation about what, for now, could be reported about the Australian special forces in Afghanistan, and what might have to wait. And when my publisher, Allen & Unwin, began to ponder the newspaper serialisation rights for my new book, I immediately suggested that Nick was the right person to edit extracts for *The Age* and *The Sydney Morning Herald*, where he was now a senior reporter.

While what was chosen was not my first choice, I could not much complain. The news industry likes arresting headlines. The Koran Ghar brouhaha would be highlighted. I had pushed for another action from the same chapter, about a perilous commando rescue mission, but could not deny it was less newsworthy.

There was every reason to see the tumult ahead. It had happened before. Back in 2006, when my book *Jonestown*, an unauthorised biography of Alan Jones, was about to be released, reporting focused on the broadcaster's secret homosexuality. It was hardly the main point of the book, but for months and years afterwards I battled accusations of having dared to out Alan. We not only have little control over our reputations, but little power to influence the debate we think matters. The book was more about Jones' power.

And in this new one, Ben Roberts-Smith was far from the centre of attention. In 600 pages he featured irregularly, one character among hundreds. Equally, the IGADF's inquiry cast a wide net, examining hundreds of incidents, the majority not involving Roberts-Smith.

But again, the story/debate was about to bolt like a runaway steer. Like the soldiers, we journalists end up fighting the war in front of us rather than the one we thought we were meant to fight. And journalism is my industry: if I wanted to moan, I should do so to myself.

Prior to the publication of the extracts he had edited, Nick separately approached Ben Roberts-Smith and requested an interview; in his correspondence he identified Roberts-Smith 'as a target for some complaints' to the IGADF.[1]

A response from Mark O'Brien Legal mirrored that received by Allen & Unwin. Mark O'Brien accused McKenzie of 'falsely linking' Roberts-Smith to the inquiry, 'purely for a headline grabbing purpose'. The lawyer asserted that any such publication represented 'a most despicable and indefensible defamation'.[2]

Neither in the extracts nor in the book was Ben Roberts-Smith accused of breaking any laws. The wicked problem of whether to shoot an unarmed Afghan at Koran Ghar was fairly presented—not as a war crime, but reflecting the mountain of challenges confronting combatants.

There was no cause to sue. The reporting of Koran Ghar, even with all its deviations from the official version, inflicted no enduring injury to Roberts-Smith's reputation.

But Ben was not of a mindset to let things go.

CHAPTER 11

UN-AUSTRALIAN

It was supposed to be a party.

Early in November 2017, the warring tribes gathered. Journalists and soldiers are not an easy mix.

At my own expense, I booked a room at the Royal Automobile Club in Sydney. Beer and wine on the bar. Appetisers on trays and a pile of books in the corner. *No Front Line* was now published.

In the ADF, they have an unofficial 'carton rule'. If a soldier is the subject of publicity, they must turn on a carton of beer for their mates. Presumably the aim is to restrain bragging.

Among special forces operators, obliged to stay in the shadows, the need for secrecy is even more severe. My colleagues across the media turned up with an express understanding that this would be a no-publicity event. Chatham House Rules would apply. I thought it a good opportunity to break down some barriers.

I had made some good friends in the special forces community. Many had stuck their necks out. I often say that the only way you win trust is to earn it, and I wanted now to honour the trust.

There was another divide in the room: between the Commandos and the SASR. Like warring bikie gangs, the boys eyed one another across the room. They did not mingle as I'd hoped. Too much wine was spilled, but it was a memorable occasion all the same.

One sour note came later, when I was told the proceedings had been secretly tape-recorded and allegedly passed to a Ben Roberts-Smith supporter. With so many secret squirrels in the room, this should not have been too much of a surprise, but it was disappointing all the same.

In the month leading up to publication, I had copped a beating in Kerry Stokes' *The West Australian* and in the national broadsheet, *The Australian*, which are both, of course, rival publications to Fairfax's *The Age* and *The Sydney Morning Herald*.

It began with a phone call from *The Australian*'s editor, Paul Whittaker, who asked about serialisation rights. When I told him Fairfax had them, battlelines were drawn. This had happened before, when *Jonestown* was also serialised by the Fairfax papers.

Just prior to the book launch, *The Australian* splashed a headline: 'VC hero Ben Roberts-Smith: I did nothing wrong in Afghanistan'. A swathe of further reporting followed. The war hero offered up to the newspaper's reporters my long list of failings, prominent among them the scoundrel sin of being 'un-Australian'.

Via the reporters, Ben Roberts-Smith posed twelve questions, presumably for them to prosecute. The first was about Matt Locke: the prospect that I was causing distress to his family by painting the now deceased soldier 'in a bad light'.

I had written respectfully and positively about Locke at Koran Ghar. Regarding communication with the families of deceased soldiers, I had reached out to all for whom I had contact details. An arrangement had been struck with Defence for them to contact others, if there was a perceived need—for example, if any content might be unknown to them or might cause upset.

Defence had seen no need to contact Locke's family and nor did I. In my view it was more Roberts-Smith who dragged his family into the story. Ben did not need to highlight Locke's role. My account asserted no wrongdoing by Locke; indeed, it commended him: 'There is no denying his bravery moving forward to take on the enemy alone . . .'[1]

Ben Roberts-Smith also asked for details of my 'official access' to Defence and whether General David Morrison had been involved. It was a query that appeared to emanate from deep recesses of mistrust and opportunism.

In 2013, the Chief of Army, Lieutenant General David Morrison, became famous across the world, both revered and reviled, after a landmark speech. With help from his speechwriter, former Lieutenant Colonel Cate McGregor, Morrison confronted entrenched misogyny and sexual abuse. 'The standard you walk past is the standard you accept,' he said.

It was no surprise then that the tough-guy mafia in the ADF and special forces hated Morrison. I could see how he fitted any conspiracy theory. It was, of course, absurd. I knew him only slightly, and there had never been communication between us regarding the book.

That did not stop Roberts-Smith from launching protracted and expensive freedom-of-information searches. Addisons Lawyers, acting on behalf of the Seven Network, requested access to my deed of agreement. It was passing strange—a media company, which employs hundreds of journalists, was probing the affairs of a journalist.

My guess is that Roberts-Smith was on a mission to prove a conspiracy had been forged between senior Defence personnel and me. Along the way I had picked up that such a rumour existed—to the effect that 'Masters was paid by the brass to do a job on Special Forces.' In fact, there was no commercial arrangement, and no conspiracy.

When we spoke in April, Roberts-Smith had offered me a hint of all this fear and loathing. He told me, 'Now the IGADF is involved, because they have seen what you gave SOCOMD.'

Addisons Lawyers also sought documentation relating to my employment at the Australian War Memorial (which had unceremoniously ceased). Between 2013 and 2017 I had worked on a range of galleries as well as the documentary project; more work that had been flagged did not eventuate. I presume I was suddenly persona non grata. Within the institution, the Addisons freedom-of-information inquiry seemed to generate panic, not about the false history I'd uncovered but about how I'd accessed this information.

Soon after *The Australian*'s strident defence of Ben Roberts-Smith, a handwritten note, with lots of underscoring in red, was sent to Trent Dalton and Rory Callinan, the two journalists who wrote the October 2017 front-page story headlined 'VC hero Ben Roberts-Smith: I did nothing wrong in Afghanistan'. The anonymous author suggested, 'perhaps you both better warn that UnAustralian—fuckwitted—traitorous (so called) journalist Chris Masters (despite defence-facilitated) better watch his back . . .'[2]

I can't say I handle well being beaten up by fellow reporters. My view is that there is a shared responsibility. We work first for the public, so there should be some shared values and purpose. This was a tough story. But I would be a fool to expect a soft ride. Institutional competitiveness, generally seen as a positive, is much less so in the media.

The Australian's reporting on the war crimes now under scrutiny, and especially on Ben Roberts-Smith, was flimsy and partisan. Probably because they had not done the work, because they were incapable of catching up and had an ingrained oppositional stance to Fairfax, and because they could not resist the spoils of a drip-feeding by Roberts-Smith's lawyers. For many months ahead, *The Australian* would defend Roberts-Smith and maintain its criticism of the IGADF inquiry.

Their reporters may have thought I would not be too fussed, given the maxim that any publicity is good publicity. At the time, Rory Callinan wrote to me: 'Not sure this controversy is a bad thing for the book.'[3] And they were probably acting under editorial direction. An indirect message from an unknown journalist at News Ltd was forwarded to me by one of the soldiers: 'If you are in contact with anyone at Fairfax let them know that despite a lot of pressure, not all of us are prepared to publish what we are told.'

The West Australian followed suit. Kerry Stokes' newspaper, well read by members of the Perth-based SASR, was even more strident in its challenges to the book and the IGADF. In the months and years ahead, the paper ran strong support for Roberts-Smith while unfavourably referencing my work on the whole and never once calling or writing to me. Perhaps they were too ashamed.

Even before my book's release, a firmament of anger framed public debate. The Australian War Memorial's director, Dr Brendan Nelson, became the highest-profile defender of Ben Roberts-Smith. He was a prominent critic of the IGADF inquiry and of Fairfax's reporting of the ongoing controversy, in journalism often jointly written by Nick McKenzie and me.

Brendan might not have been the first choice among Canberra's political elite, but, given wariness about commenting on matters under formal investigation by the IGADF, lobbying of serving politicians by pro-Roberts-Smith forces had not gone well.

Up to now, Brendan and I had not been at odds, but I came to presume that his stance against me was likely influenced by the AWM's chairman, Kerry Stokes. Not that there were any signs of a lack of enthusiasm on his part. A gifted public speaker, with an astonishing memory for detail, on multiple occasions he exuded conviction and passion. 'I don't think that any of us on the thrones of sanctimony in our comfortable lives can make judgment about what happens in the heat of battles unless there is a most egregious breach of the laws of armed conflict,' he thundered.[4]

Seven's owner appeared to be even more protective of his war hero Queensland general manager. The news website *Crikey* quoted an unnamed *West Australian* reporter: 'Kerry Stokes was feral in defence of Roberts-Smith.'[5]

Another former reporter from *The West Australian* told me that in his time Kerry Stokes had not been particularly interventionist, except when it came to stories about the SAS. One officer recalled Stokes at a pre-deployment drinks quietly telling the proprietor to open the bar and send him the bill. Stokes was further admired for having offered immediate aid and comfort following the Blackhawk helicopters crash in 1996, which killed fifteen members of the regiment.

My contacts in Perth thought the septuagenarian billionaire, who was well known for his heartfelt views on the Anzacs, looked on members of his beloved regiment as a 'protected species'. That respect appeared not to extend to those members who believed that their time-honoured values had been betrayed.

While there was a chance of challenging misinformation in the east, in Western Australia it was more difficult. Perth is a one-newspaper town. The one-sided coverage was not only damaging to truth but also disadvantageous to goodwill.

In our age of fake news, the loudest voice tends to win. And, as ever, Fairfax's critical coverage triggered extensive abuse on social media. 'Cam' texted me: 'How you could have the nerve to discredit any of our forces beggars belief . . . to denigrate our VC winners is beyond me.' 'Scott' bellowed: 'Who the fuck do you think you are . . . if I was you don't walk down any dark alleys and I'd watch that spineless back of yours.'

Opponents were keen to depict Nick and me as enemies of the Australian soldier and special forces, and we knew there was a danger that our key allies in the regiment might turn away from us. They were always being told no good would come of contact with the media. Prospective supporters were more likely the quieter voices. The SAS had long prided itself on humility, professionalism and understated excellence.

Looking back, getting into a fight with Australia's most decorated soldier and a billionaire might not seem to have been our smartest move. But even if Nick and I had wished for a different alignment of the stars, our course was set. In an op-ed piece for Fairfax, I remarked on the irony: 'Who would have anticipated that my opponents would be neither the government nor the Defence Force, but a constellation of friends, fellow journalists and a television network?'[6]

CHAPTER 12

WHISKEY 108

Even now it is hard to pinpoint the exact moment when we learned of a second alleged execution by Ben Roberts-Smith. His angry response to negative reporting had something to do with it. It ensured that Roberts-Smith, long a figure of controversy, was discussed even more widely, and so the events at Whiskey 108 came to our notice.

The compounds where Afghans lived were coded. This particular compound was near Kakarak, in Uruzgan; it was numbered 108 and stood on the west (W) side of the Dorafshan River. It had long been a Taliban hotspot.

An SAS soldier had been wounded near there a year earlier. And on 16 March 2009, Corporal Matthew Hopkins from the 7th Battalion of the Royal Australian Regiment (7RAR) was shot nearby while returning fire. The young father's life was ended by a Taliban bullet to the head.

In the following weeks, fighting persisted around Whiskey 108, on both sides of the river in what was termed a high-activity zone (HAZ). 7RAR continued its patrolling; rifle and cannon fire echoed through the valley.

On 12 April, camped above at Patrol Base Qudus, G-Troop from 2 Squadron SASR watched on, according to one of the operators, with 'heads up like meerkats'. An air strike was requested. At 1221 hours, a 500-pound bomb streaked from the sky, smashing into the northern wall of Whiskey 108. There was a scurry of activity inside the compound, and armed fighters moving for cover were picked up by a patrolling drone.

The troop captain of 2 Squadron made a classic SAS 'who dares wins' call. In broad daylight, across open country, his squadron would launch an assault. Five six-man patrols, each with a defined role, covered one another. Ben Roberts-Smith was second-in-command (2IC) of Gothic 5; his patrol commander was The Scot.

The duo was already known for some conspicuous chest-beating. The Scot could be disparaging of some of his fellow operators for being 'soft'; those he would relegate to support roles. His denigration would later metastasise to charges of outright cowardice.

Gothic 2 and Gothic 5 would be the two primary assault teams in this offensive. Gothic 4, led by The Veteran, would lead the approach and provide cordon security for the assault teams.

On their way in, spotting fleeting movement, Gothic 4 engaged and killed three insurgents. The last was shot by the patrol's forward scout (Person 14, The Scout), through broken cover, close to the compound. Stooping to quickly scan the body, he was momentarily puzzled, seeing no obvious entry wound. The fighter had been shot neatly through the cornea.

Ben Roberts-Smith's patrol, Gothic 5, was the first to enter the compound. From outside, through a break in the wall, The Scout saw a body with a prosthetic leg thrown to the ground. And then he saw a soldier raise their gun and fire an accompanying burst. Although uncertain, he assumed the shooter was Roberts-Smith.

The details of what happened at this time would be widely, if covertly, discussed later by those who were there that day. The episode ultimately polarised the entire troop, with the witnesses divided for and against Ben Roberts-Smith.

Nothing heard at this stage was from a primary source. As was the case when we later learned of another killing inside Whiskey 108, equally blurred in detail, which was to prove very destructive of troop morale.

The soldiers, highly trained special operators, were not squeamish about killing. It was, after all, their job. What some—hopefully the majority—did not like was outright murder. And there were intense misgivings about junior soldiers being bullied into acts they could not live with.

Here I need to backtrack a touch. By this stage, various sources had spoken to Nick and me about 'blooding'. Early in the rotation, the patrol commander of Gothic 5, The Scot, was heard proclaiming a need to 'blood the rookie'. It was rumour only, but it was thought a second victim within Whiskey 108, after coercion, had been executed by the team's newest member.

I will call him The Gunsmith (Person 4). Although new to the SASR, he was an experienced and popular soldier. The Gunsmith would become a crucial witness.

Over time, these snatches of rumour hardened to become a centrepiece war crimes allegation. In summary, what we came to allege was that after Gothic 5 and Gothic 2 entered the compound, two Afghan males were found hiding in a tunnel and, soon after, executed.

On that day, 31 SAS operators were at Whiskey 108. Thirteen years on, fourteen of the 31 would be questioned about what happened. Six, among them Ben Roberts-Smith, asserted no men were found in the tunnel and no war crimes occurred. Another seven saw otherwise, observing Afghan men being detained, and in three cases directly witnessing executions.

In the history of armed conflict it would be hard to find another operational incident that would be so thoroughly scrutinised.

CHAPTER 13

BATTLELINES

Ben Roberts-Smith and The Gunsmith had not seen each other for a while when they caught up in Brisbane in December 2017.

For much of the preceding decade, their friendship had run hot and cold. They had been together for the Victoria Cross action at Tizak in 2010; indeed, many believed The Gunsmith had done as much as Roberts-Smith, but that he'd received only belated recognition. The two men's forged-in-battle bond would come under further strain after Darwan, when The Gunsmith struggled with what could not be unseen.

At Moo Moo's Bar and Grill, over drinks and dinner that night, they shared 'warries'. As well, Roberts-Smith floated the prospect of using his influence to secure for The Gunsmith a Wandering Warriors tertiary scholarship, so as to advance his post-SAS job prospects. There was booze and blandishment. And while the scholarship would not eventuate, the evening ended with a tearful embrace and some promise of reconciliation.

The Sniper (Person 11) had also been with Roberts-Smith at Darwan in 2012. The Gunsmith and The Sniper were close; The Gunsmith had been best man at The Sniper's wedding. As the only SAS troopers at the cliffside with Roberts-Smith, both were vital witnesses—and both were showing signs of mental disintegration.

Roberts-Smith also reached out to The Sniper. In September 2017, when The Sniper was called by Justice Brereton for questioning about

Darwan, he and Ben spoke. They would deny discussing evidence, in breach of IGADF non-disclosure orders, saying it was just mates catching up. And in February 2018 they caught up again, at the Floreat Hotel in Perth.

At this stage, Roberts-Smith had had no contact with the Brereton inquiry's investigators, but, given his awareness of the interviews conducted with other soldiers, he clearly knew they were circling. In a phone conversation with a former comrade that Roberts-Smith recorded, he reveals himself as a man under siege: 'I've never spoken to them, and I've never been brought in by them . . . it's going to be what it's going to be, some ridiculous, broad sweeping thing and it really fucks everybody over, and it has no purpose, and it is not necessary.'[1]

In the same phone conversation, he was vitriolic about a group of SAS soldiers he falsely thought were conspiring against him: 'You've got to understand my position, mate, and how many people got together and deliberately targeted me by fucking colluding about a lot of shit . . . I find it pretty fucking hard to take.'[2] There was also contempt for non-compliant journalists, oddly intertwined with a Defence leadership group, whom Roberts-Smith believed were out to get him:

> I want to move on. I am so fucking sick of the Army and the unit and all the bullshit that goes on there. Just remember I was minding my own business one day and I get attacked by all these journalists in a week, just trying to do my job.[3]

Nor were things going well for him at work. If there had been a belief that the television prima donnas needed a dose of barracks-room discipline to deflate their industrial-scale egos, it was not gaining traction. Now, a few years into his $700,000 gig, his colleagues at Channel Seven Brisbane had taken to nicknaming their boss 'BRS MIA'. He was either on a plane somewhere or at lunch, as staff put it, with 'some AJ [Army Jerk] mates'.

For his part, over red wine and grilled swordfish, the general manager held nothing back about his colleagues: Roberts-Smith's commentary, covertly and legally recorded, would later feature in our reporting. Here is one example: 'They know I am close to Kerry and hate me for it because I have a direct line to the chairman. They think I am a dumb fucking soldier that Kerry gave a job, that's why I did the MBA. I don't even like the industry.'

He was now often not returning to his family of an evening. The home of Ben, Emma and their twin daughters in the Sunshine Coast hinterland was a 100-minute drive from Brisbane, not always wise after a long lunch.

At home, Emma was becoming concerned about his drinking. He would reportedly sit alone on the steps, going through multiple bottles of wine. Fearing it was the drink that was consuming him, the concerned wife confronted her husband. Later, in a text to a friend, she disclosed that 'he realises that his drinking is out of control'. At Emma's urging, he saw a doctor, Parbodh Gogna, a friend from his Army days, who in turn referred him to a psychiatrist. After this, for a time, his drinking moderated.

Another stress would likely have been the other woman in Roberts-Smith's life.

There had always been plenty of opportunities for dalliance—a glamour industry, hero worship and five-star hotels. Male colleagues, with embarrassment and envy, could not miss how their female counterparts swooned in the presence of the broad-shouldered war hero. The frequent travel and his speaking engagements put him literally on many a pedestal.

In October 2017, days ahead of the newspaper coverage of the Koran Ghar battle, Roberts-Smith began an affair with a married mother he had met at a charity function.

His life was becoming more complicated. You see it from time to time: a person under stress escaping chaos into more chaos, their thought patterns a whirlpool of vengeance and paranoia.

In Ben's mind, it appears, it became a game of numbers. He had to match or, better, overmatch the soldiers he believed were speaking against him. It was time to align his big guns to face the enemy triumvirate of former mates, military investigators and media.

Thanks to the Kerry Stokes war chest, Ben Roberts-Smith was able to assemble separate teams of lawyers to focus on the Brereton inquiry, defamation issues and FOI searches.

And there was another weapon, John McLeod. The private inquiry agent, enlisted to spy at cocktail parties, was further tasked as rat catcher. Roberts-Smith was seeking to neutralise more of those traitorous 'mates'.

His first target was The Veteran. Roberts-Smith knew the SAS sergeant had led the protest regarding Roberts-Smith's CDS.

Twenty years Ben's senior, The Veteran had the skill set of an old-school SAS operator. Within the regiment, this watery was famous for a range of unspoken exploits. He was also known for a quality common enough within the regiment's non-commissioned officer (NCO) class: he spoke his mind, plain and blunt, to all, officers included.

The Veteran had deployed with Roberts-Smith in 2009 and 2012. On one of the early missions as a patrol sergeant, he had castigated Lance Corporal Roberts-Smith for abandoning his post. He regarded the dressing-down as an important and measured professional intervention. 'I got stuck into him, but he did not give a fuck.' There were further incidents bringing the leathery sergeant to a characteristically unfiltered observation that 'RS has got balls, I'll give him that. But otherwise, he is an infant who ends up believing his own fantasies. A showboating piece of shit. Not a good soldier. A big boofhead.'

It would be fair to say that Roberts-Smith thought no more kindly of The Veteran. And he was determined to have his revenge.

In October 2017, John McLeod was persuaded to create an anonymous email address and write to the commissioner of the Australian Federal Police, Andrew Colvin. The letter alleged that The Veteran was involved in weapons smuggling and was in possession of an unregistered firearm.

Soon after, the same information was sent, via the same means, to South Australian senator Nick Xenophon, with the additional note that The Veteran was unstable and in danger of repeating the 'Los [*sic*] Vegas massacre'. (Weeks earlier in that US city, a lone gunman had fired from a high-rise building at a music festival crowd, killing 60 and wounding 413 people.)

Next, McLeod emailed *The Australian* newspaper. Journalist Andrew Burrell responded, asking if the allegation came from a serving SAS member. McLeod consulted with Roberts-Smith and replied, 'Yes'.

In November, *The Australian* published two reports, alleging that, according to an unnamed 'military whistle-blower', an unnamed SAS member was engaged in weapons smuggling.[4]

It was after midnight on 22 November 2017 when armed West Australian police came through the door. The Veteran was used to holding his nerve, but he could do little to ease the distress of his wife and children.

Across opposing battlelines in the SAS, a new frontier had just opened. Family space was now being invaded. Furthermore, Ben Roberts-Smith had engaged in the very conduct he said he despised in others: he had surreptitiously used the media to attack a perceived enemy.

After stressful hours for The Veteran and his family, with neighbours rubbernecking, police withdrew, having found nothing. No charges were laid. But all through the ranks something clear was signalled. Oppose BRS and there would be consequences.

Roberts-Smith himself said as much. When Emma Roberts-Smith read about the raid in the newspaper, dumbfounded she asked him, 'What the fuck?' In reply, he sent a text message: 'What happened to The Veteran will scare the others.'

At this stage, by Roberts-Smith's mental calculations, the 'others', who were undertaking a 'whispering campaign' to the media (and the Brereton inquiry), were five serving members of the SASR.

If the beleaguered war hero had been able to appraise the facts more calmly, he might have taken some comfort. Of the five soldiers, only one had been interviewed—for my book—and not a word had been uttered about war crimes.

CHAPTER 14

THE SCOUT

It was a breakfast meeting on the outskirts of Canberra. Early 2018.

When I arrived at the cafe, I found a lone four-wheel drive parked outside. Inside, a lone individual was seated. Thirty-something, fit, with a trim beard and moustache. The soldier was typical of the special forces paradox: they aim to be both anonymous (to outsiders) and recognisable (to each other).

Easygoing, too. Soon after the conversation opened, I was enthralled. The Scout is a natural storyteller. It was swiftly apparent that The Scout was one of those people investigative journalists live for, someone who can't help but tell the truth.

I had once hoped to interview him for *No Front Line*, but I'd been unable to connect with him before we met at the launch. With an updated edition planned for release at the end of 2018, I was keen to gather more information. And there was no denying it: there were clues that he could provide more information about Ben Roberts-Smith.

When The Scout had first gained SAS selection, he had made a deliberate choice to become a 'landy': 'The wateries were too much like a club,' he said. His first hit-out in Afghanistan was on Rotation I in 2005. He was also there on the ground for the Whiskey 108 action of 2009.

Over a strong coffee and the breakfast special, he explained that, before the Whiskey 108 episode, he had heard The Scot referring to The

Gunsmith as 'the rookie'. And he'd heard him intone, in his distinctive Scottish brogue, a need to 'blood the rookie'.

My note-taking at our meeting later became relevant, with argument about its accuracy.

In general, for background interviews, I don't use a recorder. I find this saves time: you don't have to listen twice. Furthermore, I don't take extensive and conspicuous notes, because this can put the interviewee off. You try not to inhibit candour. Rather than having a notebook, I just scribble on a scrap of paper key words, rather than verbatim quotes; this is less intrusive and the information flow is freer. Later, the scrap of paper can be discarded after I've composed a record of the interview. Those key words and hopefully my memory are sufficient for me to fill in the detail.

A weakness in this method, of course, is that it relies on memory. But for background interviews that is of less concern, because my practice is always to check the accuracy of content before publication. A reporter's research notes from protected sources are meant to remain confidential.

When my notes for this morning's conversation were later typed up, I made reference to The Scout having spotted something through a doorway at Whiskey 108. And this: 'RS had an M14 and The Gunsmith a Minimi. Understood The Gunsmith had shot an old guy with a prosthetic leg.' While the bulk of my record of interview was accurate, this detail was wrong.

Of all the soldiers I interviewed, The Scout was among the most courageous and principled. I believe that the error was not his—it was mine.

When I had paused, pen in hand, my coffee having gone cold, there was perhaps a lapse of concentration. But what I was next told certainly captured and redirected my attention.

After leaving the meeting, and before the four-hour drive home to my laptop, I reached for my phone. In breathless bursts I relayed to Nick McKenzie the first direct evidence we had of Ben Roberts-Smith's involvement in a war crime. This one, not at Whiskey 108 but in a different year, on a different mission—to Chinartu.

CHAPTER 15
CHINARTU

Insurgent figures of prime interest to the SAS were called 'objectives' and assigned code names, selected at random by computers—or by intelligence analysts with a taste for eccentricity. The target in this story was a mid-level Taliban commander who came with the tag Objective Stolen Idea.

Taliban objectives were kept under constant surveillance. When a voice signature on a cell phone or Icom UHF radio 'pinged', assault teams at Camp Russell would scramble to the ready room and launch from the adjacent tarmac. On 12 October 2012, the ping resulted in a mission to Chinartu, in Uruzgan.

Such is Uruzgan's complex tribal tapestry that there were two Chinartus. One was known as 'Good Chinartu' and was friendly to the Coalition. And then there was this one.

A few years back, convoys of Bushmasters would have taken all day to cover this distance, slogging along over IED-strewn dirt tracks, but now the Blackhawks, with their Apache escorts, took just twelve minutes to get there.

The Scout was strapped into the back row of one of the choppers. The patrol commander, Corporal Ben Roberts-Smith, was up the front.

As ever, the teams had earlier been assigned specific roles—assault, cordon protection, overwatch, detention management and tactical questioning. But as they were about to land, The Scout heard Roberts-Smith shout a change of plan. Something like 'Fuck the cordon! We will head straight for the VRI [very reliable intelligence]'—meaning they would abandon detailed groundwork and instead go straight for the target.

While Roberts-Smith, with a team of Australian SAS and Afghan partner force members, hurried in single file towards the targeted compound, The Scout and another soldier set about providing security and attending to prospective threats from the bypassed compounds. At these compounds, they found fighting-age males who were familiar with the routine; they were compliantly assembled and a 'PUC train' was formed so they could later be 'tactically questioned' (or TQ'd).

The Scout then moved to the main target compound, where he saw in a room Ben Roberts-Smith with a bearded, middle-aged Afghan male dressed in a white traditional robe. Alongside Roberts-Smith were Afghan partner force soldiers and their leader, The Lieutenant (Person 12).

The fact that this soldier was present on that day would later become pivotal evidence, revealing a calculated and widespread effort to absolve Ben Roberts-Smith and mask the truth. The Lieutenant was a Wakunish commander. The Wakunish, or 'Wakas', were National Directorate of Security (NDS) commandos, better trained than regular Afghan National Army soldiers or militia. From the north, with zero sympathy for the Taliban, they could be ruthless.

Watching on from outside the room, The Scout noticed some discolouration in one of the compound's perimeter walls. Curious, he swung his boot twice at the patch and uncovered a cache: two pink and white bags of ammunition, two AK-47s, rocket-propelled grenade (RPG) warheads and binoculars.

Combat engineers swiftly took over. The find appeared to seal the fate of the man in white. In that moment, the mood in the compound room was transformed.

As The Scout watched on from the courtyard, it was as if, in an instant, the setting was a courtroom—and the verdict already clear. He saw Ben Roberts-Smith point to The Lieutenant and say: 'Tell him to shoot him, or I will.'

The Afghan interpreter, who we will call The Terp (Person 13), hesitant, queried: 'What?'

Roberts-Smith repeated: 'Tell him to shoot him, or I will.'

The Lieutenant conferred with his soldiers. One Wakunish, with his face masked, stepped up, trained his suppressed M4 on the man in white and methodically pulled the trigger. The man dropped. More rounds punched into the prone body.

At 1539 hours, a radio call was made: 'One EKIA.' (An EKIA designates an 'enemy killed in action.')

Some consternation followed, less about the summary execution as about the fact that the PUC numbers didn't add up. The Blackhawks were approaching, and the space was already allocated.

Two EKIAs at Chinartu were reported that day. The timing of the reported killings would have importance. One of the victims, not the man in white, was identified as Objective Stolen Idea.

The Scout's clear and consistent recollection of what occurred was not matched by that of his comrades. A soldier who had been by his side from the time they stepped off the helicopter would later have no memory whatsoever of the mission.

And Ben Roberts-Smith, as well as a further two comrades, came to condemn The Scout's account as a complete lie.

CHAPTER 16

THE SERGEANT

I won't deny a friendship. Some of it might have been forged over a shared interest in the rugby codes. But more so, The Sergeant proved helpful when I was researching *No Front Line*.

We met at the end of 2015. I had already heard the SAS sergeant was regarded as one of Perth's solid, unassuming, well-respected operators. Even rival Commandos spoke well of him.

He had joined the Army in 1994, after reading an Anzac Day newspaper supplement. His imagination had been caught by a German soldier's account of Australians fighting at Tobruk. The German wrote that he had at first lived in terror of bayonet-wielding Australian soldiers who were said to be merciless. But, he then explained, after he was wounded and left helpless in no-man's-land, an Australian soldier crawled up to him, applied first aid and effectively saved his life.

In 2001, having been selected into the SASR, The Sergeant embodied the regiment's core value of understated professionalism. The idea of the tough but fair Anzac, which had first fired his imagination, clung to him over the years and retained its grip. On a 2005 deployment to Afghanistan, when coming upon a wounded Taliban, he and a comrade pulled out a medical kit and applied the same treatment to the Afghan as had their forebear at Tobruk.

By then something of an amateur historian, The Sergeant was reading widely. Like Ben Roberts-Smith, he fought in the famous Battle of Tizak in 2010. After many a gunfight, he was now less starry-eyed, but he had developed a more rounded yet still respectful adherence to the notion of civilised soldiering.

He was not alone in holding to these hard-earned values, nor in recognising that, for others, the longest war had worn them down. Successive rotations had induced in some soldiers a preference for what the manual called 'direct action', and many men came to call 'killing bad guys'. But for old-school SAS types such as The Sergeant, that went against the grain. Staying in the shadows, collecting intelligence and suppressing violence was more the go. As was often said, 'The shot not fired can be more important.' And as The Sergeant himself would say, 'We are not Genghis Khan's raiders, we are Australian soldiers.'

It became clear to me from our earliest meetings that The Sergeant had a low regard for Ben Roberts-Smith. There was no denying that some passion and invective emerged whenever his name came up. But it always seemed to me that this anger sprang from an offence to professional principles, rather than from anything personal. After all, in 2011, when Ben Roberts-Smith was awarded his Victoria Cross and The Scot was awarded his Star of Gallantry, The Sergeant accompanied them on a promotional tour.

It is important also to say, because it was to become a matter of contention, that during my initial interviews for *No Front Line*, the issue of war crimes was not discussed with The Sergeant. I sensed that war crimes were not a topic he was eager to talk about, then or later.

Only long after our interviews for *No Front Line* and my contact with other sources—and after persistent questioning—were some incidents prised out of him.

In March 2010, I learned, during a compound clearance, The Sergeant's patrol came upon a man in a foetal position, catatonic with fear. His immediate thought was: 'Jeez, this bloke is shitting himself. We'll give him a moment and then we'll attempt to detain him again.'

At that moment Roberts-Smith appeared. As The Sergeant recalls: 'Didn't say a word. He got down on one knee. Then three or four quick-fire punches into the side of the Afghan's head, and then two knees into the chest/stomach area.'

The Sergeant said: 'Whoa, whoa, whoa! What are you doing? We're looking after this. Get out of here.'

Without a word, Roberts-Smith walked out of the room.

In August 2012, there was something similar. During another compound clearance, The Sergeant came upon Roberts-Smith holding an Afghan by the shirt against a wall. When the man was released, a tiny Afghan girl, in distress, ran to him crying. The Afghan squatted, cradling her in his arms.

Roberts-Smith stood glaring at them.

When The Sergeant challenged him, the following conversation ensued.

'What's going on here, RS?'

'He's a fucking bad cunt,' Roberts-Smith replied.

There was another incident, earlier on the same rotation. The Sergeant came upon Ben Roberts-Smith in the ready room, rummaging through their assault bags. There was an extraordinary exchange, a warrior soldier's version of a pre-game motivational rev-up. Roberts-Smith, now with VC, MG after his name, declared to The Sergeant: 'Hey mate, I'm going to talk the talk. I want you to make sure I walk the walk . . . Before this trip is over, I'm going to choke a man to death with my bare hands. I'm going to look him in the eye, and I'm going to watch the life drain out of his eyes.'

It was from such incidents, and more, that an assessment of Ben Roberts-Smith began to make the rounds: 'a dead-set psychopath, a fraud, the Lance Armstrong of the ADF'.

But of further concern was evidence that, even before Roberts-Smith was deployed in 2012, the path to blooding and murder was set. One particular scene, played out at Lancelin, a training area near Perth, stuck in a few memories.

Eleven years into the Afghanistan conflict, mission rehearsal training could seem as arduous as the mission itself. For five months a squadron would practise: live fire, helicopter insertion, dog-handling, detention management. Drill after drill at either the massive Cultana complex in South Australia, itself a mini-Afghanistan, or north of Perth, at either Bindoon or Lancelin.

For all the Coalition partners ensnared in Afghanistan, detention management had become a hot-button issue. Rough handling and locking up Afghans was hardly the way to win hearts and minds, so procedures were now in place to ensure humane treatment and to enable the collection of evidence so a prisoner could be accurately classified as either an innocent farmer or a committed Taliban.

One day at Lancelin, Corporal Ben Roberts-Smith was bedding down his new hand-picked team. The Sergeant watched on from a high vantage point; he had already been bothered by Roberts-Smith's absence from much of the pre-deployment training, when his VC duties had interfered.

Post-VC, the always confident Roberts-Smith was showing signs around the regiment of further emboldening. This was to be his first tour as a patrol commander, and members of his team were new to the regiment, one having no Afghanistan experience.

'Fucking kill him!' ordered Roberts-Smith. The Sergeant could see that the courtyard below had been configured to replicate a typical Afghan compound, with an SAS soldier (Person 9, The Dog Handler) role-playing as a prisoner, on his knees facing a wall. In a semicircle around him, armed with M4 assault rifles, stood three troopers with their patrol commander, Ben Roberts-Smith, in front.

The new member hand-picked to his patrol, yet to deploy to Afghanistan, we will call The Trooper. He was momentarily stunned by the order, The Sergeant saw, as he hesitated, confused. The manacled 'prisoner' twitched.

'Shoot him!' Roberts-Smith repeated.

Perplexed, but beginning to catch on, The Trooper pulled the trigger and uttered two words: 'Bang, bang!'

Even from a distance, The Sergeant could sense the relief of the 'prisoner'. Then he saw Roberts-Smith place his hand on his rookie's shoulder. 'Are you good with that?' The Sergeant heard Roberts-Smith ask him. 'Because that's how it's going to be when we get over there.'

Afterwards, at a nearby car park, The Sergeant caught up with the decorated corporal. 'Hey, RS, you got a second?' He could see Roberts-Smith was annoyed. They came face to face. 'What was that shit all about?'

Roberts-Smith: 'What shit?'

'You know what shit I'm talking about. Pull your head in. Grow up and wake up to yourself.'

Roberts-Smith turned and walked towards his car. The Sergeant heard him mutter, 'Fucking war.'

So, prospectively, an episode at Lancelin in May/June 2012 loomed large. Was this an indicator that allegations of murder in Afghanistan, if true, were far from flashes of fury born of chaos? That, instead, they were calculated, premeditated, months, if not years, in the planning?

CHAPTER 17

BLUE-ON-BLUE

It was 15 July 2012, two weeks into Rotation XVIII, a milestone for The Trooper and his patrol commander, Ben Roberts-Smith. It was not only Roberts-Smith's maiden mission as a lead planner, but also The Trooper's first serious venture outside the wire.

Another factor elevated the mission's status. They were going back to a compound of interest (COI) known as 'The Hilton', a Taliban hotspot in the Chora Valley, where an SAS old hand had been killed two weeks earlier—Sergeant Blaine Diddams, a friend of Ben Roberts-Smith. The target was the insurgent commander deemed responsible.

Two patrols, one led by Roberts-Smith, would walk in from a combat outpost the night before and take up blocking positions. The rest of the troop would later insert by helicopter, with the objective of driving squirters towards the secreted ground troops.

The two foot patrols arrived at the target area at dawn and assumed their blocking positions. As they did so, shots rang out. One round passed within centimetres of one of Ben Roberts-Smith's team (Person 22, The Rifleman). That soldier, along with Roberts-Smith, moved into the open to marry up with the other patrol.

While they were doing this, The Trooper, carrying a Minimi machine gun, went to ground behind a mound to provide covering fire. As he did so, he caught a fleeting glimpse of what he thought were two insurgents.

He started 'drake shooting'—that is, he started firing in the direction of likely cover to discourage enemy manoeuvring.

After a series of short bursts and clearing stoppages (when ammunition fails to feed), he heard his patrol commander yell, 'Cease fire! Cease fire! Cease fire!' Then, from the target area, a woman carrying a birdcage and a child were seen, thankfully unscathed.

The mission was blown. Worse, it transpired that the original shots had not been fired by the enemy but by the other SAS patrol. It was a 'blue-on-blue', sometimes unkindly referred to as an 'Irish ambush', and prospectively embarrassing for Ben, given this was his first planned mission.

Upon their return, the patrol commanders attended a troop debrief. It was admitted that the errant shots came from the other patrol. Poor planning might have been the issue.

But Roberts-Smith directed the blame squarely at his young trooper. In the meeting he railed, 'That cunt, that cunt, I fucking gave him an opportunity. He's gone and let me down. His eyes rolled in the back of his head, and he was blazing away uncontrollably with his Minimi.'

Back in the patrol room, The Trooper was seated on a couch when his lofty boss charged in and stood before him. 'Stand up!' The Trooper rose; the rest of the patrol watched on. Ben Roberts-Smith swung his fist into The Trooper's face, propelling him back onto the couch. Roberts-Smith berated the junior soldier.

In the jailhouse milieu of the special forces, a thump on the chin hardly ranks as a high crime, but in the Army, under the *Defence Force Discipline Act*, assaulting a subordinate is an offence. It was bullying. It was poor leadership. It was hardly exemplary mentoring. Worst of all, to many of The Trooper's peers, it was straight-up scapegoating. Here was another example of someone else taking the blame for Ben Roberts-Smith—in this case, for his less than auspicious beginning as a patrol commander.

The Trooper shouldered the blame. He admitted he was at fault in firing in the direction of the mother and child. In most cases, given his inexperience, this might have been considered excusable, but in this case, by the estimation of some onlookers, it was used to cover up the blue-on-blue.

The Trooper was given a formal warning, and for the rest of the rotation did not go outside the wire. He later resigned from the Army.

In 2013, while in the process of leaving the SASR, he prepared a statement explaining what had occurred. Ben Roberts-Smith intervened, pressuring The Trooper to ensure that his report aligned with Roberts-Smith's version. According to The Trooper: 'He threatened to report me to The Hague if I did not state that I was firing on the other patrol, essentially the blue-on-blue.'

Ben Roberts-Smith also contacted The Mechanic. You will recall this was the other new soldier in Ben's patrol, who lost his Army career after ammunition was found in his car in Perth. Telephoned by Roberts-Smith, The Mechanic was to pass on a warning to The Trooper: 'You tell that cunt, he'd better not say anything. Otherwise, I'll get him charged for war crimes.'

Corporal Roberts-Smith VC, MG maintained his role as patrol commander for Rotation XVIII. He was further rewarded with a CDS. In 2017, he told me:

> I did not want to leave the regiment until I had achieved patrol commander responsibilities. Out there it is often irrelevant as experience kicks in. I wanted to be a leader of a team and would not knock back an opportunity to be in a fight and be the one making the decisions.

Ben Roberts-Smith also said he had self-reported his assault of The Trooper, but nothing came of it. It appears the Victoria Cross had provided another layer of Teflon coating to an already protected persona.

CHAPTER 18

PERTH

At the beginning of March 2018, Nick and I needed to get to Perth.

This was a big story, but it was still unpublishable. More evidence was needed—and crucial corroboration. We needed to get up close and personal. Face to face is what counts. The people we were chasing rarely said much over the phone.

After presenting some background to Fairfax management, it was agreed we could have a few days in Perth, so we boarded a packed flight, arriving after dark. An Uber to a budget motel and hoofing off in search of a cheap meal.

I had seen some good years in investigative journalism, but you'll never find Hollywood budgets or celebrity employment packages. In my time at the ABC, cost cuts were as seasonal as floods and fire. And now the digital age was steadily eroding what was left of the traditional revenue base for important news journalism, whether in the broadcast or print media.

Getting difficult stories published takes a while. Investigative journalism is resource-intensive and subject to eternal budgetary pressure. For a freelance investigative journalist like me, the deal is a miserly one. We get the conventional dollar-a-word rate, irrespective of the time and effort applied. And anyone who knows anything about the Australian publishing market knows there are no great fortunes to be made in books.

For all that, the allegation that Nick and I were simply money-grubbers was a constant from the very well remunerated Ben Roberts-Smith. Brendan Nelson chimed in: 'It is strange that Defence has given access and assistance . . . for a book that will be written for profit.'[1]

Nick and I shared an enthusiasm for hunting down important truths. There is excitement in discovery. We had plenty of experience demonstrating to the nation the value of serious, risky journalism. And we understood our privilege. There are few media organisations left that will fund such a venture. Research, travel, legal support and all that time with nothing to show for it—all this cranks up the costs. And for what? Even more trouble.

Our working relationship was organically forged. Nick and I shared our research; he wrote the news stories for the front of *The Age* and *The Sydney Morning Herald*, while I provided the more reflective feature articles. The main purpose of our budget-stretching Perth trip was to convert allegations into reportable facts, but this proved hard going.

When I was researching *No Front Line*, it had been much the same. Alone in the West at that time, appointment after appointment had fallen through. I remembered long and fruitless waits for a call back.

And now the post-publication controversy over the book had rendered the traditionally shy SAS mob near mute. Some soldiers were found who were willing to talk, but there were more who backed away. A key witness politely declined. Another, who had earlier told me he was happy to meet, was now not answering his phone.

Nick, accustomed to the grind of daily journalism, urged me to be more aggressive. But it wasn't working. Investigative journalism is time-critical. A key reason we had got this far was through patience. The long lead time of the book had meant I was allowed months, even years, to build trust. In contrast, if you pressure people over the phone amid the tidal pull of the news cycle, the conversation swiftly drowns.

But you get used to knockbacks. Particularly early in the piece. After a long day of slim pickings, we would take stock. Nick's thing is to hold court. Over a beer he would summarise the evidence so far—dictating play, calling bullshit, anticipating the next move, highlighting amusing moments. His face would become suffused with something close to joy. He loves the hunt.

And then there is the other side of investigative journalism. One morning, I found him at breakfast hunched over a laptop, at a corner table, phone pressed hard to his ear. A conference call from the paper's lawyers in Melbourne. He had been sued again. Voice clipped, brow furrowed. I let him be.

We kept up the struggle. What we were encountering in Perth was a kinship of silence. It was commonly pressed on the operators that the reputation of the regiment overrides everything else. Appalling, but there it was. The sin of not having a mate's back was greater than the virtue of exposing war crimes.

'People don't want to dob in mates,' as one interviewee put it.

We caught up at a Fremantle coffee shop while he was halfway through a morning run. He came highly recommended by the soldiers. One said he had saved his life. A unit psychologist, he was helpful, more for the sake of context and a regimental brainscan. 'We want a functional psychopath,' he explained. 'They have got to want to hurt. We want them controllable and reintegrateable, but if they become attack dogs you can't control . . .'

There were no names named. Nick and I asked how often allegations of war crimes featured in routine post-deployment debriefings.

'It came up a lot. Soldiers would broach the subject as a hypothetical: "For example, what if this occurred?"' When he told them he would be obliged to report it, they would go quiet. He thought some of the officers had learned to not ask questions. So did we. The failure of curiosity was palpable, but with key exceptions.

Pete Winnall and I had become friends. I wanted Nick to meet him, and there he was at a spare laminex table in an Asian food court along the

Hay Street mall. A retired major, he still loved the regiment and had vivid, impassioned recollections of his tours, but not the happiest memory of his departure. Major Winnall was never forgiven for standing up to the bullies in the NCO mafia.

Now in business, he was putting it behind him. We ordered $5 stir-fries. Pete told us he worried that the unremitting Afghanistan deployments may have confused a defensible SAS culture of bending the rules with an indefensible one of breaking the law. 'The soldiers were expected to know the difference,' he said. 'There was always a pushing of the boundaries, but never at the expense of the values of the organisation. As a collective, there was always a strong sense of right and wrong.'

We did not talk about Ben Roberts-Smith. Pete knew Ben, but they had not deployed together.

It was good to catch up. Pete was already a precious source of reason. And a moral comfort. Going against the mob can be lonely and unnerving. It might even be true that from time to time we sought each other out for therapy. Mutual counselling can become a feature of the reporter/source dynamic.

Also, he had a mate who would become a further invaluable ally.

CHAPTER 19

'H'

The military loves its acronyms. Even its people can be reduced to a digitised descriptor. It was time to meet Andrew Hastie—or, rather, 'H'.

When the men call you 'boss' or some other personalised moniker, it can convey a form of respect. To an officer, it is often a compliment. Much the opposite to being declared 'sir', particularly when expressed with vehemence and unmissable contempt.

The officer/NCO bond is hard won. A young lieutenant, fresh out of Duntroon and taking command of a gang of experienced subordinates (sometimes insubordinates), can struggle. Be too nice to them and they will trample all over you. Too tough on them, and every response is a masterclass in obstinacy.

In the SASR, you can multiply that by ten. In general, the officers cycle through for shorter terms. The men, and particularly the NCOs, are there much longer. When you attach combat tour after combat tour and a jangle of gallantry medals to the curriculum vitae of a corporal or sergeant, the new-boy captain might have to dig even deeper for that voice of authority.

Since its inception, the SAS has struggled with the challenge of popularity over leadership. There are cruel examples of senior officers being booed from the mess, and of the humiliating 'Cock of the Year' award being conferred on junior officers at what was once the annual Stirrers' Parade.

The fact that the NCOs essentially run the selection program for the regiment adds the risk of nepotism and compliance to the mix. Outsiders could not fail to notice the number of brothers and sons swelling the ranks of the SAS; they might suspect that at least some of the junior leaders might be winning their places by demonstrating a willingness to become one of the boys.

But that is not Andrew Hastie's story.

Andrew Hastie had joined up just as his granddad had done. As he put it, he was 'long intrigued by military service as a rite of passage'. There was family pride in Norman 'Bill' Hastie DFC, who in 1945, as a wireless air gunner on an RAAF Catalina, was seriously wounded while rescuing a downed Beaufighter aircrew.

The younger Hastie is one of the 2001 generation, having enlisted as a reservist in that fateful year. Commissioned as a full-time member of the Australian Army in 2006, he first deployed to Afghanistan as a cavalry troop lieutenant in 2009. Seeing the SAS as 'the peak of soldiering', in the following year he completed selection.

His initiation into special forces soldiering was brutal. In 2013, on his first mission as a young captain, Hastie was posted to the perennially unsafe Shahid-e-Hasas district of north-western Uruzgan Province. He was there to defend a checkpoint manned by local Afghan security forces, condemned to a kind of suicide watch.

On 28 February, electronic indicators identified a looming attack. Two US Apache gunships were summoned, and their target was fixed. Sixty 30mm cannon rounds pounded the hillside.

But the Apache crews had committed a tragic error. As it turned out, their intended target was 300 metres away; it shared almost identical physical characteristics with the place they had pounded. Two small boys gathering firewood had their lives obliterated in an instant, while two Taliban spotters scuttled to safety 300 metres away.

Andrew Hastie immediately reported the ugly, undisguised facts of what had occurred to his superiors, and days later he made his way to the home of the boys. He was there to deliver a compensation payment and, however impossible, to attempt to make amends.

'I stepped into the centre of the room with the uncle and brother,' he related, 'and I said to them: "I'm the commander; I was the guy who made the decision." And I said, "I'm sorry. If I could take it back, I would." The uncle smiled warmly, nodded and said, "I forgive you."'

His next major testing moment came later in the rotation. It was an episode that received world attention.

On 28 April 2013, while in pursuit of a national priority target, the infamous Objective Rapier, SAS operators killed four insurgents. With helicopters swiftly approaching and in the rush to get biometric evidence that might identify the dead men, a corporal kneeled beside the bodies, produced a scalpel and severed the right hand from each of three of the men.

When he saw what had occurred, Captain Hastie challenged this procedure and, back at base, following further inquiry, instructed it to cease in future. But the issue passed up through multiple tiers of command and 'hands' became a cause célèbre, generating consternation among Americans and Afghans and a lot of media back in Australia. Though he was the one to call it out, he became known to some henceforth as Andrew 'Hands' Hastie—such is the iniquity of ill-informed public debate.

So you might say Andrew Hastie has form in raising matters that cause discomfort, even to himself.

When he returned to Australia in July 2013, the SAS captain immediately joined the Liberal Party. And in 2015 he was elected to the federal parliament as the member for Canning, Western Australia.

Early in 2017, when first contacted, it was as if Andrew Hastie was waiting for my call. It was as if we had already had a long conversation. Unsurprising in a way, given we were in touch with many of the same people.

For example, three years earlier, my contact—The Sergeant—and Andrew Hastie had shared concerns about undercurrents from Afghanistan. Looming large in their ruminations had been the spectre of Big Ben.

Around the base, Hastie and Roberts-Smith knew of one another, and there had been a brief interchange abroad. Prior to the 2013 mission, a 'famil'—a regular familiarisation exercise ahead of a full deployment—had been staged. It was on such an exercise that H and RS first crossed paths.

In October 2012, on a mission to Syachow, close to the border of Helmand Province, Andrew Hastie's curiosity was stirred when he saw something that did not add up. What he heard on a radio transmission was someone saying 'shots fired', but to his ears there had been no gunshots at all. Soon after, Ben Roberts-Smith walked past, offering as a brief aside: 'Just a couple more dead cunts.'

Had there been an execution? Had there been a blooding? He did not know.

But the 'famil' helped arouse in Hastie a determination that no one under his command would do anything their conscience could not live with, nor breach the rules of engagement. 'When I arrived, I felt it was time to reinforce what we stood for,' he said. 'Some blokes had been desensitised over time. They had been on multiple trips. Many had lost friends or had friends wounded.'

At our first meeting, he told me Roberts-Smith had given him nightmares. 'And I wake up fearful and my whole day is ruined . . . It is not what I have seen, but what I have heard; and the moral trauma, calling to account what will ultimately come to some people. And because I am part of that institution, I share in it.'

Many conversations later, when we caught up in Perth, Hastie drove me to his electoral office, in Mandurah. The hour-plus journey gave us time for another 'deep and meaningful'. A philosophy graduate and practising Christian, H has some talent for D&Ms.

We talked about a lot, including downtime at Camp Russell. 'The Fat Lady's Arms', a less-than-secret SASR drinking hole, was not off limits. 'I did drink overseas,' he said. 'There were many bigger battles to fight, and quite frankly I needed a drink once in a while to get to sleep.'

But after he returned to Australia, a related issue helped accelerate his decision to resign. In 2014, the story of 'Grattos' (the Gratwick Club, which adjoined Campbell Barracks) employing topless barmaids was laid bare in the Perth media. Andrew Hastie had been one to confront 'Strippergate'. His fate might have been sealed as far back as 2011 when he took a position and gave his reasons for not contributing to the stripper entertainment fund.

'I thought, we spend so much time away from our wives and families, it is completely wrong to be boozing up with these women who aren't in a privileged position,' he said. 'It was completely at odds with what I believe was the right thing. I had to take a stand, and it cost me. That was when I started to realise: okay, it's the NCOs that have a lot of influence in this place. And for this I was being bawled out by senior leadership.'

Nick and I came to notice that the ethos of 'principle before popularity' had followed Andrew Hastie into politics. Much to our relief, he probably did more than we know to limit political opposition to our work. As you might expect, as the IGADF inquiry came into sharper focus and parliamentarians wanted background information on the SAS and Afghanistan, they turned to one of their own.

We were told that, when he discussed our work with the editor of *The Australian*, Paul Whittaker, Hastie told him that although Nick and I were from rival newspapers, we were well informed. Not that we can say that particular intervention proved to be of any help.

Without faltering, Hastie remained consistent and open in his support for the Inspector-General's inquiry. And here you see bare moral courage. Backing the Afghanistan probe, which was perceived by many as an attack on the beloved Perth-based regiment, was likely to make him enemies in the west. Hastie could expect opposition from local media magnate Kerry Stokes, for one.

There had long been local defensiveness about the prospect of the SASR being relocated. And reciprocal concern in the 'Big Army' that the regiment's isolation and autonomy represented an ongoing challenge to Canberra's command and control. At worst, if the IGADF inquiry found that there had been serious misconduct by SAS members, the beloved regiment risked not only relocation, but also disbandment.

CHAPTER 20

THE TANGLED WEB

Immediately following our trip to Perth, Ben Roberts-Smith contacted the SASR's regimental sergeant major and complained that Nick and I had been attempting to telephone members. And that some alumni were speaking out of turn.

While Ben was the regiment's most famous soldier, his cachet was not converting to unconditional fealty. An earlier attempt to reach the Chief of the Defence Force to complain about me got nowhere.

And his claim that his VC was the cause of all this heat—having raised him to tall poppy status—was not how many closer to the action saw it. As a former regimental sergeant major put it to me, 'You don't get all this trouble with the other VCs, such as "Donno"'.

After Trooper Mark Donaldson of the SASR received his Victoria Cross in 2009, his career of humble service calmly continued. VC duties can be a burden, and Mark never took to the limelight. But he knew his duty and he turned up. The boy from Dorrigo, New South Wales, who never went to university, became a natural statesman.

Mark and I knew one another. When the angry clouds began to gather, he gave me a call, presumably following some prompting by Ben. It was said they did not get on. After a brief discussion, we agreed it was unfair for Mark to be dragged into the gathering storm. The subject was, in future, avoided between us.

At this time, Roberts-Smith was calling in a lot of favours. His phone was running hot, with grassfires on all flanks. He was worried about The Gunsmith. Brotherly love, rekindled in December 2017 at Moo Moo's Bar and Grill, had again soured. The feedback we received was that The Gunsmith was now telling others that 'RS can get stuffed'.

The Sniper, in contrast, was hanging in. But, having been questioned by the IGADF about Darwan and more, he was worried. To ease his concern, Roberts-Smith promised to arrange financial and legal support for him via Kerry Stokes.

In February, Roberts-Smith flew to New Zealand for similar discussions with another prospective witness. We will call him The Hunter (Person 35). Also important to Roberts-Smith, he had been on the ground (but not at the cliff) at Darwan. He was also on the Chinartu job, and his presence at Whiskey 108 was a prospective game-changer. The Hunter had been a long-time BRS friend.

In 2008, when he'd transferred from New Zealand's SASR to Australia's, he counted Ben as one of those who welcomed him and helped the new-boy Kiwi acclimatise. A decade on, having resigned from the Australian Army, he was back in New Zealand. Ben's visit was ostensibly about a joint venture business deal. While this did not eventuate, Roberts-Smith went on to lend him $45,000.

On top of all this keeping-old-mates-happy stuff, Roberts-Smith had an ongoing battle to keep his marriage together. Emma and Ben were now attending marital counselling. Through January and February there had been a number of sessions.

It didn't help when, in the midst of all that, his girlfriend rang to tell him she was pregnant. More furtive telephone calls. At the end of February, they agreed to terminate the pregnancy. The procedure was scheduled for 6 March in Brisbane.

Oh, what a tangled web. Roberts-Smith was unsure of the truth. He was suspicious that his girlfriend wasn't carrying a baby.

Tension amplified. More frantic texts. The girlfriend was distraught. On 2 March she received a message: 'Don't fucking abuse me again because it won't end well.'

It was time for Roberts-Smith to again call for the fixer. He spoke to John McLeod, arranging for the private inquiry agent to conduct surveillance at the Greenslopes Day Hospital. He showed McLeod a photograph of his girlfriend and told him she was a Channel Seven executive.

McLeod travelled first to Brisbane Airport to track her arrival, and then to the surgery to cover the only entrance. After some confusion, he caught sight of her and videoed her at the nearby hospital. He then sent the short recording to Ben Roberts-Smith.

Later that day, at Brisbane's Milton Hotel, the Seven general manager and his girlfriend caught up. He confronted her about the pregnancy. He said he knew she hadn't had a termination that morning because she had been followed. He showed her the footage and demanded she do a pregnancy test in his presence. When she explained she'd suffered a miscarriage and showed him her positive result (which usually continues for some weeks after a miscarriage), the tension between them eased.

At dinner that night, Ben Roberts-Smith told his girlfriend that he was 'a good friend to have'.

CHAPTER 21

THE GREAT HALL AND THE BLACK EYE

Australian service personnel are not always enthusiastic about a posting to Canberra. It's fine if your kids are of school age and you need time out for professional networking, but wars aren't meant to be fought in offices.

To Perth boys, in particular, Canberra was regarded as Shiny Bum Central. But for Ben, since his departure from the Army, the national capital now had appeal. Given the range of his formal appointments and official functions, he was visiting often. And be it the Hyatt, the East or the Realm, Canberra's hotels offered to Ben Roberts-Smith VC, MG right royal treatment.

There were new friends too. A Canberra power couple, Richard and Debbie Rolfe, became members of Ben and Emma's inner circle—Richard was the owner of a large motor dealership, and Debbie a partner at a local law firm. Well-known philanthropists, they were honoured to have Ben as a friend. And, in a sense, they served together: Richard Rolfe was a board member and Ben Roberts-Smith the chairman of the National Australia Day Council.[1]

There was further kinship. One of the Rolfes' sons, Zachary, had also served in the Army and aspired to join the SAS. Instead, in 2016 he joined the Northern Territory Police Force. Zach Rolfe, who would later attract national headlines over an unrelated matter, regarded Ben Roberts-Smith as a mentor.

Three weeks after he organised the surveillance of his girlfriend in Brisbane, Ben Roberts-Smith flew with her to Canberra. They booked into the Realm on National Circuit, just down from Parliament House.

Wednesday, 28 March 2018 was a day to take it easy. In the morning, Ben had an interview appointment at the Australian War Memorial. And then it was a short drive, wheeling past Russell Offices and Duntroon, to the Pialligo Estate winery for lunch.

Some respite. They were enjoying themselves. The romance of autumn light, farm-to-table food and lots to drink. A cocktail. One bottle. Two bottles and two hours later: 'When you can manage it, the bill.' Back to the Realm and another drink in the courtyard, before a change of clothes and on to the Great Hall at Parliament House.

Roberts-Smith was to join the prime minister, Malcolm Turnbull, and would share the role of master of ceremonies with ABC presenter Virginia Haussegger, at the Prime Minister's National Veterans' Employment Program awards.

Ben was on the head table. With duties on stage, he had reason to be measured in his alcohol intake. For his plus-one, described as a Channel Seven employee, a seat had been arranged at a neighbouring table. She was seated between the Veterans' Affairs minister, Darren Chester, and Vice Admiral Ray Griggs.

The girlfriend was less restrained. For her, it was a heady occasion, and she consumed more wine. Up on the stage with Prime Minister Turnbull, Roberts-Smith may have worried about what his significant other was sharing.

As the proceedings wound down, he motioned for her to leave. He became frustrated when she took her time. At the entrance to the forecourt basement, she searched for Ben. A man came to help. Navigating the stairs, she turned and fell, injuring her forehead and thigh. Two Australian Federal Police officers came to help. By now Ben had been found and there was discussion about the need for an ambulance.

Roberts-Smith, persuaded that an excess of alcohol was the major problem and confident of his own first-aid training, advised the COMCAR driver to instead take them back to the hotel.

What then happened in their hotel room would later be keenly disputed. The girlfriend claimed Roberts-Smith struck her, an allegation he would vehemently deny. The pair flew back to Queensland. The bruising would fade, but the hurt remained. A week after the Great Hall event, he telephoned her to say, 'We need to end this.'

Two days later, they met again and spent the night together. The next morning, when Roberts-Smith was showering, the girlfriend went to his wallet, found his driver's licence and noted his address. She then drove to Ben and Emma's Ilkley home, where she told Emma about the affair, which was now most certainly over.

CHAPTER 22

STAY KIND

It was April 2018 and Ben Roberts-Smith had offered his services to a worthy endeavour, recording a public service video for the Stay Kind initiative, which had emerged from the tragic, random, one-punch fatal assault on Thomas Kelly at Kings Cross in 2012.

In a dark suit, white shirt and mauve tie, bearded and stern, Roberts-Smith faced the camera, reading from an autocue.

'People know me foremost for my prior role as an Australian Army soldier. My family has for several generations shared a vision of the importance of patriotism and the protection of the Australian people. Stay Kind resonates with me in relation to these values . . . Stay Kind is about being selfless and caring for others . . .'

You might imagine the hoots of derision among former colleagues as the video was shared around.

Perhaps a Jekyll and a Hyde lurked within. On a psychological tight-rope, a capacity for abject cruelty was balanced perilously alongside unabashed self-belief. While there was much to indicate severe insecurity within Australia's most decorated soldier, his capacity for introspection was not so apparent.

In the same month, the departing Chief of Army, Lieutenant General Angus Campbell, issued a challenge to his organisation's inner self. He was transitioning to the big job, Chief of the Defence Force, and he used the occasion to publish a directive titled 'Use of Symbols in Army'.

The first two paragraphs of the minute stated:

> On visits across Army and our deployed forces, I have occasionally come across the use, display or adoption of symbols, emblems and iconography at odds with Army's values and the ethical force we seek to build and sustain. While sometimes formal, more often these are informal patches, badges or symbols, on display by force elements from section to unit level.
>
> I refer in particular to the use of what could be termed 'death' symbology/iconography, for example the pirate Skull and Crossbones (maritime outlaws and murderers), the Phantom or Punisher symbols (vigilantes), Spartans (extreme militarism) or the Grim Reaper (bringer of death). Such symbology is never presented as ill-intentioned and plays to much of modern popular culture, but it is always ill-considered and implicitly encourages the inculcation of an arrogant hubris and general disregard for the most serious responsibility of our profession; the legitimate and discriminate taking of life.[1]

The ink was barely dry before the heckling began. Campbell was scorned by commentators for promoting a 'Kumbaya Corps'. In *The Spectator*, columnist Mark Powell flew to the defence of the Jolly Roger: 'The point is clear. The reason the military has its symbols is to help them win our wars. Obviously, the traditions need to be ethical. But we need warriors, not snowflakes.'[2]

As insiders knew, water operators from Ben Roberts-Smith's Epic 1 patrol wore the Skull and Crossbones Jolly Roger patch. Roberts-Smith himself proudly sported a Spartan tattoo. And when deployed in 2012, he took to posting a kill board on the inside of the door to the team room.

Although the timing might have been off, far from being a silly demonstration of political correctness, Angus Campbell was marking out important ground. But, watching from the sidelines, I wondered whether the Chief of Army's directive might have been subjected to less ridicule if the Inspector-General of the ADF had by now reported. A common presumption in Defence had been that the inquiry would have wrapped up within two years, and thus delivered some important context.

At the 24-month mark in Australia's longest inquiry into Australia's longest war, the IGADF still had a long way to go. It did not surprise me that the pace of investigative lawyering would be any less glacial than that of investigative journalism.

Since 2017, Brendan Nelson had maintained public criticism of the wearisome wait: 'Justice delayed is justice denied.' To *The Weekend West*, he worried: 'I'm concerned about the impact of the inquiries on the members of the SAS and the Commandos, particularly the impact on them psychologically.'[3]

But there was in fact progress. At the beginning of April, inquiry investigators interviewed The Scout. Further important witnesses were scheduled.

However, as Nick and I were finding, the SAS's cone of silence continued to hold firm.

In the way of investigative journalism, we needed to find another door, around the side, around the back. Another way through, somewhere. Tightly bound SAS operatives might stand loyally silent, but outsiders—medics, combat engineers, translators—might offer more promise.

Nick had been chasing such a witness. And later in the month, close to Anzac Day, he made a breakthrough.

CHAPTER 23

THE TERP

Before we journalists ask our viewers and readers to believe our reporting, we must first believe it ourselves.

We had heard of an interpreter attached to 2 Squadron who was described as a character. Outspoken, a bit of a punk, sporting a mullet. The interpreters—'terps' for short—were generally Afghan Americans. Obviously, they were fluent in Pashto; they were also well paid, and deserved to be, given the acute risks they took by accompanying soldiers into the jaws of battle.

Mark Donaldson's Victoria Cross was earned in part because he rescued a badly wounded interpreter at the height of a blazing gunfight. The terps were not allowed to carry weapons, so it fell squarely to the operators to keep them safe.

Of course, we were working hard to find witnesses who might corroborate the Darwan story we'd first heard a year earlier. It still rang in our ears: an Afghan kicked off a cliff by Ben Roberts-Smith and then executed. One prospect was the interpreter there on the ground on 11 September 2012. Some of the soldiers had stayed in touch with their former support personnel and eventually Nick made a breakthrough.

Further, we were collaborating at the time with the ABC. Reporter Dan Oakes had already commissioned a visit to Darwan by a local Afghan journalist, and was sharing with us some of his findings.

Interviews had been recorded with locals who spoke of 'a big guy—he kicked him', referring to the victim, now identified as Ali Jan Faqir. 'He was thrown down from the cliff. Afterward they dragged him and placed him under a berry tree. He was alive and then he died.'[1]

So witnesses from different corners of the globe—in Afghanistan, Perth and the United States—all told a common story. For further confirmation, Fairfax newspapers would send their own stringer correspondent to Darwan, seeking further witnesses and additional verification.

Ben Roberts-Smith had not followed through with the threats of defamation action made against me and my book publisher by his lawyer Mark O'Brien in 2017; those had related to my account of the shooting of the spotter at Koran Ghar. The Darwan allegation, far more serious, would certainly reignite that fuse.

If we proceeded, our objective would be not only to assemble the facts, but also to assemble enough evidence to allow us to defend ourselves against legal action. And that last bit was much harder. We needed also to engage with Roberts-Smith.

On 15 May, Nick wrote directly to Roberts-Smith, requesting an interview, either on or off the record. Here was an opportunity for him to present his side of the story. After all, he was telling others that the stuff being said about him by journalists was complete bullshit and easily disproven.

At the time this email was sent, we did not know that Roberts-Smith was in London, meeting the Queen. He was reportedly furious.

On that very day he was one of 24 living Victoria Cross and George Cross holders gathering for a reception at Buckingham Palace. In a photograph to commemorate the occasion, Roberts-Smith is standing tall in the back row. Other living Australian Victoria Cross recipients—Mark Donaldson, Daniel Keighran and Keith Payne—were also present, with a smiling Queen Elizabeth II at front and centre.

Nick's email, sent to Roberts-Smith's Channel Seven office, had been forwarded to him. When there was no response, Nick persisted. He identified three alleged executions: at Whiskey 108 in 2009, at Chinartu in 2012 and, that same year, at Darwan:

> On September 11, 2012, you are alleged to have kicked a detainee, Ali Jan Faqir, from the top of a small cliff and were then party to an agreement with a small number of soldiers, including partner force soldiers, that Faqir would be executed, as he was. What is your response to this allegation?

The correspondence ended: 'I appreciate these are very serious allegations and we will talk to you if you wish—on background if you prefer—at a moment's notice.'[2]

As previously, it was Mark O'Brien who fired back: 'The allegations are false, constitute a gross and indefensible defamation, and provide further evidence of a malicious smear campaign against BRS.'[3] He promised to commence defamation proceedings if the allegations were broadcast or published.

The IGADF inquiry by now also knew a great deal. Given its comparative wealth of resources and powers, it would be fair to assume that the Inspector-General knew more than we did. At the time of the flurry of emails, the IGADF requested a further interview with The Sniper, Ben Roberts-Smith's offsider at Darwan. The Sniper immediately phoned Roberts-Smith, who followed through with his pledge of legal support.

On 3 June 2018, following a referral from the Chief of the Defence Force, Air Chief Marshal Mark Binskin, the Australian Federal Police commenced an investigation into the murder of Ali Jan and the alleged executions at Whiskey 108.

CHAPTER 24

THE SSE

Think of it as the military version of CSI, crime scene investigation. The soldiers call it 'SSE'—sensitive site exploitation. One of the NCOs from 2 Squadron had developed some expertise in it when its practice was being refined in 2009.

That was the year of the counterinsurgency (or COIN), a revitalised attempt to achieve something resembling success in Afghanistan. Coalition forces were trying to introduce modern rule-of-law principles in a wilderness of remote valleys and medieval villages, where for centuries no concept of functioning governance had existed.

The idea was to lawfully arrest, prosecute and detain offenders. A first step was SSE—gathering and processing the evidence, such as fingerprints on detonators and explosives, collected at a 'sensitive site'. A decade into the conflict, the Coalition was assembling a massive biometric database, a who's who of suspected Taliban commanders and bomb makers.

The NCO—we will call him The SSE—was one of those who contributed to the biometric collection. After many an op, he would take DNA swabs and fingerprints while gloved up and kneeling at the scene. After depositing them in a sealed and labelled evidence bag, he would step back and photograph the contorted dead. A grim task, undertaken by a grimly professional, experienced and reliable soldier.

The SSE had assumed this role at Whiskey 108 in 2009. He had also fought alongside Ben and The Scot at Tizak, coming away from that famous battle with reservations about the appropriate dispensation of honours and awards.

Importantly, he was a friend of The Gunsmith, who was central to the fallout from the Darwan action in 2012. The Gunsmith had told him about the unforgettable scene of a man being kicked from a cliff and callously murdered.

It was no surprise, then, that Ben Roberts-Smith would be worried about The SSE.

On 8 May 2018, this was accentuated. When Roberts-Smith's close friend The Scot was called to an interview with IGADF investigators at Campbell Barracks, he noticed The SSE also waiting in the wings. The two men were told to separate, and then each was interviewed.

That night Emma Roberts-Smith heard her husband on the telephone to The Scot. It was a tense conversation. The Scot told Roberts-Smith to 'prepare himself' for a 'witch-hunt'. She later texted a friend, revealing that The Scot was 'drilled for hours'; that there were 'lots of questions about Ben, and even to the point of questioning his VC action'; that her husband 'didn't get much sleep'; and that 'it's obvious that someone has said a hell of a lot about Ben'.

So who was that 'someone'? Ben Roberts-Smith had The SSE near the top of his list of suspected rats in the ranks. He and The SSE were not friends, and they had served together on missions now under scrutiny. He knew The SSE had been interviewed by the IGADF, and he believed he was leaking to me.

On this last point, he was wrong. I had never met The SSE. But at about this time, a different witness, hitherto unknown to us, came forward.

Later in May, Nick McKenzie was contacted by Ben Roberts-Smith's now former girlfriend. She was hurting. Aware of our reporting and having heard Roberts-Smith griping about intrusive journalists, she contacted

Nick at *The Age*. As she later explained in court, she hoped Nick could help her better understand what she was caught up in.

'Strange things' were spooking her. She had received a cease-and-desist email from a purported lawyer, Danielle Kennedy. The correspondence, bearing a letterhead and photograph of 'Danielle', warned her there would be dire consequences if she continued to contact Ben. The photo—and, for that matter, the lawyer—were fakes.

She was also worried about a threat put to her by a stranger: that compromising photos of her would be released.

At the end of the month, there was a meeting in Melbourne, where Nick heard her account of the alleged assault. Nick encouraged the woman (later known as Person 17) to report the assault to the police.

We now know that, throughout this period, Ben Roberts-Smith was orchestrating his own 'black ops' campaign. He set up encrypted lines of communication with his mates. And he was behind the false 'Danielle Kennedy' email to his ex-girlfriend.

While his ex-girlfriend was heading home to Queensland after her meeting with Nick McKenzie, Ben was out shopping. He purchased envelopes, a ream of paper and some rubber gloves, which he brought home in a grey shopping bag.

At this time he suddenly developed a keen interest in philately—specifically the study of, rather than the collection of, postage stamps. He quizzed a family friend, who had worked at Australia Post, about how stamps could be traced. So out he went again, to various shops to buy stamps. And then to the Bunnings store at North Lakes, just off the Bruce Highway between his home and Channel Seven, where he met John McLeod.

Ben was now in frantic-executive mode: 'I'm under the pump. I'm flat out, can you post these for me? . . . The names are there . . . and I'll get you the addresses tonight.' He handed the private inquiry agent a blue folder containing stamped and sealed envelopes, together with slips of paper with names on them.

McLeod challenged him: 'You're not that fucking stupid to send anything silly in the mail?'

Ben Roberts-Smith assured his friend, the fixer, that it was all innocent. It was something to do with guarantees for limited-edition SAS watches.

That night Roberts-Smith was in contact with McLeod again, providing him with just two Perth addresses. One was a post office box in Claremont, and the other was at Campbell Barracks. Soon afterwards, the fixer drove across the NSW border to Tweed Heads to post the letters.

The two letters were sent to the same person, The SSE—who, two years later, would give key evidence to the defamation trial as Person 18.

CHAPTER 25
LEONIDAS

In my business, news is news. What counts is not so much whether it is good news or bad news, but whether it matters.

On the weekend of 9–10 June 2018, in the tradition of great newspapers, *The Age*, *The Sydney Morning Herald* and *The Canberra Times* ran big on a story that many readers did not want to know—and, further, which might cost a fortune to defend. It was the culmination of the investigative journalism that had preoccupied Nick McKenzie and me during the past twelve months.

On their front pages on the Saturday was a news report headlined by all three papers as 'SAS's day of shame'. It revealed the Darwan cliff kick, but Ben Roberts-Smith was not named. Instead, the alleged perpetrator became 'Leonidas', because Ben's actual descriptor, 'Achilles', was deemed a tad too close to home. No one wanted to be slapped with a defamation writ. We were 100 per cent convinced of the truth of our report, but if a court case eventuated, we knew witnesses would be hard to assemble, and their testimony would be subjected to unsparing challenge.

Inside was a large feature, straddling two pages. The *Herald* headlined it, 'Did the SAS kick a cuffed man off cliff?' It was accompanied by an artist's impression of the incident, and led with the words: 'An Afghan father set off to get flour. He ran into some Australian soldiers. He never came home.' For the first time in print, the alleged execution of an Afghan at Chinartu that year was also mentioned.

The feature reached back to the beginning of the IGADF inquiry and mentioned that the Special Operations Commander, Jeff Sengelman, had called for letters from members of the regiment to help him identify concerns. Andrew Hastie provided perspective on the bigger picture of mission drift in Afghanistan; the SAS captain, by now a member of parliament, described soldiers 'grasping for operational clarity in a sea of ambiguity'.

Forewarned of the publication of this material, the ADF issued a press release pointing out that 'Current allegations related to Special Forces have arisen from within our own community', and provided details of a counselling helpline.[1] It was issued by the Chief of the Defence Force, Air Chief Marshal Mark Binskin, who five days earlier had referred the allegations of the murder of Ali Jan Faqir and the Whiskey 108 executions to the AFP.

On 10 June, *The Sunday Age* ran another feature, titled 'A law unto themselves'. This one, under my by-line, provided a sociological thread through the news reporting, looking into SAS culture and the longest war's dehumanising toll. 'Further into the Afghanistan mission, after multiple deployments, soldiers began to refer to some of their members having gone "Up the Congo", into the moral wilderness of novelist Joseph Conrad's *Heart of Darkness*,' I wrote.

The feature also detailed the three major transgressions by rogue special forces operators. The first—'The Initiation', or 'Blooding'—provided context for the alleged executions at Whiskey 108 in 2009. This included the first account of a bizarre battlefield trophy: the prosthetic leg from one of the victims, which had been purloined for use as a drinking vessel back at the 2 Squadron mess.

The next transgression was 'The Throw Down', the practice of planting weaponry or other incriminatory evidence on the dead, to legitimise killings.

And then there were 'The Executions', about competition killing, kill boards and the discredited metric of body counts. In short, this had led to the creeping, unsanctioned practice of ensuring 'bad guys' were not left alive on the battlefield.

In the middle of this reporting blitz, Ben and Emma Roberts-Smith flew from Brisbane to Perth. Ben made a point of showing up at the office of *The West Australian*, which predictably continued to champion his cause.

That weekend, *The West* led with 'Not fair on SAS. SAS probe criticised'. Shane Wright wrote: 'Concerns have been raised for the welfare of the nation's elite soldiers because an ongoing investigation into claims of alleged war crimes had dragged on for so long, it is denying them natural justice.'[2]

The visit to his old home town appears to have had another purpose as well. Ben Roberts-Smith's offsider at Darwan, The Sniper, was due for a third IGADF interview. Having declared himself unfit, an appointment scheduled for the preceding week had been adjourned. Roberts-Smith and his friend met that weekend.

Roberts-Smith had also sought help from a family friend to obtain two prepaid sim cards and phones, telling her: 'I want to be able to contact the guys in the unit without our phones being tapped.' The phones came to be referred to as 'Handbag 1' and 'Handbag 2'.

It was at that time that a letter turned up at Campbell Barracks, addressed to The SSE. He opened it, read it and immediately handed it to his commanding officer. It purported to come from 'A friend of the regiment'. On a single page, a double-barrelled threat:

> You and others have worked together to spread lies and rumours to the media and the IGADF inquiry. You have one chance to save yourself. You must approach the inquiry and admit that you have colluded with others to spread these rumours and lies about certain individuals or you will become their focus. We are very aware of your murderous actions over many tours of Afghanistan and we have specific mission details, dates and witnesses who now are willing to

> expose you to the authorities so that you are criminally investigated. Just like when you participated in the execution of two PUCs from the Taliban's makeshift medical compound following the battle in Tizak. You know what you have done and so do we. Approach the inquiry and admit to working with others to concoct lies about other SAS members. You have until the end of the month to tell them the truth and don't forget this because it will not go away. You will go down. Better to take a reprimand than murder charges.

On 14 June, The SSE received an identical letter at his Claremont post office box address. Again he handed it to his commanding officer—this time unopened. A letter intended for The Redhead was not sent when it was realised he was on an overseas posting.

CHAPTER 26
'YOU WEAK DOG'

Australian investigative reporters have a much-loved bush telegraph, which reaches from one end of the continent to the other. Along it the story of the threatening letter came to us. So, on Friday, 15 June, the Fairfax press, under the headline 'SAS link to "mafia" witness threats', reported: 'Defence sources have confirmed that a key inquiry witness and member of the Special Air Service Regiment was sent a letter earlier this week threatening retaliation if he did not recant his testimony to the inquiry led by NSW Supreme Court judge, Paul Brereton.'

In response, the ADF had issued a statement confirming the threat, which was described as a 'criminal offence'. It declared that 'witnesses are protected by law from intimidation and from liability for what they tell the inquiry'.[1]

When Emma Roberts-Smith read about the threatening letter, it triggered a recollection of Ben coming home with envelopes, stamps and a ream of paper. She questioned him: 'What the fuck are you doing? What is this all about?'

They walked out onto their terrace because Ben was conscious of the possibility of listening devices. There he told Emma: 'I sent a letter to The SSE.'

She responded: 'No more fucking lies, Ben. You know they can trace your fingerprints and where the letters were printed.'

Roberts-Smith: 'No, I used gloves and printed the letter at the Channel Seven office. I wanted The SSE to withdraw his testimony to the IGADF.'

Gathering up what stationery remained unused, Ben carried it to the firepit and set it alight.

Then there was another bonfire. In the same month, Emma Roberts-Smith observed her husband gathering up his portable computer, dousing it in petrol and striking a match. A few years on, the Curious Case of the Flaming Laptop would inspire many a comedic meme.

Onward. There was more housekeeping to deal with.

Roberts-Smith summoned his fixer again. They arranged to meet at their now common haunt, the Milton Hotel in Brisbane. When John McLeod arrived at the car park, Roberts-Smith approached the private inquiry agent, calling out, 'No phones! No phones! No phones!' McLeod turned his mobile off and left it in his car.

Then they walked to the side of the building, where Roberts-Smith asked whether the PI was keeping up with developments in the media.

McLeod had not followed the news reporting. But when Roberts-Smith began to explain things, the penny dropped. He realised the letters he had been asked to send were menacing—that he had been unwittingly engaged in blackmail.

Roberts-Smith tried to reassure him: 'They're not fucking threats, it was just a touch-up.'

McLeod bristled: 'If you've put me in the frame, you've compromised me somewhere, you better get me a good lawyer.'

Roberts-Smith attempted to placate him—'There's no need for that'—while at the same time asking McLeod to accept all responsibility. 'All you got to say is that you're a supporter of mine, and that you sent the letters because you were sick of the way I was being treated.'

It would be their last conversation. John McLeod spat at Ben Roberts-Smith: 'Fuck that, you weak dog!' And then he walked away.

Roberts-Smith was having more success with other mates.

Soon after returning to Brisbane from Perth, he was on a plane to Sydney for a catch-up with allies from the regiment who had stuck firm. On 13 June, The Sniper was due to be questioned again by the IGADF, and Roberts-Smith, having just connected with him in Perth, wanted to see him again. Emma was worried this could be interpreted as collusion, but Roberts-Smith insisted his mate was suicidal and in need of support.

And rallying to the cause was another mate. The Freefaller was close, a godparent to one of Ben and Emma's daughters. Another SASR patrol commander, he had been on the ground at Tizak. He had also served with Ben on exchange in the United States. The Freefaller was later known in court as Person 29.

He was happy to drive to Sydney and have a meal with his mates, Roberts-Smith and The Sniper. They would later insist, as per their legal obligation, that they did not discuss any of the evidence then before the IGADF inquiry. The Sniper testified that the dinner was the idea of his wife, who, given all the stress he was under, felt that getting him together with his friends presented an opportunity for him to 'unwind'.

Ben Roberts-Smith's other friend, The Scot, was on the phone to Ben for hours after his IGADF 'grilling', before then flying out to the United States. The Scot then prepared and sent a three-page email to Roberts-Smith, which he forwarded to his legal team. The Scot described all this as a complaint about the conduct of the IGADF—and in no way an act of collusion in which he had revealed the sensitive evidence he had given to the inquiry. This proposition was later contested by lawyers, albeit behind closed doors and not in open court.

Mark O'Brien Legal was also active in support. On the day after Ben and the boys got together over dinner, Roberts-Smith's lawyer wrote to Nick McKenzie and me, making clear his view that 'Leonidas' was a 'thinly veiled reference to our client'. He sought an undertaking that there would be no further reporting that linked Ben Roberts-Smith to war crimes.

Another letter went from O'Brien to the IGADF, complaining about leaks to journalists and requesting an inquiry into how this had happened. According to Team BRS, mischief and collusion was signature conduct for sure, but among his foes rather than his friends. O'Brien claimed The Veteran 'has approached serving and ex-SAS members and asked them to provide to Chris Masters false and disparaging claims about our client's service in Afghanistan'.

There was a further complaint: that The SSE had been approached by The Veteran to talk to me, and that The SSE 'did share information with Masters'. Again, untrue. It seemed like it was the season for heady accusations.

On 28 June, another letter was sent to the IGADF from Mark O'Brien on behalf of his client. It alleged that, at a social function, a lawyer working for the inquiry warned an 'acquaintance' of Ben Roberts-Smith to avoid doing business with him. 'It is highly unsatisfactory that our client has been the subject of defamatory gossip by members of the Inquiry's staff.'[2]

A convoluted and time-consuming investigation followed. The IGADF ultimately produced a thirteen-page report on its extensive search, in which it chased witnesses all over New South Wales. 'Ultimately, there is no evidence whatsoever that any lawyer or other person working for or associated with the Inquiry made any statement to the effect alleged,' it concluded, 'or anything like it. The complaint is dismissed.'[3]

There was no doubting the power of Ben Roberts-Smith. He was able to appropriate resources aplenty to substantiate a scenario that was alive only in his imagining.

CHAPTER 27
EMISSARIES

When Ben Roberts-Smith received an approach from former AFP commissioner Mick Keelty, he was nervous. He had cause to worry about the cops joining the posse of IGADF lawyers on his tail.

At Keelty's initiation, they set up an appointment, which occurred around the same time as that meeting with John McLeod at the Milton Hotel car park. This one, on 15 June 2018, was just around the corner, at La Dolce Vita, a cafe/restaurant.

The former commissioner said he wanted to help. He had been told by someone connected to Kerry Stokes that Ben was in a 'world of hurt'. Keelty said his approach had been approved by the AFP leadership of the day. At this stage, the fact that the ADF had referred to the AFP the Darwan and Whiskey 108 murder allegations was not public knowledge; nor had Roberts-Smith been named in media reporting. But the buzz around Ben was strong. The two men discussed the prospect that, given his high profile, Ben Roberts-Smith VC, MG was at risk of being 'knocked from his pedestal'.

Five days later, they met again. Keelty had spoken to AFP deputy commissioner Ramzi Jabbour about the feds' Roberts-Smith investigation. Contentiously, he now disclosed the AFP referral to Roberts-Smith, and explained to him that a referral did not necessarily lead to an investigation.

Early in July, while Nick McKenzie was holidaying on Magnetic Island, he received a call from Mick Keelty. Nick called me straightaway to inform me of the approach. Both Nick and I have done a lot of police reporting in our time, so we were well acquainted with the former commissioner, who suggested we get together for a chat. But it would take some weeks before we could align our schedules. Nick was travelling to Sydney from his home base in Melbourne more often than usual, because a merger was occurring between Fairfax and the Nine Network. (It was publicly announced on 26 July 2018.) Having taken an interest in our war crimes reporting, the Sydney-based *60 Minutes* TV program wanted to get involved.

On 17 July, a meeting at the Sydney *60 Minutes* cottage at Artarmon was arranged; there was time before that for us to catch up with Keelty in the CBD. We met in the foyer of the plush Sheraton Hotel, hoping that Mick would pay for the overpriced coffees.

We found a quiet table. Keelty explained that he had had two meetings with Ben Roberts-Smith, but that Ben was not aware of this meeting we were having. He expressed concern that Roberts-Smith was under stress and might be on the edge of a breakdown.

We told him we were confident of the facts underpinning our reporting. There was agreement on one point, however: given that Ben Roberts-Smith professed to have nothing to hide, he should make himself available to investigators.

Afterwards, there were handshakes and a warm farewell. I can't remember who paid for the coffees.

I was uncertain what the point of the meeting had been. Mick described it as a welfare concern for Ben Roberts-Smith. I presumed—wrongly, as it transpired—that Kerry Stokes might be opening a line of communication.

Another approach from another emissary, this time with a clear Stokes connection. Early in July, on that same investigative reporters' bush telegraph, we picked up another tip. This time, that a former colleague, Ross Coulthart, had been employed to interrogate our work.

I had worked with Ross at *Four Corners*. Throughout his career, this lawyer turned journalist and author had occupied a range of media posts, more recently at *60 Minutes*. Over the years, his work had garnered many awards and some credit, but his standing took a hit following an exposé of a paedophile ring in Britain's highest corridors of power, allegedly complicit in murder, rape and torture.

In July 2015, Ross described this 'special investigation' as 'the biggest political scandal Britain has ever faced'.[1] But the sensational allegations were sparked by a man who was later revealed as a fraudster. In February 2018, after revealing the story's profound evidentiary weaknesses, the ABC's *Media Watch* adjudicated the reporting as 'not *60 Minutes*' or Ross Coulthart's finest hour'.[2] When his contract was not renewed at Channel Nine, Coulthart took a consultancy position with Cato & Clegg,[3] the public relations firm that had been contracted to provide advice and assistance to Ben Roberts-Smith.

One of the curiosities of the news industry is that practitioners who have trained and worked together can routinely deploy to enemy camps. But when a journalist, acting as a public relations adviser, is there to simply ensure their client gets a fair go, we can't complain. And Ross initially explained that he was trying to rescue us from catastrophic error. Although he and I had more history, he spoke to Nick rather than me, appearing to try to drive a wedge between us, telling my colleague I had betrayed sources.

When Nick questioned Ross about who was funding him, my former *Four Corners* colleague declined to answer and instead texted our boss, group executive editor James Chessell: 'I'm happy to sit down with you for an off-the-record chat but I don't want to get yelled at by Nick McKenzie just because I'm doing him a favour by offering to help fix a looming disaster for him and the paper.'

It was no surprise to learn in time that the commercial director for Channel Seven, Bruce McWilliam, also a close Kerry Stokes ally, had commissioned Coulthart's work. Late in June, a report by the journalist cum PR consultant was submitted to McWilliam and Stokes. It was never shared with us. Curious that he would claim to have evidence from many witnesses that would vindicate Roberts-Smith, yet we were never allowed to see it.

Following Mick Keelty's approach to AFP deputy commissioner Ramzi Jabbour, the corruption watchdog ACLEI—the Australian Commission for Law Enforcement Integrity—investigated the intercession. Jabbour was stood down and later left the AFP.

The former police commissioner came to regret reaching out to help a former soldier he had never met, which was always a peculiar mission.

The other emissary for Ben Roberts-Smith, Ross Coulthart, went on to write a book about UFOs.

CHAPTER 28

SEVEN VS NINE

After the June 2018 Darwan war crimes revelations, detailing the murderous rampage of the as-yet-unidentified 'Leonidas', Nick and I prepared for Round 2.

On 7 July, *The Sydney Morning Herald* ran a report headlined 'Victoria Cross war hero under scrutiny'. It identified Ben Roberts-Smith as 'one of a small number of soldiers subject to investigation by a quasi-judicial inquiry looking into the actions of Australian special forces soldiers in Afghanistan'. This report also ran in *The Age* and *The Canberra Times*.

Ben Roberts-Smith declined to answer a series of questions we sent him a few days later. He would have been busy, given this was the week he received a notice from the IGADF requesting production of documents.

On 8 July, Seven West Media issued an internal memorandum stating that Mr Roberts-Smith had shown 'great leadership' as general manager of Seven Queensland and had 'the confidence of the Chairman and the Board', and that the assertions were 'unsourced and unverified'.

Seven's principal competitor, Nine Entertainment Company, was now finalising its merger with Fairfax; in some quarters it was perceived as a takeover. By the end of the month the deal was done. Internally the reaction was mixed. While the Nine partnership improved Fairfax's prospects of survival, there was widespread speculation that journalistic standards would drop. The whispers reached our ears.

As the whisperers put it, Nine was more about populist reality TV than revenue-sapping journalism. In commercial media, economic principles regularly trump journalistic principles. We feared the new entity would not want a costly legal battle with a rival network. Ben Roberts-Smith's lawyer, Mark O'Brien, had been a long-term Channel Nine stalwart, and had represented the network previously in many high-profile defo stoushes. Ross Coulthart had also worked for Nine, and his new boss, Sue Cato, in the recent past had provided Fairfax Media with well-paid advice.

But our fears were unfounded. Nine's executives and their lawyers continued to back us, even as the stakes continued to rise. We can assume the accountants had factored in estimated legal costs relating to prospective legal action (even though these were surely nothing like the stratospheric sum the broadcaster would ultimately confront). During the rest of July, the furious momentum was maintained, largely played out behind the scenes between journalists, lawyers and spin doctors.

Led by Nick, a major feature was being drafted and redrafted. Canberra-based Nine/Fairfax national security correspondent David Wroe was working up further details around the Great Hall event of March, putting a series of written questions to Roberts-Smith. I was in the third seat.

We were well aware that revealing the extramarital affair and alleged assault might be howled down as a defamation too far. The editorial call was a tough one. There was much debate. I was concerned more about the potential damage to the goodwill we still enjoyed among some within the special forces. This was never in abundance, and no doubt an intrusion into Roberts-Smith's personal life would be seen by many as a low blow.

But news is news, and domestic violence is a burning issue of the times. We had strong evidence: a photograph of a black eye, and subsequent text messages that no serious reporter or editor could ignore.

Before publication, more questions went to Ben Roberts-Smith via his lawyer Mark O'Brien. There were queries about an assault on a fellow soldier, the anonymous written threat to another soldier, the use of fake communications and the alleged assault at the Realm Hotel.

Mark O'Brien has the look of someone who in his earlier days might have been a good fit for the front row of a Wallabies scrum: not one to take a backward step. He labelled the assertions 'outrageous and false'.

Peter Bartlett is a senior partner at MinterEllison and was being retained by Nine/Fairfax. He is urbane, polite and every bit as tough.

Over the weekend of 4–5 August, outside of court, O'Brien and Bartlett went head-to-head. It was off the record. Listening around the edges, I heard that I was being accused of having fired up Nick McKenzie. I thought it was more the other way around.

Our story, still under review, was scheduled to run the following weekend. Mark O'Brien briefed Arthur Moses SC to seek an injunction. Moses was one of ultimately three senior counsels retained to represent the war hero. He had strong military and legal credentials as a reservist squadron leader in the Royal Australian Air Force and president of the Law Council of Australia.

It was after hours on Friday, 10 August when an urgent *ex parte* interlocutory application was heard in the Federal Court. Arthur Moses argued the proposed publication 'was in wanton breach of Commonwealth law'. Sandy Dawson SC, for Fairfax Media, said that, if so, the action taken should have been against the Commonwealth rather than the publisher, and that the 'horse has bolted', given that the story was published at 6 am [online] and 'has been read by thousands'.[1]

The injunction failed. The 4000-word feature, 'Beneath the bravery of our most decorated soldier', was followed up in the print versions of *The Age*, *The Sydney Morning Herald* and *The Canberra Times* on Saturday, 11 August.

As we read our own words, we held our breath. 'A recipient of the ultimate bravery award, Ben Roberts-Smith has become a leading figure in Australian public life. Why are so many questions being asked about his past?' There was acknowledgement of his public service, of his membership of the Australia Day Council and the Prime Ministerial

Advisory Council on Veterans' Mental Health, of his role in the selection of domestic violence campaigner Rosie Batty as an Australian of the Year.

And an unfolding catalogue of devilry. The pre-deployment mock execution. The assault on a comrade in Afghanistan. The alleged assaults on Afghans. The 2006 shooting of the spotter and the decade of bullying that followed. The 2009 blooding. The challenge to his CDS. The AFP raid on The Veteran and the intimidatory letter sent to The SSE. As well, in raw detail, the alleged assault on his girlfriend.

We like to say in journalism we try to give the public 100 per cent of what we know. Little was left out, but we did not link all this with the 'Leonidas' article and the alleged Darwan cliff kick execution, which had been published two months earlier. Our necks were out far enough.

On the day of publication, *The West Australian* parried with a Roberts-Smith response, describing the girlfriend violence allegations as 'malicious', and our report 'a catalogue of lies, fabrications and misrepresentations'.[2]

The Australian also weighed in. It had been quiet on the subject for months, but with a new defence editor putting his foot on the accelerator, the paper turbocharged its defence of Roberts-Smith.

CHAPTER 29

SECRETS, LIES AND NEWSPRINT

The Weekend Australian's front page of 11 August 2018—published on the same day as our story burst in the weekend Fairfax papers—carried a photo of Ben and Emma Roberts-Smith together, holding hands. Ben in dark blue jeans and a pale blue shirt, Emma in a loose-fitting grey sweater, jeans and boots. She looks sad.

Journalism is neither mistake-free nor pain-free. If you take the job seriously, you know your work will inflict hurt. If you are chasing down a second mortgage scam artist who has robbed retirees of their scant life savings, this comes as little bother. But not so if, camera ready, you knock on the door and come face to face with a bewildered wife, her children clinging to her knees.

On that Saturday, there was guilt as I looked at that front page. But the picture and accompanying 'exclusive' report headlined 'War hero lashes his accusers' by defence editor Paul Maley hardly told the full story. Emma was certainly sad, but that was not all down to our reporting.

The day before, while out with her daughters at Maleny, near where they lived, she had heard fresh allegations about Ben's affair and assault on another woman. Embarrassed, she rushed home from the excursion to confront Ben. As she stood with him in their bedroom—with their daughters in the lounge room nearby—Emma was told by her husband that, if she did not lie and say they were separated while he was with another woman, she 'would lose everything, including them', and he pointed towards the girls.

Emma did not want to lie or to be interviewed but, fearful of his threat, agreed to the photo shoot. A public relations officer from Seven rang her to ask what she was wearing, and to tell her to look sad. Emma did not want the media in their home, so the couple walked down the road and posed next to a fence line.

In the accompanying report, *The Australian*'s Paul Maley quoted an 'emotional' Roberts-Smith pleading, 'My family and I sit here and wonder, what's next?' Tucked under the solemn image of Ben and Emma was another 'exclusive', headlined 'PMs warn against rush to judgment on SAS'. Four of the prime ministers who had overseen the Afghanistan conflict—John Howard, Tony Abbott, Kevin Rudd and Julia Gillard—were interviewed and had 'thrown their support behind the Special Air Services [*sic*] Regiment'.

On the following Monday, *The Australian* ran another 'exclusive', interviewing Brendan Nelson, who thought the girlfriend violence allegation 'did not gel'. 'Look, I've been in public life for 30 years and I've seen some pretty low things, but I don't think it gets much lower than this,' he said.[1]

There were further challenges in *The Australian* about the integrity of the girlfriend violence complaint, and on Wednesday another lengthy feature by Paul Maley championing Ben Roberts-Smith: 'A hero in the crosshairs'. A glowing account of the Victoria Cross action began the report. The 2006 fighting and his 'Medal of Gallantry' [*sic*] were also cited. The feature repeated the falsehood that Roberts-Smith was separated at the time of the alleged assault on his girlfriend and refuted that incident altogether: 'The "violence" never happened.'

Addressing the issue raised by Fairfax—why were so many questions being asked about his past?—Roberts-Smith portrayed himself as the victim of a whispering campaign by disgruntled former colleagues. 'The best way I can describe it is, the more successful I've been on the outside of the military, the worse a soldier I was.'

The same day, Vietnam veteran and Victoria Cross recipient Keith Payne supported Roberts-Smith's proposition that 'jealousy' could be behind attempts to discredit him.[2]

To cap a week of veneration, an editorial in *The Australian* appealed for perspective, chiding disobedient politicians: 'While most current politicians have been conspicuous in their silence, Australian War Memorial director, Brendan Nelson, a former Defence Minister and Liberal Party leader, has provided vital insights and leadership on the controversy.'[3]

On the other side of the continent, the Kerry Stokes–owned *West Australian* followed suit, tapping a direct line into Roberts-Smith paranoia: 'Sources told *The West Australian* they believed there is no question that senior officers in the Army have been behind providing false and malicious information that has formed the basis of the attack on Mr Roberts-Smith by Fairfax Media.'[4]

It was not only senior leadership alleged to be fuelling our reporting. A few days later, again according to the *West*: 'The reports were based on leaks from an inquiry by the Inspector-General of the Australian Defence Force into actions of Australian forces in Afghanistan.'[5]

For the record, I had no contact with senior command since the months prior to the publication of *No Front Line* in October 2017. Nor were there leaks from IGADF. And at no stage did senior officers make allegations or provide derogatory information about Ben Roberts-Smith.

Channel Seven, which was more measured in its reporting on Roberts-Smith, circulated an internal memo to staff penned by CEO Tim Worner:

> All.
>
> What seems to have started out as a publicity and marketing campaign for a book, has turned into a relentless attack by a rival newspaper company on the character and reputation of our colleague, Ben Roberts-Smith.
>
> This has been a slur on him personally and on his inspiring military service record.

Today, Ben spoke directly with his teams in Maroochydore and Brisbane. He outlined to them how he would take this fight on with dignity and honour.

As part of that, he will be issuing defamation proceedings tomorrow against Fairfax and the two journalists concerned.

Ben and all our people in television in Queensland have our respect and total support.

They should be proud that they are already delivering a record breaking result in 2018.

As Ben conveyed with great emphasis, we will not allow anything to distract us from continuing that great work.

Onwards, TW[6]

The coverage, and perhaps the memo from CEO Tim Worner, brought forth a gush of leaks. Ben did have friends among staff members at Seven, but they were not the ones who reached out to us. Over drinks at a long lunch, the Queensland general manager had vented. His tirade, secretly (and lawfully) recorded, was duly passed on to us.

On journalists: 'Now it is personal. Now I am going to do everything I can to fucking destroy them. All those journalists. That's my sole mission in life.'

On a mooted Murdoch merger with a struggling Seven—and the other benefit of acquired media assets: 'They're not going to want to take on someone else's debt. But it's worth taking the loss here if other parts of the business are going well, because it means you have political influence. That's why politicians are scared of people that own media networks.'

On his workplace and the boss who heaped praise: 'Everything is fucked. When I go to Sydney, they all look at the ground. They know I am close to Kerry and hate me for it. Tim Worner hates me because I have a direct line to the chairman.'

On 17 August 2018, Ben Roberts-Smith filed a writ in the Federal Court launching defamation proceedings against Fairfax Media, Nick McKenzie, Chris Masters and David Wroe.

CHAPTER 30

HISTORY WARS

It was the end of August 2018. I had accepted a longstanding invitation to contribute to a symposium titled 'The Real Charles Bean'. The venue was Old Parliament House. Brendan Nelson and I were both on the card, and a who's who of politicians, bureaucrats and journalists filled the room beforehand. This was the infamous 'Canberra bubble', and within it there was much humidity, keenly felt.

The mingling was sweat-inducing awkward. It stung when former defence minister John Faulkner chided me for reporting Ben's affair. And his view appeared to be widely shared. Further, the 'SAS's day of shame' headline had not gone down well. Australia's most famous regiment had protected species status among much of Canberra's ruling elite.

But as to Ben Roberts-Smith himself, attitudes were mixed. The static around a looming BRS vs IGADF scandal had ricocheted within the bubble long before Nick McKenzie and I transmuted rumour and scuttlebutt into hard news.

I looked for a gap in the crowd so I could speak to Brendan Nelson before we joined the panel on stage, but he was tight in conversation and had barely a greeting to offer me. Although we were now positioned in opposite corners, I thought the last time we had spoken had signalled that some residual goodwill existed.

In November 2017 we had had a snatched conversation at a chance encounter in the Australian War Memorial bookshop. His mood then had reflected more sorrow than anger. He told me it could have all gone differently, that Kerry Stokes might have funded an authorised biography of Ben Roberts-Smith. As to the schism: 'He is the chairman—what can I do?' When it came to choosing allies, a common journalist appeared to rank well below a philanthropic billionaire.

The symposium commenced. It is never easy to speak after Brendan has spoken with his customary passion and eloquence. I listed point by point the qualities I admired in Charles Bean, who was a gifted writer, an indefatigable worker, selfless and empathic, who went on to establish an iconic institution. Yet he had struggled to communicate discomforting truths. In his private diary, he referred to bad behaviour by Australians at Gallipoli—malingering, cowardice, cruelty and treachery. He noted: 'I've never written higher praise of Australians than on this page, but the probability is that if I were to put it into print tomorrow the tender Australian public, which only tolerates flattery and that in its cheapest form would howl me out of existence.'[1]

At the end of my contribution at Old Parliament House that day, I went to the subject that was then occupying so many minds. Despite Charles Bean's affection for the Anzacs, this in no way stopped him from describing the meanness, the horror and the ugliness of warfare. He wrote of Australian soldiers' participation in the rioting in the Wazzir at the beginning of the Great War, and in the Surafend massacre at the end of it. He reported angry Australians, having suffered losses, bayoneting Germans who had surrendered. On this he reflected: 'The Germans in this case were entirely innocent, but such incidents are inevitable in the heat of battle, and any blame for them lies with those who make wars, not with those who fight them.'[2]

Brendan Nelson was sitting in the front row. I hoped he would get the point. The reporting in Fairfax Media was not about split-second, heat-of-battle incidents, but clear criminal breaches of the rules of armed conflict.

But if he took in the words, they made no impact. Three weeks later, on 19 September, Nelson addressed the National Press Club in

Canberra, a red poppy badge gleaming on his lapel. Dan Keighran VC sat approvingly in an audience dominated by members of the press gallery. Nelson condemned our coverage, particularly of Ben Roberts-Smith: 'Our comfortable lives breed easy indifference to sacrifices made in our name . . . Context is everything. Judgements being made about the Commandos and the SAS and what they have done in Afghanistan have been made without context.'

Historians at the Australian War Memorial, working on the official history of the Timor and Afghanistan conflicts, must have wondered at the proclamation Nelson had made in mid-August in an interview with Alan Jones, when he declared that we should leave alone all but the 'most egregious breach of the laws of armed conflict'.[3]

Certainly academic colleagues were alarmed at this. A former principal historian at the Australian War Memorial, Peter Stanley, took our side when he was invited to respond: 'We need to know the truth, whatever it is.'[4]

Edward Cavanagh, an Australian research fellow at Cambridge University, agreed: 'People need to be able to ask hard questions about how war is conducted.'[5]

The respected Frank Bongiorno, Professor of History at the Australian National University, considered 'the idea that there are no-go areas that belong to the sacred, that journalists, historians and other academics shouldn't encroach on, is dangerous to democracy'.[6]

And Peter Rees, a Charles Bean biographer, offered the insight that his subject 'was of the strong belief that any incidents that might reflect on the Army negatively still needed to be included because some reference or other to it is sure to get into future histories, and it will appear to have been covered up'.[7]

At his September National Press Club address, Dr Nelson—his voice all but breaking—wound up by invoking our heroes: 'Where, I ask, where is the national interest in tearing these people down?'[8]

A compelling and central fact was being ignored: the complaints about Roberts-Smith had originated not from pampered, irresponsible media, but from battle-hardened colleagues. Similarly, Nelson's often-professed view—that we need to know our military history if we are to know ourselves—was undermined by his curious insistence that we should know only so much.

Considering his plea, we could equally wonder: where is the national interest in shrinking from the truth?

CHAPTER 31

FASIL

'I shot that cunt in the head . . . I pulled out my 9-mill, shot the cunt in the side of the head, blew his brains out, and it was the most beautiful thing I've ever seen.'

The Medic (Person 16) remembered Ben Roberts-Smith saying these words after they returned from a mission on 5 November 2012. The two men passed each other in a corridor at Camp Russell; the words came in response to a question from The Medic: 'What happened to that young fellow that was shaking like a leaf?'

The Medic would become an important witness. These three sentences, inerasable, unforgettable, were repeated many times to Nick and me. And, much later, to a crowded courtroom. The words were like bullets piercing a forever consciousness.

Wheel back a few days. Helicopters were descending on Fasil, eleven minutes' flying time south of Tarin Kowt. The target was Objective Sole Inheritance. A common mission task was vehicle interception, and this was what occurred.

The Medic and an Australian combat engineer took positions on either side of the road leading to the village. A Toyota Hilux, as ubiquitous in the wilds of Afghanistan as in Australia's Bunnings car parks, approached the checkpoint and was stopped. The soldiers gestured for the occupants to get out of the vehicle and be searched.

Four men were detained. The Medic had a strong memory of the one in his late teens, not only because of his youth, but also because he was 'trembling in fear'. While the Afghans were being processed, the vehicle was searched. Two rocket-propelled grenade (RPG) warheads were discovered and assessed to be components for roadside bombs. A radio call reporting the find was transmitted.

Ben Roberts-Smith's patrol then arrived, collected two of the hand-cuffed men and walked them away. The Medic moved to another compound; he presumed the Afghans had been removed for tactical questioning.

At 1000, less than an hour after the helicopters arrived, another radio call was made: 'One EKIA.' Nine minutes later, a further enemy killed in action was reported.

When the troop returned to Camp Russell, The Medic was unaware of the fate of the two men he had detained. That was why, when he passed Ben Roberts-Smith in the accommodation hallway, he asked his question. He later recalled that Roberts-Smith had added at the time that he'd been told by his commander not to kill anyone on that job.

This sorry story would have some resonance with other troopers on this rotation. It was late in the war, and questions were being asked about kill counts in Uruzgan, which to Coalition Command seemed excessive. And in Camp Russell itself, a kill board on the door of Patrol Commander Ben Roberts-Smith's team room was a talking point. A comment overheard on the eve of this, their last mission for 2012, took on special significance: 'Hey fellas, we're on eighteen. We need two more to get to twenty.'

Later, when examining SSE photos, The Medic confidently identified one of the victims as the frightened adolescent. And it would be contended that an AK-47 'throwdown' had been placed on his body.

The Medic was brave, consistent and unflinching in his account of what occurred. When Nick and I asked him how he responded to

Roberts-Smith's words, he said he probably said something like 'Cool, mate'. Why? Although he was shaken, he knew it was unwise to show any outward sign of disapproval.

A common question asked of investigative journalists is how we find our sources. There are many answers. The best way is to be out there, with your antennae tuned. We talk to one person, hopefully creating trust, and a recommendation to speak to someone else results.

What we find, and it is some comfort, is that any attempt to close down our lines of communication is counterproductive. In a functioning democracy, when people are told to shut up, you can almost guarantee a degree of disobedience. That happened, for example, with the Seven Network's employees.

It was my workmate Nick who found The Medic. This followed his befriending a different medic, Sergeant 'Dusty' Miller, who in 2018 was doing it tough. Medics have a duty of care. Six years earlier, Dusty had been attached to 3 Squadron SASR. The rotation had exposed him to brutality, tweaking his conscience.

One incident left a horrible mental scar. Having attended a wounded Afghan, he later inquired what happened to him, only to learn he had been dragged away and killed.

Dusty Miller came to us to tell his story, which we hoped would help his healing. And along the way he introduced us to his friend. The Medic was attached to Ben Roberts-Smith's 2 Squadron in 2012.

Investigative journalism—working beyond the churn of the 24-hour news cycle—deepens journalists' attachment to their sources. Undeniably, this comes at some cost to objectivity. But friendship is organic and, in a way, unstoppable. It is a maelstrom, but we do our best to retain a clear head.

Nick and I were as one in accepting that the forging of a personal friendship with a professional source brought with it responsibility. We would not only do everything we could to protect our sources, but we would also maintain a faithful relationship.

Towards the end of 2018 and beyond, when our meetings with lawyers gathered pace and our requests for witness cooperation intensified, that bond, that trust, came into its own.

CHAPTER 32

SHOWDOWN AT THE EAST

> Hey Scout it's RS. Hope your well mate, Freefaller said he touched base and it was fine to me give your number. I know you guys spoke so I'm keen for catch up. I will be in Canberra and free for a brew at 0900 Friday, I'm at the East hotel in Manuka if that suits? It has coffee shop in reception. Looking forward to it mate.

It was 17 October 2018. This text message from Ben Roberts-Smith pinged on The Scout's phone two days ahead of the proposed meeting. The two men had not spoken since 2012. Roberts-Smith was reaching out now, a week after he had received from his lawyers a copy of the defence filed by Fairfax Media—a development that had put him on full alert. Now aware that both the AFP and the IGADF's investigators were leaning in, it became paramount for him to fortify his defamation case against Fairfax.

In August, Roberts-Smith had travelled to New Zealand to again catch up with The Hunter, who was sticking firm. The Freefaller was also onside, and The Sniper, although suffering ongoing stress, was sticking to his guns. But The Scout was a worry. He had been at Whiskey 108 and Chinartu, and was known to be close to Roberts-Smith's perceived enemies, The Veteran and The SSE.

After receiving the text, The Scout phoned The Freefaller, who told him: 'Ben heard your name mentioned in relation to the Fairfax allegations.

Fairfax will subpoena you and RS doesn't want you thrown under the Fairfax bus. RS is happy to offer you legal and any other assistance you like.'

The East is a boutique hotel, a short walk from the Manuka shops. Ben Roberts-Smith arrived a few minutes after The Scout had found a seat in the coffee bar. They shook hands and exchanged the requisite small talk, which gave Roberts-Smith the opportunity to boast about the two teams of lawyers he had assembled, each led by prominent senior counsel.

Roberts-Smith had with him a document Fairfax had filed as part of its formal defence. The Scout could see black lines, redactions, names replaced by witness numbers. Ben said, 'I want you to read this.'

The Scout hesitated, responding: 'I'm not signing anything, mate.'

Roberts-Smith said he was not asking for a signature, just that he read it.

The statement, with his name redacted, was The Scout's own account of the October 2012 alleged execution of an unarmed Afghan at Chinartu. After The Scout had read it through, Roberts-Smith, who had figured The Scout was the source, said, 'That's obviously not true, right?'

The Scout looked up at Roberts-Smith and said, 'Well, that's how I remember it.'

As if a curtain had suddenly drawn shut, the mood shifted.

Roberts-Smith: 'So, it's going to be like that, is it?' More hesitation, then he continued: 'Well, it's your word against The Sniper.'

There was discussion about The Scout and others talking to the IGADF. Ben told him that if his name came out (in public and within the regiment), there would be career consequences. He cited the witnesses against him as largely limited to The Veteran, The Sergeant and The SSE. The Scout disagreed that he was one of only a few opposing witnesses. 'I am not going to name anyone, no, that is not true, this is 2 Squadron-centric,' he said.

Their discussion then turned to the alleged 2009 executions, also mentioned in the statement. The Scout looked at Roberts-Smith. 'The incident at Whiskey 108, you were pretty loose,' he said. 'I was there. I heard the burst of gunfire.'

More hesitation.

Roberts-Smith: 'You wouldn't have seen it. No, it was in TIC.'

TIC stands for 'troops in contact'—Roberts-Smith meant the insurgent was killed in legitimate combat.

There was one very menacing moment when Roberts-Smith complained about 'journos ringing people'. Leaning forward, he said: 'Be careful who you fucking talk to.'

The Scout: 'That's how I remember it. There's no way I am going to get up on a stand and lie, and I hope no one else does.'

After what was later said to be a 'massive' pause, Roberts-Smith looked out the window. Turning back, he said: 'I don't even know what to say. That's it, then.'

The Scout: 'Thanks for the coffee.'

The meeting lasted 45 minutes.

Ben Roberts-Smith had been careful. His wife later said he had been worried the encounter might be taped. While he never expressly denied the alleged incidents of war crimes, neither did he confirm them. The most he had said to The Scout was, something like, 'It will be the word of you and some raggedy Afghans against the testimony of my supporters, such as The Sniper.'

Word got around afterwards. Within the craven cloisters of social media, The Scout would be trolled, castigated for talking to journalists and ratting on a mate. But some in their cohort also felt envy. You do see among these men an admiration for bold action. The Scout had been unhesitant, and he had seized the opportunity to show moral courage—to stand up to and stare down Roberts-Smith. I was struck later when one of his SAS mates told me, with apparent conviction, that he wished it had been him.

That night Ben Roberts-Smith appeared on Murdoch's Sky News. He was composed, convincing, coached perhaps, in a sharp grey suit and plain green tie, but there was also, understandably, strain in his voice. The interviewer asked about the raft of additional allegations listed in the Fairfax defence. Roberts-Smith described them as 'bewildering' and 'completely untrue', as 'scenarios in battle that have been twisted and in many cases falsified'.[1]

Since its barracking for Ben in August, the Murdoch press had kept up its bashing of his accusers. In subsequent months, they were handed some big sticks.

When Ben's former girlfriend withdrew her complaint against him, they offered prominent coverage of this development, stretching the facts. *The Australian*'s account on 25 September was headlined 'War hero cleared of violence claim'. In fact, the woman had not recanted her evidence but—as is all too common, so as to maximise her privacy and minimise her anxiety—had dropped the case.

Another drip from Mark O'Brien was received by the Murdoch press with evident relish. This time *The Australian* was given an opportunity to bash not only Fairfax but also a rival it disdained even more, the ABC.

Their renewed attack began with: 'Roberts-Smith pursuit "malicious"'. Mark O'Brien's evidence for this claim arose from some texts composed by ABC reporter Dan Oakes: 'Mr O'Brien said Oakes had made "his motive very clear" in his investigation of his client, saying in one text, "Sometimes karma needs a helping hand" and, "The Australian public has been sold a lie, and it needs to be exposed. It is as simple as that."'[2]

In pursuit of information about Roberts-Smith, Oakes had made contact via social media with a person he thought was The Redhead. As it turned out, Dan had the wrong man; subsequently, his text exchanges with this person, and his attempts to persuade him to provide information, made their way into court evidence.

I did not see Oakes' 'karma' comment as proof that he was incapable of fair reporting, but it was unhelpful. In time, the ABC's coverage of the war crimes saga would be picked up and effectively pursued by another colleague, Mark Willacy. But from this time on, the national broadcaster's inquiries into Ben Roberts-Smith also came to a halt.

Murdoch's bombardment tied Nick McKenzie and me to Dan Oakes. There had been an alliance between him and us, but it had ceased months earlier.

Nick and I generally spoke every day. Since the defamation proceedings had got underway, it felt like we spoke every hour. Queries from the lawyers and round-table or video conferences filled the calendar. In journalism, the deadlines don't go away and the time you need to service the eternal demands of the court is heaped on top of everything else.

Being sued is not fun. But at least we could turn to one another. Our Fairfax colleague David Wroe, who was named as third respondent in the defamation case, was not as embroiled as we were because he had been involved in only part of the coverage. Even so, it was no fun for him either.

Being bashed day after day by *The Australian* & co. did not make life any easier. Time and again, through gritted teeth, I would say to Nick: 'Never mind, try to ignore it. We will do the news, let them do the PR.'

My colleague, much younger than me and with a career more grounded in the merging forces of media and media management, disagreed: 'No Chris, we have to do the PR too.'

CHAPTER 33

KILLER ANGELS

We were now engaged not just in a contest of the law, but in a battle for public opinion. Tough going. Throughout the tumult, the argument that we should leave alone what happens on the battlefield appeared to gain traction.

In Letters to the Editor columns, on both sides of the Fairfax/Murdoch divide, we were taken to task. A *Sydney Morning Herald* letter-writer: 'The media sensationalism re allegations of improper conduct by Ben Roberts-Smith is nothing short of utter contempt for those sent to partake in a war in which we ought never to have been involved.'[1] And this in *The Australian* the next day: 'There is something deeply disturbing in the attack on the character of Victoria Cross recipient, Ben Roberts-Smith, and on the integrity of his war service. Something seems to have gone out of the robust decency that made the Australian character so admirable.'[2]

Summarised, the case against us appeared to be that if he was wearing an Australian uniform, it can't have been a war crime.

To counter that widely held belief, readers needed background and context. In the months and, as it turned out, years before the trial, we would try to reach beyond the what, when and where, and get to the how and the why.

The culture of the exalted SAS was a good start. The skill set for entry into the regiment was itself a paradox. What was required were compassionate psychopaths, PhDs who could win a knife fight in a phone booth. The 'killer angel' ability to be able to apply lethal force without hesitation, but also to know when it is necessary—and when it is not—is not found in ordinary mortals. One SAS officer told me they needed men who were capable of doing something to be proud of in the dead of night and then never speaking about it. Humility should be their hallmark.

There were individual troopers who exemplified this ideal in some memorable incidents.

We wrote of an incident earlier in the Afghanistan War in which an SAS patrol, crouched in a hide, caught sight of a group of armed men moving towards them. The soldiers—from 3 Squadron SASR—brought their weapons to their shoulders as the Afghans came closer. They unlocked the safety catches and curled their fingers around the triggers.

And then—to the surprise of his men, and perhaps to the disappointment of some—the troop captain laid down his rifle and stood upright. The approaching Afghans hesitated but also lowered their weapons, then moved off in a different direction.

Well-schooled in the tenets of modern warfare, the captain knew that a man with a gun in Afghanistan was not necessarily an enemy, and that taking lives was not the point of his mission. Former SASR warrant officer Person 102 had once written of the virtue of the shot not fired: 'I personally take pride in the fact that I led patrols that went undetected and without contact and we worked with the locals and developed intelligence that was valuable down the track.'[3]

We also wrote of the padre who was posted to the SASR in 2010, a year when hubris was beginning to trump humility. It should have been a career pinnacle for him, but he was sidelined and dismissed as an irrelevance. We wrote of how the longest war was wearing away at hard-earned values. The 'rock star' persona was becoming prominent. This phenomenon was applauded by some commanding officers, to the disquiet of many old-school SAS operators.

In this regard, the worst offenders were the wateries. As with their US counterparts, the Navy SEALs, the unquestionable capability of the wateries was becoming tinged with arrogance.

When the padre arrived, he found rampant bullying within the ranks. It got under his skin. So he took the wateries on in the language they understood. An accomplished boxer, he offered to fight them one by one. He then carried his boxing gloves to the gym, where he sat all day. Nobody turned up.

Concern was growing within the ADF that after a decade in Afghanistan, Australian special forces were overused. The regiment had been cycling in and out of Afghanistan, one squadron at a time, since 2001. A dehumanising descent was hard to arrest.

Suicide bombers presented soldiers with an impossible choice. *Is that a pregnant woman on her way to the clinic or am I about to be blown to bits?* Out in the rural areas, a farmer might transform into a fighter in what seemed a split second. Put down a hoe, pick up an RPG and bring down a helicopter, extinguishing the lives of fifteen comrades. Maybe his only weapon was a handheld radio, used to deploy someone else to fire the fatal rocket.

So spotters became legitimate targets. So too did squirters. A presumption was allowed to develop among the soldiers that if a fighting-age male was still in a combat zone when shooting erupted, he was likely a bad guy.

Of course, it could also be true that the man with the radio was not a Taliban at all. He might have been listening to Afghanistan's top 40. And an Afghan who appeared to be 'moving tactically' might be a simple farmer, understandably eager to get out of the way.

Getting it right mattered. Killing the innocent was the opposite of the point. More than morally offensive, in counterinsurgency warfare it was strategically counterproductive. So, as rumours swelled, rules tightened. ADF inquiry officers became a feature of life at Multi-National Base Tarin Kowt (MNBTK).

To many soldiers, the prospect of armchair investigators subjecting them to months of interrogation over a life-or-death battlefield call was making a difficult war beyond impossible. The counterinsurgency mantra was 'Clear, Hold, Build'—but out there on the ground, it appeared only the first box was being ticked. The Coalition forces cleared valleys, but soon the Taliban were seeping back in.

Operators, understandably intent on survival, were perplexed by what they saw as counterproductive oversight. The fact was that if a detainee was brought in for processing, and he was bruised and bloodied, there would be endless questions. If he was left dead on the battlefield, more than likely that would be the end of it.

With conventional forces, transparency was more readily applied. There were plenty of eyes on them and a much less aggressive posture. But with special forces, secrecy was encoded, along with a bias for offensive action. Justification emanated from their counter-terrorism remit. Clandestine operations against terrorist cells remain secret because there is no logic in signalling to the enemy your intentions or capability. With the SASR's mission consigned to a grey zone of international law, it became unusually challenging to apply effective command and to manage integrity.

Furthermore, the regiment's officers were kept at a distance. In contrast to the Commandos, who operated in larger numbers and with officers engaged in the close fight, small SAS patrols regarded it as more expedient to keep their officers outside a target area until it had been secured.

Australian cultural cringe and a streak of vanity was also on show. There is an international cousinage of special forces, a kind of bristled brotherhood, with the Aussies routinely demonstrating keenness for acceptance and approval.

Across the global network of special forces units, there is a spread of skill sets and specialisations. The United States ranks its units such as the Navy's SEAL Team Six and the Army's Delta Force as 'Tier One'. While this designation relates to resourcing and tasking rather than status, the black-ops rock stars tend to get the cool missions, such as hunting down Osama bin Laden, and thus the envy.

Because of interoperability, the exchange of personnel and the fact that Australia deployed the third-largest Special Operations Task Group to Afghanistan (after the Americans and the British), Australians were exposed to significant influence from the cousinage.

In 2015, *The New York Times* published an extensive investigation of the Navy SEALs, detailing the evolution in Afghanistan of a 'kill fest' in which the victims were too often unarmed civilians. SEALs were using customised weapons, such as what the newspaper described as 'primeval tomahawks', and practices such as 'canoeing' (splitting open a victim's skull). There was a similar reputational blight reported in Britain, with its famed Special Air Service (on which Australia's SASR is modelled) accused of planting weapons and unlawful killing.

It now seemed undeniable that the Australian special forces were exposed to the same dehumanising influences. Nick and I quoted Lieutenant Colonel Steve Hart and Major Tom McDermott from their research paper 'Armouring against atrocity', where they wrote that 'small units within the military are easily seen as primary groups'. They concluded that 'groups are inherently less moral than individuals', and that '[w]hen the group is "virtuous" there is often a positive outcome; however, where the group norms are shifted and the behaviour is atrocious, individuals in the group are often unable to apply the brake'.[4]

One of the Australian SAS padre's deployments was through those tortured months of 2012. By then the regiment's moral compass was spinning wildly. Soldiers, under peer pressure to 'leave their faith at the door', would secretly seek him out. Junior members, distressed by what they had seen, were coming to seek consolation.

When he spoke to us, he would not go into detail, but for him an enduring memory of Camp Russell was the smell of blood on the clothing of operators as they returned. 'All that killing,' he said. 'It stirs a hornets' nest and makes it worse.'

Not all of it was demoralising. 'The best fighters were not the rough men,' he said. 'While I encountered plenty of dark hearts, I was struck by the many who remained principled and true.'

At this stage in the battle for public opinion, Ben Roberts-Smith VC, MG continued to stand tall. But we began to notice that his personal stew of bitterness, aggression and entitlement was starting to corrode the goodwill he had previously amassed. Too often, Ben's own worst enemy was Ben himself.

CHAPTER 34

A GAME OF ARITHMETIC

A big man-hug for Ben. As the dignitaries were assembling within the VIP enclosure, this physical, public declaration of love and trust was unmissable. Brendan Nelson was resolute in support of his friend Ben Roberts-Smith—and what dissenters saw as a sharp right turn at the Australian War Memorial.

It was 1 November 2018, and Australia's top landmark (according to Tripadvisor, ahead of the Sydney Opera House and Harbour Bridge) was unveiling its $500-million overhaul.[1]

While both sides of parliament supported the grand expansion plan, there was some sideline discord. What about funding for other museums? Why was sponsorship from arms manufacturers permitted? Some feared that a sacred institution was being transformed into a military theme park.

On Armistice Day in 1941, when the Australian War Memorial opened, Governor-General Lord Gowrie had spoken of its purpose: it would act 'not only as a record of the heroic deeds of those who fought and fell in the last war but would also be a reminder for future generations of the brutality and the utter futility of modern war'.[2]

But Nelson was forthright about the revamp. He told the Nine Network: 'I'm completely unapologetic about it. This is for veterans, it is for them and their families.'[3] And in his speech that day: 'It is within that building that we reveal our character as a people, we reveal our soul. It is not only a shrine, not only an archive, this place is part of the therapeutic milieu. This is how these men and women come to terms with what they've done.'[4]

As these words were being spoken, many of Ben Roberts-Smith's comrades in arms were stressing about the forthcoming defamation court case. Gathering witnesses was crucial to both sides. At this stage, Fairfax had declared to the Federal Court that seventeen serving or former members of the SASR would be called as witnesses in support of our case. Some had made this commitment from the start and were co-operative. Others had to be advised, as gently as possible, that, if necessary, they would be required to appear under subpoena. It is fair to say that not one of them relished the prospect.

Ben Roberts-Smith's witness list was roughly equivalent. We presumed there was a game of arithmetic underway: you find twenty witnesses who say I did it, and I will find twenty-five who say they are wrong. While some of his witnesses expressed enthusiasm for helping their mate, among others there was anxiety equal to that suffered by our witnesses.

And right in the middle were three witnesses with an even greater cause for dread. The trio were all alleged to have executed detainees on the instruction of Ben Roberts-Smith. All had suffered ongoing psychological trauma, at varying times receiving psychiatric treatment. They were now caught up in a kind of tug-of-war, with an eloquence of lawyers on both sides competing for their cooperation.

In Brisbane, following the issuing of the defamation writ, Roberts-Smith was secretly recorded speaking to his mates: 'They fucked up. Nine doesn't want this . . . Fairfax has gone. Their lawyers have been talking quietly . . . they're in fucking trouble.' He obviously harboured some hope that, faced with the breathtaking costs, the newly merged Nine/Fairfax organisation would shrink from the fray.

Far from it. In response to his statement of claim, Nine/Fairfax had mounted a robust defence. Six alleged unlawful killings had been identified. Nine/Fairfax argued that its reporting had not defamed Roberts-Smith, but that, if required, the publisher would rely on a defence of truth.

Backing away from the fight might have made sense from a commercial perspective. The costs were frightening: senior counsel charged around $10,000 a day, and that was just the beginning. Australian defamation laws are widely regarded as unfriendly to media, and a truth defence, particularly in the hostile judicial climate of New South Wales, presents as a very high bar. But there was no retreat whatsoever.

On the day of the Australian War Memorial's big expansion announcement, on the lawns of the sacred ground, strewn with kangaroo poo, Brendan Nelson addressed the psychological fallout of warfare, though obviously he regarded his friend as a victim of this rather than a perpetrator: 'As far as I am concerned, no element of the media should be judge and jury on any of these things. Leave it to the inquiry. But I say to the people doing the inquiry: can you damn well get on with it.'[5]

Political silence had so far shadowed the war crimes saga, but that morning Prime Minister Scott Morrison had told broadcaster Alan Jones that 'those who are responsible for that [advancing allegations against Roberts-Smith], they're not showing any of the values [as seen in the Victoria Cross recipient]'.[6] No doubt Roberts-Smith saw this as a small win; he was likely also relieved at this breach of what had been an infuriating silence.

But the IGADF inquiry was still yet to report. It was now two and a half years since it began. *The Australian* reported that its schedule had 'blown', despite there being no formal deadline.[7] For me, it meant the updated edition of *No Front Line* had to be abandoned, given that I had planned to include in it the inquiry's findings.

Returning to Queensland after the Australian War Memorial event, Ben Roberts-Smith had work to do. He was consumed by it. Emma texted a friend that Ben was acting 'like a Zombie'.

His long-awaited interview with the IGADF was scheduled for late November 2018. Already he had called for help from comrades. In the early weeks of November they sent him USBs and various imagery, including of Whiskey 108. His data usage spiked. He asked a friend to purchase more SIM cards, and to 'top up handbag'—code for refreshing his supply of burner phones.

Justice Paul Brereton had previously been sharing his inquiry duties with his NSW Supreme Court commitments, but he was now devoting all his attention to the Afghanistan inquiry. The secrecy provisions surrounding his inquiry made it extremely difficult for us to get a sense of how it was going. We had heard the investigators were busy and that Brereton was closely engaged, interviewing witnesses in their homes. The feedback, which reached Ben Roberts-Smith as well as us, suggested that the investigators were well prepared. They had operational summary reports, after-action reports, SSE data, imagery, the lot. This would help them identify, quite precisely, the movement and location of individuals.

Ben Roberts-Smith was interviewed for two days. He was represented by Arthur Moses SC. Nick and I presumed Roberts-Smith would be well prepared. We knew the man could be consumed, even 'Zombie-like' at times. He could flare up at the slightest threat. But he could also be statesman-like, a man who could snap to attention. His argument that he was a victim of jealous rivals was now well known.

The response from his friends—to supply pictures and the like—could assist his case immensely. 'Das Boot', as it was known, was a conspicuous example. The prosthetic leg from the Whiskey 108 mission had been souvenired—not by Roberts-Smith, but by his nemesis, The Veteran. It had been used as a drinking vessel and featured in many incriminating photos.

A cache of useful evidence was coming together. It could be used not only against other soldiers who dared to break ranks, but also against those hypocrites above them, the pissant bosses who had joined in the drinking games and allowed the 'witch-hunt' to take off.

If Ben was going to pay, so were they.

CHAPTER 35

PROTECTED IDENTITY

I spoke to [my husband] . . . he reacted exactly as you predicted. I think he believes me but is a bit sceptical.

I thought he would . . . what did you say? Does he think I did it?

Yeah, he did to begin with, and he didn't believe that I'd fall down stairs. I just told him what I talked about . . . I've some other bruises, including a massive one on the right side of my body, which will hopefully make the falling story more believable.

On 20 November 2018, the text message exchange between Ben Roberts-Smith and his then girlfriend, following the alleged assault at Canberra's Realm Hotel, was revealed in court. So too was a photograph of her black eye.

She said that she had not pursued action against her former lover because she 'held genuine fears for her safety and that of her children' if she was identified.[1]

Justice Anthony Besanko had now been assigned to the Roberts-Smith defamation case. The 64-year-old Adelaide-based Federal Court judge would preside in Sydney. Inscrutable, hard to read, as you would expect from a judge, he was described to us as both very smart and very fair. Experienced, too, having been appointed to the Federal Court in 2006.

For the moment, the small matter of a suppression order was being sought. Justice Besanko had previously granted temporary protection to the witness designated as 'Person 17', who was Roberts-Smith's ex-girlfriend. Our defence team sought to have her name suppressed permanently, but this was opposed by Roberts-Smith's team.

Person numbers had been assigned to soldiers and an interpreter called by both sides. By law, protected identity status applied to special forces personnel, given the sensitivity of counter-terrorism tasks. In the past, particularly in the United Kingdom, soldiers identified in media reporting had, along with their families, endured threats, harassment and the risk of assassination.

The former girlfriend, now Person 17, feared something similar. Our lawyers made it clear that it was not Roberts-Smith himself who was seen as a threat to her; rather, it was his sprawling, anonymous cheer squad. Social media attacks from the Digger Diaspora, otherwise known as Misogyny Central, took the customary form of viciousness and vitriol.

One post showed an image of a man with a gun, and the words: 'Me when anyone insults our prophet, Ben Roberts-Smith.' In response to coverage of the hearing, this charming post appeared on social media: 'Just another woman making false allegations to discredit a guy because she has a vagina so it must be true. She smells money today's women are so toxic to the point you have to tar all of them with same brush and not get involved with them.'

Bruce McClintock SC, acting for Ben Roberts-Smith, dismissed the risks to Person 17's safety as 'nonsense'. Boss and mentor Kerry Stokes decried Roberts-Smith's predicament, releasing a statement on 23 November:

> At present Ben is in an unjust position whereby his accusers get the benefit of anonymity but the attacks on him are reported in full with the hearing some time away . . . Knowing Ben as I do, both personally from his days of service and in his more recent executive role at Seven West Media I have every confidence that when he gets the opportunity to tell his story, his version will be borne out.[2]

Justice Besanko retired to consider his judgment. As he did, the year wound down and Ben's campaign to assemble allies moved further underground. Signal, Telegram and WhatsApp accounts were set up near his home address. New sim cards were activated, and numbers stored on the burner phones. In addition to The Scot, The Sniper and The Hunter, two more numbers were added to his electronic contacts list. One was a former SAS trooper we will call The Bodyguard (Person 38), and the other was one of the three soldiers alleged to have executed detainees at Roberts-Smith's direction.

The silly season was upon us. In *The Sydney Morning Herald*'s CBD column of 4 December 2018, a snippet appeared:

> CBD thought it a bit odd seeing Daily Telegraph deputy editor, Anthony DeCeglie wandering through Pyrmont last week, far from News Corp's Holt Street bunker. It turns out he was there for good reason, breaking bread with Kerry Stokes' Seven West Media executives, which yesterday announced he would be editor of the West Australian (where we look forward to more objective coverage of Ben Roberts-Smith).

At around this time, Nick and I met up in Sydney for lunch, and another long yarn. We both have December birthdays, but there was only the mildest celebration. Ben Roberts-Smith would not be enjoying the waiting game, and nor were we. He had complained of a 'shifting sands' approach in the argument we were assembling—what the lawyers referred to as our 'case theory'—and he was not completely wrong.

As a result of the corroborative evidence we had amassed, we were confident of the essential accuracy of our reporting. But we could not say the same about our confidence of winning in court. The labour involved in making an allegation is 1 per cent of what is involved in defending it. Our research base would bulge and shape-shift as information flowed in. There was more to know and a lot of work still to do in continuing to cover the story and in meeting the accelerating demands of our lawyers. We could complain, sure, but we were lucky to have such lawyers on our side. Serious investigative journalism cannot happen without them.

Nick was keen for us to work collaboratively for his new employer and to provide material for the Nine Network's *60 Minutes* program. When we gathered in the Nine boardroom, we met not only the program makers but also a pulsating battery of lawyers. There was lots of work for them to do as well.

We felt great relief when, at the end of January 2019, Justice Besanko ruled that the identity of Roberts-Smith's ex-girlfriend should continue to be suppressed—'to protect the safety of Person 17', as he put it.[3]

A date for the defamation trial was yet to be set, but the general sense was that it would commence later in the year. If 2018 had been turbulent, 2019 would be full of anticipation and the unexpected.

CHAPTER 36

THE WHISTLEBLOWER

Major David McBride was one of many ADF legal officers ('legalos') I had come to know over the years. At first we got on well, but then the war crimes saga unfolded.

In 2018, a year after he was medically discharged from the Army, McBride took a turn at comedy and set up a website called *The Ops Room*. In February that year, his Canberra flat was raided by the AFP while he was in Spain. Also on the search warrant were the names, 'Daniel (Dan) Oakes' and 'Samuel (Sam) Clarke' [*sic*].

In September 2018, McBride was arrested at Sydney Airport and charged with theft of Commonwealth property. 'The Afghan Files' was a report by Dan Oakes and Sam Clark that was broadcast in July 2017 on the ABC's *7.30 Report*. It was a catalogue of alleged atrocities in Afghanistan and quickly became famous. David McBride made no secret of the fact that he had leaked this material.

Yet McBride was not happy with the way the ABC had used the material he had provided. His primary concern was not for the Afghan people but for Australia's special forces soldiers, whom he saw as being dangerously restricted by the rules of engagement and punitive oversight. He agitated for the operators to have more freedom of action. He criticised Defence leadership for increasing the risk to their soldiers for the political dividend of avoiding civilian casualties.

It was this position that put us at odds. I agreed with McBride that there was a degree of suspicion and hostility towards the special forces in the wider defence community, but thought he was never going to win this campaign.

In 2019, in response to another of *The Australian*'s eulogies of Ben Roberts-Smith, David McBride posted on Facebook: 'man who put his life on the line for Australia more times than can be counted: they deliberately leaked the story to distract the news cycle from my allegations against them'.[1]

The proposition that senior leadership had leaked against Ben Roberts-Smith—a false belief he shared with Roberts-Smith himself—was added to McBride's angst about our access to the Crompvoets report. McBride and his supporters wanted to know why the police were not investigating us. I can say with complete certainty that Sam Crompvoets did not leak her report, nor was it made available to us by Defence leadership.

In June 2019, the ABC's headquarters at Ultimo was subjected to a notorious raid by the AFP. The trove of files from McBride was the cause. Journalists are condemned for disclosing sources—but the same is not true for sources who out journalists.

Ultimately, the AFP decided against charging Dan Oakes and Sam Clark, but persisted with its case against David McBride for allegedly breaching the *Defence Act*. Well versed in the law, McBride has refused any deal that might lessen the charges and see him avoid imprisonment.

Sources within Defence expressed no eagerness over the prosecution of McBride. I felt that was the right decision. David had a bad run with alcohol and prescription medication. He has acknowledged issues with mental health. He is thoughtful, likeable—but was very much on the wrong tram.

A huge amount has been written about him. There are petitions and crowdfunding campaigns. There is a documentary, a mobile billboard and T-shirts stamped 'Truth Is A Lonely Warrior'. But an article written about McBride soon after the ABC raid by David Wroe, our co-respondent in the Roberts-Smith defamation trial, to my mind did contain a lonely and contrary truth:

> At the extreme end of his theory, McBride argues the government amplified the 'rules of engagement' for Australian soldiers, knowing it could increase the risk to their lives, but that politicians were content to do this because attending soldiers' funerals would look good on television and boost their ratings. They did so with the complicity of obedient Defence leaders. This is universally seen as preposterous and indeed offensive. Even McBride's sympathisers won't touch it.[2]

The article also made reference to David McBride's father, Dr William McBride, world famous for his discovery of the link between thalidomide and birth defects, and for a dramatic fall from grace when he was later found to have falsified research results in a bid to prove the harmfulness of a different drug. It quoted a friend who regarded this history of his father's fall from grace as 'pivotal', a 'turning point' for David McBride.[3]

The David Wroe article was one story I did not see David McBride repost on social media. And it did not appear to be a story people wanted to hear. Driven by gusts of faith, the war crimes whistleblower narrative sailed on. That wind helped change David McBride's position. He ultimately became an enemy of war crimes and helped draw useful attention to a cause he had formerly disavowed.

I hope that, by the time this book goes to print, David McBride is free of jail, punishment and his demons.

A useful rule of thumb for dealing with whistleblowers is to try to find them rather than the other way around. Of course, the heroic status of some purveyors of dangerous truths is well deserved and should be protected. But journalism is not stenography. The source is not the story.

I am still puzzled by an unwillingness in my industry to report a more honest and rounded story. To McBride's credit, he was out there, offering plenty of insights into the turmoil within. Maybe hero whistleblower works a lot better than misguided martyr.

At the risk of being howled down as a heretic, I make this point: sometimes whistleblowers are not what they claim to be.

CHAPTER 37

GLOBAL WARRIORS

On Anzac Day in 2019, Ben Roberts-Smith, now not appearing in public so often, led the march in the national capital. He was invited to do so by the Canberra RSL and told *The Australian*: 'After that, I'll catch up with my friends and colleagues and we'll probably have a beer.'[1]

The IGADF's Afghanistan inquiry by this stage had interviewed hundreds of witnesses. Roberts-Smith was yet to face a further grilling, and he continued to receive assistance from close friends. Early in July he emailed The Freefaller for further details about Whiskey 108, and he received more pictures from The Scot, who had moved to the United States.

Roberts-Smith might have felt reassured at this time when he heard the news that US Navy SEAL Eddie Gallagher, in a war crimes trial with striking parallels to his own battles, had been acquitted of the charge laid against him. He had been accused of ten offences, including stabbing an injured seventeen-year-old Iraqi.

In 2017, Special Operations Chief Petty Officer Gallagher had led Alpha Platoon of SEAL Team Seven at Mosul in the war against ISIS. Going into theatre with a fresh squad, Gallagher was on his eighth deployment. He had fought in Afghanistan as well as Iraq, receiving multiple decorations, including two Bronze Stars. Known for his aggression, Gallagher was intimidating, even untouchable.

Alpha Platoon set up sniper teams in a neighbourhood where ISIS fighters moved among civilians. Its members were surprised when, instead of providing oversight, Gallagher preferred to settle behind a sniper rifle.

One of the new men in the platoon, Special Operator First Class Josh Vriens, was in a separate observation post. As he watched four teenage girls walking through the shattered streetscape, he heard a shot and saw one of the girls buckle and look up, clutching her bleeding stomach. Vriens was later told Gallagher had taken the shot.

Special Operator First Class Dylan Dille similarly watched two old men walking, representing no threat. He heard a shot and saw the man on the right fall. Again, he was told it was Gallagher who had fired.

The indiscriminate shooting continued. The men reported what was going on to their immediate superior, but nothing happened. Perplexed, they took to firing warning shots so that civilians would stay behind cover. Josh Vriens was troubled. 'I didn't join SEAL Team Seven to terrorise a population,' he said. 'I joined to protect them. What am I doing here?'[2] The men took to nicknaming their leader 'El Diablo'.

And then, as they saw it, the line was crossed in one giant leap. On 3 May 2017, the platoon's signals intelligence operator called an air strike on an ISIS stronghold. As the dust and debris settled, a wounded teenage ISIS fighter was found and brought to the Americans. Eddie Gallagher insisted on treating him. A helmet camera captured much of what occurred, but was then turned off. According to three of his team, Gallagher reached for his hunting knife and stabbed the teenager in the neck.

As with Australian SAS operators returning from Afghanistan, it was not until they were back home that the Americans began to compare notes. The first to report Gallagher to the Naval Criminal Investigative Service was a medic, Petty Officer Corey Scott, who had witnessed the stabbing.

In September 2018, Special Operations Chief Petty Officer Eddie Gallagher was charged. The case became a cause célèbre in the United States, variously described as good versus evil, boy scout versus pirate, and brotherhood and silence versus accountability. As in Australia, ranks divided between those urging loyalty and those defending integrity. And, as in Australia, there was intimidation. The names of Gallagher's accusers, described as traitors, were leaked. There were death threats against them.

Murdoch's Fox News Channel actively advocated for Gallagher with a rallying cry much like that heard Down Under: condemnation of armchair critics, denunciation of the besmirching of heroes, contempt for craven leaders who had betrayed their men.

Top cover for the accused was enlisted in the form of no less a person than the commander-in-chief of the United States Armed Forces, President Donald Trump. When the Navy sought to remove Eddie Gallagher's sacred SEAL trident pin, Trump countermanded the directive and ordered him reinstated.

In July 2019, under extraordinary circumstances, Eddie Gallagher was acquitted. The prosecution was stunned. His former comrade, medic Corey Scott, the initiator of the war crimes investigation, had received indemnity and claimed responsibility for the killing. He later told comrades that he did so because he did not want Eddie to go to jail.

Instead, the man his comrades described as 'freaking evil' had his fame burnished. And the man to take the fall was the man who had dared to prosecute him. After the presidential intervention, US Navy secretary Richard Spencer received a call from his boss, who said: 'The Gallagher thing has gone too far. I'm going to have to fire you.'[3]

Richard Spencer had vainly hoped politics would stay clear of a matter he saw best adjudicated by Gallagher's peers in the armed forces. 'I don't think [Trump] understands the real definition of a war fighter,' he commented later. 'A war fighter is a profession of arms, and a profession of arms has standards that they have to be held to and they hold themselves to.'[4]

The Eddie Gallagher story is comprehensively covered in a documentary series, *The Line*, which might have been of interest at the time to the IGADF's war crimes investigators. Certainly the Nine/Fairfax lawyers took note. Aspects of the Gallagher case would later resonate in ours.

The Line closes with Eddie Gallagher, having been cleared, admitting he 'helped along the way' the teenage Iraqi to his death. Richard Spencer's response was: 'I am gobsmacked. That is a travesty of humanity . . . it violates everything that the special warfare community is about. Everything.'[5]

Spencer was rightly concerned that, given the outcome and other prosecutions that soon fell away, American soldiers would in future be much more cautious in calling out apparent war crimes.

In the United Kingdom it was much the same story. The first war crimes case to emerge from Afghanistan was of a summary execution by a Royal Marines sergeant, Alexander Blackman, which was caught on helmet cam. In 2013, he was dismissed from the military and sentenced to life imprisonment, with a minimum of ten years before he would be eligible for parole.

The following year, the Royal Military Police commenced Operation Northmoor, which examined hundreds of alleged unlawful killings, predominantly by the SAS. Investigators complained of internal obstruction. Politicians and the populist media blamed human rights lawyers for drumming up business and trumping up charges.

In 2017, following a second appeal, Blackman's conviction was reduced to manslaughter and he was released from prison. And in 2019, Operation Northmoor was closed down; the Royal Military Police claimed to have uncovered no evidence of criminality.[6]

In the United Kingdom and the United States, then, minimal enthusiasm for prosecuting service personnel was apparent. In the Anzac colonies—Australia and New Zealand—there was little reason to think the public was any less squeamish.

CHAPTER 38

THE PHONEY WAR

In August 2019, the trial date was set for 15 June 2020. The writs, of course, had been issued a year before, on 17 August 2018, and—as ever in such cases—between the issuing of the writs and the commencement of the trial there had been a kind of phoney war. A lot of expensive, brain-sapping fighting, most of it done on paper.

Competing parties have a right to discover the evidence held in the other camp that is relevant to the case. 'Interrogatories' allow them to probe each other's evidence. 'Discoveries' allow them access to all records of relevant communications—emails, text messages, notebooks, imagery and the like. Only 'privileged' information—legal advice, essentially—is exempt.

On 31 May 2019, Nine had filed outlines of evidence (effectively witness statements on behalf of each of our proposed witnesses). In proceedings such as these, the applicant—in this case Ben Roberts-Smith—is gifted the advantage of seeing what he is up against, and is accordingly able to ask specific questions of his own witnesses. He had six weeks to do so. Within that time frame he was in contact with supportive witnesses, such as The Hunter. Evidence in reply from Mark O'Brien Legal had arrived at MinterEllison on 12 July.

One of the first moves by Peter Bartlett, senior partner at Minter-Ellison, retained by Nine and running our case, was to assign a young

Melbourne-based lawyer to manage the engine room. Dean Levitan is short of stature and large of brain. Easygoing and persistent, the media specialist would become a walking encyclopaedia on all things Roberts-Smith.

Within the bundle of documents received from Mark O'Brien was a series of witness statements from a range of Roberts-Smith witnesses. There is a common language to witness statements, discordant to an ordinary reader but coherent to a court. Lawyers generally draft these statements, based on what witnesses have told them. The witness checks the content, amends if necessary and signs off.

So a familiar pattern of legalese, from one statement to the next, won't necessarily raise a lawyer's eyebrows—but in one tranche of evidence there was a commonality that caused Dean Levitan to reach back and read again and again.

Ben Roberts-Smith's band of brothers/witnesses was continuing to expand. Among his new supporters were The Scientist (Person 27), one of many SAS members who came to the regiment with impressive other-world qualifications. The Corporal (Person 32) was another to have fought alongside Ben at Tizak in 2010. The XO (Person 39), like The Scot, had transferred from British special forces; on Rotation XVIII in 2012, he was the squadron's executive officer. All provided extensive written statements.

What Dean Levitan noted when reading through them was a very similar description of one incident, involving The Lieutenant, the commander of the National Directorate of Security, the Wakunish, that was the SASR's partner force.

First, The Scientist:

> I recall that early in our deployment, in about July/early August 2012, the Commander of the NDS, The Lieutenant, was removed from participating in missions with the SASR after he shot a dog and the bullet ricocheted hitting another Patrol Commander in the leg.

Next, The Corporal:

> While I am not sure of the exact date, I recall that early in our deployment I believe around the end of July 2012, The Lieutenant was stood

> down as commander of the NDS soldiers following an incident during a mission in which an Australian Patrol Commander was hit by shrapnel from a bullet fired by The Lieutenant.

Third, The XO:

> I recall that on or about 31 July 2012, The Lieutenant was removed from command of the NDS due to an incident on the mission when The Lieutenant acted dangerously and a Patrol Commander ended up with shrapnel in his leg. Given the prevalence of 'green-on-blue' attacks at the time, the incident was taken very seriously.

Fourth, Ben's friend The Hunter had witnessed the shooting:

> On or about 31 July 2012 we were on a mission in the Chora Valley where we had secured a compound. There were a number of dogs chained up. I was about 4–5 metres away from The Lieutenant when I saw that he was preparing to shoot a dog. Before I could stop him he shot the dog. The bullet went through the dog, into the door behind the dog, and shrapnel hit another Australian Patrol Commander's leg . . . I recall that The Lieutenant was escorted off our base and I never saw him on the base again.

And lastly there was Ben Roberts-Smith himself, who recalled being told that The Lieutenant had been removed as a result of the dog and bullet incident.

The departure of The Lieutenant in late July 2012, if true, would have massive ramifications. It would virtually destroy The Scout's account of the alleged execution at Chinartu on 12 October 2012. His evidence was that he had seen and heard Ben Roberts-Smith arguing with The Lieutenant and ordering the killing.

It would also be relevant to the alleged execution at Darwan on 11 September 2012. In an earlier defence document, based on testimony provided by an Afghan interpreter, we had placed The Lieutenant at Darwan.

So two key allegations would be knocked out. Devasting if true, and we were suitably alarmed. Furious checking ensued—and then there was relief. Photographs were found showing The Lieutenant in Uruzgan after July 2012. Subpoenaed Defence records also placed him at Chinartu. True, he was not at Darwan, but that was evidence we no longer relied upon.

In such matters, our understanding of what took place was often refined. On both sides, as the picture cleared, evidence was modified. This was sometimes seized upon as proof of previous recklessness and dishonesty, but it was more a case of having more witnesses to draw upon, and having the opportunity to see the records received under subpoena from Defence. Operational summaries (OpSums) would prove crucial. Load plans and manifests showed who was on which helicopter. Real-time chats, which recorded content and the timing of radio transmissions, were useful in finetuning the truth.

Our earlier belief that The Lieutenant had been present at Darwan was later discarded. We came to understand that on this point the interpreter had been incorrect. However, this inconsistent detail in no way disproved the allegation that Ali Jan was kicked from a cliff and murdered. And, equally, we knew he was not the soldier who shot the dog: The Lieutenant had not been removed from the 2012 mission.

Later in the year, when *The Australian* reported that we now accepted that The Lieutenant had not been at Darwan, Paul Maley led with 'War crimes defamation case: "Witness wasn't there"'. His report depicted this revelation as a 'major blow' to our case.[1]

Ultimately, the opposite was shown to be true, with an important question emerging from the strange tale of the stray dog and the stray bullet. Five witnesses had asserted that The Lieutenant was not at Chinartu. But this was shown to be false—or, if you like, 'phoney'.

How could all five have made the same mistake?

CHAPTER 39

60 MINUTES

My car was a phone booth.

It was February 2019. Nick McKenzie and I met in Sydney for the drive to Canberra. I could hardly get a word in. His mobile buzzed constantly. Mine was comparatively quiet. I was supposed to be retired.

At the peak of his career, Scoop was the busiest person I knew. Utterly prolific. Though we spoke regularly, it was often news to me when I picked up the paper and saw another Nick McKenzie front page on a casino scandal, a sex-slave racket, a white supremacist exposé or the like.

In 2019, the McKenzie workload at *The Age* increased when the Nine merger began to draw him into the *60 Minutes* fold. Previously he had had a working alliance with the ABC and had occasionally reported for *7.30* and *Four Corners*. But since the Nine Network and the ABC were competitors, this arrangement had ceased.

I joined Nick at *60 Minutes* at the start of 2019, acting as a freelance producer on their war crimes stories. Although at times it could seem as though the two of us had become professional defendants, we were, and are, reporters first. And we like to think we serve the public first.

Most of the phone calls that day to the mobile phone booth zooming down the motorway at 110 kilometres per hour were from the lawyers. A judgment unfavourable to Nine in a defamation action brought by

Chau Chak Wing had just come in. A further action by the Chinese businessman was pending against a program Nick had reported.

Most journalists don't get sued. In our industry, where risky publication is closely linked to retributive punishment, the most pervasive limit to freedom of speech is self-censorship. The worst feature of Australia's harsh defamation laws is the deterrent to risk. I don't blame journalists, caught in the 24-hour moil, for ducking a writ, which can be both damaging to your psyche and, prospectively, to your career. Nick and I both understood and accepted that while we enjoyed the benefit of having more time than daily journalists to undertake our research, the cost of this was that we stood more risk of attracting litigation. If you are given the privilege of reaching further, and you see journalism as a vocation, then taking risks on behalf of the public becomes a professional responsibility.

Andrew Hastie evidently felt much the same in his role as a politician. A federal election was due in 2019. There was no clear political dividend for him if he supported the war crimes inquiry, but whether he was worried about electoral fallout or not, he went ahead with an interview for a *60 Minutes* program Nick and I were preparing that would challenge the reputation of a national hero. The newly minted MP added moral rationale and perspective.

Andrew Hastie on political accountability: 'Everybody wanted to be there for the medal ceremonies and people turned up for the funerals. Your responsibility doesn't end there. You have to be engaged intellectually. The nature of war is inherently chaotic. And so, you need to be constantly revisiting your policy, adapting your policy.'

On the chain of command: 'I've seen people deeply affected by this. Sure, people need to be held to account at the pointy end, but I would be upset if people just hung out the soldiers and didn't reflect [on] how the system contributed to some of the behaviour.'

And on speaking up: 'There's two forms of courage in war, moral courage and physical courage. But moral courage is the greater form of courage and these guys have shown that, and I'm very glad and the Australian people should be glad that we have men of that calibre in the SAS.'

He was referring to Soldiers 1 and 2. At this stage, their interviews were in the can. Both were to the point, calling out Ben Roberts-Smith.

Nick: 'So you are accusing him of engaging in war crimes?'

Soldier 1: 'I am.'

Nick: 'Who do you think kicked the man, the prisoner of war?'

Soldier 2: 'The individual who kicked the detainee off the cliff was Ben Roberts-Smith.'

Although these two interviewees were not identified by name and spoke from the shadows in replicated voices, they were taking a big risk. After lengthy discussion and much misgiving, the two experienced SAS operators agreed to say their piece.

We all felt it was important to do so. What continued to go missing in the public debate about Ben Roberts-Smith was the plain truth that his alleged misconduct was called out by fellow soldiers, rather than by muckraking journalists. The soldiers complained first, not to the media but up their own chain of command. Those complaints went unheeded.

Of course, we promised anonymity. Source protection is another professional responsibility. Strict protocols applied. The soldiers were interviewed separately. The audio tracks were transcribed. Actors later revoiced the transcripts.

When speaking of their regiment, ingrained pride was tinged with nagging regret.

Soldier 2: 'The majority of soldiers were highly professional, used impeccable judgement, were morally and ethically above board.' But he also spoke of a rogue element, who were '[a] law unto themselves, [with] very little respect for command. Couldn't be told what to do.'

Soldier 1: 'I think they actually thought they were above the law. I think they actually thought they won't be caught. That it was a free-for-all.'

It was a long haul. In investigative journalism, getting heads on camera is always difficult. For this story it was ten times harder.

Other important interviewees were in far-off Afghanistan. With the help of a local journalist/fixer, arrangements were made. Nick flew to Kabul and met members of Ali Jan's family in a safe house. It was another dangerous journey. Darwan, and for that matter Uruzgan, was by now under Taliban control. While we were organising this filming, we learned that the AFP also collected interviews from Darwan witnesses.

Bibi Dorkho, Ali Jan's widow, and his brother Achmed gathered in a courtyard. Ali Jan's three children were also present. Their father, husband and brother was missing and they could make no sense of why he had been taken from them. His wife and his brother both insisted that Ali Jan was not Taliban. He knew nothing about guns; he feared the Taliban. Dorkho pleaded: 'Why did such cruelty happen?'

The cast list of Australian special forces alumni prepared to speak up and be identified was tiny. David Wegman, very much his own man, was unafraid. He deployed four times to Afghanistan with 1 Commando, a reservist special forces element. The regular units—unfairly, in my view—treated reservists with disdain, as common 'chocos'. While it wasn't a full-time job, the reservists, all highly trained, brought supplementary specialist skills from civilian lives, as police officers, paramedics, lawyers and more.

David Wegman had trained as an architect. At his yoga retreat in the shadow of the Victorian Grampians, he settled before the camera to do his *60 Minutes* interview. He had earrings and a hippie-like coiffure. If you think special forces is all bristle and brawn and protein powder, you are off the mark. The personality matrix is a patchwork. David Wegman, for instance, is a born philosopher, and much that he said stayed with me.

'When you set the conditions for a culture to breed and grow in a certain way,' he said, 'the special forces culture is built on superiority and entitlement and heroism and sacrifice and courage. But also there is a lot of ego in the game.'

Nick asked him: 'How important is it to have moral authority on the battlefield?'

David Wegman: 'It's absolutely essential. The second that you erode your own sense of what is right, you've lost the game. These old adages of "it's not whether you win or lose, it's how you play the game" are rooted in some of the most essential wisdom that we've managed to extract as a culture. The reason you've got to play a straight game is for your own sake.'

Another interviewee who made a profound contribution to understanding that other war that carries on after the guns fall silent was Sergeant Dusty Miller. He was well known to Nick and he keenly felt the medic's responsibility. When in 2012 a wounded Afghan was taken from his care and killed, Dusty was dogged by guilt.

'It's something I think about often,' he said. 'It's one of the intrusive thoughts I get. It just feels like I lacked intestinal fortitude at the time, that I should have stopped it and I didn't, and I know there are more others out there that feel the same way as I do. You can't keep this stuff to yourself. I thought it was the noble thing to do—let's keep it in-house—but it's not. There needs to be accountability and the truth needs to be told.'

Among many a returning Afghanistan veteran, conscience was biting. Shame was felt for what had been done to Afghans; probably more so, there was collective hurt for the many comrades burdened by unrelenting guilt. Soldier 1 and Soldier 2 saw the big step of helping the IGADF inquiry, and the even bigger step of talking to *60 Minutes*, as part of a cleansing process.

It took many months to put the program together. The 2019 federal election came and went; Scott Morrison's Liberal/National Coalition had been re-elected. Finally, over a big weekend in September 2019, our program was screened on Nine, supported by feature coverage in *The Age* and *The Sydney Morning Herald*.

60 Minutes is populist current affairs, typically leaning towards storytelling rather than hard journalism. Tabloid media in general flatters, rather than confronts, its public. But this program was different. The formula ticking clock cadence was still there, but there was also a challenging, awkward and unpalatable truth. In her introduction, Sarah Abo offered a clue: 'You may not like what we are about to reveal . . .'

The critics of the Nine/Fairfax merger had predicted a dumbing-down of the newsprint partner, and had given little thought to the prospect of an opposite form of cross-pollination. *60 Minutes* personnel were proud of this particular program, as were Nick and I.

The most strident decrier, beyond Ben Roberts-Smith himself, was a broadsheet newspaper. In *The Australian*, Paul Maley, quoting Ben Roberts-Smith, wrote:

> 'I categorically deny the allegations made against me in tonight's *60 Minutes* program,' he said in a statement. 'I am concerned that tonight's story and the previous publications by the *SMH/Age* are an attempt to improperly influence the outcome of the [IGADF] inquiry.' Mr Roberts-Smith said the two anonymous sources quoted on the program spoke in a way that suggested they had not actually witnessed the alleged killing of Ali Jan. 'None of the witnesses on tonight's broadcast provided any direct evidence of any sort to support their allegations,' he said.[1]

So Ben Roberts-Smith denied the allegation, but he seemed to make more of a perceived evidentiary weakness in our case. He had not served with David Wegman and Dusty Miller. While he would have been afraid of Andrew Hastie, he knew the former SAS captain had not been at Whiskey 108 or Darwan. He knew there were only two other SAS members with him at the cliff, The Sniper and The Gunsmith. He figured The Gunsmith was not one of the *60 Minutes* interviewees and would be an unlikely witness for Nine/Fairfax. He had The Sniper onside and there was feedback from his camp dismissive of the credibility of any Afghan witnesses.

Ben and his legal teams were not obliged to prove his innocence. The onus of proof was on us. We had to convince the court that, on the balance of probabilities, it was Ben Roberts-Smith who kicked Ali Jan off a cliff at Darwan in 2012. He was correct in his presumption that it would not be easy for us.

CHAPTER 40

EXODUS

The aftermath of the September 2019 *60 Minutes* report saw an uptick of argument in newsprint and talkback. Ben Roberts-Smith accused Nine of publishing false claims that were 'malicious and commercially motivated'. He characterised himself to *The Australian*'s Paul Maley as a victim of 'abuse of power'.[1]

Pressure for the IGADF to get on with its Afghanistan inquiry again amplified. Paul Maley returned to Brendan Nelson: 'I struggle to understand why an inquiry of this nature should take as long as a royal commission into institutional abuse of children.' *The West Australian* echoed with a headline: 'SAS probe goes AWOL'.[2]

In a series of articles in which reason and some barracking for their man ran side by side, Maley represented Ben Roberts-Smith's side of the story. He reported that none of the allegations against Roberts-Smith had been fully tested or proven, and that the alleged assault of his girlfriend had been dismissed for lack of evidence. He proposed the Darwan allegation as a prospective graduation of 'digger whispers'.[3] He presented a sympathetic account of the war hero as the victim of toxic rivalry, and 'the only one fighting in the open'.[4] He challenged the competence of the Brereton inquiry and Defence: 'The failure to properly resource and prioritise the inquiry is beyond negligent, it is culpable.'[5]

We agreed with Maley in one respect. It had seemed to us that the IGADF, particularly in the beginning, was insufficiently resourced. But we had sympathy too, given our exposure to similar challenges. By now the IGADF investigators had travelled to Afghanistan, building more evidence, and in Australia more witnesses had trickled forward. When you gather information from one source, new avenues of inquiry open, demanding attention you had not anticipated giving.

The Age and *The Sydney Morning Herald* responded to the criticism levelled at them head-on with a small Q&A:

> Q. Why were we investigating our own soldiers?
> A. Rules of engagement distinguish professional soldiers from criminals.
>
> Q. Isn't this improperly influencing the IGADF inquiry?
> A. There is no suggestion that the IGADF is not independent or impartial or would be improperly influenced by media reporting.
>
> Q. What is the justification for airing unproven allegations?
> A. Reporting investigations underway . . . is crucial to keeping the system, including the justice system, honest. Should the media have waited for the burglars in Watergate to have been jailed before they reported the story?[6]

The latter months of 2019 also saw an uptick in the paper war between MinterEllison and Mark O'Brien Legal. Between the legal citadels, categories of discoveries were agreed to and queried.

On 11 November, Ben Roberts-Smith claimed he had not retained all the communications he had sent or received. This was untrue. At his Sunshine Coast home, he was secreting hundreds of photographs and videos supplied by allies. The three-page account of The Scot's IGADF grilling was withheld. And there were emails between himself and The Freefaller.

Nick and I were also in a quandary. Mark O'Brien Legal sought 49 documents containing notes, correspondence and records of interview. This presented us with a dilemma familiar to journalists: the need to substantiate evidence to our lawyers, while adhering to source protection pledges. The pressure for discovery had intensified since the *60 Minutes* report.

Bruce McClintock SC, for Ben Roberts-Smith, argued that, by providing outlines of evidence from witnesses, we had effectively outed our sources and waived the right to journalistic privilege. We saw that as a fishing expedition. In the Federal Court, Sandy Dawson SC argued it was unfair to expose privileged documents, 'to confirm the speculation, fill gaps, draw inferences or make links that the applicant himself is unable to establish based on information before him'.[7]

The legal skirmishing ran parallel to an ongoing public information war. The ADF and the government had good reason to worry that this sad and weary scandal, dragging on year after year, was bad for the reputation of the Army and for its attempts at recruitment.

In mid-November, Roberts-Smith struck again, this time more at his former employer. Two years after the news reporting began, he finally received a call from the ADF to check on his welfare. Roberts-Smith revealed his anguish at being ignored for so long to his go-to reporter, Paul Maley. 'The call came just days after he publicly criticised the leadership of the ADF for failing to look after soldiers after they left the military,' Maley wrote.[8]

The Sydney Murdoch tabloid *The Daily Telegraph* fired the other barrel. On the front page: 'War hero's advice: "Don't join the ADF"'. Sharri Markson wrote: 'War hero Ben Roberts-Smith says the top of the Australian Defence Force need to go for shamefully protecting their own careers at the expense of rank and file soldiers.'[9]

Events were heating up, in more ways than one. The reporting came at the time the east coast of Australia became imperilled by catastrophic bushfires. New South Wales and Victoria were facing up to a summer from hell.

Ben and Emma were planning an overseas holiday, but events on their personal front were also catching fire. Because Emma acted as manager of Ben's personal business affairs, she had access to some of his communications and was becoming increasingly suspicious.

There was stress on other fronts. In early December, Roberts-Smith was again before Justice Paul Brereton. In a closed hearing, for three days, he answered a further round of questions. While this was taking place, he arranged for his friend The Freefaller to visit Sydney.

On 4 December, after emerging from Brereton's questioning, he joined The Freefaller and Monica Allen at dinner on the fringe of the CBD. Ben told Emma he had provided notes to his friend, ahead of The Freefaller's appearance before the IGADF.

Two days later, on the anniversary of their marriage, Ben and Emma took off on a holiday—of a sort. With their daughters they flew to New Zealand. There they met up with The Hunter. But recreation and nuptial nostalgia did not appear to be priority number one. Ben would prowl about, talking to himself and exercising maximum caution when using the phone.

Soon after, it was made public that the AFP had opened a new inquiry. A second team had been tasked with probing the Whiskey 108 allegations from 2009.

As this news was breaking, *The Australian* ran its 'witness wasn't there' story.[10] The report referred to The Lieutenant and, as I've previously explained, was portrayed as a major blow to our case.

A bigger dump came three days later. I do not buy *The Australian*. It makes me sick. But bad news travels fast, and I soon learned that my picture was on its front page, alongside Ben Roberts-Smith and a headline: 'They're calling me a murderer: War hero Ben Roberts-Smith'.

It was in response to *The Age*'s and *The Sydney Morning Herald*'s reporting of the second AFP investigation. Paul Maley quoted passages from a statement by Seven: 'Nine's reporters were clearly panicked by a Court report in Saturday's *Australian* about the serious deficiencies in their purported evidence.'[11]

Maley's report concluded:

> Nine claimed Mr Roberts-Smith had 'attacked' the inquiry now in its fourth year, after learning it was examining his alleged involvement in a number of incidents, Mr Roberts-Smith said the claim was 'totally false.' 'I have made no criticisms of the Inspector-General and I unequivocally support the IGADF in its investigation,' he said.[12]

In Seven's statement, Roberts-Smith further denied bagging his former bosses: 'Again, this is not the case. I have merely stated my concern that the ADF needs systemic change in order to better manage the needs of veterans and I do not resile from those comments.'[13]

On the following day, Michael Bachelard at *The Age* countered these prevarications:

> In August 2017, the Inspector-General asked for serving and ex-soldiers to come forward with information or rumours about misconduct by special forces soldiers. Roberts-Smith responded: 'I don't think these soldiers should be suffering through this ridiculous notion of being investigated for a rumour. When have you heard of a judicial process initiated off the back of rumours? It's just a joke. We should be looking after our soldiers not persecuting them.'

The source for Roberts-Smith's words quoted here was *The West Australian* of 26 October 2017.[14]

As for attacks on Defence leadership, Bachelard wrote:

> In an interview on Sky News last month, Roberts-Smith:
>
> - questioned whether young people should join the defence forces anymore because they would 'not be supported', and the problems were 'all about the leadership';

- said it was 'shameful' how returning soldiers were treated, and again blamed the leadership;
- was asked if there needed to be new leadership at the top of the Defence Force, and responded, 'Absolutely';
- said 'we're actually being let down by our own military' . . .[15]

While these blows were being traded, Prime Minister Scott Morrison was flying out for a sneaky family holiday in Hawaii, a decision he later regretted, given that New South Wales and the ACT were choking on smoke, and desperate householders were fleeing from the flames.

As Scotty was touching down in the United States, Ben Roberts-Smith and his family were landing there too. He met with his friend The Scot in ski country at Beaver Creek, Colorado. As well, Ben and family caught up with Kerry Stokes at Vail in the same state.

Roberts-Smith could still claim a cohort of solid and powerful friends. But he was about to lose his most valuable supporter. It was not the family's best Christmas. Within a month, a sixteen-year marriage would be over.

CHAPTER 41

ANNUS HORRIBILIS

Despite his lies and betrayal, Emma Roberts-Smith's instinct had always been to protect her husband, often from himself. She had worried when The Freefaller came to stay with them in late December 2019, and then soon after overheard Ben planning a trip to Perth to see The Sniper. She feared he was being watched and the meetings would be seen as collusion. They argued but he went anyway, claiming he needed to visit his sick father.

In Perth, Roberts-Smith had dined once more at the Floreat Hotel with some SAS mates. When he returned, the fighting resumed.

Emma Roberts-Smith had just turned 45. Like every Army wife, she too had served—and, as they will tell you, a special forces wife does extra duty. All those absences. All that worry. It had been seventeen years since she'd worked a paid full-time job in marketing. When they first met, Emma had been earning more than Ben, but starting again would be tough.

Of concern to her, beyond securing an adequate divorce settlement, was the prospect of being trapped by a lie that had been pressed on her by her husband to excuse his own infidelity. In April 2019, Emma had provided a witness statement to Ben's legal team stating that he had 'moved out of our home in about October [2017] to about April 2018'. She knew that was not true and she was frightened it might be used against her.

She was in regular communication with her friend Danielle Scott, and as 2020 began they discussed the predicament. If Emma were called to give evidence in the defamation case, which was now just months away, she would likely be cross-examined by Nine's lawyers. In a later text exchange, Emma told her friend: 'He thinks I am going to lie for him.'

Danielle replied: 'He thinks you will lie for the sake of the girls.' And later: 'He thinks he knows you. He thinks you will not admit it is not true.'

Clearly, the now real separation of Ben and Emma would have an impact on the defamation proceedings, but the split and Emma's dilemma were unknown to Nick and me at this time.

As 2020 dawned, Nine's legal team was flat out 'getting up' our case for trial. Sandy Dawson's junior, Lyndelle Barnett, was lost for a time due to other commitments. It was a blow, but there was compensation.

We were still awaiting judgment on the December 2019 application by Roberts-Smith's team for the suppression order on our sources and on 49 documents to be lifted. Junior counsel Chris Mitchell had been drafted into our team to assist with our source protection argument.

For Nick and me—and of course for our sources—it had been an anxious Christmas. In defamation matters, and particularly in source privilege arguments, we tend to expect the worst. So we felt great relief on 7 January when we learned that our team—Sandy Dawson SC, assisted by Chris Mitchell—had prevailed. Justice Besanko stated in his ruling: 'It is important to bear in mind that the person whose identity is protected is an informant, that is to say a person who gives information to a journalist. That person is not necessarily an eyewitness or a person whose information would be admissible evidence in a court.'

Given the ongoing workload, our own rookie, Chris Mitchell, now blooded, was asked to stay on. He had previously worked on war crimes prosecutions at the United Nations Criminal Tribunal in The Hague, and this experience, plus his eye for detail, would prove invaluable. Throughout a frighteningly costly exercise, Nine Entertainment had put no limit on the work the lawyers believed was needed. Now, the need for another barrister was queried but soon accepted.

Even so, hired gun for hired gun, we were still overmatched. Ben Roberts-Smith's team, also flat out, boasted three senior counsels. Matthew Richardson SC (the son of former politician Graham Richardson) had assisted Bruce McClintock SC in the source protection case. At this stage, their third senior counsel, Arthur Moses, was more focused on the IGADF battlefront.

On 3 February 2020, Roberts-Smith received notice to provide further information to the IGADF. And a few weeks later he would be interviewed by the AFP. Paul Maley in *The Australian* later reported that the interview was at Roberts-Smith's own initiative, and quoted him as saying: 'Following [the media reports] I asked my lawyers to contact the AFP and offer my assistance with any investigation.'[1]

Two months into the year and the smoke hung heavy. Two and a half thousand homes had been lost and 26 people killed in NSW bushfires. As one disaster dissipated, another applied its lethal grip. On 25 January, Australia's first case of Covid-19 was reported in Victoria; on 1 March came the first of thousands of deaths. An *annus horribilis* indeed.

The tribulations of Emma and the blight of Covid would have a telling influence on what was beginning to be described as the defamation trial of the century.

CHAPTER 42

THE KILLING FIELD

We were pleased when Mark Willacy took on responsibility for the ABC's Afghanistan war crimes reporting in mid-2019. The AFP raid on the ABC and the threat of charges against Dan Oakes and Sam Clark (which would be abandoned later in 2020) had unsettled us all. It was good to have the national broadcaster back in the hunt.

Mark is a mate and an excellent reporter; I might later have thought him a bit too good. As friends and rivals, we cooperated—up to a point.

I was aware when he began preparing a *Four Corners* program because he spoke with me along the way. He was searching for whatever visual material was available, which is always a struggle when you are making television about special forces.

The Defence community is commonly scornful of mistakes by civilian journalists. Programs purporting to be about special forces but which use footage of conventional forces—soldiers carrying different weapons and travelling on different vehicles—were not taken seriously. Given the covert role of special forces and the prohibition of any identifying details, accurate vision is always hard to come by.

The ADF had an 'HH' (handheld) imagery policy, restricting the shooting of images to 'task and purpose', and with storage of all photos and video being kept in-house. In 2011, an SAS captain told me, *sotto voce*, that no good ever came from a camera taken into the field.

The use by Commandos of helmet-cams was better known, but, as I came to learn, the SAS also had footage. The vast majority of the SAS material was kept on personal hard drives, and fused with sexy pictures and heavy metal soundtracks to create highlights reels that were shown at end-of-year members-only piss-ups. Over time, the men's compliance with the official HH policy had lapsed. To soldiers of the millennial generation, who had grown to adulthood in a world of GoPro and YouTube, the old restrictions were increasingly antiquated.

I helped Mark as best I could. I told him I had footage collected by Commandos, but next to nothing from the SAS. He did not say much, but somehow I detected a hint that my mate was better placed than he was letting on.

It turned out that, four months earlier, an email from an anonymous source had landed in his inbox. That had ended up putting Mark in touch with Braden Chapman. Chapman was, in the vernacular, a 'Bear'—a signals intelligence operator. So he was from the more talkative ranks of SAS support staff.

At their first meeting, Braden Chapman passed Mark an SD card, which for folks like us was like a Lasseter's Reef of gold. It contained twelve hours of video footage. Much of it Chapman had not seen; in all, it would take Mark ten days to view it.

On the last of those days, at 6 pm in an empty office, he reached FILE0185. It ran for thirteen minutes and twelve seconds.[1] Mark watched it, recovered his breath and then called his editor.

The *Four Corners* program 'The Killing Field' was broadcast on Monday, 16 March 2020, and what we saw was reality television. Not the common contrived version, but its true form.

Helmet-cam vision took us on a mission. It was late May 2012 and a patrol from 3 Squadron SASR was helicoptered into Dehjawz-e-Hasanzay, a hotspot. In 2006, this place had been the scene of a perilous night raid, when Australian helicopters and Commandos rescued a trapped Canadian special forces unit, but this 2012 mission was in broad daylight.

The camera affixed to the helmet of the SAS dog handler chased the action through a wheatfield and along footpaths in pursuit of a man who'd been spotted from the helicopters. When he was within sight, the dog was let off its leash, and it had soon pinned the Afghan to the ground. An SAS operator who came to be known as Soldier C, but was later revealed as Trooper Oliver Schulz, stood over the man and levelled his M4.

Dad Mohammed, a local farmer, married with two daughters, clutched his red prayer beads. He had no weapon. He looked up at Soldier C, two metres away.

'You want me to drop this cunt?' Soldier C yells to the corporal behind him.

The camera swings as the dog handler turns. The corporal responds, seeking higher authority: 'Hit [the patrol commander] up.'

Soldier C shouts his question two more times: 'You want me to drop this cunt?'

Mark Willacy writes in his book *Rogue Forces* that, after having the audio professionally enhanced and analysed, the patrol commander appears to say 'yes'.

Then the mechanical *tap, tap, tap* of three suppressed rounds.

Dad Mohammed was dead. The Blackhawks took off and carried the men in the patrol away. The locals complained. There was an inquiry. Soldier C was not questioned in person. Dehjawz-e-Hasanzay was not visited by any inquiry officer investigators and the killing was deemed lawful. It was claimed that Dad Mohammed had been 'tactically manoeuvring' and carrying an Icom radio.

Via the camera microphones, the apparent indifference of the other soldiers present at the Dehjawz-e-Hasanzay site was amplified. On the other hand, commentary by others who had been present across this rotation revealed suppressed despair: 'Fucking bullshit. I'm not happy with it.' 'It's wrong on so many levels.' 'We're definitely not trying to win the war anymore.'

When asked if, in general, he could have done more, Braden Chapman replied, 'Looking back now, I'm not sure how a complaint would have went at the time if I had voiced my concern. But I feel now that, even if it had have ruined my career back then, I probably should have made the complaint.'

Mark Willacy: 'Do you think it would have gone anywhere?'

'Nowhere.'

The credits rolled. I was stunned, envious and, above all, congratulatory when I rang Mark. In my view, what I had just witnessed would shift the war crimes debate. Not only in Australia, but wherever these images were screened.

The program had not mentioned Ben Roberts-Smith; it concentrated in the main on the 3 Squadron tour of Afghanistan in 2012. Roberts-Smith's 2 Squadron arrived in the middle of that year to succeed them. One sequence was devoted to a 2 Squadron raid in late August 2012, in the immediate aftermath of the insider 'green-on-blue' attack, when a rogue Afghan National Army sergeant had killed three of his Australian comrades.

As the SAS pursued Hekmatullah, the perpetrator of this outrage, at Sola, on the outskirts of Tarin Kowt, two Afghans were shot and killed. Ben Roberts-Smith and The Gunsmith were involved in one of these killings. *Four Corners* reported the matter as under investigation by the IGADF, but it did not mention Roberts-Smith's involvement—most likely, I assumed, on the advice of the ABC's lawyers.

Even so, the *Four Corners* program was immensely helpful to our cause. The persistent argument that reports of unlawful killings by Australian soldiers were nothing but empty-headed media beat-ups immediately lost its impetus.

It was good for our own morale too. Here was healthy competition from another broadcaster doing its job. This stood in stark contrast to the activities of our print competitors, particularly *The Australian*, which, as far as I could see, paid little attention to investigating the facts around war crimes. Its focus instead was on advocating for Ben Roberts-Smith and undermining our work.

Another outcome was some deflection of the social media vitriol. Much of the attack previously directed at the 'Fauxfax' reptiles would now target the ABC 'leftards' such as Willacy. In this logic-free media zone, *Four Corners*' graphic evidence was never going to make much difference.

I was a shade of green about Mark finding Braden Chapman and that compelling film footage. Chapman's motivation for coming forward was in part a result of the ABC's 2019 reporting of the plight of his comrade, Dusty Miller. We too had reported the Dusty Miller story, but we were not fortunate enough to be approached by Chapman. It did make me miss my old workplace; I assumed the ABC's status as the nation's most trusted broadcaster might have influenced Chapman to reach out in its direction.

There can be no doubt at all about the incredible impact and power of visual material. Strong images are like lightning strikes: they awaken the truth and can forever shift the public's mindset. *Four Corners* had done it before with Caro Meldrum-Hanna's footage of the manacled teenager in the spit hood at the Northern Territory's Don Dale Youth Detention Centre. Sarah Ferguson did it with footage of the torment of animals caught in Australia's live export trade. Those pictures, in the best tradition of the fourth estate, had generated direct reform. Now Mark Willacy had done it with his amazing pictures from an Afghanistan wheatfield.

But this story still had a long way to go.

CHAPTER 43

THE LUNCH BOX

On the same day *Four Corners* revealed its Killing Field footage came another discovery. Its impact would be felt a little further down the track.

Now confronting cheerless divorce proceedings, as you would expect, Emma Roberts-Smith's mind turned to sustenance for her girls and herself. Before their separation, Emma had noticed Ben repeatedly withdrawing money. And she and the housekeeper wondered what he had been doing poking around out in the garden. Emma suspected he might be burying cash.

On 16 March 2020, she discussed this with her friend Danielle Scott, who was visiting. The women prepared breakfast for the girls and then went looking. Emma found a rock near a hose reel; it appeared to be a marker. With a pitchfork, they dug down just below the silty coastal topsoil and found a lunch box that belonged to one of the girls. It was clear plastic with pink tabs.

Emma opened the lunch box. Rather than being stuffed with cash, it housed six USB drives, double-sealed in plastic ziplock bags. She deduced that the USBs were likely to be those sent by Ben's friends. They gathered up the find, went inside and Danielle copied the contents of the USBs onto a laptop. They then returned the USBs to the lunch box and reburied it.

Soon after, Danielle flew back to her home.

Across the nation travel restrictions were tightening. That week a cruise ship, the *Ruby Princess*, docked in Sydney Harbour, disgorging over 2000 passengers, many coughing and spluttering. Soon the state premiers began to close their borders—none of them more aggressively than the premier of Western Australia, Mark McGowan. Given that the defamation case was to be heard in Sydney but most of the witnesses were resident in Western Australia, this became a serious complication.

In the next months it was masks in supermarkets, where the shelves soon emptied of toilet paper. Hand sanitiser in every handbag and briefcase. Purchases of exercise bikes and home entertainment systems on the rise. Pedestrians anxiously social distancing. Families exiled. For my grandkids, Facetime became a norm.

And online legal conferences galore. We tried to get used to Zoom. Nick was stressing. The lawyers were demanding more. We were fortunate that a core band of witnesses had stuck with us, but there were others who knew more. In this numbers game, both teams were compiling rival banks of witnesses. Our position was line ball.

Indirectly, we had heard of a further witness to the alleged executions at Whiskey 108. We tried to make contact. And we heard of another: a young soldier suspected of having been blooded, who was now suffering acute remorse. Again, it was indirect; but we had no direct line to the witness.

A month out from the scheduled commencement of the trial, another hurdle was erected, and a further shroud of secrecy was thrown over proceedings. The federal attorney-general, Christian Porter, invoked the *National Security Act* so that evidence at the trial deemed to be 'sensitive' would be suppressed. This was going to further crowd the bar table, as it gave the Commonwealth a prominent seat there. Managing what could and could not be ventilated in open court would add an extra layer of complexity.

In response to the attorney-general's suppression order, Bruce McClintock SC argued that open court was 'fundamental to his [client's] vindication'.[1] Sandy Dawson SC stated that we 'shared for different reasons the applicant's desire to have as much of this matter heard in open court as possible'.[2]

As we had begun to expect, the trial was now postponed. The *National Security Act* gag order contributed to this decision. It would be impossible to keep a lid on evidence communicated via videolink. While some evidence would have to be given this way, all parties preferred testimony to be delivered in person. Truth seeking, whether in journalism or in a court case like this, is best conducted face to face.

Justice Besanko explained: 'This is a trial where the credibility or reliability of the key witnesses may well be crucial in circumstances where the alleged imputations arising from the matters complained of are . . . very serious indeed.'[3]

Ben Roberts-Smith was disappointed. It was close to two years since he had commenced these proceedings, and he wanted his day in court. *The Australian* reported that for him, 'speaking requests had dried up and he did not receive a single invitation to be involved in any commemoration on Anzac Day this year. He was also suffering from anxiety and severe insomnia.'[4]

By May 2020, the Channel Seven Queensland general manager had upgraded his single-bedroom flat in Brisbane to better accommodate his daughters. Emma, still concerned about his drinking, had contested access. But now an agreement was reached for the girls to visit him on alternate weekends.

Early on 5 June, Emma received an email from Ben requesting a different kind of visit. He said he wanted to return to Ilkley to recover possessions he had left behind. She replied, telling him his personal belongings were packed in boxes in the garage and that he could collect them between 2.30 and 3 pm that day.

Before he arrived, Emma Roberts-Smith photographed the area of the garden near the hose reel where the rock marked the buried lunch box. Once Ben arrived, she stayed out of his way while he gathered up his belongings. When he had left, she returned to that patch of ground and again photographed what was clearly disturbed earth.

CHAPTER 44

ENTITLED PRICKS

It was now seven years since Special Operations Command had deployed a task group to Afghanistan. It was five years since Major General Jeff Sengelman had requested members of the SASR to provide him with tell-all letters.

Sengelman had since moved on. His 2017 departure was not exactly a happy one. The bearers of bad news and catalysts for overdue reform are rarely thanked. Given the close ranks of special forces, there was every likelihood that some of Sengelman's former friends would be unforgiving.

Defence's senior command remained top-heavy with SAS alumni. The Chief of the Defence Force, Angus Campbell, and the Chief of Army, Rick Burr, had both earned the sandy beret. But, given sensitivities about the prospect of a special forces protection racket, their current Special Operations Commander, Major General Adam Findlay, like Sengelman, had come to the job a cleanskin, with nothing from operational service likely to haunt him.

Soon after the *Four Corners* 'Killing Field' report, Adam Findlay addressed the Perth-based regiment. Although pride had taken a stumble, most of those assembled before him were exempt from personal shame, having had no experience of Afghanistan. Special forces has a high churn rate. Operational pressure is wearing, and because its members are older, they often have growing families. Their broad skills base can also be attractive to civilian employers.

'You are probably sick of hearing about it,' Findlay began. 'But I am going to give you the real news up front.' He was in no mood for back-pedalling; the time for 'nothing to see here' excuses had passed. The nation had witnessed on their television screens a prospective war crime. Even within Defence precincts, there had been shock at this footage, compounded by the casual indifference of the vainglorious warfighter caste.

Findlay was angry—in his own words, 'disgusted and appalled': 'It [the war crimes stigma] will be here by my estimation as a factor of life in SOCOMD [Special Operations Command] for a decade. So, young troopers in the audience—you will be patrol commanders. You captains in the audience—you will be commanding officers by the time this has washed through. Prepare for the long haul.'

The preceding evening, the major general had been briefed by Justice Paul Brereton, whose report was near completion. As we thought, the delay was largely down to an ongoing scramble to manage new leads. Findlay informed his audience: 'One of the reasons it is going on is because new people come to light.' So far Brereton had interviewed 300 people, he said, and he applauded the soldiers who had spoken up. 'They have shown moral courage, hence the IGADF. But there are still people out there who haven't told the whole truth. Now this is a problem for you.'

Their red-tabbed boss reminded the men of who they were. The SAS is supposed to get the selection right. There is supposed to be a virtuous balance to the 'killer angel' persona. 'We are a first-world army,' Findlay said. 'We represent the best of our Western civilisation. We are highly selected. No one is here by accident.'

He spoke in the soldiers' own language about the reasons for moral and reputational failure, for the corrosive encroachment of mob rule: 'It's poor leadership. In fact, it is poor moral leadership.' And it had come about due to the rise of a particular character familiar to all the SAS squadrons. Findlay described this character as 'the self-righteous, entitled prick.'

If there were proper checks and balances, he said, such men would be reduced to barking from the sidelines. But as the war had dragged on, they had become the big dogs. Major General Findlay wanted no more of them. 'Why would you be an entitled prick and alienate everyone?' I hope his audience was listening attentively. Soldiers take only so much notice of their officers.

The major general also spoke of something close to my own heart. When I was reporting on Queensland police corruption in the 1980s, I'd felt that what I was seeing was an irredeemable mess. But recovery can be amazingly swift. Although corruption is never vanquished, when I peered at Queensland again a decade later, I saw a very different place. This was invoked by Adam Findlay: 'There were egregious breaches of law in the Queensland police service. People went to jail. Now Queensland has the best police service.'

However, the Special Operations Commander was probably not so happy, soon afterwards, to read excerpts of his speech in the morning press. A recording of his speech also found its way into our inbox.

Defence Media is customarily unnerved if it finds itself wrong-footed when it is attempting to control the narrative, but this time the leak to Nine newspapers could have been seen as a plus. Adam Findlay's smackdown indicated that the senior leadership was as horrified as were the many other Australians who had witnessed that shooting in the wheatfield.

With the June trial date now postponed, we had more time to strengthen our case. Accordingly, an application to amend our defence was lodged.

At an interim hearing on 2 June, Sandy Dawson SC submitted that, in addition to the five alleged unlawful deaths already pleaded, there were two more. The Sola killing, referred to in the *Four Corners* report, was added, as was an alleged blooding at Syachow.

Dawson further particularised the Darwan allegation, no longer arguing that it was an Afghan partner force member who had inflicted the *coup de grâce* on Ali Jan, but rather Ben Roberts-Smith or his comrade The Sniper.

As *The Age* reported:

> Mr Dawson said the newspapers could not say who of Mr Roberts-Smith or The Sniper killed Mr Jan, 'but on the law we don't need to'. The death was a murder, the barrister said, because Mr Jan was handcuffed when kicked off the cliff before he was shot, and at the very least Mr Roberts-Smith was complicit and responsible for the death.[1]

High drama ensued in the Federal Court. Bruce McClintock SC exploded:

> Yes, he's won a Victoria Cross. Yes, he's a soldier. Yes, he saw a considerable amount of action. Yes, there can be no question about his courage . . . But he's still a human being, Your Honour, and to confront allegations like this put forward by a large and powerful media organisation in circumstances where it turns out that what they actually said in the articles is insupportable—and now they want to change position.[2]

Ben Roberts-Smith's barrister also got stuck into me over the alleged murder at Fasil. Initially we had dated the incident 21 October 2012. 'Where is Mr Masters to explain how, in his defence, an allegation that he must have known was false, appears?'[3]

In *No Front Line*, I had placed Ben Roberts-Smith on that date not at Fasil but at Char Chineh. The error was not in the book, but in our determining when the alleged Fasil execution occurred. Pinning down dates was always difficult. For the soldiers, one mission blurred into the next; it took subpoenaed Defence records for us to be sure. McClintock was correct in identifying an initial mistake, but wrong in his accusation that it was deliberate.

Roberts-Smith himself publicly lambasted the reinforced allegations as 'designed to distract from the fact they are backtracking on their most prominent allegation and have admitted they don't know what their case is on the death of Ali Jan'.[4]

Behind all this bravado there would have been some concern. Our backroom lawyers had been busy. With some help from Nick McKenzie and me, Peter Bartlett and Dean Levitan had produced further witness statements.

Critically, one detailed prospective evidence from The Gunsmith, the other SAS operator who had been there at the cliff at Darwan. If he appeared in court, and his testimony was believed, Ben Roberts-Smith would have further cause for worry.

CHAPTER 45

D&MS

When I was embedded with conventional forces in 2010, they used to joke about the 'deep and meaningfuls' that took place out at Patrol Base Wali. You might think the most intense human communication occurs at sandstone universities, the cathedrals of parliament or within the communal sanctity of the church. For me, looking back, as often as not it was while perched on an ammunition box or sharing a brew in the fading light of another crowded day.

When you're deployed as a reporter in a war zone, one basic objective you have is to make sense of what is going on around you. So you lean towards those who have experience and insight. Reaching for people's inner thoughts is always challenging, and particularly so, perhaps, among Australians. Diggers, since their earliest days at Kapooka Training Ground, have been conditioned to require the permission of the group before 'gobbing off'.

All of the above explains why I ended up spending so much time with the padres. They had lots of experience with 'D&Ms', and they did not need the consent of their mates or the boss to do so. I am glad to say that, in time, I became a more familiar and less threatening presence; the conversations I enjoyed across the ranks then became less inhibited.

Really, this should not surprise. Soldiers are obliged to become philosophers: they share a deep need to comprehend profound experience.

To reconcile the challenge of inflicting harm with the purpose of doing good is an eternal task. When they are risking their own lives, there can be no false confidence about the worth of doing so. If they do not achieve an honest reconciliation, there is some risk they will be tormented for all their days. Avoided questions have a way of coming back to haunt you.

I blame the D&Ms for a request that came through from the chaplaincy in January 2019 for me to provide an essay for their annual journal. The subject was 'Empowering Morality'. This was a topic that gripped all who were close to this war crimes saga. Major General Adam Findlay grieved the absence of moral leadership. But where was that little voice that is supposed to be in all of us, saying 'No, Australian soldiers don't do that'? Why was it not allowed to rise and, via a collective conscience, be heard?

An enduring concern for me, across the decades of my reporting on the ADF, was the often-feeble relationship Defence and its service personnel have with the media. I felt it was my duty to do all I could to help bridge that divide. So I seized all opportunities: I gave talks at the Royal Military College, at Canungra, at Lavarack Barracks, at Staff College, at Robertson Barracks and more. The reward for me personally was a broadening of my knowledge and a deepening of my contacts.

So I agreed to write the piece. There was much to draw on. In those D&Ms, many a moral dilemma had surfaced.

Commando Private Warren Loudon will never forget bursting in on sleeping civilians during a dead-of-night compound raid.

> On this particular night I ripped the sheets off a lump on the floor and it was a little girl, approximately three years old, with her hands above her head and a look of complete terror on her face. I was wearing night vision goggles and it was in a room with very little light, so I doubt she could really see me; but I could see her as clear as day. Something about her stopped me cold. I don't know if it was the

> look of fear on her face or if it was my complete lack of compassion; but it stopped me for a short time while I did a quick assessment of what I had become.

An SAS non-commissioned officer remains troubled to this day about not being able to evacuate a child who had been wounded in a gunfight. It made no difference that the child was a victim of the insurgency, rather than the Coalition.

Another soldier told me of catching an armed insurgent in his scope, but not firing because he saw a boy nearby who might have been the man's son. The decision not to shoot was his own. In that split second, the soldier was halted by his consideration of the future impact on the son if he saw his father die like that—and his decision not to shoot created in him a new consciousness.

Working with Afghan partners who routinely engaged in *bacha bazi* ('boy play'—which is to say, paedophilia) troubled many SAS consciences. The appalling treatment of women was commonly witnessed. Soldiers saw children with disabilities abandoned to the elements. Those soldiers simply had to reconcile themselves to such experiences. We were in their country; complaints to Afghans about conduct that offended Western values had little purchase.

Soldiers could turn to the psychologists or the chaplains, all of whom heard a million stories. While soldiers received plenty of general resilience training, I doubt if many anticipated the charred landscape of moral injury that lay ahead of them.

The longer the Afghanistan conflict continued, the more ubiquitous were the warning signs. More T-shirts bearing 'I Kill Terrorists' logos. Death-symbol iconography passed without question, even though this was officially a peacekeeping mission. One of Australia's helicopter support units was the US 101st Combat Aviation Brigade, which proudly bore the motto 'Expect No Mercy'.

Pejoratives like 'ragheads' slipped more readily into the soldiers' vernacular. An expression drawn from Joseph Conrad's *Heart of Darkness*—the novel that underpinned the Vietnam War movie *Apocalypse Now*—also entered the lexicon: after multiple deployments, soldiers were heard referring to some of their members as being in danger of heading 'up the Congo'. Some from the SAS said they saw evidence of this in Ben Roberts-Smith.

Within the architecture of command, there is space for empowering morality and reinforcing humanity. The commanding officer of Roberts-Smith's 2012 rotation, Lieutenant Colonel Ian Langford, was worried when the lust for revenge gripped the entire command after the murder of the three Australian soldiers by their Afghan colleague Hekmatullah.

Langford had already drawn his padre into his command group. He wanted the little voice amplified. 'Soldiers aren't religious,' Langford told me, 'but there is definitely a spiritual element to soldiering in that they think about life and death, particularly with the special operations rotation. It does give them a unique perspective.'

One hundred years ago, when attendance at chapel was greater, so too was the value of the padre. You only need to look at the headstones from the Great War battlefields: 'Known Unto God', 'Thy Will Be Done', 'We Cannot Lord Thy Purpose See But All Is Well That's Done By Thee'.

A century on, with the erosion of trust in organised religion, where was that voice to be heard? In Karl Marlantes' book *What It Is Like to Go to War*, he writes of encountering a similar need during the Vietnam War. Marlantes found that few of his fellow US Marines spoke to the chaplains; instead, the role of 'unit spiritual helpers' organically formed among characters who had an aptitude for communion and counselling. Over time he came to wonder whether the system could be formalised. 'I think if more of this was done, atrocities would be less likely to occur,' he wrote. 'Infantry platoons have medics for the body. Why not for the soul?'[1]

The idea of a 'medic for the soul' made some sense, although I will admit it does sound like the job description of the chaplain.

I shaped these thoughts into an essay that I submitted to the chaplaincy association's annual journal. I was told it was gratefully accepted and prepared for publication. But that never happened: the edition was pulped.

No one called me to offer an explanation. But I guessed the order to obliterate it was connected to the Ben Roberts-Smith trial. Probably the ADF did not want to give the appearance of publicly aligning itself with one of the respondents.

I hope that shutting me up was not an attempt to stifle debate about what had gone wrong in Afghanistan. Within Defence, an active process was in place to learn the lessons from our participation in that war. Structural reforms had been formally proposed; they were designed to strengthen oversight and better merge the warring special forces tribes. But, informally and less visibly, influence was being exerted by the 'put it behind us and move on' lobby. The SAS had many powerful backers who thought the regiment had taken enough of a beating.

For the Ben Roberts-Smith vs Nine/Fairfax matter, a war crimes trial in another guise, there were many beyond the direct participants who were anxious about what the outcome would reveal. And, in parallel, another unknown: was there, in Defence, the collective courage to see the reform process through?

CHAPTER 46
REVERSE FERRET

The expression emanates from the Murdoch camp, coined by Kelvin MacKenzie, stalwart Rupert ally and infamous former editor of his London tabloid *The Sun*. To 'stick a ferret up their trousers' was taking a poke at the establishment. And the 'reverse ferret' was the sudden and rarely explained U-turn a media organisation takes when it becomes apparent that it is on the wrong tram.

In the latter months of 2020, with the Brereton report now imminent, Rupert Murdoch's *The Australian* was poised for a U-turn. It did not take a genius to figure that five years of intense IGADF scrutiny had moved beyond the examination of mere rumour.

In June 2020, the national security editor, Paul Maley, ceased employment at the newspaper. Nick McKenzie and I were probably relieved, knowing we would no longer be ducking his missives, but we weren't to know a reverse ferret was in train.

Soon after, foreign affairs and defence correspondent Ben Packham took on the war crimes beat. A full-page article that ran in September 2020 hinted at a shift. 'Pawns in a deadly game' was a lengthy feature about 'moral injury'.[1]

Anticipating Justice Brereton's findings, it acknowledged that the inquiry was not concerned with 'heat of battle' incidents. It named Ben Roberts-Smith as a person under scrutiny. It cited the shocking *Four Corners*

'Killing Field' imagery and queried the accountability of Defence leadership: 'There is also growing disquiet in ranks of the nation's Special Forces regiments, particularly the Special Air Service, that the "higher ups" will avoid punishment for the darkest stain on the country's military in living memory.'[2]

'Darkest stain'—it looked like a reverse ferret to me.

The following month, Ben Packham reported on an SAS internal document he had obtained which investigated the alleged bullying of The Redhead by Ben Roberts-Smith, following the 2006 action at Koran Ghar. This was the episode I outlined in *No Front Line* that had triggered the first series of attacks by *The Australian*.

The Redhead was one of two soldiers who disputed the official account of what initiated the firefight that had earned Ben Roberts-Smith the Medal for Gallantry. In the aftermath, Roberts-Smith accused The Redhead of cowardice. The Redhead in turn reported that his accuser had threatened to shoot him in the back of the head, and had subjected him to ongoing years of bullying.

There was no acknowledgement in *The Australian* of a change of direction, even though the newspaper was now reporting that 'the investigating captain concluded in 2013 that, despite the seven-year gap between the alleged incident and the complaint, "there is reasonable suspicion that an incident of unacceptable behaviour did occur"'.[3]

And then, on the eve of the release of the IGADF's report, an editorial appeared in *The Australian* on 13 November 2020 under the heading 'Nation's moment of truth on alleged war crimes'. Its theme was accountability, essentially of senior leadership. It contended, unremarkably, that overuse of special forces had worn down mental resilience.

> Some may have grown callous and indiscriminate in the use of force . . . Charging a handful of corporals and sergeants while senior leaders receive honours and promotions would breach the remaining cohesion of the SAS, already at breaking point after years of leaks to selected media . . . This process has already gone on far too long. The culture of the SAS is basically sound. That is why so many of its

members provided vital evidence to the IGADF inquiry—a measure of moral courage and integrity.

The Australian's editorial thinking had clearly travelled a long way from its editorial of 18 August 2018, when Ben Roberts-Smith launched his defamation action: 'It is high time for the imbroglio surrounding Victoria Cross and Medal of Gallantry [*sic*] winner Ben Roberts-Smith and the Special Air Service Regiment, whipped up by Fairfax media, to be put in perspective.'[4]

That editorial had cited Brendan Nelson as providing that perspective, championing the VC recipient: 'Australian soldiers are at home with their families today because of the courage of Mr Roberts-Smith.'[5] It had mirrored Nelson's lament about 'tearing down the reputation of heroes'.[6] It had concluded with a recitation of the 'fog of war' justification, later abandoned: 'it would be an immense injustice to overlook the pressures faced by soldiers forced to make split-second decisions in "kill or be killed circumstances" during a brutal guerrilla war with the Taliban and its affiliates. Their advice is worth heeding.'[7]

In the 2018 editorial, there was wall-to-wall bombast about Ben. In the 2020 editorial, he does not rate a mention. *The Australian* appeared to be walking back from an absolute defence of Ben Roberts-Smith, while holding to a view we shared: that responsibility for misconduct reached beyond the soldiers in the line.

Like many journalists, for many years I had defended my colleagues at News Corporation, where I had worked for a time. The Australian news industry is incestuous. Half our peers are employed by Rupert, and from them we have seen plenty of fine work.

But also like many of my colleagues, I had now given up on Rupert's minions. For me, the 'years of selected leaks to selected media' comment in the 2020 editorial said a lot. The editorial itself read like a leak from the precinct of allied power elites.

By way of contrast, our journalism was not driven by leaks. We reported from the ground up, as we are supposed to do. We made connections, we obtained evidence, we applied critical analysis and we wrote it down. The more you do that, the more information comes your way.

Murdoch's papers lived in a world of select leakage; conditioned to that mode of reporting, they could not compete. It was as if they had forgotten, or surrendered, the entry code to investigative journalism. And as if they had come to believe, as many in the public believe, that the entire news industry is nothing but a dancing puppet on a fraying string. No wonder we are all disrespected.

One of *The Australian*'s reporters, obliged to check something to help validate an impending attack, told me: 'I know you would not report any of this, Chris, unless you were 100 per cent sure, but I have a job to do.' I came to think that here was someone who should no longer call themselves a journalist.

As for *The Australian*—if it was no longer interested in facts, it should no longer pretend to be in the news business.

CHAPTER 47

THE PAPS

During the final phase of the IGADF inquiry, the PAPs went out. These 'potentially affected person' notices from the Inspector-General gave soldiers caught up in the inquiry an opportunity to respond to findings before public release of the report.

After four years, and with coercive powers similar to a royal commission and an expanding pool of witnesses, Paul Brereton and his team were across the big picture. In contrast, the Nine/Fairfax team of journalists and lawyers had detailed knowledge of the core of the major incidents, but more broadly we were looking through a glass darkly.

We presumed that Ben Roberts-Smith had been issued a PAP, and that within this notification there would be considerable detail of interest to us. But we were up against it. The IGADF and the Commonwealth opposed disclosure on the grounds that witness confidentiality would be breached and the integrity of the inquiry undermined. Effectively, the PAPs were procedural fairness notices.

In September 2020, at a hearing before the Federal Court's Justice Craig Colvin, Sandy Dawson SC argued that it was procedurally unfair for their side, the applicant, to have access to material denied to our side, the respondents. For example, if Roberts-Smith had received a PAP (as we strongly suspected), he would see details of the evidence that had been gathered against him. Dawson undertook that if that material were disclosed to us, it would not be published; and that access to it would remain restricted to our lawyers, Nick McKenzie and me.

The following week, Justice Colvin ruled that we should have access, but gave leave to the Commonwealth to file a confidential affidavit to furnish further reasons why disclosure should be opposed. After consideration, the Commonwealth decided against submitting further argument.

But on 7 October, Arthur Moses SC, for Ben Roberts-Smith, having previously stayed out of the fight, launched a bid to reverse Justice Colvin's ruling. In response, Dawson argued that the applicant had already had 'ample opportunity' to oppose this and should not be rewarded with 'a second bite of the cherry'.[1]

A month later the ruling came in. It was a win for us, and a crucial one. The preliminary findings by the IGADF concerning Ben Roberts-Smith would be disclosed to our legal team and us. Hundreds of pages. But there were caveats. National security information would be redacted. Information acquired coercively would not be revealed, so as not to jeopardise prospective criminal proceedings. We could not simply cut and paste evidence from the IGADF preliminary findings to our matter—but we already understood that.

Access to the PAP was great news, received with a mixture of elation and relief.

It was 13 November, and I was due to enter a media lock-up in Canberra with the release of the IGADF report imminent. I was booked to stay that night at the East Hotel, the scene of The Scout's previous showdown with Ben Roberts-Smith. My car managed to get me to the hotel from my home outside Sydney; a whining noise, which could not be sourced to my own sense of self-pity, troubled me all the way.

When I hopped out and donned my facemask, there were startled looks. Canberra was not as locked-down and masked-up as in the bigger smoke.

In the foyer at the East, metres from where Roberts-Smith and The Scout had stared each other down, I picked up that morning's *Australian* and glowered over its editorial volte-face, timed to coincide with the release of the report.

But, as it transpired, both *The Australian* and I were out by a week. Upon my arrival, I discovered that the long-awaited release had been a late scratching. It had been stymied by a pre-emptive presser from the prime minister.

At his press conference, Scott Morrison announced that a special investigator would be appointed, to advance the IGADF's remit by continuing the investigations and preparing cases for prosecution. An independent oversight panel would also be appointed to report to the defence minister on cultural, organisational and leadership issues.

Justice Brereton's report had been received in Canberra a week ago, on 6 November, and the PM was one of a small inner circle who had been briefed. Morrison said the findings would be 'difficult and hard news for Australians' and would reveal 'brutal truths'.[2]

With the media lock-up postponed, I drove back home, my ear tuned more attentively to the engine. The acquisition of an affordable replacement alternator became a fresh item on my to-do list.

CHAPTER 48

'POSSIBLY THE MOST DISGRACEFUL EPISODE . . .'

I came back to Canberra on Thursday, 19 November 2020. My registration for the press conference having come through, I made sure I got there early.

Out the front of the ADF's Russell Offices is a sprawl of car parks. While these spaces empty quickly in the afternoon, at the beginning of the working day it is like *The Hunger Games*. Defence personnel must be conditioned to early starts. Somehow I managed to find a space.

The media lock-up was scheduled for 9 am in the ground-floor theatre of Defence R1 Building, where the top brass are to be found. Notebooks, takeaway coffee and g'days all around. Familiar faces taking their chairs. Mark Willacy waved. Ben Packham introduced himself, and I thanked him for straightening the reporting at *The Oz*. He acknowledged the unusual degree of difficulty there is confronting the special forces' cone of silence.

The assembled reporters were then given a bound volume of 465 pages. We had to absorb very rapidly four years of work and read around large tracts of blacked-out copy. Atop the pages in red: 'OFFICIAL (redacted for security, privacy and legal reasons)'. We had to do all this in two hours and to prepare the questions we wanted to ask at the scheduled press conference.

The numbers were confronting. They were more than I expected: a total of 39 individuals killed, 25 current or former ADF personnel as perpetrators, 36 matters to be referred to the AFP.

There was vindication here. The findings confirmed our reporting of a proliferation of 'throwdowns', 'bloodings' and summary executions. Given the wholesale redaction of names and other identifiers, trying to find our way quickly through the pages called for guesswork, aligning the incidents detailed in the report with what we already knew.

Sometimes a date offered a clue. One reference to an engagement 'wilfully misreported' might have been Koran Ghar. Equally, it looked like Whiskey 108 was there, in a dual reference to 'unlawfully causing the death' of detainees.

When turning to the year 2012, entire pages were blacked out. But one further incident—of inflicting 'severe physical and/or mental pain and/or suffering upon a male Afghan non-combatant'—might have referred to Ali Jan and Darwan.

Then, in Chapter 2.50 on page 103, we read the words: 'What is described in this Chapter is possibly the most disgraceful episode in Australia's military history.' That certainly made the room sit up. This sentence would soon ricochet around the world.

More guesswork. The material in Chapter 2.50 was so heavily redacted that we were left wondering what it actually contained, and whether this powerful indictment was being made of the totality of the Roberts-Smith story. After all, it seemed to be a valid assessment of a series of alleged executions and bloodings between 2009 and 2012, in patrols where he was either the leader or second-in-command, with a further indication from pre-deployment training that some of the murder spree was premeditated.

The allotted reading time quickly passed. Chief of the Defence Force General Angus Campbell then spoke. I doubt he would have looked forward to this. Important ADF communiqués are these days more commonly delivered by the minister, which is a source of disappointment, both inside and outside Defence, as it denies them a direct line of communication to the general public. But at today's gig, the 'shit sandwich' belonged to the CDF.

Campbell came across as a touch uncomfortable. But he was also heartfelt: he acknowledged the bad news and accepted a 'duty to set things right'. In trying to explain what went wrong, he said: 'It starts with culture.' In this he was referring to one particular sentence in the report: 'Some domestic commanders of Special Air Service Regiment bear significant responsibility for contributing to the environment in which war crimes were committed, most notably those who embraced or fostered the "warrior culture" and empowered, or did not restrain, the clique of non-commissioned officers who propagated it.'[1]

Given that it was now acknowledged there was evidence of war crimes having occurred, and occurred repeatedly, attention inevitably swung to the command chain. But Justice Brereton had uncovered 'no evidence that there was knowledge of, or reckless indifference to, the commission of war crimes, on the part of commanders at troop/platoon, squadron/company or Task Group Headquarters level, let alone at higher levels such as Commander Joint Task Force 633, Joint Operations Command, or Australian Defence Headquarters'.[2]

The Commander of Joint Task Force 633 in 2011 had been the man standing in front of us—Angus Campbell. After his twenty-minute address, there were questions. Karen Middleton from *The Saturday Paper* asked if the report let him 'off the hook'. The CDF replied, 'I don't think it lets anyone off the hook.' Perplexing all the same.

I asked how the public could be expected to believe that, over six or seven years, all these incidents occurred without a single officer, between a lieutenant and a lieutenant general, knowing anything about it. General Campbell said they all had had a responsibility to know, and that reflecting on this collective failure was 'distressing'.

While I still found it hard to believe no officer knew anything, neither Nick McKenzie nor I had come upon any evidence directly implicating command. And, quite obviously, neither had the IGADF. Lawyers, like journalists, need evidence. However unsatisfactory it seemed, nothing had emerged.

Released into the sunlight, I phoned Nick. We had reporting to do: me on today's events, and my colleague on the IGADF's long road leading up to this day.

As might have been expected, Ben Roberts-Smith continued to be in the news. Despite some reporting to the contrary, he still had Kerry Stokes' support. In June 2020, the Seven West chairman's private investment company, Australian Capital Equity, had offered a loan to fund Ben's legal costs. Some $1.9 million was already spent. As collateral, Roberts-Smith's medals, including his Victoria Cross, could be retained by Kerry Stokes and donated to the Australian War Memorial.

Directly after the release of the IGADF report, the media magnate phoned his Queensland GM 'to reassure him that he was still firmly in his corner', as *The Australian* duly reported.[3] Seven West was also paying Roberts-Smith's annual salary, even if it had been reduced in these straitened Covid times from $700,000 to $550,000.

It had been a particularly stressful period for the war hero since the postponement of the trial. His legal team complained that Ben was being 'continually crucified' with 'a dire impact on his mental welfare'.[4] His professed response to the Brereton report's shattering findings was relief. He welcomed the prime minister's announced establishment of the Office of the Special Investigator, 'with expertise and experience to consider evidence not rumours and make decisions based on evidence rather than unsubstantiated rumours'.[5]

Positive spin was at play here. The IGADF inquiry had been tasked with determining whether there was 'any substance to persistent rumours of criminal or unlawful conduct', and Roberts-Smith was correct in observing that it was not required to make 'findings of fact in relation to rumours'.[6] The threshold determinant instead was whether there was 'credible information' of war crimes. On this score, Justice Brereton found plenty.

A trial date was now set for 7 June 2021 with the bar lifted a notch. The onus of proof fell to us to demonstrate truth in our reporting, on the balance of probabilities. Justice Besanko would determine which side had the stronger case.

CHAPTER 49

BRERETON BACKLASH

Now the steepest section of the marathon loomed before us. But, as it happened, we caught a breath.

The Covid pandemic, which announced itself in the first half of 2020, produced millions of losers and a few sheepish winners. Had our case gone to trial that June, as originally planned, we would not have been as well placed as we ultimately became. The delay gave us the PAP result, which immediately provided us with the prospect of five new witnesses. None could be accused of having been tainted by contact with media, and all offered testimony supporting the Whiskey 108 allegations.

It was a turning point, but there was still a lot for us to do. Testimony before the IGADF could not be used in our or any other trial, but leads were opened that advanced the prospect of obtaining further direct evidence.

Some development on Ben Roberts-Smith's personal and domestic fronts during the delay in the commencement of the trial were fortuitous for us. In August 2020, he was photographed in Brisbane holding hands with lawyer Monica Allen. They would deny a romantic relationship, but Emma Roberts-Smith was having none of it. Her husband and their lawyer—she felt doubly betrayed.

Having found her mobile number, Nick McKenzie sent a text inquiring whether she might speak with us. Recognising the likelihood of being subpoenaed to give evidence at the trial, Emma was now giving thought to how she might respond.

In December 2020, the Roberts-Smith divorce was finalised.

Pre-Christmas is usually a fallow period for the media, but the bombshell Brereton report continued to cause shockwaves.

During the opening rounds in this skirmish, way back in 2017, I had picked up a threat from the Roberts-Smith camp that they might sic Alan Jones onto me. It took a while for that to happen. Early in December 2020, the Sydney broadcaster had a spray in his show on 'Sky After Dark' (otherwise known as SAD): 'It seems that some years ago, Defence agreed to have a book written on the SAS in Afghanistan. What process did Defence use to determine who should be the most appropriate person to write the book? How was the chosen person, Chris Masters, appointed?'

My unauthorised biography of Alan, *Jonestown*, was now nearly fifteen years old. As with *No Front Line*, no one had appointed me to write it. It was my own decision. We are not all marionettes.

Alan's tirade made no difference. Thankfully, over those fifteen years his power had waned considerably. Now the best thing about his attack was that it took me three weeks to find out about it.

However, the backlash to some of the Brereton recommendations was of concern. When he released the report, General Campbell had undertaken to action the recommendation to revoke the Meritorious Unit Citation (MUC) that had been awarded collectively to the Special Operations Task Group. Justice Brereton had said: 'They all share in the triumphs, and they must all share in responsibility for shortcomings.'

This infuriated populist commentators, as well as the great many operators who had done no wrong. Revocation of the MUC was intended as an important correction of the record: for a period that had been shown to be bloodstained with abuse to be formally anointed as 'meritorious' was poor. But populism held sway, and Prime Minister Morrison announced that no decision had been made on this matter.

Another dispute played out in the media courtesy of duelling photos. In private holdings across the nation were compromising photos of special forces operators at play. Many came from the Fat Lady's Arms, the less-than-secret SAS drinking hole at Camp Russell.

The Commandos had one too, the Back Deck. While adherence to rules of engagement were now more liberally interpreted, for the entire mission one decree remained inviolable: in no circumstance would a member of a rival force element gain entry to the other's sacred space.

Photos of senior NCOs and officers cavorting drunkenly with their men at the Fat Lady's Arms had been retained, either innocently or as prospective insurance. The tolerance of immoderate drinking by special forces personnel, a privilege not extended to conventional forces, and wisely so, would prove to be a catastrophic mistake.

Among these mementos were photos of 'Das Boot'. This was the prosthetic leg retrieved from one of the victims at Whiskey 108 on Easter Sunday in 2009. It had become a kind of macabre 2 Squadron motif, repurposed as a drinking vessel. Reporter Rory Callinan, who had taken up cudgels for *The Australian* in 2017, now wrote an article for *The Guardian* that featured a photograph of two soldiers drinking from Das Boot. They were two witnesses believed to have spoken against Ben Roberts-Smith.

In response to the reporting of this curious bar-room ritual, in the pre-trial jousting Bruce McClintock SC said Ben Roberts-Smith 'never drank from the thing . . . because he thought it was disgusting'.[1] A photo featured soon after in *The Age* showed Ben Roberts-Smith looking far from disgusted as he embraced a comrade so imbibing.

Christmas passed and, just ahead of the New Year, the *Australian Financial Review* ran a lengthy feature, 'The defamation trial of the century'. Aaron Patrick reported: 'The case is causing huge stress on both sides. Roberts-Smith, who spent 17 months in Afghanistan over six years, has said he can't sleep and gets up every morning dreading the allegations he will face next.'[2]

Given our lawyers' advice to keep our traps shut, I declined to comment. But there was no doubt about it, we were also having sleepless nights. Nick McKenzie even more so, given that a judgment was imminent in another defamation case.

The second Chau Chak Wing trial had opened in October 2020. The billionaire was suing over a 2017 report by Nick for Fairfax and *Four Corners*. Mark O'Brien Legal and Bruce McClintock SC, counsel for Ben Roberts-Smith, were also representing Chau Chak Wing. On 2 February 2021, the Chinese Australian businessman was awarded $590,000 in damages.

We hoped it was not a portent of what was to come.

CHAPTER 50

LAWYERS, LOVE AND LOSS

Sandy Dawson SC and I had crossed paths previously. He did a lot of work for the ABC, where my sins—my death by a thousand courts—meant many a defamation lawyer was known to me.

I admired the quiet, strong advocates like Sandy. While the cold-blooded bullies at the bar were more famous, for me the most effective counsels were those who were polite but insistent inquirers.

It is the same in journalism. The better-known interviewers tend to be aggressive. In some respects, they must be: the nightly political interview of seasoned politicians is a gloves-off affair. There isn't time for small talk. But there had been a time when the occasional politician appreciated such interviews as an intellectual contest, as an opportunity for them to demonstrate a command of their portfolio.

As an interviewer in the past, my favourite exchanges had been the ones where honesty and generosity shone through the camera. There had been the occasional exquisite moment when I looked across and saw the interviewee absorbed, reaching for memories and the perfect expression, having lost all sense of the presence of cameras and crew beyond the circle of light.

Such interviews were achieved via patient, empathic conversation. Without actually saying so, you communicate to the subject a sense that this is their platform—it is their story—and you want them to do their best.

In contrast, if your questions land like blows, you guarantee an aggressive, heels-dug-in response. But in journalism you are marked down if you fail to ask the hard questions. There might be occasions when it is appropriate to be rude, but in my experience they are few and far between.

While a witness box is hardly a yoga mat, the same principles can apply in court. Sandy epitomised jurisprudence. A fine lawyer and a fine man. While he found himself outnumbered at the bar table in our particular case—three SCs against one—he kept us well in the race. In the important pre-trial contests, with help from two junior counsel, Lyndelle Barnett and Chris Mitchell, he won two crucial victories for us, securing confidentiality for some of our sources and access to the PAP notices.

It was this latter development that carried me to the MinterEllison offices on the 40th floor of Sydney's Governor Macquarie Tower in January 2021. If we were to win this case, the energy, intelligence and commitment of the solicitors was at least as important as brilliance at the bar table.

The MinterEllison offices in Melbourne, just down the road from *The Age*, housed the command team of Peter Bartlett, Dean Levitan, Tess McGuire, Dougal Hurley and Dylan Dexter, but this case was to be run in Sydney. Given the need for local hands-on help, Jeremy Forbes was assigned.

Jeremy was not yet 30, slim, fit and, like many of his ilk to someone of my ilk, imponderably bright. We met in their expansive foyer overlooking Sydney Harbour, from where he escorted me to the straitened confines of the lock-up.

A corner office had been repurposed in accordance with security requirements. Access to the PAPs was strictly limited. As respondents, Nick McKenzie and I were allowed in—even though we were from the reptilian ranks of the media—on the understanding that we would not breach the national security information and public interest immunity conditions.

Jeremy took me through the protocols. All classified information that we had access to for the sake of the case was to be locked away, and nothing was to be removed from the lock-up. During the closed court sessions, no phones, tablets, laptops or recording devices were to be present. No notes could be taken, and nothing recorded. Nothing could be discussed with outsiders, only between ourselves.

After gaining access to Roberts-Smith's PAP file, I was heartened by what I was able to read, particularly his response to the IGADF findings, which felt flimsy to me.

One of the prospective new witnesses this PAP revealed was someone I had tried to reach. We will call him The 2IC (Person 40). A while back, a whisper on the rambling SAS grapevine had reached my ears, suggesting The 2IC was dismayed by what had happened at Whiskey 108. This position had led to him being mistrusted and disparaged by the likes of Roberts-Smith and The Scot. I had found his number and phoned him, but as he was still in the regiment, he refused my approach.

Nick and I decided to try again. Requesting a witness's cooperation in a mate vs mate public shaming calls for the bedside manner of an angel. A witness box was the last place these soldiers wanted to be, and inflicting a curt 'be there or else' subpoena on them would hardly augment their cooperation.

We had a lot of experience maintaining favour with witnesses. As we knew, we always needed them not only when the story was published, but later on as well, if the story had to be defended from legal or other attack. And I doubt either of us would normally place 'good bedside manner' high on the typical legal eagle's skills card.

There was also the salutary lesson drawn from the Eddie Gallagher case in the United States, which showed the importance of maintaining trust and cooperation. The prosecution had lost at that trial largely because a witness switched camps at the eleventh hour.

As it turned out, Peter Bartlett's vast contact book and Dean Levitan's accommodating nature were useful. Our negotiation with prospective witnesses was very often conducted lawyer to lawyer. Their job was to communicate the realpolitik—that we intended to subpoena the witness, but we wished to do so in as pain-free a manner as possible.

Then came a gambit from Roberts-Smith. A few weeks after The 2IC received our subpoena, he was approached by The Freefaller, his former patrol commander. The advance was similar to that made by Roberts-Smith to The Scout in 2018. The Freefaller suggested The 2IC did not have to be a witness for Nine/Fairfax, and that Roberts-Smith's lawyers could arrange for him to sign a paper that absented him from proceedings. Thankfully, the gambit failed.

Meanwhile, we persisted in reaching out to Emma Roberts, the name she had assumed after her divorce. Following Nick's initial text message, Emma had conferred with her lawyer, Jason Murakami, who then spoke to Peter Bartlett. Peter put forward our argument that it would be useful for us to meet her.

That invitation hung in midair for many weeks. Then came a phone call: 'Is that Peter . . . Bartlett? This is Emma.'

Peter's initial reply was: 'Emma who?' But he quickly recovered and waved in Dean Levitan from a neighbouring office. 'When would you like to talk with me?'

There was a hurried scrolling through diaries and an arrangement struck. 'See you on Sunday at home,' Peter said.

Sunday, 14 March 2021. Peter Bartlett, Dean Levitan and Nick McKenzie flew to Brisbane and caught a taxi to Emma's new address. It was a day when Ben was rostered to spend time with their daughters. Emma's friend Danielle Scott joined the group for a long conversation.

More outreach. This time to John McLeod, as a result of some sleuthing by Nick, who had been assiduously probing the origins of the 2017 anonymous letters to the AFP, Senator Nick Xenophon and others that claimed The Veteran was involved in arms smuggling, which had subsequently resulted in a police raid on The Veteran's home.

We knew John McLeod had been acting as a kind of 'fixer' for Ben Roberts-Smith, and we suspected he had been involved in this clandestine work. By this time the two men had fallen out, so McLeod was no fan of Ben. But, regrettably, neither was he a fan of Nick or me.

Even so, we recognised he was a valuable witness, if recruited to our cause. The lawyers reached out. Peter Bartlett's network gave us a connection to McLeod through his Gold Coast lawyer.

Initially, all requests to talk were batted away: 'No, no, no.' But the inevitability of a subpoena eventually secured a meeting with him at the Inns of Court building in Brisbane, ten days after the meeting with Emma.

We were now ten weeks out from the trial, and our confidence should have lifted. But that was not the case.

Lyndelle Barnett and Sandy Dawson had run many a trial together. Sandy was a mentor and a friend. They had worked day and night on the Roberts-Smith case, calling Afghan witnesses at inconvenient hours, wrangling with the Australian Government Solicitor to secure documents, squeezing every last detail out of Nick and me.

Lyndelle began to worry when she noticed Sandy seemed unusually distracted. He complained of headaches. The same pattern was observed at home. An appointment was arranged at St Vincent's Hospital. The result came in: a tumour.

A very cruel blow. The Dawson family was being asked to endure more unbearable pain. Sandy's sister, Katrina, had been one of the victims of the Lindt Cafe siege in December 2014.

Work went on over conference tables loaded with documents, now tear-stained. The news was devastating.

CHAPTER 51
SECRETS OF WAR

Our job is to report, so Nick and I continued to do so. I won't pretend that this caused no trouble with our lawyers. There was a risk of offending the judiciary by doing so, but the Ben Roberts-Smith vs Nine/Fairfax trial was before a judge alone in the Federal Court, so there was no jury to influence. On the other hand, there was still much the public had not heard.

Nick was not long back from Queensland with another breakthrough.

On Sunday, 11 April, he fronted *60 Minutes* with a mythbusting introduction. The classic portrait of SAS daring in the field was juxtaposed with tawdry images of the boys at play. The scene was the Fat Lady's Arms. One image captured Ben's mate The Hunter in a Ku Klux Klan cloak and hood, holding up a noose. We saw Das Boot lifted to the lips of a bare-chested operator. Someone was peeing in the corner. An officer was simulating oral sex with one of the men. Another was baring his bum to the camera.

In the program, Ben Roberts-Smith's voice was heard—it came from one of the secret recordings we had obtained. He threatened retribution to his accusers, and boasted of his litigation war chest: 'Mate, I will take it all the way and I've got the bank to do it.'

60 Minutes reconstructed the burial of the child's lunch box, in which had been hidden much of the imagery now being graphically exhibited to the nation.

Admiral Chris Barrie, a former Chief of the Defence Force (and, as it happened, my next-door neighbour for a time), was interviewed. Nick showed him an image recovered from the lunch box, of a dead Afghan with the regiment's souvenir coins covering his eyes. A bizarre practice, derived from the old myth about paying the ferryman for the journey to the underworld.

Under the Geneva Convention, as Barrie explained, trophy hunting and desecration of remains could be considered war crimes. 'That's certainly not on,' he said. 'I think it conveys a sense of increasing brutality, a sense too that somehow these aren't human beings like the rest of us.'

Former Supreme Court judge Anthony Whealy was asked about the suppression of evidence. 'If it is to do with concealing information from the Brereton inquiry, then I can only assume it is a deliberate effort to mislead or distort the outcome of the inquiry.'

Two days after the corpse and souvenir coins photo was taken, on their return to Camp Russell a dress-up party at the Fat Lady's Arms kicked off. A group photo showed the whole crew, dressed variously as The Hulk, Pinhead from the *Hellraiser* film series, a pirate, a werewolf and Mr KKK with the burning cross. Beers and cheers. Up the back, fist aloft, is Ben Roberts-Smith.

Admiral Chris Barrie: 'It's entirely inappropriate behaviour. It's a failure of leadership . . . When I was CDF, and I became aware of that kind of behaviour, those people lost their jobs very quickly . . . It's not appropriate and it's not us.'

The program detailed Ben Roberts-Smith's effort to intimidate opponents. For the first time, his involvement in the attempt to silence The SSE was revealed. *60 Minutes* reconstructed the letter drop that was central to this blackmail attempt. Beyond the lunch box revelation, the program had the details of the stationery and stamps being purchased, the letter typed at the Channel Seven offices, and the enlistment of an agent to post it at Tweed Heads. John McLeod was not named; there was no value in aggravating an important prospective witness.

One of the secret recordings revealed Roberts-Smith's reliance on Kerry Stokes' support:

> There's no fucking way I'd be able to keep paying what I'm paying for until Kerry got onto it . . . Bottom line is I'd be fucked without him . . . They [Kerry Stokes and Bruce McWilliam] are privy to everything that's gone on in the courts, they know what is going on . . . Put it this way, mate, Stokes isn't an idiot, he's not going to back someone . . . who's a loser . . . That's why they're shitting themselves now, because he's prepared to run his bank down to do it.

Roberts-Smith was giving expression to what we had long suspected was his strategy in the case. Litigation is too often a contest of deep pockets. We were two months from trial and millions had already been spent. Nine was taking a massive financial risk, with Seven—or, more accurately, Kerry Stokes—amply resourced to up the ante.

Nick had done tremendous work. We had stayed well in the hunt, largely through persistent digging of our own. But it was mostly Nick at this stage. I continued to contribute, and I had helped produce the *60 Minutes* report, but I was not a Nine employee and I worked part-time.

As had happened previously, the *60 Minutes* program, 'Secrets of War', triggered a national debate. *The Australian* reported that the officer seen simulating oral sex, now a colonel, was in line to head Special Operations Training.[1] For months and years to come, a ripple of discomfort touched some in the officer ranks. What else might there be in the photo trove?

Ben's solicitor, Mark O'Brien, issued a statement proclaiming the *60 Minutes* program as 'either an attempt to intimidate Mr Roberts-Smith into discontinuing the defamation proceedings, or to punish him for bringing them'.[2]

As ever, Seven stuck by its Queensland general manager: 'Most of the material aired is old. Seven notes it is before the Federal Court and the court process should be respected.'[3] But, after Anzac Day 2021, Ben Roberts-Smith, while retaining his salary, stepped down from Seven to focus on the trial.

Despite an order by the Brereton inquiry for Roberts-Smith to provide to it all relevant material, the hundreds of images stored on USBs and concealed in the child's lunch box had not been supplied. Nor had they been disclosed in response to the discovery notices issued by our lawyers.

Within a week of the airing of the *60 Minutes* report, and five days after being asked by our lawyers to preserve copies of the USBs, Ben Roberts-Smith wiped his laptop. He would later say it was because he was trading it in and had been instructed to do so by Apple.

CHAPTER 52

FEELING THE HEAT

The brain tumour was operable, but for Sandy Dawson the case was over—and so too, prospectively, a hard-won career. Horrible from every perspective. He had been almost twenty years at the bar, the last five as a senior counsel.

The trial was already a labyrinth, additionally complicated by national security imperatives, non-publication directives and a bafflement of military nomenclature. Lyndelle Barnett retained a commanding overview, well assisted by Chris Mitchell. But we had to find a replacement for Sandy, which was not easy given the full schedules of specialist defamation barristers. At the time, I could not see how anyone stepping in so late could possibly catch up.

Up on the 40th floor, the solicitors too were feeling rising heat. Peter Bartlett was constantly expressing 'a need to get on the front foot'. Much of the fighting at this level was an office-to-office paper war between MinterEllison and Mark O'Brien Legal.

Ongoing Covid restrictions meant conferences mostly took place via Zoom or Microsoft Teams videolinks. All of us, every Tuesday at 5 pm. This was dispiriting at times. I could see why Ben Roberts-Smith was telling people he had already won: within our witness line-up were plenty of reluctant starters.

Through the early months of 2021 there was argument over competing NTPs ('notices to produce'). There was fighting over access to medical and psychiatric records. Roberts-Smith, via Mark O'Brien Legal, sought the restriction of any information drawn from Ben and Emma's Family Court case. O'Brien raised unspecified 'concerns and criticisms' about Nick, me and *60 Minutes*. There was a row over Roberts-Smith's earlier failure to produce the lunch box USBs, followed by an excuse that this was down to 'inadvertence'.

Rising heat in the Australian precincts of justice was nothing compared with what was being felt in Afghanistan's remote communities and the coal-smoke-clouded crush of its major cities. The Taliban was moving on Kabul, and Coalition forces were in the final stage of withdrawal. The court agreed to hearing evidence from the four witnesses from Darwan. They would have to travel to a secure location in Kabul, and whether this could be practically achieved was still in doubt.

Lawyers for Ben Roberts-Smith wanted access to the evidence these witnesses had given the IGADF. So, more preliminary argument. The Commonwealth sought for this information to be protected, because the villagers might be exposed to Taliban retribution. Arthur Moses SC saw his client as more at risk. 'We should pause for a moment and think what the Taliban may or may not do to someone they think has engaged in such war crimes if they ever got their hands on him or his family,' he told *The Australian* in May.[1]

It was flat chat on both sides. We could barely keep up. While the bulk of our SAS witnesses had given detailed statements to our lawyers, there were others still beyond our reach. Summaries of their evidence for our lawyers were largely composed from what Nick and I had discovered, second- and third-hand. While these were rough around the edges, our lawyers still saw them as providing a strong base.

But it was scary all the same. When you call someone to give evidence, without being confident about exactly what they will say, your heart is in your mouth. As had occurred in the Eddie Gallagher trial, such testimony could, like a hissing IED, blow you to bits.

Peter Bartlett and Dean Levitan continued to reach out via Minter's national network of law offices, doing all they could to soften the compulsory thump of raining subpoenas.

At this eleventh hour, Dean was heartened when the phone rang. At the other end, out of the blue, was The SSE's lawyer. Another witness and another statement now refined.

At much the same time, Roberts-Smith suffered a setback. His number-one character witness had been drawn from the absolute top shelf. As Australia's governor-general, Dame Quentin Bryce had conferred the Victoria Cross on Roberts-Smith in 2011. In the intervening decade, as both were Brisbane-based, they had crossed paths. Early in the proceedings, Dame Quentin provided to Ben and his lawyers a statement of support; it was described by an associate as 'vanilla.'

Then, in April 2021, Bruce McClintock SC declared in court that the Honourable Quentin Bryce would be called as a reputational witness. But Dame Quentin had not been told about her intended court appearance and was caught by surprise. Some ground needed to be made up.

On 26 May, Ben Roberts-Smith headed to Dame Quentin's home, armed with a large bunch of flowers. With the help of his daughters, he had beforehand reconnoitred and identified the correct residence. At the portico, within range of a security camera, he rang the bell. His flowers concealed his identity.

It was early morning. The former governor-general appeared in her dressing-gown and opened the door, expecting to greet a florist. By all accounts she was flustered.

The timing was poor. Quentin Bryce had not long lost her husband, Michael. There was an awkward exchange as Roberts-Smith apologised for the surprise announcement made by McClintock in court.

Dame Quentin subsequently made it clear she had no intention of testifying for Ben, and described the early-morning floral ambush as 'inappropriate.'[2]

The loss of the former governor-general was an impediment, but slight compared to another setback. Another important woman, Ben's former wife Emma, had switched sides.

Federal Court proceedings were launched against Emma, and these threatened to further delay the defamation case. During their marriage, Ben and Emma had had a shared email account. Roberts-Smith's lawyers were now concerned that some of his communications with his lawyers, using this account, might have been passed to our lawyers, which would have been a breach of legal professional privilege. There was concern as well that other information passed to us might have been in breach of the Family Court settlement.

Bruce McClintock SC rattled a sabre. He warned that Emma would be cross-examined and our team should 'rethink what they're doing', because 'sometimes you can pay too high a price' by involving family members in proceedings.[3]

Counsel for Nine replied, declaring this an 'egregious submission'.[4]

Yes, we had a new top silk. Nicholas Owens SC had come to the rescue. We had done exceptionally well in obtaining his services in an exceptionally difficult circumstance. Owens was coming off a complex class action case flowing from the 2011 Brisbane floods. Other matters were in train, but a fortuitous settlement of them produced a gap, and with some juggling, he was on board.

Nicholas Owens SC was not a defamation specialist, but it became immediately apparent that this mattered hardly a toss. I was astonished at how quickly the tall, bespectacled, unflappable Mr Owens got his head around the defamation trial of the century.

CHAPTER 53

'CREDULOUS'

The witness scorecard was close to even. Of the SAS operators, there were sixteen in the Roberts-Smith camp. On our side the list was longer, but it was a lesser number if we counted only the known quantities—witnesses who had provided comprehensive statements and, albeit with trepidation, had agreed to testify.

A week out from the trial, I was asked to see Dean Levitan and Chris Mitchell in Chris's Sydney office. We gathered to talk mainly about Koran Ghar. Chris began to plot through a series of large folders, marked 'credit', which is lawyers' shorthand for credibility. On this occasion, he was focusing on the credibility of Ben Roberts-Smith and his witnesses.

Early in the piece, the lawyers had struggled to keep their heads above a flood of facts, sometimes to the frustration of the journalists. Now, on the eve of the trial, we were in one sense chastened and in another gratified to see the tide turn. Within those volumes was a powerful amount of clever work.

The public contest also amped up. One day out from the trial, the *Mail* ran a feature. Photographed shirtless during an early-morning workout at Woolloomooloo, Ben looked buffed and fit. 'I'm feeling good mate,' he told a reporter, 'looking forward to finally setting the record straight.'[1]

Also offered to the media were his parents, Len and Sue, who had crossed the continent from Perth, braving Covid quarantine requirements to be there for their elder son. 'The allegations have not only destroyed Ben's life but have affected us every day for the last several years,' they said.[2]

The long-awaited dawn: 7 June 2021. Because I live outside Sydney, I stay with my city-based younger daughter, who drops me in town on her way to work. Masked up, it is first to MinterEllison to sign sheafs of documents. Then a ten-minute walk to the Queen's Square Law Courts, the 30-storey imposing high-rise building containing 34 state and seven federal courtrooms, strategically located between the barristers' eyries in Phillip Street and the political stronghold in Macquarie Street.

A posse of media waits outside. I slip through, recognised only by the older ones. It must be the mask!

Through the security screen. Laptop and phone in a basket. Proof of vaccination displayed. My titanium knee replacements trigger the alarm. This procedure will be repeated for months to come.

Into the lift. Up to the eighteenth floor. As at a church wedding, demarcation is understood, Ben Roberts-Smith's team is on the left, near the windows; our crew is on the right; the Commonwealth representatives are in the middle.

I find one of the remaining empty seats up the back, directly behind our lawyers. Len Roberts-Smith is next to me. His son, Ben, in the corner. Bruce McWilliam, Seven's commercial director, sits near Ben, assiduously texting. Their PR consultant, Helen McCombie, scouts the media pack. She will not bother with us. Nine's group executive editor, James Chessell, is to my right. Nick McKenzie, locked down in Melbourne, watches via a videolink.

Then, at 10.15 am, the most galvanising ritual of all. A tap on the door. The entry of Justice Besanko and his associate, and an announcement that the court is now in session.

We had offered to go first, but the applicant held to the advantage of the first move. Bruce McClintock SC, near the end of a celebrated career, is on his feet and, as we anticipated, showing no mercy in his opening address.

Ben Roberts-Smith, 'with a deservedly high reputation for courage, skill and decency', has been brought down by jealous soldiers 'aided by credulous' journalists. The spectrum of calumny endured by his client is greater than can be covered in a day, so McClintock's opening spills over into Tuesday.

He describes Ben Roberts-Smith as being assailed for his courage at Koran Ghar by cowardly soldiers who were not up to the standard of the SAS. The accusation of murder at Darwan was never raised at the time. It is a 'ludicrous' allegation and 'did not happen'.

McClintock also scorns the alleged Chinartu murder. He has documents to annihilate that claim. The Lieutenant was not even on the mission. In a mocking tone: 'As I was going up the stair, I saw a man who wasn't there.'

Regarding Whiskey 108: 'My client's version is considerably more likely to be true.' Roberts-Smith had taken out a high-level Taliban commander, and the blooding allegation was 'false'.

The accusation of the execution by pistol to the head of a teenage boy at Fasil is 'insane'. The alleged Roberts-Smith comment of it being 'the most beautiful thing I've ever seen' are the words of an 'ostentatious psychopath'. And 'he's not that'.

McClintock engaged in counter-defamation, accusing me of knowingly reporting false information, in that my book identified Ben Roberts-Smith as having been elsewhere at the time. Ben Roberts-Smith's lawyer was wrong. Only after we accessed Defence records were we able to confirm the date of the Fasil mission as different to what was earlier presumed.

Regarding the complaints about the awarding of the Commendation for Distinguished Service: some were unsigned, and within none of them was 'one word about war crimes'.

So jealous were his accusers that in 2012 they returned to the scene of the Tizak Victoria Cross action and miserably paced the ground, attempting to disprove a citation that underscored true valour.

In the matter of the 2 Squadron novelty drinking vessel Das Boot, McClintock concedes that his client made a mistake, but that drinking from the prosthetic leg of a dead Afghan: 'in the scheme of human wickedness it does not . . . rate terribly high'. He further points out that the distasteful souvenir had been recovered by one of Roberts-Smith's accusers, The Veteran, and that he has a photo to prove it.

While rejecting the allegations against Roberts-Smith, McClintock devotes time to painting a word picture of a tortured battlespace. 'It is impossible to re-create here in the courtroom the reality of fighting and the conditions that existed in Afghanistan,' he says. The soldiers 'had no way of knowing' farmer from fighter: 'they didn't wear uniforms; they didn't carry a sign saying "insurgent"'.

Bruce McClintock emphasises the scale and gravity of the contest. 'At the end of the trial we will put to Your Honour that this justifies an aggravated damages claim, and I will put to you that an allegation of murder with no basis justifies the largest award of damages ever in this country.'

It was a strong opening, spoken with passion and conviction. But to me, as a reporter sitting at the back of the courtroom, it was unconvincing.

I cast my mind back four years, to when the argument about Ben first surfaced and we set out to discover the truth of the matter. All that followed was Ben Roberts-Smith running and hiding from the truth.

Getting this wrong would be every bit the catastrophe his counsel was now making out. Our many sleepless nights, up to this point and beyond, were largely due to the investigative journalist's inclination to think the worst. What if they did have evidence that proved us wrong? Truth evolves as further facts come to light. What if there was an unanticipated X-factor element that could blow our case out of the water?

I called Nick. We both felt relieved, but there was a long way to go.

CHAPTER 54

A TARGET ON MY BACK

Our approach to court each morning saw trolleys loaded with lever-arch files, sweeping black robes, dangling wigs and furrowed brows converging on a media scrum rising to attention. We often found ourselves on the same Phillip Street footpath as Ben. Immediately recognisable above the crowd, he would be immaculately dressed, with his broad shoulders filling a tailored suit, and a small briefcase tucked under his arm.

Often, at a distance from the court, he would be spotted side by side and in conversation with Monica Allen. But as they neared the media scrum, his lawyer would drop back; we presumed this was under advice, so as to avoid being photographed together. The hand-holding pictured from August 2020, and more particularly their social relationship, was later acknowledged by her boss, Mark O'Brien, as 'unwise'.[1]

And in that first week Monica Allen was back in the spotlight because of a separate action. In the same building, but before a different Federal Court, Justice Robert Bromwich was hearing argument about whether Emma Roberts, via her access to an email account she'd shared with Ben, had breached his legal professional privilege.

There was a moment of drama when Justice Bromwich paused proceedings. He was responding to the relationship 'rumour'; this followed media reports that, after an exercise workout that had been featured in the *Daily Mail*, Roberts-Smith had been seen entering a nearby apartment building, where Monica Allen lived. Justice Bromwich said he was compelled to raise the matter because he wasn't 'aware of any of this', and he was 'uncomfortable with the situation'.

An annoyed Arthur Moses SC assured the court that 'the applicant and the deponent are not in a relationship, full stop'.[2] Outside court, Bruce McWilliam, Seven West Media's commercial director, was also wound up, describing the treatment of Ms Allen as a 'deplorable slur': 'There's no truth attached to any of it and it's a very bad way to treat a very talented lawyer who's very good at what she does.'[3]

Indeed, according to other reporting, for months now Ben Roberts-Smith had been stepping out with a new girlfriend, a former Brisbane-based Channel Seven employee named Sarah Matulin.

The following day, Thursday, 10 June, Nicholas Owens SC, having sought permission, was allowed a brief opening address. Usually, this would occur after the applicant's case closed. But given that Bruce McClintock had commanded the narrative through much of the first week, Owens was keen, as he told me, to 'plant a flag'. Figuring Justice Besanko would not welcome him 'playing the media', our barrister kept it brief.

Owens told the court that Nine was pleading truth as a defence, and he emphasised that none of the six murders alleged to have occurred was committed in the heat of battle. It was 'inherently implausible' that the 21 current and former SAS members in line to give evidence for us were all motivated by jealousy. Owens spoke of 'friends' lives being destroyed', and how 'honourable men could not remain silent'. We would demonstrate that Ben Roberts-Smith's pattern of behaviour—threatening letters, burner phones and bullying—profoundly undermined the integrity of his evidence.

Just before 11 am, Ben Roberts-Smith—in dark blue suit, white shirt, silver cufflinks and grey-green tie—was called forward. He took the box before Justice Besanko and to the right of the bar table. A camera above captured the action of court 18D, the image reproduced on a large screen positioned on the rear wall and transmitted to the world beyond. Once sworn in, he began his evidence in chief.

I had seen this kind of polished performance from him before. Roberts-Smith can be convincing. A deep, if at times dull, voice and some facility to his vocabulary. As well, there were no evident signs of nerves from the VC.

'I spent my life fighting for my country,' he said, 'and I did everything I possibly could to ensure I did it with honour . . . and I really cannot comprehend how people on the basis of rumour and innuendo can maintain that . . . and it breaks my heart.'

Bruce McClintock took him through his Army career. Ben said he had not achieved a rank beyond corporal because 'of the tempo of operations, we just simply didn't have a lot of time in the SAS to do the required promotional courses'.

As in the opening address, McClintock spent considerable time on Koran Ghar. I wondered why, given Roberts-Smith had not sued over the *No Front Line* telling, nor did it figure in the listed imputations for this matter. Condemnation of The Redhead went beyond his failure to bring gun oil and thus compromising their firepower. 'Noodle-gate', as we came to term it, was also raised. On a different patrol, The Redhead was accused of being more interested in finishing his bowl of noodles than in responding to an enemy mortar attack.

Regarding the Whiskey 108 action, Roberts-Smith said he'd shot the insurgent in legitimate combat. The man had been running, crouching, carrying a bolt-action rifle. The alleged blooding had never occurred. Roberts-Smith said he had never heard the term 'blooding the rookie'. The proposition was 'completely ridiculous' and made him 'angry'.

As Roberts-Smith explained how the second victim at Whiskey 108 met his fate, credibility was strained. He said the Afghan was shot by another soldier, firing from somewhere behind him, and to this day he did not know who that soldier was. Given the frequent and intense interpersonal exchange of war stories between veterans, how likely was it that Ben had never bothered to find out who effectively saved his life?

It was later in the afternoon when the subject turned to the Battle of Tizak, the action that earned Ben a Victoria Cross and (in his words) 'put a target on my back'. His account was vivid. His voice broke as he spoke of that profound moment when his mates were under a smashing torrent of fire: 'when you see that, the reality is you have to make a decision'. An ashen pause. He could not go on.

Bruce McClintock intervened: 'Do you want to stop there, Mr Roberts-Smith?' He looked at the clock: 4.15 pm. 'Is that a suitable time, Your Honour?'

Justice Besanko: 'Yes, I think it is. The court will adjourn until 10.15 in the morning.'

It was a little like being at a Saturday matinee: a riveted audience carried to the edge of the cliff.

When the Tizak narrative resumed, it was now 11 June, the eleventh anniversary of the famous battle. Suitably refreshed and composed, Ben Roberts-Smith picked up where he left off: 'The decision was: could you go home and face their families if you didn't do anything?' He then described in detail the perilous uphill assault on the compound.

Again, Tizak was not in the raft of imputations sued over. Although we knew there was controversy and disagreement about who did what, in our reporting there was no challenge to the official record. That would have been a bridge too far.

But we felt no surprise that it would be showcased. A defamation case is all about reputation and, as we had witnessed, Australia's most decorated living soldier had quite a story. But the door was now open to a counter-narrative. Witnesses who were also at Tizak would be called, with accounts at variance, accounts that for many were meant to remain unspoken.

In contrast, a cornerstone allegation—the murder of Ali Jan at Darwan—had to be flattened. Roberts-Smith found dealing with it was 'like being in a bloody nightmare'. 'No', he did not kick a man. 'No', there wasn't a cliff. 'No', the man was not dragged. And 'no', he was not then shot. Roberts-Smith was 'particularly disgusted' that the allegation could be raised after he'd risked his own life to swim a river and kill an armed insurgent on that very day.

The claim that he'd struck a woman was at least as offensive. Domestic violence was 'highly reprehensible', 'deplorable', 'disgusting'. He had 'no tolerance for anyone who would ever raise a hand to a woman . . . That particular allegation, I feel, coupled with being called a war criminal, ruined my life . . . For a long time, I found it very difficult to leave the house.'

There were a few concessions in his testimony. Ben Roberts-Smith admitted there was a kill board on his team door in 2012—but this was a common enough practice, he said, dating back to the Vietnam War. He also acknowledged having punched The Trooper on the face early in the same rotation. While he regretted this, he said the soldier had giggled when confronted following the blue-on-blue incident. The young soldier had not comprehended the seriousness of almost shooting a woman and child, and 'just wasn't up to par'.

Being a witness is hard work, particularly if you are lying but also when telling the truth. Maintaining acute concentration can be exhausting, even for the easier part when you are led by your own barrister. Less than a week in, this was already a marathon, and Roberts-Smith was mostly impressive.

Certainly, if you gave no credence to the evidence against him, Roberts-Smith's claim of having been catastrophically wronged was moving and shocking. But there were also moments when he appeared pallid and worried, his confidence shaken, his commentary clipped and interspersed with nervous laughter.

There was documentary evidence he was always going to have difficulty explaining. For example, the handwritten notes retained by the private inquiry agent, John McLeod. Pre-emptively, Ben claimed that the information, in his handwriting, was for McLeod to trace addresses as he intended hiring a different private investigator to monitor the movements of soldiers he believed were briefing against him. Roberts-Smith's explanation must have seemed implausible even to his own supporters.

When it came to the buried lunch box, the story was completely denied. He had hidden nothing in the garden. As for the burner phones, they were not acquired to elude war crimes investigators, but journalists; the phone hacking scandal in the United Kingdom, which had caused so much grief for Rupert Murdoch, had been playing heavily on his mind.

Ben Roberts-Smith's evidence in chief ran for four days. He said he had not enjoyed any of it. He had gone to fight in Afghanistan at the government's behest and returned traumatised. He had followed the rules. He had seen what could not be unseen. Now, he said, 'there are moments in my life in the last three years that I just didn't think it was worth it'.

But Roberts-Smith's respect for the Victoria Cross, the Australian Defence Force and his love for his friends and family had sustained him. 'And that's what keeps me going, to set the record straight.'

CHAPTER 55

SOFTLY, SOFTLY

Thursday, 17 June. This is in a period of early starts and long train rides into town. Out at Wynyard station and a brisk walk to Minter's, busting for a pee.

The young lawyers are already in the lock-up. Camaraderie is developing. Dean Levitan and Tess McGuire, both up from Melbourne, are still learning where to find a decent coffee. It turns out I know Tess's father. Frank McGuire, now in politics, had worked with me at *Four Corners* in the 1990s.

Our barristers are in chambers closer to the court. Among us all there is discussion about how best to approach the cross-examination of Ben Roberts-Smith. It is clear he has been well-rehearsed; he is highly motivated.

The VC, MG is a fighter; his bias is for action. But, as I saw in 2017, in the rose garden interview, if you let him run he can overstep. The Sergeant, no big fan, described Roberts-Smith, when challenged, as flaring like a 'frill-necked lizard'.

Nick McKenzie joins us at the court, having escaped the Melbourne lockdown. Partway through a law degree, and sometimes sounding like one of them, he finds a seat alongside our legal team.

Nic Owens takes it softly, softly. Polite and methodical at first, locking Ben Roberts-Smith into his position on devilish details surrounding the six alleged unlawful killings.

'Mr Roberts-Smith, is it correct that at all times when you were deployed to Afghanistan, you understood that it would never be permissible to kill a PUC [person under control]?'

'Yes,' answers Ben Roberts-Smith.

'May we also take it that at all times during your deployment to Afghanistan, you understood that if you became aware that somebody was ordering, directing or encouraging another person to kill or injure a PUC, that you should take measures to prevent that happening?'

Another perfunctory 'Yes.'

For most of the morning, Owens takes Roberts-Smith through standard operating procedures (SOPs), PUC handling and permissible use of force. Also the basics of Pashto—'stop', 'get down', 'hands up'—that Roberts-Smith had at his fingertips. On his uniform, which is showcased at the Australian War Memorial, you can see such phrases taped to his sleeve.

The witness gives clear and concise answers, occasionally sipping water as the day proceeds and his throat dries. There is little evident threat in the questioning.

Owens asks about his knowledge of 'throwdowns'. Ben is aware of the term, but if it is practised at all, it is only done so by soldiers of other nations.

'Had you heard rumours of patrols in the SAS using throwdowns?'

'No.'

This takes Owens to Darwan, on 11 September 2012. He asks about the Icom handheld radio found on Ali Jan: 'Where was it?'

'It was on the ground, actually. On, effectively, underneath him.'

Owens asks about Roberts-Smith's earlier crossing of the Helmand River and his killing of an armed insurgent. 'Did you find an Icom on the body of that insurgent?'

'I don't recall.'

Roberts-Smith is shown a series of aerial photographs of Darwan and asked to mark on them the location of his and other patrols, the PUCs, partner force and interpreter in accordance with timings and movement. Owens is softly spoken but relentless. Roberts-Smith is steady, if hesitant at times, 'I don't recall' now heard more often.

On this day, Arthur Moses SC is riding shotgun for Roberts-Smith. He occasionally pulls Owens up, suggesting that his opponent does not fully understand military SOPs and is guilty of repetition. Owens, mildly irritated, carries on.

In the afternoon, the tall silk drills down to the engagement with the Darwan spotter. While we have alleged that Ali Jan was kicked from a cliff and executed, Ben Roberts-Smith and his comrade, The Sniper, contend that the victim, photographed dead on the ground, was an insurgent tactically manoeuvring as the Australians and their Afghan partners prepared for helicopter extraction.

He describes following The Sniper up a steep rise and hearing shots. Now communicating with all his body, he mimics a climbing motion, his hands gripping and pulling at undergrowth to assist his ascent. He makes pulling movements with his hands.

He was pushing on in support of his mate. The Sniper was firing at a 'spotter' who had broken cover just two to five metres away. Roberts-Smith saw the man fall in a cornfield. He says he was confident he was a spotter due to the Icom traffic heard, the atmospherics, the intelligence and because Darwan was a Taliban village. Roberts-Smith: 'I think it was a more than reasonable assessment that he was showing hostile intent.'

A satellite photograph is produced, and Roberts-Smith is again asked to mark the positions of himself, his comrades and the route to the helicopter landing zone.

When questioned about the time the operation took, he says he has no idea, but it was hours.

'Did it strike you as odd,' Owens asks, 'that this spotter chose this exact moment to appear, when you were coming up the embankment?'

Roberts-Smith: 'No, I think he was unlucky.'

There were some signs of afternoon fatigue when the subject turned to Whiskey 108. Again, there was a long preamble as Owens worked through the walk to the compound on Easter Sunday 2009. Again, maps and photographs were produced and marked to show where the bomb strike had occurred, and to infill routes taken by the various patrols.

Roberts-Smith described the entrance to the courtyard and the discovery of the tunnel, and was asked to mark that point. He recalled his friend The Hunter climbing into the tunnel to undertake a search. At this point he noticed a gap in the wall and moved to see what was outside. 'Before I could get to the edge of the building, I saw the insurgent moving at my front, and they had the engagement . . . It just happened quite quickly.'

Roberts-Smith marked the point of the engagement, describing the insurgent as hunched over and carrying a rifle.

After he'd fired two rounds, his weapon jammed. Crouching to clear it, there was more gunfire as a second insurgent was sighted and shot. Roberts-Smith marked the point on the photograph where that man fell, estimating the two bodies as about three metres apart.

As he had explained during his evidence in chief, Roberts-Smith said he did not know who shot the second man. He said he dragged one body back and another soldier he could not identify dragged the other body. They were moved to a secure position inside the compound wall. There, the sensitive site exploitation (SSE) began, as Ben moved back out to recover the bolt-action rifle.

The clock on the wall now edged past 4.15 pm and Justice Besanko adjourned.

When a witness is in the middle of cross-examination, contact with outside parties is strictly limited during the adjournment. No feedback or coaching is allowed. The evidence cannot be discussed.

For Ben, it would be a difficult night.

CHAPTER 56

THE DEVIL IN THE DETAIL

When Ben Roberts-Smith removed his mask and resettled in the witness box on Friday, 18 June, he immediately corrected his evidence of the previous afternoon. He told the court that, 'upon reflection', the second soldier did not drag the other body back. Instead, it 'lay where it fell'.

Ben explained: 'It was a mistake yesterday in my evidence, so I thought it best to correct that.' Queried, he gave an assurance that he had spoken to no one overnight; his confusion stemmed from his six Afghanistan deployments and 'multiple engagements'.

I thought I detected some unease at his bar table. Was this a turning point?

It would be a long morning. Nicholas Owens continued, patient and penetrating. Step by step, he took the witness through his version of how the Whiskey 108 victims met their fate.

We believed Roberts-Smith had shot one man with his machine gun and carried him outside, while the other man was executed inside the compound, in the blooding of a junior soldier. Roberts-Smith agreed that the man with the prosthetic leg was shot by him—but he claimed it had been in legitimate combat and outside the compound. The second and older victim was killed nearby by another, unknown operator.

Five photographs taken at the SSE were presented by the court attendant at the defence's request and closely examined. Metadata showed the time each was taken.

At the lunchtime adjournment, all parties would move to small rooms near the courtroom. Ben's team was in the first of these, just along from our courtroom's entrance; the Commonwealth was next; ours was further along the corridor, closer to the lift well. Nobody would say anything until the door was closed, and then voices would be lowered.

Lunch would be sandwiches delivered in a sealed plastic box, alongside a collection of fruit juice. A carton of bottled water in a cabinet in the corner was regularly replenished. So too a box of muesli bars, as there was not always time for breakfast. Curiously, there was always competition for the egg salad on wholemeal, while the shaved ham with tomato bleeding through often went untouched.

Jeremy Forbes, tall and without a skerrick of body fat, opted for a private reserve of sushi. The treat for all of us was a box of mixed Cadbury's chocolates. It would empty quickly. MinterEllison covered the costs, which was fine by me, given that I was on no one's payroll.

After a quick debrief, the barristers would soon retire to their chambers while the solicitors usually lingered in the small, stuffy cubicle. Everyone continued to work. I wish the law was not so costly, and I do think they are paid too much, but I can't for a second deny how hard they work.

On this particular morning, there was some intense discussion about the unexpected U-turn. Chris Mitchell, who had been a war crimes prosecutor with the International Criminal Court, knew the value of being across the detail. He told me, 'Forensics have an objective quality that witness testimony often lacks.' For example, he explained, when skeletal remains are found showing wrists and hands tied, it can be readily concluded that the person was executed.

As for Whiskey 108 and the sudden change to Roberts-Smith's testimony, a photograph of the older man, whom Roberts-Smith said was shot by an unknown other, clearly showed it could not have been moved. Next to it was brain matter, a blood pattern, and no drag marks. We suspected Ben Roberts-Smith had changed his testimony to conform with the documentary evidence.

The morning session had also turned back to Darwan, with Roberts-Smith pushed on timings. Using the operation summary and radio transmission reports, Owens had been able to pin down the patrol movements. Again, the detail was critical.

In statements from Afghan witnesses, an interpreter was remembered as being present at the last compound cleared. Ben said the interpreter wasn't there, and that he was without him for only ten minutes.

Owens had produced documentary evidence to indicate that the interpreter was there, and that the period of his absence—within the window we alleged the murder occurred—was more like 90 minutes.

Cracks were showing, and Roberts-Smith was struggling to seal them.

After 45 minutes of discussion, Dean Levitan suggested a coffee run. It was good to get outside and talk about something else. We were making ground, but we were still far from in a winning position.

And then, at 2.15 pm, back in court, the man under most pressure resumed his seat. Straight back into it, with more telling details about the spotter at Darwan. Ben Roberts-Smith revealed that, along with The Sniper, he too had fired rounds at the fleeing man, 'so he had multiple wounds'.

More photographs were produced, including confronting images of the deceased Ali Jan. Nicholas Owens asked Roberts-Smith to look at a highlighted section revealing a 'large amount of blood on his left hand and wrist', and then a straight line with 'no blood'. He asked: 'Do you agree that straight line is consistent with that man wearing plasticuffs [cable ties] around his wrists at the time he was bleeding?'

Roberts-Smith: 'No.'

Owens turned to another picture, and questioned Roberts-Smith about the tight cluster of four wounds to Ali Jan's chest. How was that consistent, he asked, with being shot 'multiple' times while running? Our barrister further queried whether larger wounds on Ali Jan's arms—apparently exit wounds—were consistent with his arms being tied behind his back.

Ben Roberts-Smith disagreed.

And then there was the jagged wound to Ali Jan's face. We contended that this was caused after he was kicked while manacled, when he was unable to protect himself and his face had struck the cliff face.

Nicholas Owens held nothing back: 'This man suffered that injury falling down a cliff on the other side of the creek bed, didn't he?'

'No.'

'And either you or The Sniper shot him?'

'That is completely false.'

Next Owens took Roberts-Smith back to Whiskey 108: 'What you said yesterday was a lie, correct?'

'No, I made a mistake.'

On to the tale of the stray bullet and the mongrel dog. Documentary evidence disproved the claims by Roberts-Smith and his supporters that The Lieutenant was responsible and subsequently removed.

Owens put to him: 'You know for a fact that it wasn't The Lieutenant . . .'

'Well, from the documents I have now, I do.'

'I put it to you that it was dishonest, Mr Roberts-Smith. What do you say to that?'

'I say it was not my intent to be dishonest.'

Then it was 4.19 pm and the second week of an anticipated ten-week trial was at an end.

CHAPTER 57

'THERE WERE NO MEN IN THE TUNNEL'

We had much ground to cover.

The third week of the trial proceeded, moving between open and closed court. From nervous start to exhaustive finish, a welter of classified content and NPOs (non-publication orders) meant there was constant movement by the robed personnel with their loaded trolleys as they shuttled back and forth between courtrooms 18D and 18A.

While the camps of the applicant and the respondents opted for as much transparency as possible, the Commonwealth remained vigilant; a public interest immunity blanket was kept at the ready to be thrown over any classified content. This meant that lawyers on both sides reserved sensitive subject matter for a private airing, and then attendance thinned to only those directly involved.

The media got a break, but not so Nick McKenzie and me. As second and third respondents, we were allowed to attend the closed sessions. But we could bring no phones, laptops or recording devices. Notes were not to be taken. And, obviously, there was to be no reporting of what was said. That rule still stands to this day, including for this publication.

As it turned out, Ben Roberts-Smith also got a break, having been informed he was a close contact at a Covid-19 hotspot on the Thursday. Tested on the Sunday, he was isolating for part of Monday, 21 June, as he awaited the result. After a negative finding, open court cross-examination resumed midafternoon.

Nicholas Owens continued to punish Roberts-Smith's version of the killings at Whiskey 108. He questioned the likelihood of two insurgents suddenly appearing in an attack so close to the compound, which was occupied and surrounded by a heavily armed SAS troop. Why was one body and a weapon dragged towards the compound while the other body with a machine gun was left in the dirt? How did Ben not know who had saved his life?

Owens queried inconsistencies in Roberts-Smith's evidence about radio transmissions, and the discovery of the prosthetic leg on the man he shot. Then he put it squarely: 'He was one of two men discovered hiding in the tunnel courtyard, wasn't he?'

'No.'

To the consternation of Arthur Moses SC, Owens confronted Roberts-Smith with our version: that two men had been pulled from the tunnel. The older man was ordered executed, and The Gunsmith borrowed a suppressor from another soldier before carrying out the order. The man with the prosthetic leg was manhandled outside and machine-gunned by Roberts-Smith himself. The weapons seen in the SSE photographs were throwdowns, recovered from a concealed cache.

Moses complained: 'My friend has put a number of propositions to the witness that are not to be found in the outlines of evidence, Your Honour.'

But the questioning proceeded. Owens identified a number of further witnesses who had observed the discovery of the two men in the tunnel.

Ben Roberts-Smith was adamant: 'There were no men in the tunnel.'

Owens' approach to cross-examination was unusual and prospectively dangerous. Dangerous, because it gifted latitude to the other side. The Nine team gambled on the 'enough rope' approach—that is, letting Roberts-Smith speak at length. We could prove our case by demonstrating the dishonesty of his case.

Given the paucity of written outlines of evidence, no one knew for sure what was coming. But warnings were sounded. Ben's lawyers should have been concerned about whether they could hold the line on their story of no men being hauled from the tunnel.

It was a cold Sydney winter's morning. I was not the only one surprised by the arrival of Nick McKenzie's surfboard. He had wangled space for it on a plane from Melbourne and as an odd accoutrement at MinterEllison. I mostly commuted to court by train from my home outside Sydney. But for this week, Nick had booked an Airbnb at beachside Bronte. There were two bedrooms, so I towed a bag into Sydney. There might be time for a quick surf in the morning—for him, I hasten to add.

Tuesday was mostly closed court, so no reporting.

On the Wednesday, we caught the bus into town, noticing fewer people and more masks as we lurched through the central business district.

The questioning of Ben Roberts-Smith now turned to his alleged threats and collusion. Roberts-Smith stubbornly refused to accept that he was behind the blackmailing of The SSE. He was taken to my alleged contact with The SSE and a connected conspiracy allegedly between him and The Veteran.

Owens: 'You realise now it's completely false, don't you?'

Roberts-Smith. 'No, I don't know that.'

As for his friend The Scot providing details in a late-night phone call about his grilling by the IGADF, Roberts-Smith dissembled.

Owens: 'At the time of the phone call, you understood, didn't you, that The Scot shouldn't be disclosing the content of his interview with the IGADF to you?'

Roberts-Smith: 'In my view, he wasn't disclosing the content of it.'

Owens: 'Well, he told you the subject matter of some of the questioning, correct?'

Roberts-Smith: 'Well, I believe he was . . . just venting.'

Towards the end of the day, Roberts-Smith's use of burner phones and his method for getting rid of personal computers captured the attention of media. Owens' proposition—that he had poured petrol onto his laptop and set it on fire, in a 'panic' at the prospect of the AFP seizing it, was rejected.

Ben Roberts-Smith: 'Sir, I've burned laptops in 2010 and '12, when I was in Brisbane with my family at my parents' property, because if I'm getting rid of a laptop, that's what I do.'

Nick and I stayed in town to talk with the lawyers and were late leaving Minter's. The city was dead. Covid had dimmed the lights all around Circular Quay, which usually bustled with tourists and diners. After some footslogging, we found a tapas restaurant, which we had pretty much to ourselves. The food could be claimed on Nine. The drinks we paid for ourselves; the days of TV journos and unlimited credit are long gone.

Thursday was another long day. Ben Roberts-Smith was questioned about his 2018 meeting with The Scout at the East Hotel in Canberra. Roberts-Smith did not remember The Scout saying he would be 'truthful and honest about what he saw in Afghanistan', and that his response was: 'It's going to be like that, is it?' He further denied that The Scout accused him of machine-gunning the man with the prosthetic leg.

Owens: 'And what he told you made you panic. Correct?'

Roberts-Smith: 'No, I was surprised, that's for certain.'

Owens: 'And you leaned forward and said, "Be careful who you fucking talk to."'

Roberts-Smith: 'That is a complete lie.'

On our side, as Roberts-Smith was challenged to reconcile his responses in cross-examination to the testimony in his evidence in chief, our solicitors scurried to locate passages in the transcripts. Swiftly identified and marked files were then passed forward. Similarly, on the applicant's side, there was constant ferrying of post-it notes between solicitors and barristers. In the back corner, Mark O'Brien and his Seven executive comrade, Bruce McWilliam, were sitting together, a double act of Sydney heavyweights.

You could feel for Roberts-Smith at times. During breaks, he would return his mask to his face and stand at the window, taking in the harbour view, clearly wearied. Dealing with a volume of complicated evidence and being forced into constant denial can be a doleful business.

In the late afternoon, attention turned to 2006 and Koran Ghar. One doubt about the flawed official reporting of the mission was the claim that, when the young Afghan 'spotter' was shot, a flare had been ignited in his chest rig or webbing. We knew that no chest rig or webbing had been observed by The Redhead or The Sig, nor had they seen smoke.

Plenty of soldiers with experience of Afghanistan doubted the likelihood of Taliban carrying flares, and of a bullet strike causing such an ignition. The doubters saw the story as a means of justifying the shooting of someone by claiming he was a combatant.

Ben Roberts-Smith, conceding the man was not armed, stuck to his story about the flare-up: 'Well, as I said, there was that translucent sort of smoke you get off a burn, off something burning, but I don't recall there being proper smoke.'

Owens asked Roberts-Smith whether his sensitivity about the Koran Ghar action was down to being awarded a medal for shooting an 'unarmed teenager'.

Roberts-Smith, angry: 'Not only do I find that a disgusting comment, it's also false.'

The following day, the Koran Ghar narrative resumed, focusing on Roberts-Smith's ensuing persecution of The Redhead. Roberts-Smith continued to regard him as 'a coward', more recently because of alleged underhanded contact with the media.

Owens asked him, 'Are you aware of The Redhead ever having spoken to the media?'

'I have no idea. I can't prove that. My view is he has,' replied Roberts-Smith.

In fact, he had not.

It was a long week, and a gruelling ordeal. Roberts-Smith's responses were mostly steady and monotone. Sitting up the back, I thought it interesting how, to me at least, he appeared most animated when The Redhead was being discussed. Roberts-Smith fielded multiple questions about alleged murder quite impassively, but he appeared to be genuinely pissed off that the diminutive ex-choco was now a sergeant, and had thus risen higher in the ranks than Ben himself had done.

Attention turned to the women in Roberts-Smith's life. Owens pushed hard on a raft of evidence, including from Roberts-Smith's own wife, that he was not separated, as he claimed, when he was conducting an extra-marital affair. He was also questioned about recruiting a private inquiry agent to spy on the woman.

Owens: 'Do you agree that hiring a private investigator to follow and secretly record your girlfriend is abusive and controlling behaviour?'

Roberts-Smith: 'No, I do not.'

Emotion was tapped once more when he was asked about his ex-wife, whom he blamed for the concealment of the USBs in the buried lunch box.

Owens: 'All of the evidence that you keep giving about your wife is false and designed to try to blame your ex-wife for your concealment of evidence. Correct?'

Roberts-Smith: 'No. It's very sad that my ex-wife has involved herself in these proceedings, Your Honour, and I take absolutely no joy in describing my wife in any way that is negative, but the reality is she is extremely bitter. She has done things, along the way, that have been detrimental to my family, and particularly to me, because she thinks it will hurt me. I don't like to have to say that, and I really am saddened by it, because of my children, but that is just the way it is, and unfortunately for me, she has injected herself into these proceedings, and she can say whatever she likes, but it's not true.'

I am sure this was heartfelt. But Ben Roberts-Smith as a victim, blaming women for his problems, might not have gone down well with at least 50 per cent of the Australian public.

The public reaction to two weeks of Roberts-Smith's evidence was hard to gauge. You might say he started from a high base, given the usual esteem for a war hero. But in the campaign for public opinion outside the court, I began to wonder whether he was losing his previously amassed goodwill. In some areas of social media, where he would have expected to enjoy favour, he was now being depicted as a cartoon villain—bleak and blameful, spying on a girlfriend, setting fire to a laptop.

Inside the court, in the contest of objective fact, we thought we had done well. Immediately following the Friday adjournment, crowded in our cubicle, with the door closed, Nic Owens was congratulated. It had been a stellar performance.

Nine's editorial legal counsel, Larina Alick, regularly in attendance, agreed. But as we raided the Cadbury Favourites, she cautioned: we were a long way from popping the champagne. We had not yet proved the truth of murder.

CHAPTER 58

'THE RESPONDENTS SHOULD BE ASHAMED'

Brendan Nelson doubled down. Maybe it was a case of 'in for a penny, in for a pound'. He fronted court on Monday, 28 June as Ben Roberts-Smith's key character witness.

But before Dr Nelson took the stand, Dr Parbodh Gogna appeared by videolink from the Bahamas, another reputational witness for Roberts-Smith. A former regimental medical officer and family friend, Dr Gogna had helped treat Ben when Emma became concerned about his excessive drinking. In court, he observed that his friend had become 'more withdrawn' and apprehensive after the 2018 media reporting.

There were more such witnesses providing support via written statements. But, after the withdrawal of Dame Quentin Bryce, Brendan Nelson—the former defence minister and Australian War Memorial director, and now the chief executive officer of Boeing Australia—was the star in the applicant's support cast.

And, once he had removed his mask, Brendan's enthusiasm for Ben, as we had come to expect, leapt forth unrestrained. 'Men and women of everyday life would want to be with him, to shake his hand and have their photographs taken with him. On some occasions I saw people fall into his arms,' he said.

But 'the most respected, admired and revered soldier in more than half a century' had endured a devastating attack. 'I will try not to get angry about this,' Dr Nelson declared, voice breaking. He revealed he had become 'very concerned' about Ben Roberts-Smith's mental health after newspaper articles appeared that seemed to be 'intent on bringing him down'.

I thought his timing was a little out, remembering how Brendan had expressed concern to me that Ben might be 'self-destructing' more than a year before that reporting began. But Nicholas Owens did not cross-examine him. This was disappointing for those of us who would have liked to hear the former War Memorial director explain why he believed we should leave alone all but the 'most egregious breach of the laws of armed conflict'.

But Brendan Nelson was not on trial. Our lawyers viewed challenging him as an unnecessary distraction.

Immediately following Nelson's deposition, Bruce McClintock re-examined his client. Now recalled to the witness box, Ben Roberts-Smith too doubled down. He invoked Matt Locke, his friend, who had also been awarded a Medal for Gallantry for the Koran Ghar battle, before he was tragically killed in action soon afterwards.

Bruce McClintock: 'How did you feel when [Owens] put to you in the witness box that you had lied, in effect, about shooting an unarmed teenager . . . because you didn't want the public to think you had won a Medal for Gallantry for such an act? How did you feel?'

Ben Roberts-Smith: 'I didn't ask for any of my medals, nor did I expect any recognition at all, because I was just doing my job. But to have the respondents instruct their senior counsel to challenge my citation for the Medal of Gallantry [*sic*], and in doing so, challenge that of my good friend and a dead Australian soldier, who cannot stand up here and fight for himself, in Sergeant Matthew Locke: I find it utterly reprehensible. No basis to do that at all. And it's even more damaging to me, particularly the respondent—or Mr Chris Masters, who has profited off what we have done in Afghanistan through his many books, as they have both benefited by tearing our reputations down to try and enhance theirs, yet they see fit to destroy the legacy of a man who is an Australian hero. It can't be seen any other way. And with no basis. Every day those articles are not answered, the Locke family listens to that. Their sacrifice is enduring. They see that every day. They feel that pain and that hurt, and that is what hurts me more than anything else, Your Honour: the fact that they have to listen to that. And they do not deserve that because they have sacrificed enough, as did Matthew Locke.'

McClintock: 'After all, he gave his life, didn't he?'

Roberts-Smith: 'He did give his life. It is utterly disgusting that it was put in those terms. The respondents should just be ashamed.'

I was not ashamed. Frustrated a touch, yes. In these proceedings, there were plenty of occasions when we journalist respondents came under attack and sat silent. We were pleading a truth defence, which meant we were not required to give evidence.

In previous cases in which I had been involved—for example, in the extensive defamation proceedings that flowed from the *Four Corners* program 'The Moonlight State' (the 1987 Queensland police corruption exposé), a different defence had been mounted: qualified privilege. For me that had meant long days in the witness box, arguing that I had acted responsibly and in the public interest. In contrast, our team's objective in the Roberts-Smith defamation case was to demonstrate the truth of what was reported.

I had questions but I had to trust the lawyers to ask the right ones at the right times.

On Tuesday, 29 June, a month-long halt was called. Covid stay-at-home orders in Sydney made managing the trial next to impossible. Justice Besanko was opposed to a preponderance of video hearings and staggered sittings. Hard borders limited the availability of the many interstate witnesses, because quarantine restrictions might prevent them from returning to their home states after they had given their testimony.

Witnesses based in Afghanistan were at greater risk. Nicholas Owens pointed out that they might not be available at all in the future, given the rapidly deteriorating security environment. So there was a lot of anxious waiting in both hemispheres.

Three weeks later, witnesses secreted in a Kabul safe house were told the Australian court would resume to hear their evidence, via videolink.

CHAPTER 59

GOOD LUCK WITH THAT!

Nick and I occasionally encountered an attitude that anything the Afghans said counted for naught.

In Afghanistan, the 'true special warriors', as some in the SAS saw themselves, were at times less than vigilant in covering their tracks. The presumption that no one would bother to come and ask the locals what had happened annoyed me. So too the 'good luck with that' scorn, emanating from some in the Roberts-Smith camp in response to the suggestion that illiterate Afghan villagers might give believable evidence in an Australian court.

To be fair, that view was probably widely shared. As Nicholas Owens SC put it, 'The more a person is "like you", the more likely you are to perceive them to be telling the truth.' And here were witnesses who could hardly be more 'different', in 'customs, language, religion and manners'.

As Western forces withdrew from Afghanistan and the Taliban closed in on Kabul, our senior counsel continued to press for an urgent sitting. Counsel for Ben Roberts-Smith expressed 'studied neutrality' regarding resumption; however, they did note that the rising Covid numbers in New South Wales raised concern about 'the public health aspects of such a hearing'.

On Monday, 19 July 2021, Justice Besanko set a start day for a limited hearing, beginning one week hence.

The logistical challenge was breathtaking. The witnesses were in a small law office in Kabul, with sound and vision beamed to a reduced court sitting in Sydney. In the middle, another world away, was a court-qualified Pashto translator in Ottawa, Canada. As far as we knew, this would be a world first: a court sitting conducted contemporaneously across three continents.

Mohammed Hanifa, in an olive tunic and black waistcoat, was first. The 28-year-old started with his background: 'I haven't lived anywhere else other than Darwan.' He had grown up with Ali Jan, his 'stepmother's brother'. He described the father of three as living a subsistence life, farming, selling wood and living two hours away at Baag. Ali Jan was not Taliban, not a 'fighter for anyone'.

Hanifa's introduction to the fateful events of 11 September 2012 was when he learned of a $500 reward that was being offered by the foreigners for information about the rogue Afghan soldier Hekmatullah. When the helicopters arrived that morning, he and Ali Jan began to move their tethered donkeys, but when shots were fired, they returned to the makeshift accommodation they referred to as the guesthouse, and tied them up.

He said soldiers wearing face paint and accompanied by a military dog found them, tied their hands behind their backs and bashed Hanifa's head against a wall. They were taken into the house of a neighbour, Mangul, where a 'big soldier' appeared before them. He was 'wet up in his chest area' and 'there was sand from the river on his uniform'.

An interpreter questioned them. Hanifa said the big soldier kicked him 'hard' in the abdomen. Then they were marched, manacled, outside. Hanifa was told to look the big soldier in the eyes. At this point Ali Jan laughed, perhaps a nervous reaction, and Hanifa told him not to, because the soldiers did not like it. The big soldier came to Ali Jan, who, with his hands tied behind his back, looked directly back—and again smiled.

Wali Shearzad, the Ottawa-based translator, told the court what Hanifa said he then saw: 'And [the big soldier] kicked him really hard and then he fell on his back.' Hanifa gestured the lowering of his head to indicate watching him fall. He said he then saw Ali Jan 'rolling down, rolling down until he reached the river'. And then a gunshot.

When the soldiers left, Hanifa went to Mangul's daughter to have his hands untied. It was a short walk down to the river, following a blood trail to Ali Jan's body.

Bruce McClintock SC challenged Mohammed Hanifa: 'Everything you've said about the events of the day in question is a fabrication, isn't it?'

Hanifa: 'No.'

'You actually didn't hear any gunshots that day, did you?'

'Of course, I heard them.'

On the following day, it was the turn of his neighbour, Mangul Rahmi, to face the camera and to participate in this curious foreign rigmarole. He recalled the same circumstances of the soldiers' arrival. He was acutely aware of the soldiers' dog being released, because it bit him. He saw Hanifa and Ali Jan outside, facing into the cliff and with their backs to the drop below. He had been grabbed by the neck and frogmarched to sit with Hanifa and Ali Jan. He remembered the interpreter interrogating them.

When the soldiers left, he found Hanifa and asked him about Ali Jan. Mangul was told what had happened. He headed down to the river and found Hanifa's sister there, crying under the berry tree beside the deceased Ali Jan. The Canadian translator provided Mangul's words to the court: 'He was lying on his back. He was shot.' He described Ali Jan's wounds, to his head and chest.

Mangul was shown a photo from the sensitive site exploitation evidence. He recognised Ali Jan and saw the Icom radio.

Owens asked: 'Did you see Ali Jan that day carrying a radio like that?'

The interpreter relayed Mangul's reply: 'No. He doesn't even know how to operate, how to work out a watch.'

Mangul's credibility as a witness was challenged.

Bruce McClintock: 'You do believe that the foreign soldiers whom you encountered in Darwan are infidels, don't you?'

Mangul: 'Yes.'

The common plight was revealed of rural Afghans trapped between a Taliban they feared and an alliance of government and foreigners they mistrusted. Mangul admitted his hatred for the cruelty of foreign soldiers: 'Yes, they killed innocent people. They murdered them.' But he denied his support for the insurgency. 'I do not agree with the Taliban. The Taliban have done injustices to us, and the foreigners have also done injustices to us.'

As July wound to a close, the security situation in Afghanistan further deteriorated. There was fear the hearings could not be sustained because of persistent power failures throughout Kabul. Fighting there prevented Bora, a prospective female witness from Darwan, from entering the capital.

On Friday, 30 July, the last witness, Shahzada Aka, Hanifa's father and Ali Jan's brother-in-law, took his seat. He too spoke of the arrival of the soldiers with painted faces; he recalled one of them who was tall and who, when standing above a steep slope, ordered Ali Jan to stand.

Nicholas Owens: 'And did you see what happened?'

The translator relayed the answer: 'Ali Jan's hands were tied up, and they made him stand up. Ali Jan was facing the soldier, and then the soldier kicked him, and he went down.'

There was divergence. Shahzada recalled the tall soldier speaking Pashto, while the other witnesses had remembered all communication being via the interpreter. Shahzada conceded he did not see the big soldier fire shots.

All witnesses were pressed regarding the money they had received from Nine to cover their travel, rent, flour, tea and medical expenses. They were questioned about possible financial compensation for them from the Afghan Human Rights Commission. The witnesses denied being motivated to speak for any reason other than to honour the truth.

We say in journalism that over time we develop a talent for detecting the truth. This is not the result of some mystical awakening; it comes more from just plain experience. Thousands of conversations processed; falsehoods sifted; objective facts prioritised; absorbing not only what is said but the way it is said.

Bruce McClintock's rigorous questioning was reasonable and justifiable as a professional testing of the evidence, but it prompted passion—and, for me, that gave credibility to the testimony of these witnesses. After repeated assertions that he was telling lies, Hanifa, in exasperation, responded: 'Look, brother . . . I am a witness. I am not afraid of anybody. Even if I die, I will tell the truth. This is the Pashtun tradition.'

Our team got the sense he thought he was under a moral duty to tell the truth, no matter the consequences to himself.

In the Sydney courtroom, we thought it went well, again more down to the detail. The witnesses were correct in describing the arrival of the helicopters, the presence of a military dog and their attendance (denied by Roberts-Smith) in the last compound. Most important were critical details that perfectly aligned with accounts by Australian witnesses.

But it's fair to say the other side were probably also feeling good. Judging by the demeanour of opposing counsel, the evidence by Shahzada that Roberts-Smith had spoken Pashto was seen as a big win, destroying his credit as a witness.

All in all, given the momentous obstacles, there was enormous relief that the evidence of these men had now been secured.

When Australia abandoned Uruzgan Province in 2013, it was sometimes said that at least we'd given them hope. Two weeks after the evidence from these Uruzgan villagers was beamed into an Australian courtroom, Taliban fighters were photographed reclining in triumph in Kabul's abandoned Presidential Palace.

It was a dispiriting sight for all who had hoped for a better Afghanistan. The scenes of panicked evacuation were hard to watch. We feared for the safe return to Darwan of the witnesses. And we took comfort from the prospect that our trial had set free an important truth from these denigrated Afghan witnesses, a truth that had come close to being obscured.

After Justice Anthony Besanko thanked the Kabul lawyer and the Ottawa translator for their expertise, patience and professionalism, the parties in Australia withdrew for what would become an even lengthier adjournment.

CHAPTER 60

PROTECTION RACKET

In November 2021, Omicron replaced the Delta strain of Covid-19 as the dominant cause of global infection. In Australia, border closures had not eased. Moving the trial to another state was debated but, given the delay relocation would impose and the uncertainty anyway about whether this would improve witness access, it remained anchored in Sydney. Justice Besanko set a case management hearing for December in the hope that the trial might resume in the new year.

Against this coughing chorus of case numbers, the war crimes saga proceeded on two further fronts.

PR jousting broke out in the second half of 2021. The Defence department had released in 2010 a photo of Ben Roberts-Smith in combat kit in action in Afghanistan. The Nine newspapers revealed that the original picture had shown a Crusader's cross sewn on the chest of his tunic, but Defence Media had airbrushed it out. Bearing an anti-Muslim symbol in a Muslim country was described by Australia Defence Association executive director Neil James as 'exceptionally dumb.'[1]

Soon after, the *Daily Mail* countered with a spread of photos featuring Ben's nemesis, The Veteran, cavorting in his underpants with an alleged swastika hanging from his neck. It was in fact an Iron Cross from the time of World War I, which had been captured from a German soldier by The Veteran's great-uncle, and which he'd worn in Afghanistan as a good luck charm. However, in the feature, when the *Daily Mail* enlarged the Iron Cross, it had been altered to become a swastika. After a complaint, the *Daily Mail* removed the article from its website, but continued to defend its reporting.

The Veteran had previously been the target of a December 2020 leak of embarrassing photos to *The Guardian*. This time he was described in the *Daily Mail*'s updated report as the '"chief source" of war crimes allegations against Ben Roberts-Smith'.[2] This was false, and The Veteran would not be called to give evidence in the defamation trial.

The next battlefront was an all-out assault on Justice Paul Brereton's recommended reforms. At the end of July 2021, the Afghanistan Inquiry Reform Plan was released. Referring to the IGADF's report of eight months earlier, it confirmed: 'Defence has accepted all findings and is addressing recommendations.'

But, as had previously happened with the overturning of the proposal to rescind the Meritorious Unit Citation, defence minister Peter Dutton was listening to critics who thought Brereton had overreached.

By the latter half of 2021, scandal fatigue had penetrated deep into the sacrosanct ranks of special forces. The impact of the Roberts-Smith defamation proceedings, of the ABC's reporting, and of the release of Mark Willacy's book *Rogue Forces*, on top of Afghanistan having fallen to the Taliban, combined to sap energy from the ADF's intention, previously expressed, to fulfil its 'duty to set things right'.

The Daily Telegraph joined the *Daily Mail* in announcing a backdown. The Sydney tabloid, claiming 'lives ruined by war crimes inquiry', reported: 'Thirteen soldiers from the Special Air Service given notices to show cause why they should not be dismissed after the Brereton report came out have now been told there is not "sufficient information" for their cases to be referred to investigators.'[3]

A range of publications also falsely asserted that some of those accused of war crimes had been cleared and deployed to Afghanistan for the August evacuation. Talkback fulminations extracted an apology from Peter Dutton. The defence minister told Sydney radio station 2GB's Ray Hadley: 'If people have been wrongly accused and they've now been cleared of that, then I do apologise for what they've been through and what their families have been through.'[4]

Nick McKenzie responded in *The Age* with an unmasking of the misinformation campaign:

> By June this year the Army had issued 17 notices that required special forces soldiers to 'show cause' as to why they should not be sacked. But 13 of these 17 had already been discharged on health and other grounds. Of the four remaining soldiers issued notices, two are reservists (one is serving with the UAE armed forces). Of the 17, this masthead confirmed only one soldier remains on active duty with the SAS in Perth.[5]

Nick quoted the Australia Defence Association chief executive, who had called out the propaganda: 'Neil James describes their contentions as "bullshit" guided by powerful individuals who have an interest in eroding public and political will for ongoing war crimes probes.'[6]

As James suggested, it was not only tabloid hecklers resisting reform. The SAS had top-shelf support. Its members had over many years provided protective security for politicians travelling abroad, and through that experience had forged useful political ties. And plenty in Canberra's security industry had the SAS brand stamped somewhere in their curriculum vitae.

On 1 September 2021, the *Herald Sun* announced, under the headline 'A good day for the SAS', that the assistant defence minister, Andrew Hastie, had unwrapped a present. On the eve of the regiment's 57th birthday, Hastie announced that his old regiment would have its command structure elevated. A full colonel, rather than a lieutenant colonel, would take its command, 'to ensure sufficient capacity and appropriate oversight for the complex missions SASR is expected to perform in the future'.[7]

Andrew Hastie recognised the need for reform, but his loyalty to his old regiment was clear. The full colonel status was sold as a means of improving accountability—but, equally, it was seen as further evidence of exceptionalism. No other regiment, not even the Commandos, has a full colonel as boss.

On the east coast, the rival 2nd Commando regiment was seriously pissed off. They had emerged from the Brereton inquiry with a cleaner slate and probably with expectations of the parity they had always yearned for. David Irvine, a former ASIO director-general, having conducted a review, had recommended joint selection and training of special forces. This mirrored Canadian and UK initiatives and was aimed at helping 'establish at an early age personal relationships spanning the current regimental divide'.[8]

What resulted instead was duelling directors-general. David Irvine's recommendation of joint selection was scrapped by Peter Dutton, with the support of another former director-general of ASIO, Duncan Lewis. Major General Lewis (ret) was quoted as asserting that it was vital 'the people coming into the unit [SAS] meet the professional and moral standards that the unit demands ... The Special Forces organisations that I know best are all in control of their own selection processes.'[9]

Duncan Lewis, a former national security adviser, became the newly anointed Honorary Colonel of the SASR, his old regiment. Many a rival Commando saw the selection reversal as 'the SAS brand being protected at all costs'.

A recommendation that Ben Roberts-Smith's old 2 Squadron be disbanded was also contested, particularly by former members. Audie Moldre, an SAS Vietnam veteran, called it 'a symbolic sham: an act of ritualised hypocrisy, emboldening our enemies who already see the West as weak and divided. It would run a dagger through the heart with all who have served with pride and sacrifice in 2 Squadron SASR.'[10]

But on this score, the ADF held its nerve. As it turned out, a planned flag-folding ceremony to coincide with the regiment's birthday was not canned; rather, it was postponed. Covid restrictions were cited as the cause. The prospect of angry and visible protest might also have advanced a mood for discretion, that better part of valour.

November 2021 was twelve months on from the Brereton report and three months out from the trial resumption. A senior officer working on the Afghanistan Inquiry Reform Plan told me, 'The general mood [among high-ranking defence officers] is that it has been squibbed.'

As for our team, we approached Christmas holding to a hope the neutrality of the court would resist a similar loss of heart for getting to a difficult truth.

CHAPTER 61

'I KNOW WHAT I SAW'

At various Christmas functions through December 2021, media colleagues quizzed me about our chances. While I privately fretted, I would of course tell them we aimed to win. In turn, when I asked for their view, the consensus appeared to be: 'It looks like Roberts-Smith is guilty, but you will probably lose.'

So I had mixed feelings as the resumption date approached. We had witnesses who would give strong evidence, but there was lingering uncertainty about how forthcoming they would be, and how well they would cope in the witness box. We also had new evidence of more alleged murders, but it would not be heard. The court was not going to allow the eternal amendment of defences; nor was the marshalling of witnesses getting easier.

—

Wednesday, 2 February. On the train in, an N95 mask and a rapid antigen test. Same court configuration, but we had moved three floors up to the 21st. We needed a strong start, and we hoped we had found it with The Cyclist (Person 41). Nick McKenzie and I knew of him, rather than knew him.

The PAP notices had helped our lawyers open the first door to co-operation with some new potential witnesses. The next step had been to obtain the contact details of the lawyers of those witnesses we intended to subpoena; those were provided to us by Commonwealth solicitors, who did not want us to make direct contact with these people.

In the case of The Cyclist, for example, Dean Levitan had been able to speak to his Melbourne lawyer, Jack Tracey, and make the case that it was in his client's interests to confer with us ahead of the trial. A Zoom video conference followed, which helped our lawyers compile a 'proof of evidence' statement. From this we knew The Cyclist could provide critical eyewitness evidence about the events of Easter Sunday 2009.

When The Cyclist entered the witness box, we saw a man in his late 40s with a tinge of grey hair. Not exactly at home in his dark suit, he was also wearing a white business shirt and red striped tie. A keen cyclist, he was working on recovering some of the fitness he'd had thirteen years earlier, when his troop had made the danger-charged daylight approach to Whiskey 108.

As he told it, there had been an overcast sky that day and menacing atmospherics, with both the weather and the enemy manoeuvring. Five patrols had been spread out; The Cyclist's patrol, led by The Freefaller, was in the centre. The Scot's patrol, which included Ben Roberts-Smith and The Gunsmith, was to the left. They patrolled past the dead man, who had been shot by The Scout, and threaded cautiously through the rubble caused by the earlier bomb strike. Once inside Whiskey 108, they began the clearance process. Women and children were moved to safety.

The Cyclist gave his evidence with composure—he was steady and sure. He referred to Ben Roberts-Smith, who was seated in the opposite corner of the courtroom, as 'RS'. He recalled having seen RS and The Scot in the open courtyard. He also recalled witnessing his patrol commander, The Freefaller, and The Hunter discover a tunnel.

Nicholas Owens SC's interrogation edged like a flame along a fuse towards the loaded question: had The Cyclist witnessed murder? But in anticipation of that, an exchange played out that we would come to see many times. The Cyclist's lawyer, Jack Tracey, was on his feet, objecting to his client being compelled to provide an answer that might expose him to prosecution.

The witness was asked to leave the court. Tracey contended there were reasonable grounds for the court to grant a certificate protecting The Cyclist against self-incrimination. The witness was recalled. Justice Besanko explained his willingness to provide the certificate and asked whether, in that circumstance, The Cyclist was prepared to give evidence. He answered, 'Yes.'

The Cyclist explained he had been searching two compound rooms when he heard a commotion outside. Investigating, he saw Ben Roberts-Smith and The Gunsmith; squatting behind them was an Afghan male, whom The Cyclist believed was one of two men who had been hauled from the tunnel.

The Cyclist told the court that RS and The Gunsmith approached him. Roberts-Smith said, 'Hey, Cyclist, can I borrow your suppressor?'

A suppressor (sometimes referred to as a silencer) can be fitted to a rifle to reduce noise and muzzle flash.

The Cyclist recalled: 'I thought [that] a bit of a strange request at first, but I complied. I removed the suppressor from my M4 assault rifle and handed it to The Gunsmith.'

As he watched his two comrades walk towards the Afghan, a thought zipped through The Cyclist's mind: 'I think I know what's about to happen here.'

'RS then walked down and grabbed the Afghan male by the scruff of the shirt, picked him up, marched him a couple of metres forward . . . he then kicked him in the back of the legs behind the knees until he was kneeling in front of The Gunsmith. He pointed to the Afghan and said to The Gunsmith, "Shoot him." And as he said that and he stepped to the side, I didn't wish to witness what was about to happen and I stepped back into the room.'

Even so, he could not miss the sound of a single muffled round. When the suppressor was returned to The Cyclist and he refitted it to his M4, 'it was warm'. The Cyclist saw the Afghan man on the ground, lying on his back, 'shot once in the head'.

The lunch break interrupted a transfixing narrative. The witness was isolated. He was provided with sandwiches and fruit juice. It was the first day of the telling of our story, and so far it was going well.

We resumed at 2.15 pm. Nicholas Owens SC took the witness to the fate of the second man we alleged had been dragged from the tunnel and 'frogmarched' outside the compound.

The Cyclist: 'I turned to face RS to see what was happening. He then proceeded to throw the Afghan male down onto the ground; the man landed on his back. RS then reached down, grabbed him by the shoulder, flipped him over onto his stomach and then I observed him lower his machine gun and shoot approximately three to five rounds into the back of the Afghan male.'

The Cyclist said Roberts-Smith, knowing he had witnessed the execution, asked: 'Are we all cool? Are we good?' To which The Cyclist had replied, 'Yeah, mate, no worries.'

Turning to my left, I glanced towards the tall, besuited VC, MG. It was hard to gauge his reaction behind his black facemask. Roberts-Smith looked down at his phone and began to text.

In journalism we try to ask no more questions than are needed. No point in exhausting the interviewee. The unnecessary, which will have to be processed alongside the necessary, bleeds time and breeds confusion. Owens appeared to think the same. He was pointed and efficient in both cross-examining and leading evidence from our witnesses.

The Cyclist was shown photos and identified the victims as those he saw shot. He was asked about an encounter after the shootings with The 2IC, who queried what had happened to the men taken from the tunnel. The Cyclist related having told him, 'No, mate, I don't know.' He explained to the court the 'unwritten rule' about keeping quiet. '[I] figured it wasn't my business . . . I was a new trooper. My very first trip with the SAS . . . I just wanted to toe the line . . . You just go along with whatever happens.'

And so ended The Cyclist's evidence in chief.

Bruce McClintock SC was momentarily benched. It was his colleague, Arthur Moses SC, who would cross-examine The Cyclist for the rest of the afternoon and most of the following day.

Moses' first questions were about The Cyclist's impending medical discharge from the Army due to physical injuries. The Cyclist revealed that he had consulted a psychiatrist but had not been diagnosed with PTSD; he did not take prescription drugs, nor consume illegal substances.

He agreed he did not report the shootings, either in theatre or on his return to Australia—in keeping with that 'unwritten rule' of 'playing the team game'. For this, there was a practical explanation: dob in a mate and you would lose the trust of your colleagues, you would not get the interesting jobs and your career would be effectively sidelined.

The Cyclist said he had 'no issues' with Ben Roberts-Smith; he regarded him as a good and brave soldier, who could be relied upon to have his comrades' backs.

Arthur Moses took him to other relationships—with Roberts-Smith's perceived enemies. The Cyclist said he knew The Sergeant and The Scout, but he'd had no contact with them in years. He said The Veteran had visited his workplace at Swan Island, in Victoria, but they had not discussed Roberts-Smith. He accepted Moses' propositions that The Sergeant had a 'deep dislike' for Ben, and that The Veteran was a 'hater'. The Cyclist said he did not wish to speak with either of them because he suspected they 'may have gone to the media'.

The Cyclist admitted to drinking 'on numerous occasions' from the prosthetic leg retrieved from the man he saw machine-gunned to death, and said he later felt shame at having done so.

His account of lending his suppressor to The Gunsmith was dismissed as implausible. After all, why wouldn't The Gunsmith use his own suppressor? Why would it be needed, given the less-than-secretive nature of the shooting?

Arthur Moses took him to the discovery of the tunnel. 'And is it the case that you were scared when you looked down at the tunnel?'

The Cyclist: 'Well, I didn't want to go down there, no.'

This minor confession led to a major accusation of shame, cowardice and epic deceit. Ben Roberts-Smith's counsel contended that The Cyclist's fear of going into the tunnel turned to shame, which somehow motivated him to lie about the murder of the two Afghans.

Moses: 'And you left The Freefaller and The Hunter there, without you there, correct?'

The Cyclist: 'Correct.'

Moses: 'You did not have their back?'

The Cyclist: 'I didn't believe they needed it at the time. There were other areas needing to be cleared.'

Moses: 'On this day, 12 April 2009, in which you saw other members of your patrol engage in heroic acts, you were scared?'

The Cyclist: 'No, I don't recall seeing any heroic acts on that day by members of my patrol.'

Moses: 'See, isn't it the case that you've been lying to yourself about what happened that day in order to cover up for the fact that you were scared and walked away from backing up The Freefaller and The Hunter?'

The Cyclist: 'No, that's incorrect.'

Moses: 'The story that you've told to the court about what you say happened on 12 April is to assuage your own feelings of guilt about the fact you were unable to cut it that day?'

The Cyclist: 'That's untrue. I have no feelings of guilt.'

Watching on, up the back of the courtroom, I took in the effort by Roberts-Smith's senior counsel to connect a spurious accusation of cowardice with a lie that would condemn a respected comrade. There was no logical reason for The Cyclist to lie, to trespass beyond the boundary of his own 'unwritten rule'. And I could not see Arthur Moses coming close to succeeding in his attempt to undermine this important testimony. The witness, steady and dispassionate, countered every accusation of dishonesty with a measured, 'I know what I saw.'

It was an early finish that day. As the departing silks and their respective entourages converged in the corridor, conversation was muted. Too many inquisitive ears. It was not until we were across the street and settled in Nicholas Owens' chambers that dialogue unlocked. I heard our barristers—Owens, Lyndelle Barnett and Chris Mitchell—concur: 'The perfect first witness.'

Bruce McClintock SC had contended in his opening address that the case against Ben Roberts-Smith was built on the collusion of jealous rivals and credulous journalists. Yet this first witness to two murders had not been linked to Ben's detractors, and had had no contact with Nick McKenzie or me. Indeed, when asked about my book, *No Front Line*, The Cyclist said: 'I started reading it, but it got too much, so I put it down . . . I didn't find it a good read.' (The only apparent flaw in his testimony, I thought.)

News coverage was generally fair in its representation of The Cyclist's evidence. But *The West Australian* was sceptical. Its headline: 'SAS trial hears witness is a liar who drank out of dead man's leg'.[1]

CHAPTER 62

THE GREATER SIN

We owed The Scout. Eager for another strong witness, we asked if he would endure not only opening salvos from hostile lawyers but also extensive and expensive quarantine requirements that would absent him from his home and family for weeks.

The ongoing Covid pandemic continued to escalate costs. There were travel and accommodation expenses for both our witnesses and their legal counsel. In some cases we met these expenses also for the partners of witnesses.

On Friday, 4 February 2022, The Scout was delivered to the court. The protected identity status of SAS witnesses meant transfer by Commonwealth car from their hotel to the underground car park of the court. Then skyward in a private lift, bypassing the snapping horde of media outside.

At the first session, the question of 'blooding rookies' was raised, in tandem with the familiar issue of ensuring the witness understood his legal rights. The Scout's barrister, Glenn Cridland, had flown in from Western Australia. He made a submission for a certificate protecting his client against self-incrimination, which was granted.

The Scout recalled a meeting in 2009 at Troop Headquarters in Camp Russell, where he overheard The Scot, in Ben Roberts-Smith's presence, declare: 'I'm going to blood the rookie.' This was before the Whiskey 108 mission, which The Scout went on to describe in what seemed to me like cinematic detail.

As I have already noted, he is a gifted storyteller. Anyone with an interest in infantry minor tactics could have done worse than be in court that day. His testimony was modest and matter-of-fact. As his patrol's scout, he led the broad daylight walk-in to an insurgent stronghold. Cold, a drizzle of rain, poppies two metres high, handrailing over makeshift bridges, muddy underfoot. It had crossed his mind that he might be wounded or killed, but 'that comes with the job'.

'I took a knee at a tree which was roughly in line with Whiskey 108,' he related. Covering his comrades, he trained his weapon on movement he had seen. It was an Afghan, carrying something. If the man moved towards the patrol, he was a threat. 'As he was turning and observing the troop, I engaged him.' Two rounds. The man was killed.

The Scout used the scope on his M4 to scan the compound. He made a radio call: no fighting-age males, just women and children. Two patrols, led by The Scot and The Freefaller, entered to undertake the compound clearance. The Scout explained to the court that he had remained outside the compound with the rest of his patrol to provide cover.

He watched. There was silence. And then:

'As I turned to my right . . . there was, like, three Australian soldiers, and a black object, which was, like, similar to a human . . . was thrown to the ground, and there was a thud . . . expulsion of air, when someone is kind of winded . . . and then a soldier raised their Minimi F89 Para and fired, like an extended burst.'

'BRRRR!' Loud. He makes the noise, sound effects thrown in. The court sits up. Even the unperturbable Justice Besanko raises his head.

The Scout was unable to identify the shooter. He said he later went to inspect the corpse and for the first time he saw the prosthetic leg.

The Scout explained that, in fading light, he set the route for the return slog, deploying night-vision goggles. When they arrived at the lying-up position, he heard The Scot say, 'I finally blooded the rookie.'

Nicholas Owens SC moved on to ask whether The Scout saw the prosthetic leg again later.

The Scout: 'Yes . . . it was in our party room, our pub, the Fat Lady's Arms . . . it ended up becoming a drinking vessel.'

Owens: 'And did you ever drink from it?'

The Scout: 'Yes.'

Owens turned to 12 October 2012 and Chinartu. This time The Scout was a member of Ben Roberts-Smith's patrol. Flying in on a US Blackhawk helicopter, they were in pursuit of a high-value Taliban target.

The assault had been carefully planned. However, on approach, he saw and heard Roberts-Smith turn and yell, 'Fuck the cordon! We will head straight for the VRI.'

The Scout was part of the team assigned to provide cordon security. VRI means 'very reliable intelligence', referring to the likely location of the target.

When they landed, The Scout continued, he saw Roberts-Smith and most of the rest of his patrol running towards a large compound. Seeing some Afghan males in a neighbouring compound, he moved towards them. As was standard operating procedure, he and another soldier, The Scientist, began to search these Afghans.

The PUCs were then moved to a tactical questioning (TQ) area. There he saw Roberts-Smith, his patrol commander, leading the tactical questioning, along with The Sniper, The Terp and partner force members, including The Lieutenant. An Afghan male faced them.

He then noticed 'a massive discolouration of the wall, like it had been recently plastered with mud . . . I gave it a kick or two and it just crumbled and disintegrated and there was a weapons cache.'

As combat engineers moved forward to secure the cache, The Scout said he noticed the mood change.

Owens asked what he heard, and requested that he try to use the actual words spoken.

The Scout: 'Mr Roberts-Smith said to The Terp, "Tell him"—pointing at the direction of The Lieutenant and his partner force—"Tell him to shoot him, or I will."'

The Scout said initially the interpreter 'stumbled', and Roberts-Smith repeated his order. And then:

'One of his men . . . I don't know who. He had a balaclava or recon wrap [camouflaged face cover] up around his nose . . . stepped out of the group of soldiers, trained his suppressed M4 on the Afghan man, and unloaded five to eight rounds . . . into this Afghan. He dropped.'

Next, Nicholas Owens took the witness to his final topic: the meeting at the East Hotel in October 2018, when Roberts-Smith had sought to dissuade him from giving evidence for Nine/Fairfax.

The Scout explained how Roberts-Smith showed him the Fairfax defence, which listed the Whiskey 108 and Chinartu allegations.

The Scout: 'I read it and a few minutes expired . . . I looked up at him . . . and I said, "Well, that's how I remember it."'

He recalled Roberts-Smith responding: 'So, it's going to be like that, is it?' And going on to say, 'Well, it's your word against The Sniper.'

The Scout described the meeting ending with him telling his former comrade, 'There's no way I am going to get up on a stand and lie, and I hope no one else does.' A massive pause, and Roberts-Smith's parting words: 'That's it, then.'

At 4.18 pm, for the final session of the day, Arthur Moses SC rose to cross-examine The Scout. His job: to undermine the witness's credibility.

It would be gruelling. First up was establishing The Scout's friendship with Roberts-Smith's nemesis, The Veteran, which was acknowledged.

Some dirt was thrown. Moses asked, 'Do you remember assaulting a female US soldier?'

The Scout responded, 'No, that's absurd.' Indeed, he said, it was the other way around: he recalled some trivial horseplay, which occurred in Roberts-Smith's presence, and confessed, 'I got towelled up that day.'

The Friday session ended before 5 pm, with The Scout consigned to 48 hours of soulless isolation.

Monday, 7 February. Day 26. Refreshed in a black suit, black shirt and grey striped tie, The Scout is back. At 10 am, as is the routine, he is asked about any outside contact over the weekend. He says he has spoken with his wife and lawyer, but that there was no discussion of his evidence.

On Whiskey 108, there was hair-splitting. Arthur Moses SC points to an inconsistency: in The Scout's written outline of evidence, he had referred to the object thrown to the ground and machine-gunned as 'dark'; in Friday's court testimony, it was 'black'. The Scout saw the depictions as 'synonymous'; when pressed, he settled on 'dark'.

Perhaps depending on what side of the court you were sitting in, the lengthy cross-examination this day was either meticulous or tedious. The Scout stood his ground and denied he had rehearsed his evidence. Moses challenged every detail.

Tuesday, 8 February, and we assemble again. The trolleys are hauled in. Forests of paper and volumes of patience. A long way yet for the trial and The Scout. Arthur Moses SC questions him about his attitude to Roberts-Smith's honours and awards.

He conceded that he had 'doubts' about Roberts-Smith having fairly earned the CDS and VC. He acknowledged he was not present for the VC action at Tizak, and that his opinion had been shaped by his discussion with teammates.

The cross-examination skipped back and forth over myriad topics. Once an answer was given, 'I'll come back to that' was frequently heard. It sometimes felt like the barrister was setting a trap. Unnerving, perhaps. But The Scout remained steady.

Moses returned to the 'dark object being thrown to the ground and machine-gunned': 'It didn't happen, correct?'

The Scout: 'No, that 100 per cent happened.'

Moses: 'You've made that up, haven't you?'

The Scout: 'One hundred per cent have not made that up.'

The prosthetic leg was reprised: 'And why did you drink from it?'

The Scout: 'It helped me decompress. Let off steam. Bond.'

To the discovery of the cache at Chinartu: 'If you kicked [the wall], it could have actually blown up the whole compound if there were explosives there, correct?'

The Scout accepted that he assumed there were explosives there, but that they were not primed.

Moses: 'Why do you think they weren't primed?'

The Scout: 'Well, why would an insurgent prime his own explosives in his own wall?'

Moses later ridiculed extensive details of The Scout's account of the alleged execution at Chinartu.

Moses: 'You have lied to the court when you said that Mr Roberts-Smith said to The Lieutenant, "Tell him"—pointing in the direction of The Lieutenant and his partner force—"Tell him to shoot him, or I will." That's a lie, isn't it?'

The Scout: 'No, it's not.'

Moses: 'You've made that up, haven't you?'

The Scout: 'No, he said it twice.'

Moses: 'You've lied, correct?'

The Scout: 'One hundred per cent I have not.'

At 10.16 am on Wednesday, 9 February, the cross-examination resumed. The Scout had previously well defended his account of what he had witnessed in Afghanistan, but on this day he was less successful in defending his contact with Nick McKenzie and me.

Ben Roberts-Smith's lawyers had a copy of a declaration The Scout had made to his regiment that he had had no contact with the media. This was now revealed as false. The Scout had not lied to the court, but—and we thought this forgivable—he had been less than honest with his chain of command. It was a turning point and, for us, not a good one. Justice Besanko ruled that The Scout was required to answer questions about his contact with journalists.

Roberts-Smith's lawyers went for the jugular, insisting they were 'not about hunting down sources' but testing the 'reliability' of the witness. For much of the day, The Scout was interrogated about our meetings.

He admitted to receiving an approach from me and attending the launch of *No Front Line*. He told the court of my intended second edition of the book and of our follow-up meeting in Canberra. He was quizzed on the detail of what he told me.

He was asked about his contact with Nick McKenzie and acknowledged a meeting. This took The Scout into hotter water. There was some justification for speaking with me, as my book project had been officially approved by the Army, but *The Age*'s investigative reporter, Nick, who was introduced to him by me, was another matter.

Arthur Moses called successfully for the notes of conversations between The Scout, Nick McKenzie and me. The proceedings then moved into closed court.

We ended the day despondent. The Scout had struggled to explain discrepancies between my notes and his evidence. While there was consistency for most of it, the few differences were seized upon. I felt for him and was angry with myself.

As I explained earlier, I do not use a recording device when interviewing sources. My background notes are raw and produced from memory; I always intend to confirm the details later. When I wrote up my conversation with The Scout, I did not expect that it would end up in court and he would have to answer for my inconsistencies.

My promise to him of source confidentiality—something all journalists hold sacred—was broken by a circumstance out of our hands. The feeling in our camp was that Justice Besanko's original ruling, providing us with source protection, had been outflanked. Our lawyers sought to offer me some comfort. 'Think of it as a game down, but a set to go,' I was told as we left the court.

The proceedings did not emerge from closed court until the afternoon of Thursday, 10 February.

The Scout is a fighter. He later revealed to our team that, while he was waiting in the anteroom, he reached within himself for even greater fortitude. He asked himself: 'What am I going to say when I am asked by my kids about this in twenty years' time?' And answered himself out loud: 'The fucking suppressor is coming off.'

Arthur Moses SC: 'You are a liar, aren't you?' The Scout was again being accused of dishonesty over what he saw at Whiskey 108 and Chinartu, as well as over his contact with Nick and me.

Back in 2018, when I typed up my notes, I interposed a presumption that at Whiskey 108 Ben Roberts-Smith carried an M14, and The Gunsmith a Minimi.

Moses: 'Did you tell Mr Masters that?'

The Scout: 'No.'

Moses: 'You were speaking rubbish to Mr Masters, weren't you?'

The Scout: 'One hundred per cent negative.'

He was repeatedly asked why in my notes I sometimes referred to Roberts-Smith as 'Achilles'.

Moses: 'Did you tell Mr Masters that Roberts-Smith's nickname in 2012 was Achilles?'

The Scout: 'No, Your Honour.'

Arthur Moses pressed.

The Scout: 'For the fourth time, Mr Moses, no.'

It was 3.45 pm when The Scout was finally relieved. From where we sat, he had pulled off an impressive, spirited recovery. It is always a risk keeping a witness too long in the box, and Roberts-Smith's lawyers might have made that mistake.

During The Scout's last day of evidence, Nick and I, watching on, wondered what might be regarded as the greater sin—the commission of a war crime, or contact with a journalist?

CHAPTER 63

'THE MOST BEAUTIFUL THING'

The Army's 'Contract with Australia' calls for a soldier to be 'an expert in close combat', to be 'physically and mentally tough' and to be 'courageous' and 'compassionate'.[1] Compassion is part of the ethos. One of the nation's most famous soldiers, Colonel Sir Edward 'Weary' Dunlop, saved countless lives while a prisoner of the Japanese during World War II.

There were many expressions of toughness, courage and combat expertise by Australian special forces in the soulless battlespace of Afghanistan. Given that, it is worth noting that many operators also managed to honour the totality of the contract, retaining empathy for their fellow human beings.

Our next witness was The Medic. He was a man of short stature. As he entered the witness box, the physical contrast to his former comrade, who was seated fidgeting in the opposite corner, was apparent. It was Friday, 11 February 2022.

Nicholas Owens SC took him back to 11 September 2012. The Medic remembered seeing Ben Roberts-Smith at Darwan: 'I seen him walking past me saturated from the waist down.' He also remembered shepherding a large 'PUC train', but nothing else of significance.

Owens then took him to Fasil on 5 November 2012. The Medic's evidence was consistent with what he had already told us. He told the court of intercepting a vehicle, removing four occupants, one a younger male 'shaking with terror'.

The four Afghans were handcuffed, and their Toyota Hilux searched. IED componentry was found. Ben Roberts-Smith and The Sniper escorted the frightened teenager and another Afghan male to a nearby compound for tactical questioning.

Under further questioning from Owens, The Medic told the court: 'So, about fifteen to twenty minutes after detaining or handing over the two PUCs that I placed under constraint to Ben Roberts-Smith's patrol, I heard a call go over the radio by Ben Roberts-Smith saying "two EKIAs" [enemies killed in action].'

The Medic was shown SSE photos of deceased Afghans.

Owens: 'Do you recognise the person in those photographs?'

The Medic: 'The person in these photographs looks like the young Afghan male I detained from the Toyota Hilux.'

Owens: 'Now, you will see that in these photographs, that the person is holding, or has an AK-47 variant weapon placed on their body. Do you see that?'

The Medic: 'Yes, I see that.'

Owens: 'Did the young Afghan that you detained from the Hilux have on him an AK-47 variant weapon?'

The Medic: 'No.'

After the now routine process of requesting and receiving a certificate protecting him from self-incrimination, The Medic agreed to answering further questions.

Owens asked about the encounter in the Camp Russell hallway with Ben Roberts-Smith a day or two later.

The Medic: 'So, I crossed paths with Ben Roberts-Smith, and I said to him, "What happened to that young fellow that was shaking like a leaf?" and he said to me, "I shot that cunt in the head." And he said, "[His superior] told me not to kill anyone on the last job, so I pulled out my 9-mill [pistol], shot the cunt in the side of the head, blew his brains out, and it was the most beautiful thing I've ever seen."'

The Medic told Owens of his shock at the response, and his subsequent silence on the matter. Owens asked why.

The Medic: 'There was a code of silence in the regiment . . . I would have been ostracised. I also think that my personal safety would have been in danger by making such allegations against someone so influential.'

Ben Roberts-Smith, in his usual corner seat, was still and impassive. His lawyer Monica Allen moved back and perched beside him, whispering.

Owens went on to ask the witness of his recollection of Roberts-Smith's reputation before he, The Medic, joined the SASR.

The Medic: 'He had a reputation as being a no-nonsense individual who didn't suffer fools.'

Owens: 'After you were posted to the SASR, among the circles in which you moved at the time, did Mr Roberts-Smith have the same or a different reputation?'

The Medic: 'There were two camps, there were those for and those against. And those against see him as being someone who was belligerent, a bully. Yes, [he] would trash and tarnish others' reputations.'

One hour before the lunch break, the session moved to closed court. It resumed after 2 pm in open court, with Arthur Moses SC cross-examining.

Moses took The Medic back to the for and against camps. The witness identified individuals such as The Veteran and The Sergeant as opposed, and The Scot and The Sniper as Roberts-Smith supporters. He revealed that The Trooper had told him of Roberts-Smith's bullying. He acknowledged that he personally had never been treated poorly by Roberts-Smith; in fact, 'I actually admired some of his qualities'.

Arthur Moses' next tranche of questioning reached within, to what might have been seen as The Medic's soft centre.

Moses: 'Now, were there times when you felt upset as to the loss of human life in Afghanistan?'

The Medic: 'Yes.'

Moses: 'And were there times when you felt there were senseless deaths occurring in Afghanistan whilst you were there?'

The Medic: 'Yes.'

Moses: 'Did observing dead Afghans cause you any anguish or trauma?'

The Medic: 'It's never nice to see a dead person.'

The plaintiff's barrister went on to ask about flashbacks, about his psychological briefing on his return to Australia in 2012, and whether he had received ongoing mental health support and was currently on medication. The Medic answered yes to having received counselling and treatment for nightmares, but no to any continued use of medication.

Moses spent most of the afternoon taking The Medic in detail through what he had witnessed at Fasil. In particular, the barrister pressed him on how certain he was that the young man taken from the Hilux was the same person he had identified in the photograph.

Moses: 'Possible that it wasn't, do you accept that?'

The Medic: 'There's always a slight possibility.'

Moses then moved to questions about the witness's contact with Nick McKenzie, and his reading of our reporting.

Moses: 'And what I want to suggest to you is those articles have influenced your recollection of events; do you accept that?'

The Medic: 'No, because I was reading them, and I was astonished at their degree of accuracy.'

As to the meeting after the Fasil mission in the Camp Russell hallway, The Medic agreed that, when he questioned Ben Roberts-Smith about what happened to the young Afghan, he had 'had a strong index of suspicion that he had been killed'.

Moses: 'I'm not being disrespectful . . . but are you sure you're not just imagining this?'

The Medic: 'This conversation 100 per cent happened, and his reply shocked me to the core, and that's why I remember it.'

It was a late finish to a big week. When Ben Roberts-Smith rose to leave, he appeared agitated. In the courtroom after he completed his evidence, The Medic was greeted by our lawyers. He was emotionally exhausted. We were thankful and apologetic for putting him through such an ordeal.

His voice breaking, he told us of the inspiration he had drawn from those others who were also forced to reach for their moral courage. And of the relief that came from standing up to bullies.

CHAPTER 64

VALENTINE'S DAY

Ben Roberts-Smith's lawsuit against his former wife alleging that she had shared sensitive information was dismissed in January 2022. Less than a month later she appeared in court as our next witness. Day 31—Monday, 14 February—happened to be Valentine's Day.

Unlike the witnesses who had protected identity status, Emma entered the court through the public door and walked to the witness box, smart in a tailored black suit, with a white floral brooch and a Burberry handbag. She appeared frightened.

Heartbreaking. As I sat and watched, I thought: *This is why you don't sue for defamation*. The worst embarrassing details of what would normally be zealously guarded as private are on show to the world. Through the next two days, there would be plenty of tears.

Nicholas Owens SC started quietly. 'Could you tell His Honour your full name?'

Emma: 'My name is Emma Roberts.'

Owens: 'And you have previously been known by the name Emma Roberts-Smith?'

Emma: 'Yes.'

Owens moved to the warmer question of marital separation. 'Can I ask you in particular about the period from October 2017 to April 2018.

Were you separated, in the sense of not living together as a married couple, during that period?'

Emma: 'We were not separated.'

Emma was asked about the newspaper reporting of her husband's affair in August 2018. She told of Roberts-Smith requesting she participate in a photoshoot for *The Australian*, to counter the negative publicity about him. She explained how she agreed to participate despite not wanting to. She told of the 'PR person from Seven' counselling her about what to wear and to 'look sad'. Emma told the court how Roberts-Smith urged deceit about the separation.

Owens: 'Are you able to tell His Honour when and in what terms Mr Roberts-Smith asked you to lie?'

Emma: 'Yes. When he was standing in the bedroom that day and said that, if I didn't, I would lose them, and pointed to the children in the lounge room.'

There was further evidence about what Emma had overheard when Roberts-Smith communicated with his SAS support network, particularly The Scot and The Freefaller. She told of Roberts-Smith drilling and setting fire to his laptop, and of how she found the buried lunch box.

Emma: 'I picked it up, opened it, and there were several USBs double-bagged in snap-lock bags.' She told how the contents were copied and the lunch box reburied. The court was then shown the time-stamped photographs she took of disturbed earth in the garden after Roberts-Smith returned to the property, presumably to recover the cache.

Point by point, Owens took her through the detail of Roberts-Smith's purchase of stationery, his communications with the private inquiry agent John McLeod, and what she knew of the blackmail letters sent to The SSE.

Emma: 'He [Ben] said that John McLeod had driven over the border and posted them.'

The evidence in chief ended with a question about *The Guardian*'s coverage of Das Boot, the prosthetic leg turned drinking vessel, and the picture she had already seen on Roberts-Smith's laptop of The Scout and The Veteran drinking from it.

Owens: 'What did he [Roberts-Smith] say?'

Emma: 'He said, "Fuck them. They can take some of the pressure for once."'

Cross-examination began just before the lunch break. It was the turn of Bruce the Fearsome. At the Sydney bar, the otherwise charming McClintock SC has a take-no-prisoners reputation.

Addressing the witness as 'madam', he challenged Emma about the affidavit she swore in 2020, alerting her to inconsistencies with the testimony just given.

McClintock: 'When you signed this affidavit, on your evidence this morning you must have known this passage was false; that's correct, isn't it?'

Emma: 'No, it's not.'

And then came respite as the luncheon adjournment was called. Emma was escorted to one of our small briefing rooms on another level of the court building; our lawyers advised Nick and me to find somewhere distant, to avoid any risk of collusion or contamination (or any such appearance). Nick knew her better than me. I briefly met her only once, but I felt great admiration for her fortitude, both in being here and in facing all she had endured.

When she returned to the box, I saw soft, sad eyes. Her former parents-in-law were seated opposite, alongside her former husband. Once close, she and they were now a world apart.

McClintock sternly reminded her of accounts she gave before the estrangement, when the 'Leonidas' reporting was published in 2018. He pointed to a quote from 'one of your children': 'Why does Dad not smile anymore?'

Emma, sobbing. McClintock, sympathetic: 'Please forgive me . . . would you like a moment to compose yourself?'

Justice Anthony Besanko ordered a brief adjournment.

Ten minutes later, McClintock returned to the 2018 reporting: 'It must have been humiliating for both you and my client at the time?'

Emma: 'Yes.'

McClintock: 'People broke off friendships as the result of those articles, didn't they?'

Emma: 'Yes, they did.'

The questioning turned to when Roberts-Smith moved out, in January 2020, and a text message Emma had sent to her friend Danielle Scott.

McClintock: 'Could you read it out?'

Emma did so: '"I'm actually feeling so fucking angry today . . . I want to punch the fucking cunt in the face."'

More examples of Emma's anger were revealed. Picking up pace, McClintock's questions became steady and remorseless, like a pneumatic hammer. He queried her about the lunch box.

'In fact, I want to suggest to you that this entire story about discovering the lunch box is a fabrication, Ms Roberts. Do you agree with me or not?'

Emma: 'No, I do not agree.'

McClintock again: 'You fabricated the entire story to harm my client, didn't you?'

Emma: 'No, I did not.'

McClintock: 'And the reason was, by that stage, you had come to hate him, hadn't you?'

Emma: 'No.'

The Monday session closed. We had expected Emma Roberts would be in the box for two and a half days, but Bruce McClintock SC signalled he would require only a further hour.

Questioning resumed on Tuesday at 10.15 am. A now initiated Emma appeared fortified, more confident.

McClintock continued to probe the edges of her lunch box evidence, and queried her contact with Nick McKenzie and MinterEllison about their meeting to discuss her prospective subpoena.

McClintock: 'The real purpose was to pay out on your husband, wasn't it?'

Emma: 'No.'

Ben Roberts-Smith's barrister provided further examples of angry text messages.

McClintock: 'You see, what I want to put to you is, at that point in November 2020, you hated my client. That's right, isn't it?'

Emma: 'I was very frustrated in a very bitter divorce, yes.'

McClintock: 'You hated him, didn't you?'

Emma: 'I don't think I hate Ben, no.'

Bruce McClintock's querying of Emma Roberts' March 2021 contact with Nick McKenzie sought to establish that she had provided information for the *60 Minutes* report on the lunch box revelations of the following month. This was denied. McClintock asked whether Danielle Scott provided the material.

Emma: 'I am not aware.'

A little further on.

McClintock: 'You would like to see my client lose this case, wouldn't you?'

Emma: 'No.'

McClintock: 'In fact, you're here to inflict as much damage on him as you can?'

Emma: 'I hope Ben survives this nightmare.'

It was a powerful moment. That last sentence was expressed wearily but, for me, with conviction.

The *60 Minutes* report was screened to the court just ahead of the luncheon adjournment. I was surprised: reminding the judge of these assertions of Roberts-Smith's wrongdoing might not, I thought, be to the applicant's advantage. But then, I am not a lawyer.

Monday's anticipated further hour of cross-examination ran through to the Tuesday afternoon session. There was a brief re-examination by Nicholas Owens SC. And at 3 pm, Emma Roberts' ordeal was over.

Just watching her had been gruelling. The defamation court is sometimes referred to as a forum for hurt feelings, and today was no exception, with too often more losers than winners.

CHAPTER 65

TUNNEL VISION

Accomplished behind the wheel, we will call him The Driver. To the court, he was Person 42, another witness press-ganged to our cause via the PAP notices. Still serving as a warrant officer in the SASR, on 16 February 2022 he reported for duty to speak the truth—under subpoena.

A decorated veteran of multiple Afghanistan tours, The Driver fought in The Freefaller's patrol at the Battle of Tizak in 2010, and had also been with him at Whiskey 108 a year earlier.

As Nicholas Owens SC revealed through questioning, this placed The Driver at the forefront of the entry to the compound, and on the scene when an important discovery was made. The Driver recalled encountering women 'making a noise' and 'indicating to us there was something else'. This led the soldiers to the tunnel entrance, which had been 'covered with a mat' and 'some grass'.

Crucially, given Ben Roberts-Smith's testimony to the contrary, The Driver then saw Afghans emerge from hiding. 'They came out unarmed. They came out freely. They came out relatively quickly once given the command to come out, or hands up, whatever the command was we gave them.'

He described the Afghans as compliant when they were searched; The Driver himself had patted down one of the men. He was not sure about what happened to them after that.

———

This evidence in chief had been brief. For the cross-examination of military witnesses, the reservist RAAF Squadron Leader, Arthur Moses SC, was more often the chosen silk. His early questioning elicited acknowledgement from The Driver that over multiple Afghanistan tours he had searched not only Whiskey 108, but hundreds of compounds.

Moses: 'Without being impolite, what you're doing now is giving evidence based on how things usually happen, correct?'

The Driver: 'Correct.'

Moses: 'But sitting here today, you don't have a firm recollection of whether all members of the patrol were present at that time, correct?'

The Driver: 'Correct.'

The witness further accepted uncertainty about who discovered the tunnel.

Moses: 'Is the reason you are saying that . . . because you weren't there when the tunnel was discovered, were you?'

The Driver: 'No, that's incorrect.'

Further specifics about the tunnel's discovery were canvassed. Moses sought extensive details and then repeated his accusation that The Driver had not been present when the tunnel was discovered. They rallied back and forth, with The Driver repeating his rejection of this accusation.

An hour in, and the barrister appeared frustrated: 'Is the only thing you are certain about is that you're The Driver and you were at Whiskey 108? Is that the only thing you're sure about?'

Nicholas Owens objected, and Arthur Moses withdrew the question.

Roberts-Smith's silk then interrogated The Driver's evidence about an Afghan woman in the compound who had gestured to them. When The Driver began to answer, Moses interrupted him. Owens protested. His Honour, courteous and attentive, intervened: 'Please let him finish answering the question, Mr Moses.'

Arthur Moses continued to press The Driver on specifics. About the role of the Afghan woman in alerting them to the tunnel, about which patrol members had been present, about who was facing whom. The Driver was unsure about the details of the discovery. He thought it might have been The Freefaller who called the Afghans out of the tunnel but

Ben Roberts-Smith on Rotation XII, Afghanistan, on 6 April 2010. On his chest he bears a 'Crusader' patch, later photoshopped out when this image was released by Defence. (Australian Defence Force)

The Scot (Person 5) and Ben Roberts-Smith, his 2IC, led Gothic 5 in 2 Squadron's assault on the compound at Whiskey 108, Kakarak, on 12 April 2009. What happened there was hotly disputed. (Exhibit R4)

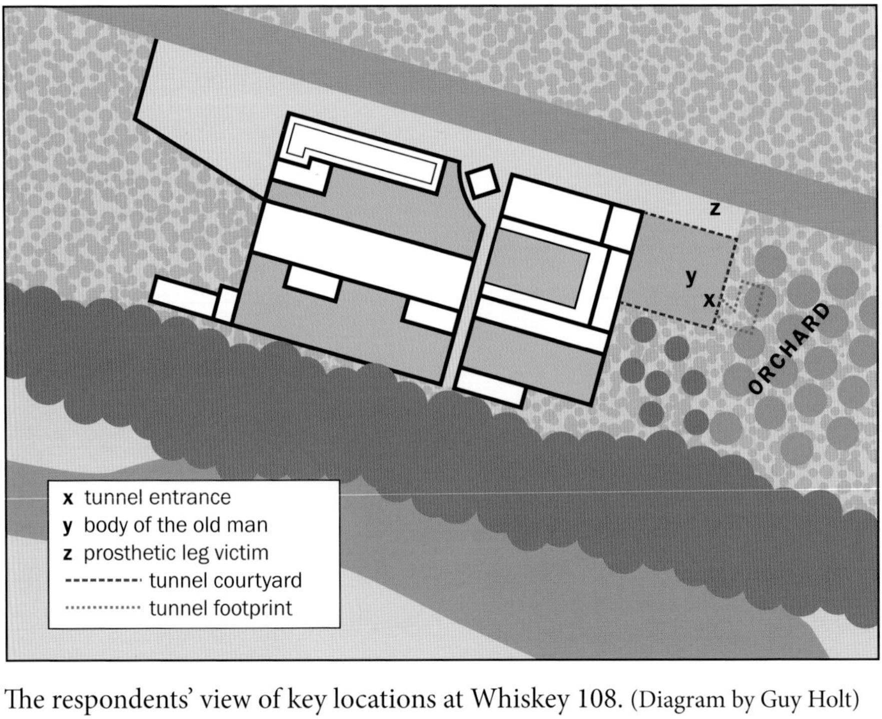

The respondents' view of key locations at Whiskey 108. (Diagram by Guy Holt)

The entrance to the tunnel at Whiskey 108, Kakarak. Witnesses for Ben Roberts-Smith said no men were found in the tunnel, while witnesses for the respondents saw two men extracted. (Exhibit R8)

Roberts-Smith with a US serviceman and the prosthetic leg, known as Das Boot, which was used as a drinking vessel at the Fat Lady's Arms. (Supplied)

Slain Taliban machine gunners after the Battle of Tizak, 11 June 2010; Ben Roberts-Smith was awarded the Victoria Cross for his actions in this battle. (Supplied)

The door of Roberts-Smith's 2010 patrol room at Camp Russell. On the sign, the names of four members have been replaced with court pseudonyms. Note 'Rookie Fuck' at bottom right. (Exhibit R210)

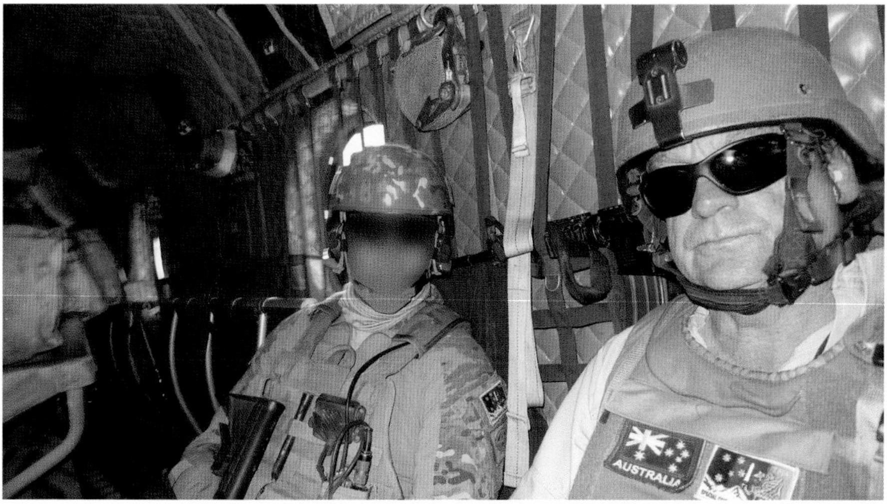

The author embedded with Australian special forces in Afghanistan in 2011.
(Chris Masters)

Following the awarding of the Victoria Cross, Corporal Ben Roberts-Smith attended Buckingham Palace to meet Queen Elizabeth II in November 2011.
(AFP/Getty Images)

Darwan, the site of the killing of Ali Jan Faqir on 11 September 2012. (Exhibit R2)

The cliff at Darwan is to the right of the man at the centre of the photograph. (Supplied)

The sign on Echo Troop's 2012 patrol room door at Camp Russell. The troop was sometimes referred to as Ego Troop. (Supplied)

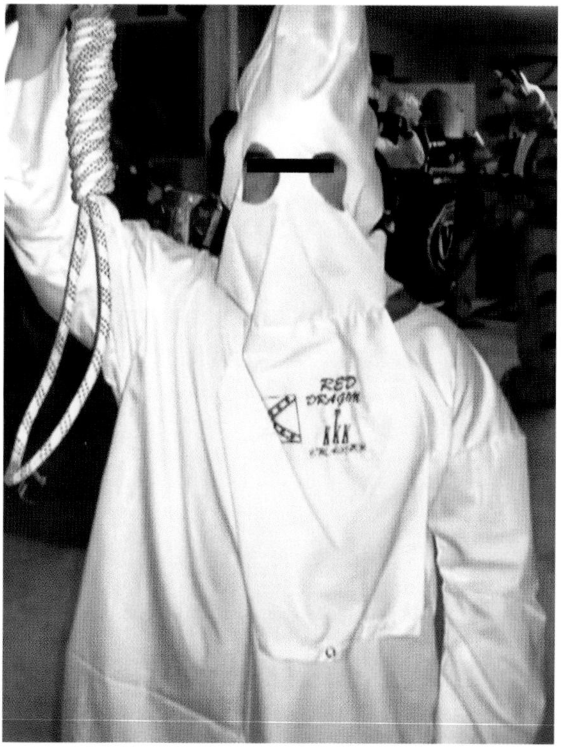

The Hunter (Person 35) in his Ku Klux Klan outfit at the Fat Lady's Arms. (Supplied)

Daniel Arzani is a teenager set to make World Cup history
DOMINIC BOSSI
SPORT

20-year-old Julia Cooney buys Sydney home for $8.7m
NEWS PAGE 16

ANTHONY BOURDAIN
Beloved TV host dead at 61
WORLD PAGE 20

Weekend

The Sydney Morning Herald

Issue No. 56,367 $4 (inc GST) INDEPENDENT. ALWAYS. June 9-10, 2018

HERALD INVESTIGATION

SAS's DAY OF SHAME

War crime allegations: bound detainee kicked off cliff and executed

EXCLUSIVE

Nick McKenzie
Chris Masters

An Australian special forces soldier kicked a handcuffed Afghan detainee off a cliff before endorsing his summary execution, according to allegations made by direct witnesses.

The case is one of two alleged executions involving a single Special Air Service Regiment soldier in late 2012, and which have been described in detailed testimony of first-hand witnesses.

Yesterday, the *Herald* published leaked details of a Defence Force inquiry from 2016 that described "unsanctioned and illegal application of violence on operations" and a "complete lack of accountability" involving some of Australia's elite special forces.

Federal Defence Minister Marise Payne has said the allegations of war crimes in Afghanistan are being "thoroughly examined", while Labor has demanded a confidential report containing the claims be made public.

The revelations are the first

Continued Page 10

An Australian Special Operations Task Group soldier in Afghanistan.
Photo: Australian Department of Defence

EXCLUSIVE

Get Real? Champs eye off Sydney

Champions League winners Real Madrid are eyeing off an opportunity to play in Sydney next year, but a major promoter says the NSW government has taken a "hiatus" from attracting major international sporting teams.
NEWS PAGE 9

EXCLUSIVE

Albo: People's Choice to lead

Friends say Anthony Albanese stands ready to lead as Bill Shorten fails to inspire people with Labor trailing in a number of seats for upcoming byelections.
NEWS REVIEW PAGE 21

EXCLUSIVE

NGA's ambitious new director

Nick Mitzevich says he wants to change everything in Australian art. Artist Bill Henson photographed the incoming director of the National Gallery of Australia for the cover of today's magazine.
GOOD WEEKEND + NEWS PAGE 17

EXCLUSIVE
$50m FOR GREAT NSW WALKS
NEWS, PAGE 2

Breaking the story on the front pages of *The Sydney Morning Herald* (SMH) and *The Age* newspapers on 9–10 June 2018. (Exhibit A2)

In August 2018, the front page of *The Australian* featured a staged photograph of Ben and Emma Roberts-Smith. (Exhibit R71)

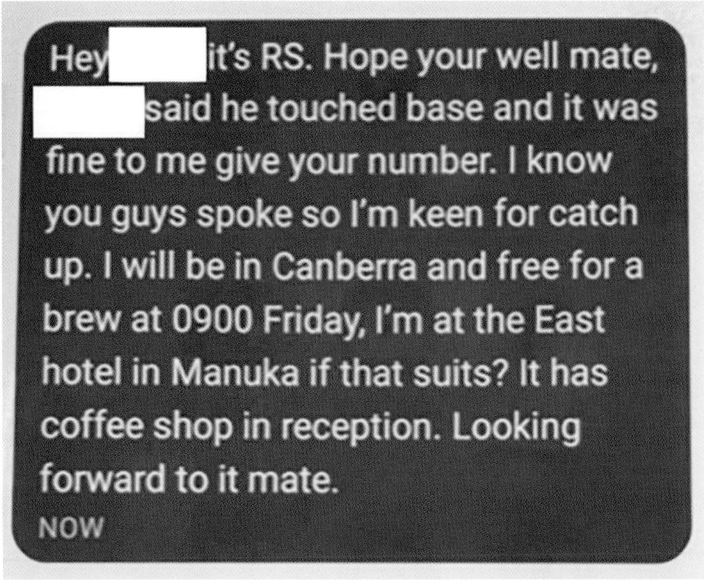

The text sent by Ben Roberts-Smith to The Scout (Person 14) on 17 October 2018. (Supplied)

The director of the Australian War Memorial, Dr Brendan Nelson, became an outspoken advocate for Ben Roberts-Smith. (Andrew Meares/SMH)

Chief of the Defence Force General Angus Campbell with Ben Roberts-Smith's employer and financial backer, Kerry Stokes. (Alex Ellinghausen/SMH)

The location of the lunch box buried in Ben Roberts-Smith's backyard and dug up by Emma and her friend Danielle Scott on 16 March 2020. (Exhibit R114)

Ben Roberts-Smith leaving court on day one of the trial, 7 June 2021, with one of the three senior counsels who represented him, Bruce McClintock. (Sam Mooy/Getty Images)

Ben Roberts-Smith had loyal supporters in his parents, Len and Sue Roberts-Smith, who were regularly in attendance at the court. (Janie Barrett/SMH)

Andrew Hastie, former SASR captain turned member of parliament, was an important witness for the respondents. (Supplied)

Arthur Moses SC (centre) was a lead counsel for Ben Roberts-Smith. He is flanked by solicitor Paul Svilans (left) and barrister Phillip Sharp (right). (Kate Geraghty/SMH)

Solicitor Monica Allen is questioned by Channel Seven reporter Chris Reason on her way to court. To her right is Seven's commercial director, Bruce McWilliam. (Janie Barrett/SMH)

Nicholas Owens SC was an eleventh-hour replacement as lead counsel for the respondents after Sandy Dawson SC became seriously ill. (Edwina Pickles/SMH)

Dinner to mark the end of the trial in July 2022. *Clockwise from front left:* Tess McGuire, Jeremy Forbes, Chris Masters, Peter Bartlett, Dean Levitan, Nicholas Owens SC, Chris Mitchell, Lyndelle Barnett and Sandy Dawson SC. (Courtesy Nicholas Owens/Tess McGuire)

Justice Anthony Besanko handed down his judgment on 1 June 2023. Afterwards, Chris Masters and Nick McKenzie spoke to the press. (James Brickwood/SMH)

The Sydney Morning Herald

Friday, June 2, 2023 **$4.00** (inc GST) | INDEPENDENT. ALWAYS. | First published 1831 No. 57,921

■ Roberts-Smith a war criminal ■ Defamation case thrown out ■ Appeal flagged

TRUTH WINS

Michaela Whitbourn, Harriet Alexander, Matthew Knott

A Federal Court judge has found decorated soldier Ben Roberts-Smith murdered four unarmed prisoners in Afghanistan, in a historic victory for the media outlets at the centre of his multimillion-dollar defamation suit.

In a landmark decision yesterday, Justice Anthony Besanko found *The Sydney Morning Herald*, *The Age* and *The Canberra Times* had proven Roberts-Smith was a war criminal who unlawfully killed and assaulted unarmed Afghan prisoners. Besanko also found the Victoria Cross recipient had bullied a fellow soldier.

He did not find the outlets had proven the former Special Air Service corporal committed an act of domestic violence against a lover, but in light of other proven allegations, Besanko found that allegation did not further harm Roberts-Smith's reputation and his case should be dismissed.

Roberts-Smith, who was photographed in Bali on the eve of the judgment, did not appear in court in Sydney yesterday. His barrister, Arthur Moses, SC, foreshadowed that his client may lodge an appeal.

James Chessell, Nine's managing director of publishing, said the decision was a vindication not only of award-winning investigative journalists Nick McKenzie and Chris Masters but the brave SAS soldiers "who served their country with distinction and then had the courage to speak the truth about what happened in Afghanistan".

McKenzie described the case as "the toughest fight of our journalistic careers" and said the decision marked "a day of some small justice for the Afghan victims of Ben Roberts-Smith". He paid tribute to the SAS soldiers who had testified and were vindicated by the result.

Masters said the newspapers made "a great call" in June 2018 to run the stories, and "I think it will go down in the history of the news business as one of the great calls".

Ben Roberts-Smith - pictured here in front of a portrait titled *Pistol Grip*, which hangs inside the Australian War Memorial in Canberra - unlawfully killed and assaulted unarmed Afghan prisoners. Photo: Jay Cronan

Roberts-Smith took leave from his role as general manager of Seven Queensland during the defamation case and remained on leave yesterday.

Seven West Media chairman Kerry Stokes, who bankrolled the lawsuit using private funds, said in a statement that "the judgment does not accord with the man I know".

"I haven't had a chance to have a discussion with Ben as yet, but I will when he has had a chance to fully absorb the judgment," Stokes said.

University of Sydney professor David Rolph, an expert in defamation law, said the decision marked "a comprehensive victory for the media outlets" and was "a vindication of the journalism in question".

"Defamation losses have a chilling effect for the media, particularly for serious investigative journalism," Rolph said. "This decision should give media outlets some confidence that they can undertake public interest journalism and prevail."

"Australia's defamation laws have a reputation for being plaintiff-friendly. This case shows that it is possible, sometimes, for publishers to prevail."

The war veteran's defamation trial was launched in 2018 against *The Sydney Morning Herald* and *The Age* owned by Nine, and *The Canberra Times*, now under separate ownership, and concluded in July last year after 110 days, 41 witnesses and more than $25 million in legal costs.

It is among the largest and most expensive defamation trials

Continued Page 2

WAR CRIMES 'TRIAL OF THE CENTURY' FULL COVERAGE

MATTHEW KNOTT

A reckoning just beginning

ANALYSIS **PAGE 4**

Blow for billionaire backer Kerry Stokes

Employer and key financial provider 'yet to speak' to former soldier.

NEWS **PAGE 2**

HARRIET ALEXANDER

Choosing Bali over courtroom

ANALYSIS **PAGE 3**

'You machine-gunned him'

Dean Tilley thought he would die in Afghanistan. Instead, he saw another man murdered, writes **Nick McKenzie.**

On a brisk spring morning in 2018, two special forces veterans of Australia's war in Afghanistan entered a busy Canberra cafe and, after pleasantries, began a grim-faced meeting. To the public servants sipping their coffees nearby, the pair would probably have stoked interest.

At 198cm, Ben Roberts-Smith, VC, was hard to miss. On the morning in question, Roberts-Smith was the most decorated Commonwealth veteran to have served in Afghanistan, an ex-soldier whose portrait hung in the nearby war memorial in testament to his status as the noble face of the conflict.

The war hero had also more recently intensified his very public campaign to clear his name of allegations detailed months earlier in the *Herald* that Australia's most revered military figure may also be a war criminal.

The meeting at the Muse cafe was part of a clandestine operation to prevent that truth coming out. It was aimed at ensuring none of his SAS comrades turned against him. Its genesis was a mission 10 years before, in a much more dangerous place.

FULL STORY **PAGES 6-7**

The Sydney Morning Herald

Verdict proof our work is essential

The *Herald* has prevailed in defending itself against the charge of defamation, but this case has still exacted a huge toll.

An Australian who received the highest military decoration our country can bestow, whose words and actions became part of the fabric of the Australian War Memorial, has been shown to have committed crimes in a war waged on our behalf. And in a distant land, fathers and sons have been cut down unjustly by foreign forces – our forces. EDITORIAL **PAGE 24**

1HERSA1 A001

The Sydney Morning Herald's front page the day after the judgment, 2 June 2023.

could be wrong. He was unclear on who pulled back the covering; this uncertainty took Roberts-Smith's barrister back to his central point: he refused to accept that The Driver had been present.

In the afternoon, after everyone returned from lunch, Arthur Moses pounced on The Driver's admission that he might have been wrong about The Freefaller doing the call-out. Then counsel wanted to know on how many missions The Driver had been involved in entering compounds. The Driver accepted that he could not put a number on that—but as to clearing tunnels, there had only been one occasion.

Moses: 'Okay. Is it possible there may have been more?'

The Driver: 'It's possible. We had cleared some other tunnel-like areas. I'm unsure when they were. But tunnels within a compound that had people in it, only one.'

Ten minutes into the afternoon session, Arthur Moses SC declared no further questions and thanked The Driver. Our solicitor Tess McGuire saw him to the secure exit. Back in our briefing room, as the team filed in, the chocolate box was raided and some words of praise spoken.

We saw The Driver as a strong witness on a range of counts. He stuck to no more than what he knew. He had not expressed a view about Ben Roberts-Smith. There was no clear alliance by him with any of Roberts-Smith's detractors, and he'd had no contact whatsoever with Nick McKenzie or me.

When Ben Roberts-Smith began his action, he must not have anticipated witnesses such as The Driver being called. There would be more.

CHAPTER 66

'A BULLET IN THE BACK OF THE HEAD'

Thursday, 17 February 2022, and public curiosity about the case is on the rise. As 10.15 am approaches, there is competition for the few remaining seats. Len Roberts-Smith is forced to move to the overflow room.

Five minutes later, The Redhead, the witness designated Person 1, took his seat. He was short and stocky, in a grey suit, dark tie and black facemask. I saw something of his dad in him.

His early evidence was about the difficulties he had, as a former reservist, being accepted by experienced, hardened regular soldiers such as his 2IC, Sergeant Matthew Locke, and Locke's close mate Ben Roberts-Smith.

The Redhead told Nicholas Owens SC that during pre-deployment driving training, 'If I hit something, a rather large bump, the applicant [Roberts-Smith] would reach down and slap me across the back of the head . . . He also said that he was going to do everything he could within his power to have me removed from the team.'

The evidence in chief moved on to the Koran Ghar episode in Afghanistan in 2006, of The Redhead's hauling the Minimi machine gun up the hill and manning an observation post with The Sig. The Redhead told of sighting a young, unarmed Afghan male; he believed he and The Sig had not been sighted.

The Redhead: 'We call it the dinner-plate eyes. If someone sees you, then generally they will give you the dinner-plate eyes, so the large eyes, the shock of seeing something they weren't expecting.'

He proceeded with his account of the Afghan disappearing and reappearing carrying a 'satchel bag', and Sergeant Locke coming to ask what he had observed and why he had not engaged. He said he replied, 'We're in an OP.'

Justice Anthony Besanko intervened, querying his meaning.

The Redhead: 'We're in an observation post.'

His Honour: 'Thank you.'

The Redhead: 'The idea being not to compromise yourself.'

The witness went on to describe Locke and Roberts-Smith moving off to engage the Afghan; he heard, rather than saw, the shots fired. Locke later told him a flare was ignited 'from the person they engaged'.

Owens asked the court attendant to show the witness the operations log from that day, and an entry: 'At time, OP spotted one armed ACM [anti-Coalition militia] with AK variant weapon.' And: 'ACM member appeared to be aggressively patrolling.' The Redhead told the court he had not seen a weapon, nor aggressive patrolling, and believed their position, after the shooting, had been compromised.

He described the battle that then commenced. The Redhead was told by his patrol commander to 'watch and shoot'. He fired short bursts, but had to re-cock after repeated stoppages.

Owens: 'Do you have an understanding as to why the weapon had those repeated stoppages?'

The Redhead: 'It wasn't correctly lubricated.'

Owens: 'Right. Why wasn't it correctly lubricated?'

The Redhead: 'I lubricated prior to the mission; however, I didn't take gun oil with me on the mission.'

Owens: 'Should you have taken gun oil?'

The Redhead: 'Yes.'

The witness accepted that criticism of his performance at Koran Ghar was fair. He was less sanguine about what happened afterwards, when Roberts-Smith attacked him in the room they shared. The Redhead remembered words to the effect: 'If your performance doesn't improve on our next patrol, you're going to get a bullet in the back of the head.'

Owens: 'What impact did it have on you?'

The Redhead: 'It made me fearful for my own personal safety.'

The witness said he reported the threat. 'Next thing I saw, the applicant approached me, looked down on me and said, "If you're going to make accusations, cunt, you better have some fucking proof."'

He said the harassment persisted. 'So, being a small base, we would see each other relatively often. If we were walking past each other, he would try to make eye contact with me and, when we got close, he would spit on the ground in front of me. If we were walking into a building, he would hold the door for me and let it slam in my face.'

Owens moved on to subsequent years, eliciting from The Redhead the improvement he achieved in his performance rating as his career progressed, up to the time when he was moved to make a formal complaint about Roberts-Smith to his regimental sergeant major, The RSM. Despite the passage of seven years, promotion and general accumulated respect, the persecution of The Redhead had persisted.

The Redhead: 'Being a young SAS trooper, I believe, is the best job in the world. You work very hard to get into that position, and people earn their position there. I believe the actions of the applicant stole those years where I should have been enjoying myself there by his behaviour in undermining my credibility at the squadron. Him speaking to my oncoming patrol commanders and trying to undermine my credibility in the squadron. Trying to get me removed from the troop. And the death threat I received from him, particularly the one in 2006. It made me fear for my own safety. Not only do I have to worry about the Taliban, but I also have to look over my own back at my own people in my own squadron.'

He paused and took a breath. 'Pardon me. It resulted in years of lost sleep and worrying about my position, my future, about my employment and my chosen career. And I believe it hamstrung my career for many years and slowed my career progression from my peers.'

There was a closed court session before cross-examination commenced in the midafternoon. Spoiling my theory that Arthur Moses SC would question the military witnesses, Bruce McClintock SC stood at the crease. Questioned about Koran Ghar, The Redhead accepted that the Afghan teenager shot was a likely Taliban spotter.

McClintock: 'Yes, and that has always been your view, isn't it—that this was a legitimate engagement?'

The Redhead: 'Yes.'

He was questioned about what we had come to term 'Noodle-gate'. It had been alleged that The Redhead failed to engage the enemy one time in 2006 because he was intent on finishing his lunch.

The Redhead: 'I don't recall the incident.'

McClintock: 'Right, there's nothing funny about it, is there?'

The Redhead: 'Which section are you referring to?'

McClintock: 'About the noodles?'

The Redhead: 'There's nothing what about it, sorry?'

McClintock: 'Nothing funny about it.'

The Redhead: 'I wasn't suggesting it was funny.'

McClintock: 'I'm not suggesting you were at all, but it's a . . .'

His Honour: 'Well, what was the suggestion, Mr McClintock?'

McClintock: 'There was something put to my client along those lines, Your Honour.'

His Honour: 'By the witness?'

McClintock: 'No, by my learned friend.'

Owens: 'Where?'

In the background, there was a scurrying for transcripts. Minutes later:

McClintock: 'The word "funny" was not used, but the word "trivial" was . . .' He continued. 'The refusal to drop your noodles, get in the car and get away. That's not trivial?'

The Redhead: 'If it occurred, no, it's not trivial.'

———

The legal teams reassembled the following morning, Friday, 18 February. Some wind was taken from Roberts-Smith's Force Ten fury about The Redhead being an alleged source of mine. The former trooper, now an SAS sergeant, was able to tell the court that he and I had never met. I did know his parents and had made an approach to him, but to no avail.

Bruce McClintock SC secured further acknowledgement that in 2006, at that infant stage in the trooper's career, he had not risen to the required standard.

The Redhead: 'I certainly had performance issues at that time, yes.'

McClintock: 'And if my client said to you, "You're not up to the standard of an SAS operator," that would be true, wouldn't it?'

The Redhead: 'As you mentioned earlier, sir, he was a fellow trooper. It's not really his position to say something like that. It's more of a team leader or 2IC's role.'

And regarding the death threat:

McClintock: 'You see . . . you didn't believe for a second that my client was genuinely going to kill you?'

The Redhead: 'Yes, I did, sir.'

McClintock: '. . . the answer you've given is false and you know it's false, don't you?'

The Redhead: 'I don't believe it's false.'

And finally the questioning moved to Sergeant Matthew Locke:

McClintock: 'Now, the phrase "bullying behaviour" directed towards you: you regard the late Matt Locke as part of that bullying behaviour, don't you?'

The Redhead: 'Sir, you're putting me in an awkward position commenting on an Australian war hero who can't defend himself.'

Bruce McClintock pressed for an answer.

The Redhead: 'Matt Locke and I didn't get along. I respected him as my 2IC, and I respected him as a soldier.'

After further pressure, the witness acknowledged bullying behaviour by Locke.

For the rest of the morning, there was an unrelenting onslaught of attacks on The Redhead's competence. Sitting just metres away, I felt he was in the metaphorical equivalent of the medieval stocks, having excrement pelted at him. I mean no criticism of Bruce McClintock SC, who was doing his professional best—but in the courtroom, as in many military barracks, you might say, bullying has a form of sanction. In the courtroom, sustained character attacks are not meant to be taken personally.

SASR selection is a test of character as well as of physical and mental toughness. For me, The Redhead had endured remarkably well, and survived as a professional soldier. In the witness box, too, he remained stoic, passive, unruffled, succinct.

In contrast, Ben Roberts-Smith, seated just metres away, glowered. His deep animus for The Redhead had been apparent when we spoke in 2017, and from his corner in the courtroom, five years on, it felt to me undiminished. This was odd, I thought, considering The Redhead had never levelled an allegation of war crimes against his tormentor.

The Redhead was relieved before the lunch break, and he and I again failed to cross paths. Another punishing day for this career soldier, although I hoped it might have been in some way cathartic.

CHAPTER 67

COOLNESS UNDER FIRE

Day 36. Monday, 21 February 2022. There are ongoing logistical difficulties securing witnesses through the national Covid quarantine grid, and anticipating how long they will be required. A further challenge to smooth running in the Federal Court is a snap train shutdown across Sydney. So it's another stressful early morning in the bunker at MinterEllison.

When the hearing began, we proceeded with The Peacekeeper (Person 21), who appeared via videolink from an undisclosed location.

He identified himself as a 34-year veteran who had served as a UN peacekeeper. Before transferring to the officer ranks in 'Big Army', he'd served ten years in the SASR, deploying to Afghanistan as a patrol commander in 2006.

And there some of those peacekeeping skills had come to the fore. After Koran Ghar, The Redhead was switched to The Peacekeeper's patrol, where he was to be 'evaluated for his performance'.

Looking down the camera, The Peacekeeper recalled to Nicholas Owens SC his then impression of The Redhead: 'He was nervous, unsure . . . asked a lot of questions, and if he made a mistake or needed to be trained . . . he picked up that information well and applied it to future situations.'

He related for the court how the young trooper had described his acrimonious departure from his earlier patrol. The Redhead had said words to the effect: 'Ben Roberts-Smith told me he was going to fuck me off out of the unit. "You're never going to be a war operator again." And he said words along the lines . . . he threatened to kill me.'

Owens: 'Were you ever involved in a contact [combat] situation with The Redhead?'

The Peacekeeper: 'Yes.'

Owens: 'And how did he perform in that contact situation?'

The Peacekeeper: 'He was calm. He was collected. He followed instructions. He made good decisions. He did not need to be directed or told what to do, and overall I was impressed by his coolness under fire.'

Bruce McClintock SC limited his cross-examination to five minutes. The Peacekeeper acknowledged that The Redhead joined his patrol following 'a commander's warning', and that The Peacekeeper had not been present for the Koran Ghar battle.

One more witness for the day. He appeared in person, but under tighter security constraints. He was a lieutenant colonel who had deployed in 2006, although then as a captain. His exact role was not declared, other than to say he worked in the command centre at Camp Russell. We will call him The Analyst. To the court, he was Person 69.

Nicholas Owens asked the day's second witness to provide his recollections of The Redhead from that rotation. They had spent time together in the Electronic Warfare accommodation hut when The Redhead sought asylum from Roberts-Smith.

The Analyst remembered The Redhead describing what had happened at Koran Ghar—the shooting of the unarmed teenager and his weapon stoppages—and explaining how, as a consequence, 'the patrol ostracised me'.

Owens: 'Is there any reason why you recall [that conversation]?'

The Analyst: 'I had never worked with the SAS . . . and I was shocked that they weren't a collegiate team. I had worked with other special forces, and they seemed to help people who were making mistakes.

Everyone makes mistakes . . . I couldn't believe that a junior trooper would get abused for not doing what was the right thing rather than being supported. That's why I remember it.'

The Analyst had another luminous memory from that rotation, of witnessing the bared fangs of the SASR's wolfpack persona. Taken to the Fat Lady's Arms by two working colleagues, he was seated about a metre away from Ben Roberts-Smith, who was overheard talking about the Koran Ghar action.

Owens: 'What do you recall happened after that?'

The Analyst: 'I then turned over my shoulder, looking towards Ben Roberts-Smith. He saw me, turned to me, and said, "What the fuck are you doing here? . . . I should smash your face in."'

Owens: 'What was your rank at the time?'

The Analyst: 'I was a captain.'

Owens: 'And what was his rank, if you know?'

The Analyst: 'He was a lance corporal.'

One of The Analyst's colleagues, shocked by what he had heard, told Roberts-Smith to 'pull your fucking head in' and then they left.

Bruce McClintock SC's cross-examination was again brief. He drew from The Analyst a concession that The Redhead's failure to pack gun oil was an 'elementary error'. The Analyst also conceded he had not reported Roberts-Smith's insubordination at the Fat Lady's Arms. Roberts-Smith's barrister was contemptuous of the prospect that a threat to 'smash your face in' would be made to a superior officer.

McClintock: 'In fact, it's ludicrous to think of a lance corporal saying it to a captain, isn't it?'

The Analyst: 'That's why I remember it when it occurred.'

McClintock: 'It never happened, did it?'

The Analyst: 'It absolutely did.'

Another early finish, Justice Besanko adjourning a banged gavel before 3 pm.

If truth is a jigsaw puzzle, this contest of the facts was of the jumbo variety, a thousand pieces. And on this day, two small but useful bits had been fitted into place.

Stepping back, however, the big picture remained indistinct. We were a long way yet from making our case, and Ben Roberts-Smith's witnesses were yet to be heard.

CHAPTER 68

DODGING A BULLET

My kayaking friend, The Mechanic, was designated Person 19. From earlier conversations, I knew he was not looking forward to giving evidence.

It was no surprise to me that soldiers would find the prospect of fronting a public court more daunting than trading bullets with the Taliban. A battle of wits, in an arena owned by the interrogator, calls for something other than physical courage. And you can imagine how for special forces soldiers, inured to silence, the witness box is a worst-nightmare, ground-zero discomfort zone.

On Tuesday, 22 February, The Mechanic was sworn in. The air conditioning appeared feeble; I was sweating. But The Mechanic, however reluctant, did not seem nervous.

He was quickly taken by Nicholas Owens SC to the episode at the Lancelin training facility, prior to 2 Squadron's deployment in 2012. The Mechanic described the PUC handling scenario that had been played out, with Ben Roberts-Smith as patrol commander directing The Trooper in the presence of other patrol members, The Gunsmith and The Sniper. Playing the role of an Afghan was The Dog Handler. According to The Mechanic, The Dog Handler was kneeling on the ground as Ben Roberts-Smith explained 'what we would do at this stage of the assault'.

Owens: 'So Mr Roberts-Smith said . . .?'

The Mechanic: 'Mr Roberts-Smith said to The Trooper, "I want you to shoot the PUC," which was referring to the person that had been captured . . . who was kneeling on the ground. I remember that distinctly because it was unusual, and I remember seeing the look on The Dog Handler's face, as they were quite surprised as well.'

Owens: 'So what happened after?'

The Mechanic: 'To the best of my recollection, I remember The Trooper saying either "Bang" or they shot the ground, but it was to the effect that they had shot the person.'

Owens moved on to further instructions from Roberts-Smith at the Bindoon Training Area. The Mechanic described a group discussion about sensitive site exploitation: 'At this stage, Mr Roberts-Smith said that any enemy combatants will be . . . well, first of all they described the process of moving any unmanned aerial vehicles, which are the drones, which can see what's going on—they pushed them off to observe another area, so they weren't observing what was occurring in the compound.'

He continued: 'Mr Roberts-Smith said that the officers would be kept outside the compound until we were ready to receive them, at which stage Mr Roberts-Smith said that . . . any people that we suspected of being enemy combatants, we take them into the room and shoot the cunts.'

The Mechanic also remembered a discussion of what to do then: '[I]f the requirement arose . . . you could put down a throwdown weapon on a body and photograph them and it could be submitted as evidence that they were killed in the conduct of the assault.'

Owens: 'Do you recall any specific occasion when you heard the term "blooding"?'

The Mechanic told of meeting Ben Roberts-Smith and The Gunsmith at a cafe for breakfast during this same period: 'I heard Mr Roberts-Smith say that The Trooper needed to be blooded or "blood the rookie" and that he "needed to prove himself". And then Mr Roberts-Smith said that I didn't need to prove myself as I had already done a number of deployments.'

Owens: 'Had you heard the term "blooding" before that?'

The Mechanic: 'I had heard the term discussed previously by The Scot.'

Owens: 'Did you have an understanding of what the term "blooding" meant?'

The Mechanic: 'Yes, I did.'

Owens: 'What was that?'

The Mechanic: 'It was essentially new members of the troop or patrol who had never deployed before or had never shot anyone. They had to prove their worth by having the—I'm not sure what the term is—the fortitude to shoot, to shoot a prisoner if required.'

Knowing that it was certain to be raised, The Mechanic owned up to his embarrassment over doing time in a military prison, instead of deploying to Afghanistan for Rotation XVIII in 2012. He told of how his car was stolen and ammunition in it was recovered by police; and how he had been charged with losing service property and, in addition, with prejudicial behaviour in recklessly gaining a financial advantage over an undue rental allowance.

This admission in no way disarmed Arthur Moses SC. When he rose to cross-examine, there were repeated questions about The Mechanic's court martial, including whether he blamed Ben Roberts-Smith.

Moses: 'Is it the case that you harbour anger towards him because he had to raise matters concerning the ammunition in your vehicle with the unit?'

The Mechanic: 'No.'

As had been anticipated, The Mechanic was questioned about his relationship with Roberts-Smith's perceived detractors. With respect to contact with The Trooper, he said they had met some months ago for breakfast.

Moses: 'Can you recall what you discussed?'

The Mechanic: 'We discussed how we could get out of the subpoena and if there were any options, because we both didn't want to appear in court here as part of the proceedings. He discussed that you could potentially get off your subpoena with mental health grounds, but he said it was very difficult.'

Arthur Moses queried The Mechanic about whether he had discussed with anyone what had happened at the training exercise. He said the mock shooting had been raised afterwards with The Sergeant, and separately, directly after the incident, with The Trooper when they drove back to Perth.

The Mechanic: 'I said words to the effect, "Can you believe that bullshit?"'

Moses continued to punish the witness over his dismissal from the Army, extracting his acknowledgement that the charges he faced were serious, and that he took personal responsibility for what he had done at that time.

The Mechanic: 'I was very disappointed. I had lost a fourteen-year career because of a couple of very silly errors of judgement.'

Moses: 'Yes, quite serious errors of judgement.'

The Mechanic: 'Yes, I don't dispute that.'

Moses: 'Yes. And you were upset about the fact you couldn't go to Afghanistan?'

The Mechanic: 'Yes, I was disappointed.'

Moses: 'And you were upset about the fact that what you had done placed your career in jeopardy?'

The Mechanic: 'It ruined my career.' The Mechanic reiterated his position of blaming himself rather than his patrol commander. Moses asked him whether indeed his patrol commander, Roberts-Smith, had challenged him about the quantity of ammunition recovered by the police being greater than he had formerly admitted.

The Mechanic: 'I don't recall that conversation. In fact, I recall him saying that, "Don't say anything about this and it will go away." I recall that conversation.'

Moses: 'What you've just told His Honour is a lie. Isn't it?'

The Mechanic: 'No.'

The Mechanic was pursued over his contact with me. He confessed to our shared kayaking trips and our maritime ruminations (which were largely about life in general). Arthur Moses SC called for notes I had made of our conversations (which I had created for *No Front Line*). The Mechanic was then questioned about his cafe meeting with Roberts-Smith and The Gunsmith, and the allegation of the plan to 'blood' The Trooper.

In our shared back row of the court, I looked across at Ben, who was giving his former comrade, The Mechanic, the stink eye. This had been an old practice of his in the mess at Camp Russell. Juvenile, pissing-contest stuff. Commandos remember him fixing his gaze on his green beret rivals, whom the sandy-bereted SAS regarded as pretenders, and attempting to stare them down.

Here in court, The Mechanic (a former Commando) appeared not to notice Roberts-Smith. He was focused, unhesitant in his responses, more confident with every passing hour. He is a fighter. As we saw with many witnesses, the harder the interrogator pushed, the higher he rose to the occasion.

The Mechanic confirmed his recollection of Roberts-Smith saying, 'You don't need to prove yourself, but The Trooper does.'

Moses: 'And what I want to suggest to you is that that is a lie; do you accept that?'

The Mechanic: 'I disagree.'

Moses then took my paddling mate into dangerous waters. The barrister asked whether 'blooding the rookie was widely discussed'.

The Mechanic: 'Yes.'

Moses: 'In the unit?'

The Mechanic: 'Yes.'

I sat up, a little surprised. This was news to me, and I thought it significant. The proposition to this point was that knowledge of alleged blooding and executions was confined to a very small group of operators.

Moses: 'Well, let's put the cafe meeting to one side. You said it was widely discussed in the unit at the time?'

The Mechanic: 'Yes.'

Pressed further, the witness recalled: 'Yes, well, I was aware of other people discussing it as well.'

Moses: 'Yes, and what did they tell you?'

The Mechanic: 'That the practice was occurring, that people had been shooting . . . whether you want to call them "PUCs" or "people". But people were being dragged into rooms and you were having to shoot someone in front of your patrol commander.'

Moses: 'Did you tell Mr Masters about the conversation at the cafe?'

The Mechanic: 'No.'

Moses: 'Sorry?'

The Mechanic: 'No, I did not discuss this with Mr Masters.'

Dead right, I thought, stopping myself saying it out loud. What was revealed was new to me, and stunning. How could the callous reality of Afghans being systematically executed by novice troopers be routinely discussed by junior soldiers, but not by anyone else up the command chain? This revelation would cause ructions. I might not have been the only open-mouthed onlooker.

Arthur Moses returned to the alleged incidents during mission rehearsal. The Mechanic's honesty was attacked regarding bloodings, throwdowns and pushing unmanned aerial vehicles off station so that 'bad cunts' could be shot. Moses also drilled down for further detail—for example, about who else was present.

The Mechanic: 'I can't remember the specifics of exactly who said what . . . I can remember very vivid parts of that encounter. I just can't remember the whole conversation and exactly who said what.'

Moses: 'Yes, yes . . . what you're doing now is saying what you think needs to be said in order to damage Mr Roberts-Smith, aren't you?'

The Mechanic: 'I completely reject that statement.'

The aircon was at half-strength. A steamy February day. Ben Roberts-Smith had removed his jacket and the temperature continued to rise.

Moses: 'You reject the statement, do you?'

The Mechanic: 'I'm saying that . . . your insinuation that I'm lying is incorrect.'

Moses: 'I'm telling you that you're lying. Do you accept that?'

The Mechanic: 'Well, that's incorrect.'

Owens: 'Your Honour, I object to that form of question.'

Justice Besanko was firm, twice telling Ben Roberts-Smith's barrister that the question was disallowed.

Arthur Moses returned to The Mechanic's contact with me. Having called for my research notes, there was a further barrage of questions.

Moses: 'And did you discuss with him a conversation in which it was said that Mr Roberts-Smith was a protected species?'

The Mechanic: 'Possibly, I don't recall.'

Moses: 'Did you say to him you were hung out to dry?'

The Mechanic: 'I was to some degree, yes.'

Moses: 'And that you were a scapegoat?'

The Mechanic: 'Yes.'

As lunchtime approached, Arthur Moses SC asked that the adjournment be a little longer than usual so he could review my notes.

It was almost 2.30 pm when The Mechanic was recalled.

As with the cross-examination of The Scout, it was excruciating to listen to him being forced to answer for my words. I was of the view that The Mechanic had lost his career partly because loose practices in accounting for ammunition returned from the range had long been commonplace. And when the system was found wanting, it was easier for the institution to blame an individual.

Moses: 'Do you accept, in the proceedings before the judge advocate, there was no suggestion made by you . . . that you had been charged in respect of these matters because it was a way of protecting the unit?'

The question was disallowed.

Moses: 'I will put it this way: did you tell Mr Masters that Mr Roberts-Smith did not tell the full truth?'

The Mechanic: 'Yes, I did.'

There was another half-hour of the soldier answering for his friendship with a journalist. Before moving to closed court, Arthur Moses put to The Mechanic: 'You've come here today, haven't you, to give evidence to try to support Mr Masters in his defence of his claim, haven't you?'

The Mechanic: 'No. If I had a choice, I wouldn't be here.'

After the proceedings closed, there was the opportunity for me to have a very brief conversation with The Mechanic in the anteroom. I apologised for the release of my notes. My friend was forgiving.

Our lawyers were pleased. His assertion that he did not want to be in court was persuasive. From my many conversations with him, I knew he experienced no joy in dumping on a former colleague.

Another character we regularly saw up the back of the courtroom was present, as best we understood it, to provide an overwatch for law enforcement. The Mechanic's evidence had been noted.

Getting dragged further into the Roberts-Smith saga was hardly on The Mechanic's wish list. But you could not miss the irony. At the time it happened, losing his career just before deployment had appeared to be a perfect storm of bad luck. But had he, so to speak, dodged a bullet? Being dragged along as a member of Ben Roberts-Smith's patrol back in 2012 might have been far more hazardous.

CHAPTER 69

THE PI AND THE VC

A wet Wednesday in Sydney, and another witness who would rather be anywhere else. The blunt force of a subpoena had secured the witness who had initially told us, 'No, no, no.'

The private inquiry agent James (John) Alexander Douglas McLeod is 70-ish. A mid-blue suit with trim pocket handkerchief, suede boots, balding, a ruddy complexion and the grimmest expression. He settles in the witness box, in the opposite corner to his former friend Ben Roberts-Smith, who sits hunched like a boxer, reprising yesterday's stink eye.

Nicholas Owens SC eased into the story of the curious alliance of the PI and the VC, establishing the relationship as it was. John McLeod explained how he had helped the Roberts-Smith family settle into Brisbane and establish local contacts: he would '[a]ssist with, you know, picking up stuff, suits and whatever. Picking up and organising Ben's medals on occasions. A lot of mundane—just mundane things. It was a bit of everything, really.'

Asked whether surveillance work was required, he detailed the videoing of Roberts-Smith's former girlfriend, explaining that at the time Roberts-Smith had identified her as a Channel Seven executive. His surveillance video at the Greenslopes private hospital was played to the court, and McLeod confirmed that it was the tape he had sent to Roberts-Smith.

Further questioning from Owens covered his role in precipitating the police raid on the home of The Veteran. He described Roberts-Smith telling him, 'There was a SAS bloke that was unhinged, an alcoholic, prone to domestic violence, that had acquired a weapon from special forces visiting from the States,' and that he was a public danger.

After receiving further details on a USB, McLeod set up an email account—blowerW2@gmail.com—to inform the politician Nick Xenophon, the *Australian* journalist Andrew Burrell and Australian Federal Police commissioner Andrew Colvin. McLeod told the court that Andrew Burrell replied, asking whether the anonymous tip came from 'a serving member of the SASR.' He said he asked Roberts-Smith how to respond and was told, 'It's not from you; it's from me.'

Owens turned to John McLeod's unwitting role in threatening The SSE. The Roberts-Smith confidant detailed receiving a blue folder, envelopes and two addresses, and then posting the letters from Tweed Heads, in New South Wales. The court attendant showed the witness photocopies of the envelopes and two pieces of paper.

Owens: 'Do you recognise the handwriting in those bits of paper?'

McLeod: 'It's Ben's handwriting.'

He further recognised the envelopes he posted, and was asked what had happened to the paper and envelopes not posted. John McLeod said they were passed to his lawyer.

Owens: 'All right. Do you know what he has done with them?'

McLeod: 'The AFP have been handed them.'

McLeod's subsequent bust-up with Roberts-Smith was also detailed, with the PI telling His Honour of the meeting at Milton in Brisbane, when 'the penny dropped' and he came to understand he had been used. Asked to try to recall the words used, the former policeman (who probably therefore had experience of the witness box) was explicit: 'I said, "Mate, if you've done something stupid, put your hand up for it, because the cover-up is ten times worse than the offence." [Roberts-Smith replied:] "No, no, no. All you got to say is that—just tell them that you're a supporter of mine, and that you sent the letters because you were sick of the way I was being treated."'

It was an unpretty end to the friendship.

McLeod: 'I just looked at him, and I said, "Fuck that, you weak dog," and I walked away.' There had been no subsequent contact between the two men, from that day to this.

Nicholas Owens asked whether the witness had any involvement in the *60 Minutes* exposé about the buried lunch box and the threatening letters, and received an emphatic response: 'No.'

Owens: 'Have you ever spoken to any journalist or media organisation whatsoever in relation to Mr Roberts-Smith?'

McLeod: 'No, I despise the media.'

McLeod's evidence in chief ran less than an hour. Cross-examination usually takes longer, but it seemed unlikely that the plaintiff's lawyers would allow such a damaging witness to linger. The defamation veteran Bruce McClintock SC was back, bulldog-like, though he started quietly.

Asked about why he left the Queensland Police, John McLeod told the court it was because he had witnessed something 'horrific'.

There was a brief delay when McLeod was shown printouts of WhatsApp messages between himself and Emma's friend Danielle Scott: McLeod grappled with the double problem of a congenital reading difficulty and his failure to bring glasses. After he had borrowed his lawyer's spectacles, he was taken by McClintock through exchanges revealing what appeared to be occasional boastful overstatement on the part of the PI.

Asked about the odd jobs performed for Roberts-Smith, he denied providing 'security' at social functions, but rather: 'I pretended to be a barman to listen to the conversations that were happening and report back to Ben of the conversations that were happening.' He said this occurred when Roberts-Smith was new to the Channel Seven job and wanted to know what staff thought of him.

McClintock quickly returned to the text messages and sought to establish the relationship between the witness and Danielle Scott, and the formation of an alleged alliance with Emma after she and Roberts-Smith separated.

McClintock: 'At some point after that, but in February 2020, you commenced performing services for Ms Roberts, didn't you?'

McLeod: 'No.'

Through McClintock's attempt to establish McLeod's ongoing contact with Emma, a snapshot of a broken marriage, banal and dismal, was revealed to the court. The witness was asked about Emma giving him Ben's Army uniforms. He said: 'I picked them up from the rain . . . They were all thrown over the driveway and they were in the rain.' He told His Honour that he collected them and kept them for the Roberts-Smiths' daughters.

More text messages.

McClintock: 'You refer to my client as a prick, don't you?'

McLeod: 'I did.'

McClintock: 'If you look at the entry at 2056 [a transcript annotation], you will see that you refer to him as a psycho?'

McLeod: 'Yes.'

McClintock: 'There's a degree of hostility in those references, isn't there, Mr McLeod?'

McLeod: 'A degree of frustration and disappointment.'

John McLeod denied a 'longstanding' personal friendship with Danielle Scott. He said he had maintained some communication with Emma Roberts out of concern for the children. He said he did not recall whether he was told that Scott was speaking with journalists.

Pointing to communications between Danielle Scott and John McLeod in the weeks preceding the *60 Minutes* 'lunch box' report, aired on 11 April 2021, Bruce McClintock SC sought to establish a link. A message from Scott to McLeod after the broadcast queried, 'You good?'—to which he replied, 'They will come for me!!' And then he asked her: 'Do you think it was enough to wake up Kerry?'

John McLeod told the court he did not know what this referred to.

Bruce McClintock appeared unconvinced: 'I don't want there to be any doubts about this. I will ask for the particular program to be played.'

I was surprised by this request. The program, hardly flattering of McClintock's client, would be rerun. It had also been played during Emma Roberts' evidence. Perhaps the thinking was that *60 Minutes*' tabloid puffery might offend judicial sensibility.

It was intended that the program be screened before the luncheon adjournment, but His Honour queried whether there would be enough time. McClintock pointed out that, despite its title, 'I think Mr Littlemore [fellow barrister and former ABC reporter Stuart Littlemore] used to call it "35 Minutes" on *Media Watch* years ago.' Even so, the clock had run down.

We retired to our cubicle. The sandwiches had lost their appeal. Dean Levitan, Tess McGuire and I headed off on a coffee run. Dean had been with Peter Bartlett at the original meeting in Brisbane with John McLeod in March 2021.

I felt McLeod was a strong witness and wondered why the other side were allowing him such latitude. We had just now learned that the applicant had confirmed a line-up of twenty witnesses, which did not suggest any loss of confidence—or maybe Roberts-Smith and his backers were in too deep.

After the adjournment, the *60 Minutes* report was played, and Bruce McClintock SC backed his considerable interrogatory skills to strip this confronting witness of his credibility. McLeod was asked about the recordings of Roberts-Smith's voice; he denied that he had played any part in them ending up at Channel Nine.

John McLeod agreed he had seen 'bits and pieces' of the program. He was vague on details of when this occurred. He was taken to the specifics of his role in sending the threatening letters, but said he had 'no idea' how Nick McKenzie found out about them. He denied ever discussing this topic with Danielle Scott and Emma Roberts. He was asked whether he had told 'any lawyers about those matters', but this question was disallowed.

Bruce McClintock SC returned to McLeod's message to Danielle Scott following the broadcast, in which he had declared, 'They will come for me!!' McLeod said 'they' referred to retaliation by 'RS's people'.

McClintock: 'Mr McLeod, the answer you've given is simply a dishonest fabrication, isn't it?'

McLeod: 'No.'

There was a further reprise, this time of the, 'Do you think it was enough to wake up Kerry?' text.

McClintock: 'You see, what you wanted was for Mr Stokes to withdraw his support for my client. That's true, isn't it?'

McLeod: 'How would I do that? No, it's not true.'

Bruce McClintock took McLeod to when he had texted to Scott: 'Kerry is stoic. If not sure, it won't be enough.' McClintock asked: 'What did you mean by that?'

McLeod: 'Kerry is a stand-up bloke. He looks after, he backs his people.'

They continued to wrestle. The private inquiry agent conceded he had hoped the Australian Federal Police would intervene, and 'speak to Kerry'.

McClintock: 'Yes, and you hoped that the effect of this would be to destroy the relationship between my client and Mr Stokes, didn't you?'

McLeod: 'I was worried about Kerry.'

McClintock. 'I'm sure he's very grateful for that, Mr McLeod.'

There was an objection from Nicholas Owens SC.

McClintock: 'I withdraw it.'

And another McLeod text: 'I thought Kerry would be smarter.' McClintock: 'That's a reference to the fact that *60 Minutes* had failed to dint Mr Stokes' support for my client?'

McLeod: 'I think it's a reference to the unwavering backing of your client.'

McClintock: 'Now, just by the way, have you ever met Mr Stokes?'

McLeod: 'No.'

The barrister squeezed harder; the private inquiry agent conceded he was not on first-name terms with the billionaire.

McClintock: 'In fact, in the references to Danielle, you were simply big-noting yourself, weren't you, Mr McLeod?'

McLeod: 'I was not.'

McClintock: 'And that, indeed, that is a tendency that you have, isn't it?'

McLeod: 'It is not.'

Ben Roberts-Smith's barrister pushed into the afternoon. A dangerous witness had to be totally discredited; Bruce McClintock SC argued that Ben Roberts-Smith's former friend and fixer's lying was motivated by loathing.

McClintock: 'Now, you see, the fact is that by the time 11 April came around, you had formed a hatred for my client, hadn't you?'

McLeod: 'Absolutely not.'

McClintock: 'And you would do anything you could do to ensure that he lost this case; that's correct, isn't it?'

McLeod: 'No.'

McClintock: 'You see, that's why you're here giving evidence, isn't it, to help him lose this case?'

McLeod: 'I did not want to be here. I had no intention of being here. I was subpoenaed to appear here.'

Media coverage of John McLeod's evidence took a particular interest in the spying confessions. The private inquiry agent's account of eavesdropping on Channel Seven employees on behalf of Roberts-Smith, raised in cross-examination, had been firmly rejected.

For me, far more important was evidence of Roberts-Smith's direct involvement in blackmail, a criminal offence. And that, as John McLeod had further revealed, the Australian Federal Police had been handed the evidence.

CHAPTER 70

A LEGITIMATE TARGET?

Media coverage of the trial, which has been energetic to date, will wane for a time. It is Thursday, 24 February 2022, and a new war dominates the headlines: Russian president Vladimir Putin's 'special military operation' in Ukraine.

It will deliver no swift victory for Putin, and will quickly descend into stalemate and depravity as war crimes begin to be reported. Under these circumstances, the Ben Roberts-Smith trial and related inquiries become an open wound. How can we Australians condemn what Russia is doing if we ignore our own conduct on the battlefield?

—

Person 2, The Sig, was in the box. He had already begun his evidence in the final session on Wednesday, after John McLeod was excused. Nicholas Owens SC took us again to the beginning, atop Koran Ghar in June 2006. Over the course of the trial, *Rashomon*-like, we were exposed to different individuals' perspectives on the truth of what had occurred.

At the OP, The Sig was watching through binoculars and The Redhead was 'scribing', or taking notes. At 70 metres' distance, a 'young boy', likely aged between fourteen and fifteen, appeared, 'walking casually', carrying no weapon, wearing no webbing and with no visible radio. He disappeared behind rocks and soon reappeared carrying a hessian sack, 'walking away from us'. The Sig said: 'He didn't exhibit from body language any form of surprise, anything that indicated that he had seen us.'

Immediately after The Sig reported this activity on his radio, Sergeant Matthew Locke arrived and stood over the two of them, saying: 'Why the fuck didn't you shoot him?'

The Sig: 'I looked up and I said, "Because we're in an OP."' He explained to the court that the mission was to observe and remain undetected. He said Locke asked, 'Which way did he go?' The Sig pointed out the direction and Sergeant Locke and Lance Corporal Ben Roberts-Smith 'started running towards that direction'.

The Sig, then a trooper, was now a commissioned military police officer. Like John McLeod, he appeared familiar with courtroom protocol. Composed and articulate, he continued: 'About a minute, two minutes later, we heard about four to five shots from two different weapons, a suppressed M4 and a suppressed SR-25.' He said he did not see the engagement.

The court attendant was then asked to show him a document, which was a copy of the incident report: 'OP spotted one armed ACM [anti-Coalition militia] with AK variant weapon 140 metres northeast of OP.'

Owens: 'Was the person you saw armed?'

The Sig: 'No, he wasn't.'

He further disputed that the ACM was 'aggressively patrolling', and did not see 'smoke', allegedly emitted after the small-arms fire.

The Sig was then taken to the extended engagement that followed these events. He recalled The Redhead's weapon jamming, and then firing a burst. He described Matthew Locke climbing a steep rock feature, 'taking a knee and engaging the enemy'. He told the court: 'Ben said, "Need some support over here."' He then moved to Roberts-Smith's side.

Owens: 'And what happened once you've moved down to Mr Roberts-Smith's location?'

The Sig: '[I] took a site picture on the enemy . . . My rifle went "click". Re-cock—clicked. I thought, "Worst case, I've got a broken firing pin." I stripped my bolt.' He described getting behind a rock: 'behind some cover, mag off, bolt out, disassembled the bolt, reassembled it, pin back in, reassembled the rifle, mag on, cocked it, site picture and fired.'

Owens: 'Okay. And what happened after that? How long did that take, that whole process?'

The Sig: 'No more than a minute.'

He said he and Roberts-Smith continued to engage an enemy, 'probably about four to five hundred metres away'. He called in air support, radioed target indicators and again came under attack from rifle fire. He described the enemy coming near enough to their position for their voices to be heard, and his patrol commander ordering a 'danger close' gun run. The British sergeant (Person 33) leading their patrol assisted by the American radio operator (Person 23) then coordinated attacks by American A-10 Warthogs, and the earth shredded within metres of where their small patrol was hugging the escarpment.

But then the aircraft were diverted to another operation, and their patrol was again exposed. The Sig's communications expertise was then called on, and he contacted headquarters and made another desperate call.

Owens: 'And what did you say?'

The Sig: 'I said words to the effect, of "Zero Alpha . . ."—this is my call sign—"This call sign in close contact, requesting immediate air support. Without air, we may not be able to hold this position."'

He described the return of aircraft as night fell. This guardian angel above used its sensors to detect enemy movement, while the small, imperilled patrol used night-vision goggles to cautiously extract to safety.

Nicholas Owens SC had a few more questions for The Sig about his brief but memorable encounters with the man sitting glowering in the opposite corner. Shortly after the Koran Ghar mission, The Sig had shared picket duty with Ben Roberts-Smith.

Owens: 'Is there anything in particular you remember about the picket duty?'

The Sig: 'Ben said in the conversation, "I just want to kill cunts. I don't give a fuck. I just want to kill cunts."'

The next episode recalled, also from 2006, was of The Sig cleaning his weapon and cocking the SR-25; he ejected a round and then caught it in midair. He said that Roberts-Smith, sitting opposite, told him: 'If you do that—and I see you do that again, I'll beat the shit out of you.'

Owens asked about a third incident, when they returned from Rotation III in 2006, and following parachute training in Australia. While seated on a bus, The Sig saw Roberts-Smith 'lean over the seat in front of me and he said, "Hey, check this out", and had pictures of dead insurgents on his iPod.'

Bruce McClintock SC's cross-examination began in the final half-hour of the sitting day. The Sig was asked whether he had attended my book launch. He had not.

Questioning quickly swung to The Sig's contact with me. This placed him at risk of being in breach of ADF regulations, in that all interactions with media are supposed to be registered. As was now routine, before answering this question he sought a certificate of immunity so as not to incriminate himself. So, at the cusp of the day's adjournment, came a request for the notes I had made of my interview with The Sig for *No Front Line*.

Before we all dispersed into the afternoon light that day, there was a brief *sotto voce* exchange of views as we huddled in our cubicle.

Lawyers are inveterate judge watchers. There was animated discussion as they interpreted various furrowed-brow and light-bulb moments. I was not so confident about anyone's ability to judge the judge. Indeed, my overall experience of many courtrooms is wonderment at how His/Her Honour manages not to nod off.

But then, this particular case was no mind-numbing trawl through the *Income Tax Assessment Act 1936*. It was a fascinating case, and I had not missed Justice Anthony Besanko's rapt attention as The Sig described the narrow escape from Koran Ghar.

As the courtroom cast assembled the following morning, what caught my eye was Bruce McClintock leafing through *No Front Line*. A familiar chill went through me—anticipation of a witness about to be assaulted with my words.

His immunity certificate having been granted, The Sig now settled in the box, lifting his head like a batsman awaiting the first bouncer.

McClintock: 'You did have contact with Mr Masters prior to the publication of his book, *No Front Line*, didn't you?'

The Sig: 'Yes, I did.'

Then there was an immediate adjournment to closed court so that this admission could be pursued.

Twenty-four minutes later, we were back in open court. The Sig was challenged over the detail of what occurred in the observation post at Koran Ghar—who was holding the binoculars, who made the entry in the log, from what direction the Afghan approached, what he was carrying. The Sig said the bag slung over the young male's shoulder was not big enough for a rifle, but it could have contained food and water for possible resupply to others, given that an earlier battle had taken place on the valley floor.

McClintock: 'And that of itself made him a legitimate target, didn't it?'

The Sig: 'No, not necessarily.'

The witness was challenged over his weapon stoppage and how much time it took before he was able to support Ben Roberts-Smith when they were under fire.

McClintock: 'What I want to suggest to you is that, whether you were assembling your firing pin or engaging in other activity, you were gone from my client's side for between ten and twenty minutes.'

The Sig: 'That's incorrect.'

The barrister next took issue with the incident when The Sig caught a bullet after he had ejected it from his SR-25.

McClintock: 'It might fairly be described as showboating, mightn't it?'

The Sig: 'Not necessarily.' He explained that there might have been a need for silence and good sense in not allowing the projectile to land in the dirt.

McClintock: 'My client never said, "If I see you do that again, I will beat the shit out of you", did he?'

The Sig: 'He did.'

The alleged 'I just want to kill cunts' evidence was also challenged, with McClintock asserting The Sig had 'entirely fabricated' the comment.

The Sig responded: 'No, I did not, Your Honour.'

Equally, there was ridicule for the account of Roberts-Smith showing pictures of dead Afghans on his iPod.

McClintock: 'First, my client did not have an iPod with a screen in 2006, did he?'

The Sig: 'He did.'

McClintock: 'Right. And this incident never occurred?'

The Sig: 'It did.'

Bruce McClintock SC jumped back and forth, occasionally fishing. He asked when The Sig had last had contact with Roberts-Smith opponents The Veteran and The Sergeant. To which The Sig replied, 'Probably over ten years ago, when I was still serving in the regiment full-time.'

McClintock: 'Yes, no conversations with them since then?'

The Sig: 'No.'

McClintock: 'Right. One final thing. The Afghan male you saw from the observation post was wearing chest webbing, wasn't he?'

The Sig: 'No, he wasn't.'

There was another adjournment. Then, armed with four pages of the notes I produced for *No Front Line*, McClintock continued his cross-examination of The Sig in closed court. Matters deemed to be subject to a non-publication order were canvassed there for 30 minutes before we returned to open court.

Resettled, Roberts-Smith's barrister pointed to a reference in my notes to the Afghan sighted at Koran Ghar as being a 'fighting-age male'.

McClintock: 'Having read that, you wouldn't suggest for a second that the person that Matt Locke and my client shot was anything other than a legitimate target, would you?'

The Sig: 'I would disagree with that.'

The Commonwealth lawyer intervened, warning that the ADF's rules of engagement were not to be canvassed in open court. Bruce McClintock did not press and his cross-examination ceased minutes before noon.

Nicholas Owens SC rose for re-examination, first advising The Sig to avoid any description of the rules of engagement. Owens: 'Could you tell His Honour why or why not you regarded that engagement as legitimate?'

The Sig: 'Because the task for the mission was to observe and surveil . . . that was our primary mission. As part of that, observe and surveil in support of a larger operation was not to become decisively engaged. Decisively engaged is an engagement which potentially affects the outcome of your mission . . . By engaging the spotter, it compromised the OP, and it compromised our ability to complete that mission and remain undetected and observe and surveil as per the task given in orders.'

The Sig withdrew at 12.01 pm. Nicholas Owens advised that the next witness to be called would be Person 4, The Gunsmith. A critical witness, with evidence that might make or break the case of either camp.

CHAPTER 71

BROTHERS-IN-ARMS

'I have never felt this nervous in my entire career,' Nicholas Owens comments as we enter court 21A. With his rounded spectacles and black robes, there is a hint of Harry Potter in our reserved and resolute senior counsel. I pray for magic as we take our seats. It is Monday, 28 February 2022, Day 41.

I had never laid eyes on The Gunsmith (Person 4). There had been one brief verbal communication by phone, when he politely declined an interview request. But here he was, in the flesh: a hard-worked physique straining under his dark suit, his black hair thinning and, once his facemask was removed, a salt-and-pepper beard.

We were terrified. We understood he had given evidence to the IGADF and we believed he had confessed to involvement in war crimes, given what we were told he had said to others. But he had not spoken to us. As Owens put it, the witness was 'this huge presence hiding just behind a curtain—but we couldn't get access to him'. There was also the prospect of The Gunsmith setting aside on mental health grounds the subpoena we had served on him, given that he had formerly checked into a mental hospital.

We also knew he had once shared a profound bond with Ben Roberts-Smith. The Eddie Gallagher case in the United States, in which a key witness performed a testimonial U-turn at the eleventh hour, in the process saving a brother soldier from going to jail, continued to rattle like a distant alarm and raise our anxiety levels.

The Gunsmith told the court he had been medically discharged from the Army in 2021. Nicholas Owens moved to 11 September 2012 and Darwan. The Gunsmith described the first shooting that morning, and his role in taking a photograph from 30 to 40 metres distance of the dead insurgent, who had been killed by Ben Roberts-Smith after he waded the Helmand River. He remembered his patrol commander re-crossing the river and bringing back a rifle, a length of detonator cord and an Icom radio.

His patrol had then moved to clear the compounds. Owens requested him to mark on an aerial photograph the key locations, but when he asked The Gunsmith who had been present in the patrol at that time, the witness objected to answering, 'on the grounds that I might incriminate myself'.

Twenty minutes later, after he had been provided with a certificate protecting against self-incrimination, he identified his fellow patrol members as Ben Roberts-Smith, The Sniper and a soldier the court referred to as Person 56. We will call him The Replacement, in that he was inserted into the patrol after the removal of The Trooper.

The Gunsmith described the Afghans the patrol encountered in the last compound they cleared. When Ben Roberts-Smith was conducting tactical questioning, The Gunsmith remembered one Afghan in particular: 'That individual had an animal with him, like a donkey. The donkey itself had a distinctive Afghani rug on it, a red designed rug. And there were baskets on that donkey that was full of wood for them to use for cooking.'

He explained the man was 'PUC'ed'—handcuffed and taken to the rear—while Roberts-Smith called for the interpreter (The Terp). In The Gunsmith's account, soon afterwards, Roberts-Smith directed The Terp to return to tactical headquarters accompanied by The Replacement.

The evidence, so far, was telling. It was consistent with the testimony given months earlier by Afghan witnesses from Darwan.

Owens took his time setting the scene. You could feel the tension rising. Roberts-Smith's solicitor Monica Allen moved outside to make a phone call. She returned to confer with Arthur Moses and Bruce McClintock. Watching on, I scribbled: 'a flurry of activity'. It was approaching high noon.

The Gunsmith continued: he had observed The Terp and The Replacement walking away, and The Sniper holding the PUC next to a 'large slope'.

Owens: 'And can you tell His Honour what happened next?'

Heart in mouth.

The Gunsmith: 'I noticed Ben Roberts-Smith, he had walked to a position maybe three to four metres away, and, as I was trying to understand what was happening, he turned around and walked forward and kicked the individual in the chest.'

Owens: 'And what happened to the individual?'

The Gunsmith: 'The individual was catapulted backwards and fell down the slope . . . I saw the individual's face strike a large rock and sustain a serious injury . . . Your Honour, he had teeth knocked out, a number of teeth, including his front teeth.'

I glanced across at Ben Roberts-Smith who, head down, was texting.

Owens walked The Gunsmith through what immediately followed, when Roberts-Smith and The Sniper walked to the creek bed below, with The Gunsmith close behind. He said he did so in a state of shock, 'because it was something that I've never encountered before'.

Our senior counsel asked where they ended up. The Gunsmith explained how they found the man, dusty and manacled, with an evident 'serious facial injury'.

Owens: 'Were you able to tell if the individual was alive or not?'

The Gunsmith: 'As we were approaching, the individual . . . attempted to sit up and fell back down again.' He said Ben Roberts-Smith directed him and The Sniper to drag the man to a large tree.

He said he walked off four or five metres and looked away. At this point the Afghan had risen, standing, still handcuffed.

Owens: 'And what is the next thing you recall, after you turned back to look away from the individual?'

The Gunsmith: 'There were a number of shots rang out.' He said he then turned around and saw The Sniper 'with a rifle in his shoulder'.

There was silence in the court.

The Gunsmith proceeded to explain the SSE process that followed. He said The Sniper took photos of the slain Afghan and an Icom radio 'positioned next to his body'.

Owens: 'Did he have an Icom on his body, to your knowledge?'

The Gunsmith: 'To my knowledge, no.'

Owens: 'Did you recognise the Icom?'

The Gunsmith: 'The Icom was slightly wet. The screen had water penetrated in it. So, it was fogged up . . . I guess it dawned on me where it came from . . . from the individual across the river.'

He was shown SSE photographs and identified the dead man and the Icom. His narrative continued, the pain of the last minutes of a man's life clawing through time and space. I had heard this story before, but never so powerfully described.

Once they were back at Camp Russell, The Gunsmith said Ben Roberts-Smith gathered the patrol together, telling them: 'This is what the story is . . . we engaged a spotter while moving to our HLS [helicopter landing site].'

The witness was also asked about a curious postscript, an indicator that, contrary to what we had assumed, what he had seen at the embankment at Darwan was more widely known, albeit selectively within 2 Squadron.

The Gunsmith: 'There was a drawing on the whiteboard in the lines [SASR's barracks at Camp Russell] . . . it was a winged penis kicking an individual off a drawn cliff.'

Owens: 'Did anyone in the regiment have a particular reputation for drawing winged penises?'

The Gunsmith: 'Yes . . . The Hunter.'

Owens moved on to questions about pre-deployment training. Did The Gunsmith recall the mock execution incident? He recalled the soldier playing the part of the Afghan detainee saying he found it 'odd'. When asked about the use of 'throwdowns', after seeking and obtaining an 'immunity' certificate, he said Ben Roberts-Smith had told him they needed to carry such items to validate engagements.

The Gunsmith's evidence in chief continued after the luncheon adjournment, with the focus now on Whiskey 108. This was more problematic, given we alleged that this witness had, upon orders, executed one of the victims. The procedure of seeking a certificate was again pursued but, after it was granted, this time The Gunsmith told His Honour that he was unwilling to give evidence. Legal argument filled the rest of the sitting afternoon.

There were mixed feelings within our team as we made our way from the court. The Gunsmith's evidence on Darwan had been pivotal, albeit unchallenged to this point. His decision not to answer questions on Whiskey 108 had been disappointing, but it was not surprising.

There was still a fair amount of tension among us, not least anxiety about The Gunsmith. But we accepted that there was scant reason for him to do us any favours, given he was here under our subpoena, testifying against an old mate and on behalf of a party to this matter who had accused him of murder.

Tess McGuire had been tasked with witness management, and there could not have been a better choice. She had organised for The Gunsmith to be accompanied by his wife for support, and she herself had offered him a mighty fund of empathy. This had helped generate a modicum of goodwill in him towards us.

I brought along a coffee for Tess when I joined the solicitors in the bunker the following morning. Nick McKenzie was up from Melbourne.

Arthur Moses SC undertook the cross-examination. His first question was about The Gunsmith's medical discharge from the Army on mental health grounds.

Moses: 'And you've been seeing a psychiatrist since 2020?'

The Gunsmith: 'Correct.'

He was further questioned about his treatment by a psychologist, and his extensive regime of medications. His barrister, Dr Ben Kremer, mounted a spirited challenge as each condition, depression, anxiety and so on was detailed.

The Gunsmith was also asked about alcohol abuse.

Moses: 'Have you been diagnosed as an alcoholic?'

The Gunsmith: 'No.'

Moses: 'But you have a problem with alcohol?'

The Gunsmith: 'No.'

He acknowledged suffering post-traumatic stress disorder (PTSD), experiencing ruminations, flashbacks and nightmares. He admitted to memory impairment. The Gunsmith said he stopped taking antipsychotic medication because 'it was having a detrimental effect on my everyday life . . . it was clouding, I had no energy.'

It was another long morning of public peering at private pain. After lunch, the questioning turned to Whiskey 108.

Moses: 'When did you first become aware that the respondents were alleging that you murdered an unarmed Afghan male on 12 April 2009?'

The Gunsmith: 'I'm unsure of the date.'

Arthur Moses underscored the wicked position into which our team had put the witness, compelling him to give self-incriminating evidence that would 'exacerbate your mental health injuries' and push him to the brink of suicide. The path between the witness box and the exit became well-worn as The Gunsmith was regularly asked to withdraw to accommodate legal argument.

The Gunsmith admitted to experiencing 'ruminations', 'not long after' 2009 and Whiskey 108. Moving on to Darwan, he was asked to describe the victim. He did so in impressive detail.

Moses: 'Okay, have you had flashbacks about Taliban insurgents that you have killed in Afghanistan—that is, lawfully killed?'

The Gunsmith: 'Yes.'

Questioning persisted about the number of missions The Gunsmith had undertaken and his personal kill count. There were further objections.

Back to 2009. He was asked whom he had spoken to about Whiskey 108 since that time. The witness denied discussing it with The Veteran, The Sergeant and The Scout, but acknowledged having done so with The Sniper.

Moses: 'I just want to stop there. I think you were the best man at The Sniper's wedding in 2014?'

The Gunsmith: 'That's correct.'

So a nightmare was being redoubled. The Gunsmith was being forced to give evidence against his brother-in-arms Ben Roberts-Smith, and against his once closest mate, The Sniper.

He acknowledged his brief contact with me, and denied communicating with the ABC's Mark Willacy (who had made an approach to his lawyer). He admitted to receiving, but not replying to, a text from Nick McKenzie. He said he had reported the approaches to his superiors.

Questioned about the first reporting, in 2018, of the alleged murder at Darwan, The Gunsmith said that he had seen it, but that he did not provide me with the information. He had already told the court he had informed both The Sergeant and The SSE in 2016 about the cliff kicking episode.

Asked to detail what he told The Sergeant, he said: 'I did mention to him that I saw the individual smash his face on a rock . . . and I saw the teeth explode out of his face.'

What a way to end the day. I stayed in town that night. Nick and I had a catch-up. We found a pasta restaurant in Angel Place and lingered there afterwards for another glass of wine.

The case was a long way from over. We knew we would continue to be filleted by our courtroom opponents, and that we'd get little credit from many media colleagues. But we could be privately pleased. Our central allegation, of the cliff kick and summary execution at Darwan, had been corroborated in detail by Ben Roberts-Smith's 2IC.

The next morning brought a setback. Our magic-spinning senior counsel, Nicholas Owens, was a reported close contact. One of his sons had tested positive to Covid-19, so he was to be quarantined for seven days.

Lyndelle Barnett would step up. She is super smart and knew the case backwards. Our sidelined silk watched on in isolation angst via Zoom.

Arthur Moses SC returned to The Gunsmith's proposition that the cliff kick at Darwan was common knowledge, asking for an explanation.

The Gunsmith: 'Well, the majority of the call signs [meaning the coded identifiers of individual teams] within the troop was aware of the incident.'

Moses: 'Why do you have that view?'

The Gunsmith: 'Because . . . Ben Roberts-Smith was telling individuals and it was evident that people knew the story just through their demeanour as such.'

The Gunsmith was asked about his discussion of Darwan with The SSE in 2019. He said he had visited his friend at his home, and over drinks they'd talked for three to four hours. Asked to recall what was said, The Gunsmith repeated the cliff kick story to the court in detail consistent with how he had previously told this story.

Moses: 'Now . . . you accept, don't you, that your memory is not good?'

The Gunsmith: 'That is correct.'

Moses: 'Yes, and you've had a bad run with mental health issues?'

The Gunsmith: 'That's correct.'

The barrister pushed harder. When he emphasised The Gunsmith's use of antipsychotic drugs and their capacity to fog the mind, the witness countered, insisting that they impacted only on minor 'incidences', and 'the major elements I can absolutely recall'.

The *60 Minutes* program featuring the Darwan story, which Nick and I had produced, began to be shown. Moses reassured the judge that he wouldn't 'put Your Honour through another showing of the other program' (referring to the *60 Minutes* 'lunch box' report, which had already been screened twice).

Dr Kremer, The Gunsmith's barrister, objected that the program was irrelevant. When he expressed concern for the welfare of his client, having noted his distress, the screening was paused.

The witness was now sobbing, but he composed himself and said it was fine to continue. The start button was pressed and the program—which, to my mind, had held up well, and was strong and well contextualised—unfolded. But twenty minutes into the screening, Justice Besanko, showing concern for the emotional impact on the witness, ordered a ten-minute break.

Once the program was over, Arthur Moses asked The Gunsmith whether, when he had seen it screened in 2019, it had triggered flashbacks. The witness said it had, but he disputed that he had confused the television version with what he had seen in real life.

Moses then turned to the Battle of Tizak. The Gunsmith gave a step-by-step account of the fighting that had delivered to him a Medal for Gallantry and to Ben Roberts-Smith a Victoria Cross. This consumed much of the rest of the day. The judge, attentive as ever, paused on one occasion and suggested the witness sip some water before resuming.

After The Gunsmith concluded his account, Arthur Moses asked him why he had not received his award until 2013, two years after the VC was awarded to his mate. The witness thought he'd missed out because of a medal allocation quota; he accepted that this had caused him 'hurt and disappointment'.

In response to a suggestion that had done the rounds—that he, The Gunsmith, should have been awarded the VC—he said, 'I was upset that something as outstanding as what both Ben and myself did was politicised, and they could have, you know, accepted the fact that both of us did as much as each other on that day.'

Questioning resumed after lunch. Arthur Moses asked: 'I just want to go back, if I can, about feeling hurt and let down by the system as a result of the issue in respect of Tizak . . . Do you think it is something that has caused you to deeply resent Mr Roberts-Smith?'

The Gunsmith: 'I loved him as a brother.'

Moses: 'No. But now you hate him, don't you?'

The Gunsmith: 'No, of course I don't hate him.'

Moses persisted with accusations of jealousy, but The Gunsmith assured the court that he did not envy the life Roberts-Smith led. In response to Moses' contention that he had sought to 'diminish Mr Roberts-Smith's reputation, in order to make yourself feel better', he denied making up stories about Darwan.

Moses: 'You've come to believe that story is true, haven't you, in regards to Darwan?'

The Gunsmith: 'Yes, that is exactly what happened.'

Moses: 'You've come to believe that story is true?'

The Gunsmith: 'No, I know it happened.'

Moses: 'And what I want to put to you directly is you're delusional about that. What do you say to that?'

The Gunsmith: 'That's incorrect.'

When I caught the train home that evening, I thought of the tears shed in Court 21A. Outside my carriage, the sky was a river and the tracks were awash. It was another of those wettest weeks on record. My old home town, Lismore, was underwater. And I wondered about the D at the end of PTSD. Is the stress they feel a disorder, or simply the understandable outcome of an experience that no ordinary person could forget?

The Gunsmith was in for more torment when we resumed the following morning. And, as I had noticed with other witnesses, he was sick of repetitive assaults on his mental stamina and personal integrity.

He was asked about the medication he had taken that morning to treat his depression. Upon intervention by his barrister, the answer, identifying these medications, was excised from the court transcript.

Taken through his evidence on Darwan, he was challenged about the alleged planted Icom radio. He was then challenged about his account of the drawing of the winged penis, about the proposition that the kick was 'common knowledge', and about Roberts-Smith instructing the patrol on what to say.

Moses: 'So you were being told to tell a false story, correct?'

The Gunsmith: 'We were directed to tell it . . . you seem to forget he was a VC winner at this time . . . he was running his own narrative.'

Moses: 'Yes, the only person who's running by their own narrative is you, isn't it?'

The Gunsmith: 'That's incorrect.'

The exchange became more heated. Arthur Moses SC repeatedly accused The Gunsmith of lying and queried whether his medication was impacting on his memory.

Moses: 'You are making things up as you're sitting in the witness box because your memory is so bad, isn't it?'

The Gunsmith: 'That's not correct . . . and I would say there are questions being posed to me here that I've never heard before.'

Moses: 'Right. Yes. That's because your evidence is being tested, isn't it?'

The Gunsmith: 'Test all you want.'

Taken to the discussion at Camp Russell between himself, Roberts-Smith, The Sniper and The Replacement, The Gunsmith was asked to identify the words spoken by his patrol commander.

Moses: 'Is that what he said: "I kicked the individual off the cliff"?'

The Gunsmith: 'No, he didn't say that.'

Moses: 'What did he say?'

The Gunsmith: 'I kicked the cunt off the cliff.'

In his evidence The Gunsmith had positioned himself as being at the neutral centre between the pro- and anti-BRS camps within the SASR. To Moses' proposition that The Sergeant was a passionate hater, he responded, 'You could say that.'

Speaking of The SSE, Moses asked: '[He] told you, didn't he, that he didn't like Mr Roberts-Smith?'

The Gunsmith: 'I can't recall him saying that.'

But the witness did acknowledge that The Veteran was an avowed BRS enemy.

Moses returned to The Gunsmith's alleged sense of injustice about not being awarded the Victoria Cross. By this stage, in a sense, the witness box had become the psychiatrist's couch.

The Gunsmith poured it out. He said he did not think he deserved the VC; he thought he and Ben 'did as much as each other'. He felt his family had suffered an injustice and repeated his lament at the politicisation of the action. His *cri de coeur*—that '[t]he regiment doesn't deserve liars and cowards'—seemed to express his anguish at being part of a profound and proud experience that had turned bitter.

Arthur Moses SC leaned in harder, berating the witness for being used by The Sergeant to 'bring Mr Roberts-Smith down'.

Moses: 'You've been ruminating over that, haven't you?'

The Gunsmith: 'Yes.'

Lyndelle Barnett objected.

His Honour turned to Arthur Moses: '[L]isten to me, please . . . Section 41C of the *Evidence Act* . . . gives me the power to disallow a question if it's in a tone that is belittling, insulting or otherwise inappropriate.'

Arthur Moses, partially penitent: 'I will not withdraw the question, but I will take that in mind, Your Honour.'

The Gunsmith acknowledged being upset at being 'manipulated'. He appeared spent. This was his fourth day in the box, and it was not yet over. There was another closed court session that afternoon.

When open court resumed on the Friday morning, Arthur Moses SC persisted with questions about psychiatric treatment, medication, rumination, flashbacks and the prospect of the witness's memory being affected by media reporting. He appealed to the court that ongoing punishment of the witness was regrettable but necessary.

'We did not want to do this. The Gunsmith was brought here, despite the medical evidence that was tendered to Your Honour. This is not our doing. So I need to discharge my duty to cross-examine the witness on these matters . . . I have to do it. I don't want to do it, but that's my duty to do it, Your Honour.'

By the lunch break, it was over. The Gunsmith had accepted being used by others to harm Ben Roberts-Smith. In general, he had acknowledged psychiatric and memory problems. He had avoided answering questions about what happened at Whiskey 108. But he was potently consistent about what he had seen at Darwan.

When he departed the witness box, he looked left to his former brother-in-arms, seated in the far corner. Ben Roberts-Smith turned away and looked out the window.

CHAPTER 72

THE COUNTRY WIVES' CLUB

A few sustained beliefs help in this work. One is faith in human decency—tested at times, but important. Another is faith in the healing power of truth. The witnesses we called were hardly thrilled by the experience, but, as we learned, many ultimately found it cathartic. We heard, and hoped it was true, that the unlocking of guilty secrets delivered some relief.

As with The Gunsmith, I was interested to set eyes on The SSE. Ben Roberts-Smith's creeping paranoia had placed him as one of our informants—it was The SSE who had received the threatening letters. But the truth was we had never met.

Lyndelle Barnett led the questioning, and moved straight to Whiskey 108. On 12 April 2009, The SSE was a scout in The Scot's patrol, alongside Ben Roberts-Smith and The Gunsmith. He told the court that once they were inside the compound, a tunnel was discovered and he saw 'two or three soldiers standing around a person in white'. The Afghan male was flexi-cuffed. The smallest soldier present, The Hunter, slid down the tunnel and, as he was clearing it, The SSE said he heard a burst of gunfire.

He told the court that soon afterwards he overheard a conversation between The Scot and Ben Roberts-Smith. The Scot asked Roberts-Smith whether an ISR (intelligence surveillance reconnaissance) drone was above them. The SSE overheard The Scot radio the JTAC (joint terminal attack controller) to learn the drone had been pushed off station.

Given his expertise, The SSE was then directed to conduct sensitive site exploitation on two bodies. The first body, he recalled, had an injury to the face—a gunshot wound around the eyeball. He moved to the next body.

The SSE: 'Everything from this person's pockets was put in the bag. As I went down the . . . left-hand leg, I felt a hard appendage . . . I pulled up the pants leg and discovered it was a prosthetic leg.'

Barnett: 'Did you locate any weapons on this EKIA?'

The SSE: 'No.'

He described photographing the bodies with the evidence bag 'placed on the person's chest'. He explained the three inscribed identifiers on the bag, which were the PUC number, the person conducting the SSE and the location of the body. He went on to explain that additionally he searched a third body, 'a person in white . . . lying on his back, there was blood on the ground', inside the compound, 'roughly near the tunnel entrance'.

Barnett asked what The SSE heard when the patrol returned to their vehicles. He said he heard The Scot and Ben Roberts-Smith say they had 'blooded the rookie'.

Barnett: 'Had you heard the term "rookie" used before with reference to any person in particular?'

The SSE: 'Yes, that was a joke between myself and The Gunsmith. He had come to the troop a year prior, and it was a running joke between the two of us, because he was a good twenty years older than I was . . . It was a running joke we used from the movie *Super Troopers* that he was the "rookie fuck", and I would constantly take the piss out of him about that. Sorry for swearing.'

The questioning moved to Darwan. The SSE was not on that mission. He said that, after 2 Squadron returned to Perth at the end of 2012, there was a function at the Gratwick Club on base, which was the first time he had caught up with his friend The Gunsmith. 'It was there that he broke down to me,' The SSE said. The Gunsmith told him, he recounted, that 'something very bad happened on the last job'.

After some routine legal jousting, The SSE was allowed to continue. He recalled The Gunsmith telling him, 'I turned around, I saw one of my teammates have hold of a detainee, I then saw Ben Roberts-Smith kick him off a cliff.'

The next passage of testimony went less to critical evidence, but more to the collective psyche of soldiers and their families as they struggled to move on from the many searing experiences of a foreign war within the indifferent isolation of their home country. The SSE said he had tried to shut down the conversation that night with The Gunsmith: 'This was another night where [I was] watching friends break down over things that happened in Afghanistan . . . I was sick of it.'

He then gave an account, heard by me for the first time, of later going with The Gunsmith and two other soldiers to see The RSM. 'The Gunsmith outlined the events at the Darwan mission,' The SSE said, using words to the effect that 'he watched Ben Roberts-Smith kick a detainee off a cliff'. He said the response from The RSM 'wasn't very receptive . . . It was way out of his hands; it was way above his head. And he honestly didn't know what to do with it.'

The SSE told the court of a second meeting with another regimental sergeant major in the following year. This time, the regimental sergeant major, having initiated the meeting, was more receptive. He said what he most remembered was The Gunsmith again describing what occurred at Darwan 'as he broke down in his office'.

Lyndelle Barnett took The SSE to 12 June 2018 and his receipt of the notorious anonymous letter. The SSE described some of the contents and said he had reported it to a third regimental sergeant major. It had arrived soon after he gave evidence to the Inspector-General of the ADF. The SSE told the court: 'The threat I took seriously. I had concern for my own safety and that of my family's.'

A busy week's evidence wound up in the late afternoon. The SSE would spend the weekend in a Sydney hotel room.

On Monday, 7 March 2022, day 46, the city was a mess after a head-on smash on the Harbour Bridge. It felt like a full day was done by the time we got to court.

Arthur Moses SC commenced cross-examination of The SSE. His first questions were about his contact with Nick McKenzie and me.

The SSE was challenged about his reporting of the threatening letter and his connections to members of the reputed anti-BRS camp. It was revealed that The Scout, a friend, was previously related to him by marriage. The SSE said they had spoken, but not about the case.

The Sergeant was also a friend. There had been some discussion of Whiskey 108 with him, but only in general terms. He agreed that The Sergeant believed Ben Roberts-Smith had not deserved a Victoria Cross, and he acknowledged having spoken with The Sergeant about 'the events that occurred in Darwan in 2012'.

60 Minutes got another workout. Arthur Moses told the judge: 'I'm not going to put Your Honour through having to watch another episode . . .' Instead, an extract, related to the anonymous letter episode, was screened.

Through repeated challenges, The SSE denied supplying any journalist with any information about this, something Nick McKenzie and I knew to be true, at least in relation to us.

Tizak was next. Arthur Moses asked about the second meeting with The RSM, which he contended had been called in part 'for the purpose of listening to complaints and rumours that were being raised in relation to awards for the Battle of Tizak'.

Moses: 'You were upset about Tizak because you didn't receive an award, correct?'

The SSE: 'No, that's incorrect.'

Five SAS patrols, designated Epic 1 to 5, had assaulted entrenched Taliban in superior numbers at the village of Tizak on 11 June 2010. The SSE was a member of Epic 1, the six-man patrol that had undertaken the uphill assault on three machine-gun nests. Ben Roberts-Smith, The Gunsmith and The Corporal had attacked the left flank; The Scot, The SSE and a third soldier (known to the court as Person 8) had assaulted the right flank.

The efforts by Ben Roberts-Smith and The Gunsmith that day had been rewarded with a Victoria Cross and a Medal for Gallantry, respectively.

On the other side, The Scot had been awarded a Star of Gallantry, one notch below a Victoria Cross on the honours list.

Moses: 'Do you have the view that you should have received the same award as The Scot because you were beside him that day?'

The SSE: 'No.'

Asked whether the issue of medals was ever discussed within the team, he said that, after they returned to Australia in 2010, they gathered in a room. The SSE had accused The Scot of lacking 'humility': 'I've read your citation . . . the things that occurred here have been overemphasised.' He said The Scot reacted with anger; following that meeting, The SSE cut ties with his former patrol commander.

In countering allegations by Arthur Moses that the split was down to his own jealousy, The SSE said the fallout over the honours and awards from Tizak spread through the SASR, focusing mainly on Ben's VC. He likened the regimental rumour mill to a 'Country Wives' Club', a 'toxic environment' where rumour was expanded 'tenfold'.

The SSE spoke of 'different angles' on the truth of what happened. Asked for his own angle on Ben's VC, he said (having largely been out of line of sight, on the right flank): 'I didn't see the action he received the award for.'

The SSE told the court that, prior to the conferral, he had a 'daily phone call from Ben complaining . . . that they were both potentially going to receive the same award'.

Moses: 'You've just made that up, haven't you?'

The SSE: 'No.'

Moses: 'The reason that you've said that is because you know that The Scot and Mr Roberts-Smith are close friends, correct?'

The SSE: 'In the time I've known both those gentlemen, I wouldn't say they are close friends at all.'

The impact on him of all this disputation at that time was similar to The Gunsmith's reaction. He experienced a souring within an 'alpha environment', overwhelmed by people trying to outdo one another. He said he became 'tired of the topic'.

In the courtroom the next morning, his third day in the box, The SSE also felt weary when he had to face up to Arthur Moses SC and defend his evidence over what he had heard about Darwan, the rookie blooding allegation and what happened at Whiskey 108. The testing of evidence on both sides meant transcripts of earlier testimony were continually being retrieved and fine detail prosecuted for signs of any inconsistency in the retelling. It could at times lead to monotony. The soundscape of Court 21A became like the drone of a distant lawnmower.

The SSE confessed to drinking from the prosthetic leg. He accepted that the events at Whiskey 108 had fed into the same 'Country Wives' Club' rumour mill. He rejected feeding into that mill lies about what he saw and heard at the tunnel. He was repeatedly confronted about his contact with the media.

Questioned about a text approach from Nick McKenzie, he repeated his assurance that they had not spoken. Arthur Moses was unconvinced. The SSE said that of course he recognised McKenzie from the *60 Minutes* reporting but, 'like I said, if I saw him on the street, I don't know what, who he is'.

Back and forth, over and over . . . Darwan; his contact with The Sergeant and The Veteran; the meetings with the regimental sergeant majors. And then again to Tizak.

Ben Roberts-Smith had not sued over our reporting of the VC action. However, it was alleged that jealousy over the award was the root cause of the defamatory accusations made by SAS men against Roberts-Smith. So cross-examination returned to the battle. To my mind, this was a risky manoeuvre for the BRS team, in that it also opened the door to questions about the merit of the VC.

Asked to detail his recollections of the assault, The SSE described the two teams advancing on either side of a 'barn'-like building. He said The Scot, with his team on the right, threw over the building a hand grenade, which exploded. As they moved around the building, Ben's team, to the left, moved towards the doorway of the building. Neither team had consistent eyes on the other.

Moses drilled down, asking why The SSE doubted The Scot's Star of Gallantry. He replied: 'His action there, throwing a grenade over a building, was written up to be the saviour of the day, and I said to him, "I don't believe it really was, mate. You didn't know where the grenade was going."'

The SSE insisted his grievance was not about being overlooked; rather, it was about exaggeration and a lack of humility. On the other hand, he explained, his patrol commander's decision to attack was a show of much-admired leadership. So, in his view, an award for leadership was well deserved, but less so one for gallantry.

Moses turned to Roberts-Smith and the VC. The SSE was again plain-spoken, telling the barrister: 'I don't think he's deserving of it . . . that's been my opinion for the last twelve years.'

Moses: 'Again, the reason you express that view is because you were upset that you hadn't received a medal?'

The SSE: 'No, that's not correct.'

Moses: '[Y]ou told me yesterday that you're not taking any medication at the moment, is that right?'

The SSE: 'That's right.'

Moses: 'Have you been seeing a psychologist . . .?'

The SSE: 'Yes.' This was for the sake of marriage counselling, he explained.

Ben Roberts-Smith's barrister sought more information on why The SSE felt his client was underserving of the Commonwealth's premier bravery award, and whether he had ever expressed this to Roberts-Smith.

The SSE: 'I definitely told him that this award made me extremely uncomfortable.'

He said he had voiced this sentiment when Roberts-Smith first learned he was to be decorated and drew members of Epic 1 together at a cafe in Cottesloe. Ben had asked that the team members participate in upcoming 'events'. The SSE said his discomfort arose from this, and 'the rumours that were running wild'.

Asked to explain, he said from general conversations with other patrol members he heard 'the pin wasn't pulled correctly' when Ben Roberts-Smith threw a grenade. Also, of Ben entering a building 'with a stoppage of his weapon', and that 'The Gunsmith should have got the VC'.

Arthur Moses appeared stung: 'Well, you've heard the quote, haven't you, that rumours are carried by haters, spread by fools and accepted by idiots?'

Lyndelle Barnett objected and Arthur Moses backed off. His Honour ruled: 'All right. Well, it will be noted on the transcript the question is withdrawn.'

Arthur Moses rephrased it, querying who was spreading the rumours, and whether The SSE was a hater.

The SSE: 'No, I don't hate Ben. I don't know the guy . . . I know who he is, and I know that I worked with him twelve years ago, but as a person . . . I've no idea.'

Challenged again, he said he was not jealous and that he had made his own mind up about the contested incidents at Tizak.

The day's cross-examination ended with a chorus of familiar accusations.

Moses: 'What I want to put to you is this. That you were happy to spread rumours yourself about Whiskey 108 because you felt cheated about not getting an award at Tizak; correct?'

The SSE: 'No.'

Moses: 'And you were happy to spread rumours about what The Gunsmith had told you about Darwan because you felt cheated in respect to not receiving an award for Tizak; correct?'

The SSE: 'That's incorrect.'

But the barrage was still not over. So, a fifth night of room service and TV for this witness, still in isolation.

When The SSE took his seat again the following morning, the issue was the letter.

It struck me as odd that a witness could be under attack for *receiving* a threatening letter, but Arthur Moses SC apparently saw a chink. Two sentences from the letter had not so far been divulged.

He read them to the court: "'We are very aware of your murderous actions over many tours of Afghanistan and we have specific mission details, dates and witnesses who now are willing to expose you to the authorities so that you are criminally investigated. Just like when you participated in the execution of two PUCs from the Taliban's makeshift medical compound following the battle in Tizak.'"

Moses wanted to know why The SSE had not referred to these sentences in earlier evidence.

After a volley of interjections, and after the witness had worn a path in and out of the court, The SSE ultimately confessed to being embarrassed by the accusation. He also admitted relief that it had not been mentioned in our reporting. But he also said he had not heard this allegation before he received this letter, nor had he ever been in a makeshift Taliban medical compound at Tizak.

We had known of this accusation, but we had considered it baseless—indeed, a clumsy attempt at counter-blackmail. It is worth remembering that The SSE had immediately and voluntarily handed this letter over to his superiors, and we presumed it had later been examined by the IGADF.

Four gruelling days ended with The SSE on the back foot. But, to our mind, he had proven an excellent witness. His unchallenged evidence about where the bodies were located at Whiskey 108 was powerful. A taciturn, blunt and at times brutal truth-teller.

CHAPTER 73

THE ANTI-BULLIES

The tunnel at Whiskey 108 would be further explored. Two more witnesses were lined up. The next, called by Nine under subpoena, was The 2IC. Fellow soldiers described him as reserved and principled. Earlier on, I heard he had expressed disquiet about the 2009 mission. But any concerns he had were never shared with me. When I reached him on the phone, he politely refused further contact.

Lyndelle Barnett would again lead the evidence, with Nicholas Owens still in isolation and watching via videolink, as was our other sidelined senior counsel, Sandy Dawson. A virtue for Owens was, as he later told me, 'being able to express my opinions loudly at the screen'.

On 12 April 2009, The 2IC had been in the patrol at Whiskey 108 led by Ben Roberts-Smith's friend The Freefaller. It included Ben's other mates, The Hunter and The Bodyguard, plus our witnesses The Cyclist and The Driver.

The 2IC gave evidence of being in the compound when the tunnel was discovered, and of seeing 'two insurgents inside the tunnel . . . Once they came out, [they were] obviously very frightened. One had a distinctive limp, that's the person with the prosthetic leg. Immediately on coming out of the tunnel he was lifting his trouser, pointing to the prosthetic leg.' The second man, The 2IC said, was 'baldish', with a beard.

The 2IC told the court he then saw them marched off by Ben Roberts-Smith and The Hunter. He moved to a defensive position and later heard a 'burst of machine-gun fire'. Later he saw the man with the prosthetic leg lying prone, shot dead.

Lyndelle Barnett changed topics, asking about a more recent interaction with The Freefaller, his former patrol commander. He told of an exchange they had after The 2IC had been served with our subpoena in 2021: 'It was a Friday. Out of the blue, which took me by complete surprise, The Freefaller said, "RS knows that you're going to be a witness for this defamation case . . . you don't have to be a witness . . . if you speak to RS's lawyers, they will get you to sign some sort of piece of paper . . . if you don't, he will see you in court."'

Which was the situation that now transpired.

Arthur Moses SC again cross-examined. The 2IC disagreed that he had a 'hazy' recollection of the Whiskey 108 mission. He was tested as to his recall of the presence of an interpreter who spoke Farsi and was used to call out the Afghans in the tunnel. His competence was also queried.

Moses: 'Isn't it a fact you got sacked as the 2IC of The Freefaller's patrol, weren't you?'

The 2IC: 'No, I did not get sacked.'

He rejected further accusations that he had been removed for 'poor performance' and 'poor situational awareness'. The 2IC said it was more that he and The Freefaller 'never saw eye-to-eye, right from the word go . . . I was quite happy not to be in that patrol anymore, because it was toxic.' He considered that he disliked, rather than hated, The Freefaller, and he did not hold a grudge.

It was a short stint before the clock wound down on another day.

Then it wound up again the next morning, with The 2IC back in court, confronting a re-energised and relentless Arthur Moses SC, who had seen a weakness in the witness's story of an interpreter speaking Farsi.

The 2IC conceded he might have spoken Pashto.

The smallest details of this incident were now being pursued. Which man came out first? Which was the prosthetic leg—left or right? What colour were his trousers? Did the two men have their arms in the air? Which one had hair, and which one was balding?

The 2IC held his own, reaching back to fragments of memory from thirteen years past. But he could not recall whether he saw the men searched or handcuffed.

He did recall the presence of his then commander (Person 81, The Captain) who, he said, also saw the man with the prosthetic leg. This evidence potentially raised the stakes, given that the former captain was still in the Army in a senior command position.

The 2IC was aware that the prosthetic leg had become a drinking vessel. He saw it in use at the Fat Lady's Arms, but he did not drink from it.

Then, as he told the court, he recalled something else back at Camp Russell: he had spoken to The Driver. Arthur Moses asked what was said.

The 2IC: 'Words to the effect that that was wrong, what occurred.'

Moses: 'What were you referring to?'

The 2IC: 'The killing of the prosthetic leg man.'

Moses: 'Did you see the killing?'

The 2IC: 'No.'

The witness conceded he had not reported the incident to his superiors.

Moses: 'What I want to suggest to you is you never saw two persons coming out of the tunnel. What do you say to that?'

The 2IC: 'Absolute nonsense.'

Moses hammered the witness about assumptions, and about the blurring of fact and rumour. There was a further closed court session before the luncheon adjournment and, with it, his release and the appearance of a new witness.

———

The man known to the court as Person 43 we will call The Reader. I heard much about him when I was writing *No Front Line*. He was described as one of the thoughtful, self-effacing soldiers who was in step with the formal special forces mission profile projecting 'courageous restraint'. This put him at odds with the warrior elite, who preferred their own informal, direct-action mandate of 'killing bad cunts'.

I was told he had clashed with The Scot and Ben Roberts-Smith, and that he was undeterred from calling them out when he saw unprofessional conduct. For this he was disparaged, and often consigned to secondary roles. I knew he had fought bravely at Tizak. And I had tried to interview him—without success, as was all too common.

Lyndelle Barnett began her examination in chief on the afternoon of Thursday, 10 March 2022. Like the preceding witness, The Reader remembered The Hunter discovering the tunnel at Whiskey 108. When The Reader was calling for an interpreter, an 'elderly Afghani male with a beard' emerged. The man was 'PUC'ed' and handed over to The Scot's tactical questioning team.

The Reader was unsure whether an interpreter arrived. He said he was also unsure whether anyone else emerged from the tunnel.

Barnett: 'Did you have a conversation with anyone else about the PUCs?'

The Reader: 'Yes. The 2IC asked me when we were walking off . . . where were the PUCs, and I answered . . . something along the lines of, "You know where they are."'

Barnett: 'And did he say something to you in response?'

The Reader replied that he recalled The 2IC was upset and said 'something along the lines of, "That's effed."'

His Honour: 'I appreciate you probably don't want to use the word, but I think it is important, if you can recall the word, that you tell me.'

The Reader: 'Yes, Your Honour. He basically said, "That's fucked."'

The examination in chief was again short and to the point. In the mid-afternoon Arthur Moses SC rose to challenge The Reader. Taken through the make-up of the patrols present at Whiskey 108, he wrongly identified The Sergeant as one of the patrol commanders. He again related his account of the tunnel discovery and the calling for an interpreter. He did not recall an interpreter arriving. He thought the call-out had been in English. He said he helped pull the old man out.

Moses again stepped through the detail of what was alleged. The Reader stumbled over the exact movements of The Hunter; the accuracy of his memory was being interrogated in view of his misidentification of one of the patrol commanders. There was an ongoing challenge to his ability to distinguish between what was standard operating procedure (SOP) and what had specifically occurred.

Cross-examination resumed the following morning. The Reader, having been medically discharged in 2017, acknowledged suffering from PTSD. He said he continued to take medication, but denied that it impacted on his memory.

Arthur Moses SC returned to the tunnel. He was critical of The Reader's evidence that an insurgent was called out. He claimed that, if they had done that, it would have given them 'an opportunity to prepare to fight'.

Moses: 'I want to say to you that you did not call out to anyone to come out of the tunnel at Whiskey 108. What do you say about that?'

The Reader: 'I would say that is incorrect.'

Ben Roberts-Smith's barrister claimed that The Reader was unable to navigate the shadowland between SOPs and actuality, between rumour and fact. His role at the Battle of Tizak in 2010 also came under fire, with Moses querying whether The Reader had sought to be written up for rescuing an Afghan casualty.

Moses: 'Were you upset that you didn't receive an award for your actions at Tizak?'

The Reader: 'No.'

Moses: 'Were you upset that Mr Roberts-Smith received an award?'

The Reader: 'No.'

Moses: 'Were you upset that The Scot received an award?'

The Reader: 'No—in fact, I nominated [him].' The Reader said he had nominated The Scot for a leadership award.

Interrogated further about the Roberts-Smith VC, The Reader said there was a question mark. He believed 'there should have been more investigation before awarding it'.

Moses: 'Did you observe Mr Roberts-Smith's actions that day?'

The Reader: 'No.'

Moses: 'And you said it is in doubt?'

The Reader: 'Yes.'

Moses: 'Why is it in doubt?'

The Reader: 'Because the only witnesses [were] his team. There were no other witnesses.'

The Reader admitted he had told many people he doubted that Ben Roberts-Smith earned the Victoria Cross, and that he viewed him as a bully. He insisted he was not bitter about being denied accolades.

Moses: 'You're upset about it, aren't you?'

The Reader: 'I'm not an attention seeker. I don't want any awards.'

The Reader was released at lunchtime on Friday. Both he and The 2IC had done well, sticking to what they knew and saying no more than necessary. There were mistakes, but about this our lawyers were generally unfussed. It is normal to confuse detail. More suspicious is a parade of witnesses who, word perfect, tell the same story.

We thought the men's evidence showed they had a 'moral compass'. Their occasional frailty of memory enhanced rather than detracted from their credibility.

The lawyers continued to work through the afternoon. Dean and Tess and Jeremy would not close the door on the bunker until later that evening. The weekend to come was welcomed.

CHAPTER 74

AN EXHIBITION EXECUTION

It was Monday, 14 March, day 51 of the trial. Person 24, whom we shall call The Gunner, was in the witness box. Nicholas Owens SC was back.

During The Gunner's evidence in chief, Owens asked him about the blooding of rookies. About a week before the Whiskey 108 mission, the witness recounted, 'The Scot came to the doorway of our patrol room, and he was in a jovial manner, dancing a bit of a jig in the doorway. And he said that we are going to blood the rookie.' The Gunner had understood that the rookie in this case would be The Gunsmith.

By no means the largest soldier in the troop, The Gunner was carrying the largest weapon, a 7.62mm Maximi machine gun, when 2 Squadron advanced on Whiskey 108 on 12 April 2009. Having arrived at the compound, he stood guard outside. He said he heard The Scot yelling to The Gunsmith to 'get in here, get in here now'. Soon after, he saw Ben Roberts-Smith emerge, hauling an Afghan man.

The Gunner told Owens he thought the burst fired into the back of the Afghan was of 'eight to ten rounds'. After which, he said, Roberts-Smith's Minimi machine gun jammed, and 'he immediately turned and started rectifying the stoppage'.

Owens: 'Okay. Were you able to see any other SAS operators at this time?'

The Gunner: 'No, only The Scout, who I was with . . . I recall saying to The Scout at the time, "Did we just witness an execution?"'

Moving on, The Gunner said it became dark and night-vision goggles were fitted. He remembered seeing his patrol commander, The Veteran, 'carrying the prosthetic leg from the PUC . . . tucked in his backpack.'

He was shown a photo.

Owens: 'Okay, can you tell His Honour what you recognise . . .?'

The Gunner: 'That is the man that BRS shot with the machine gun, with the prosthetic leg.'

Owens: 'No further questions, Your Honour.'

Cross-examination began just after 11 am. Arthur Moses SC sought to erase all credibility from the word picture that had been vividly painted of Roberts-Smith frogmarching the Afghan out of the compound, gripping him one-handed by his clothing, the man's feet sometimes off the ground. 'Now, the evidence you've just given to His Honour moments ago, in relation to you alleging that you saw Mr Roberts-Smith holding somebody in his hand—that was false, wasn't it?'

The Gunner: 'I wouldn't be in a court of law giving that evidence if it was false.'

A sustained burst of accusations of lying followed. The Gunner conceded that what had occurred at Whiskey 108 was at the eye of a sweltering storm of rumour: 'Yes, it has been the subject of much talk, Your Honour, but it has always been veiled, very veiled. It's something people don't want to talk about.'

An extract from *60 Minutes* was played. The Roberts-Smith dirt file was mined. Pictures of The Gunner urinating and with his buttocks exposed elicited a concession that the photos were embarrassing. He said he'd had discussions about the *60 Minutes* episode with friends such as The Scout.

Moses pounced: 'Did The Scout tell you in the calls he has had with you recently that he has been to give evidence in this case?'

The Gunner: 'Yes . . . I gave him a welfare call on the night he was in here.'

Moses: 'And what did you say to him?'

The Gunner: 'I asked him how he was going . . . if he was all right.'

Moses: 'And what did he say to you?'

The Gunner: 'He said it was tough.'

Moses: 'Anything else?'

The Gunner: 'No. He mentioned that you went at him like a rabid dog.'

The cross-examination moved to The Gunner's contact with the media. He had attended my book launch. We had been briefly introduced, but he'd had no further contact with me or any contact with Nick McKenzie. As he explained, for him the evening 'was more about catching up with friends than it was about attending a media launch. I didn't agree with the guys going to the media . . . I am adamant that I think it is extremely unfair the way this has panned out for BRS. But yes, I was there.'

The Gunner's testimony positioned him as objecting less to what Roberts-Smith was alleged to have done as to the way he was alleged to have done it. He had sympathy for Roberts-Smith, as well as empathy for his alleged victims—that is, those victims within the SASR. But for the two slaughtered Afghans he had zero remorse. In his words: 'I have no qualms whatsoever with what happened to those people on the ground at Whiskey 108. What I am here for is to support the people who were my mates who were adversely affected through blooding.'

Arthur Moses wanted to know how The Gunner had been affected by his war service. Discharged from the SAS on medical health grounds in 2017, he had suffered, he said, a 'general anxiety disorder' and 'may have been diagnosed with depression'.

Moses: 'You've been diagnosed with alcohol dependence?'

The Gunner: 'Yes, I have.'

He was queried about the medication he was currently prescribed. He rejected having memory problems. He was asked about Roberts-Smith's

Victoria Cross and acknowledged 'murmurings among the squadrons', which he did not 'buy into'. The Gunner identified The Sergeant as questioning the legitimacy of the VC, and The Veteran as an 'avid BRS hater'.

As to Whiskey 108, he had a vague recollection of his patrol engaging in a post-mission debrief, when they discussed what they'd witnessed. The Veteran had said Roberts-Smith had 'broken the rules of conflict'.

Moses, doing his job, applied microscopic attention to hair-splitting detail. He pointed out, for example, that, in The Gunner's account, Roberts-Smith was 'carrying' the victim from the compound, but elsewhere he said he had been 'dragging' him.

The Gunner: 'Let's correct that . . . he carried him . . . You want me to make a mistake, but in my eyes dragging and carrying someone out is a very similar thing.'

Moses: 'And you've been saying that because you've been caught out telling a lie?'

The Gunner: 'I am not telling a lie, Mr Moses.'

Moses continued to turn up the heat, querying which hand Roberts-Smith had used to carry the man. By the shirt or the trousers? Where was he facing? In what direction did Roberts-Smith walk? What was the relative position of The Scout at the time? The Gunner said Roberts-Smith 'had him like a handbag', but he was not '100 per cent on the detail'.

The detail of the alleged shooting was further dissected. Arthur Moses proposed to the witness that the fusion of rumour and media reporting about blooding had blurred his accurate recollection of the events at Whiskey 108.

The Gunner, never one to rest on the back foot, counterpunched. He was sick of answering the same questions. He did not want to be here. Friendships had been severed over this issue.

Nicholas Owens rallied in support: 'This has been gone over—I've lost count.' Arthur Moses defended his approach; His Honour allowed the question. The barrister and the witness proceeded to swing at one another until the luncheon adjournment.

—

Whiskey 108 dominated the afternoon session as well. The Gunner accepted his weakness in recollecting how many patrols had been involved. And he was unsure how many times the events had been discussed in the interim. 'We've discussed the leg, Das Boot. That's how it is referred to.' He admitted doing so with The Scout.

Moses: 'And can you recall what was discussed?'

The Gunner: 'It would have been a joke, some sort of dark humour.'

The Gunner disclosed drinking from the prosthetic leg 'many times'. Unabashed, he later added: 'At the time, I thought it was hilarious that we were drinking from the target's prosthetic leg.'

The barrister searched for weaknesses in the witness's disciplinary record, reaching further into the Roberts-Smith dirt file. Moses asked about a 2011 incident when The Gunner had tossed a 'flashbang'—a non-lethal distraction grenade—at another soldier's feet.

Moses: 'You did that?'

The Gunner: 'Yes, I did.'

Moses: 'And did you get into trouble for that?'

The Gunner: 'No, I did not.'

Back to contact with the media, and the impact of this on friendships. The Gunner said it had caused him to sever his relationship with his former patrol commander, The Veteran.

'Why was that . . .?'

The Gunner: 'I didn't agree with the agenda he was pushing, and he was pushing it really hard. And I still don't agree with the fact that BRS is here and under an extreme amount of duress for killing bad dudes who we went over there to kill.'

Moses returned to The Gunner's account of the machine-gunning, interrogating his evidence about how far he was from Roberts-Smith at the time. He was pressed about his claim of being here to support his mates.

Moses: 'You're here to back up The Scout's story in respect of Whiskey 108, aren't you?'

The Gunner: 'Farcical, Mr Moses. I'm here to tell the story of what I saw on the ground, and what I don't think is fair is how . . . good soldiers have been adversely affected, not only by somebody else's actions on the ground, but also in this courtroom.'

It was a hard day's work all round by the time the court adjourned. But Arthur Moses SC was not yet finished.

On Tuesday morning, the cross-examination resumed with the usual queries about who was spoken to overnight and what messages were received. The Gunner said a friend had texted to say, 'Don't decompress too hard and keep a clear head for tomorrow.'

Moses: 'Did you decompress last night?'

The Gunner: 'I had one beer last night. I decompressed by going to the sauna and having a beer.'

More questions followed about alcohol dependency and medication. Tension again rose as The Gunner was asked to identify his medication, which he said he had been taking since 2015.

Moses: 'Were you diagnosed with a major depressive disorder?'

The Gunner: 'I don't recall it being a major depressive disorder, but I was diagnosed with depression, Your Honour.'

Both blood pressure and emotion were on the rise. Arthur Moses demanded The Gunner identify the friends he said he was here to support. When he pinpointed The Gunsmith as the first of these friends, as a person he had encouraged to join the SAS, he lost his composure: 'He's a good soldier . . . he's a great person. And to see how his life has been turned upside down . . .'

His Honour: 'Do you have some water there . . . Can the witness be given some water?'

The Gunner: 'Thank you. I find it heartbreaking, Mr Moses.'

Asked about other soldiers he was here for, he nominated The Redhead and The Trooper as both being 'adversely affected' by Roberts-Smith, and a further operator he did not know personally, The Replacement.

The Gunner told the court he had directly heard Roberts-Smith speak of The Redhead 'in a derogatory, aggressive manner'. His knowledge of The Trooper being 'ostracised' by Roberts-Smith was gleaned more from others.

Turning yet again to Whiskey 108, Arthur Moses pointed to identifiers on a map and pressed for an explanation about discrepancies between what The Gunner had marked and what he had said. The Gunner conceded the possibility of 'disparities'.

Moses: 'I want to put this directly to you. The evidence that you gave yesterday to His Honour, that you saw Mr Roberts-Smith exiting the compound, was false. What do you say about that?'

The Gunner: 'What I say about that, Your Honour, is that there is no reason for BRS to have exited that compound with that Afghan male in his hand [frogmarching him] . . . What I think is that it was an exhibition execution. He wanted people to see that he was going to kill someone out there in front of everyone.'

Another comment that would resonate: The Gunner was contending that, far from this being a covert killing, Ben Roberts-Smith at Whiskey 108 in April 2009 had gone looking for an audience.

Back to the alleged 'blooding the rookie' comment by The Scot. Asked who was present when this was said, The Gunner snapped back: 'There were other members there, but if I say, "I think it was this person," we will go around on the Mr Moses Merry-Go-Round for the next hour.'

Moses: 'Is the reason why you don't want to say who you remember being there because you don't want to be caught out telling a lie?'

The Gunner: 'I am not telling any lies, Your Honour . . . I am not making this up. I am as uncomfortable as any other person who has been coming through here . . . I do not want to be here. I'm here because I was subpoenaed . . . and, as I said yesterday, I find it extremely difficult to stomach having to give evidence against that man in the corner.'

Moses, taking a breath: 'Okay. Would you like a break . . . would you like a break?'

The Gunner, wound up: 'No, let's crack on.'

There was not a lot more cracking on, at least in open court. Closed court sessions consumed most of the rest of the day. And then The Gunner was thanked and released.

The Gunner's was a complex, even contradictory account. He did not want Ben Roberts-Smith to pay for eliminating people he said his nation had sent them to kill. Equally, he wanted to support members whom he said had suffered because of the man sitting in the opposite corner.

In the closed court hearings and at a later sitting, however, we lost ground. Some of the evidence The Gunner had given to the IGADF was shown to be inconsistent with the testimony he had given here.

Our lawyers sought to frame this as The Gunner telling half-truths rather than lies. But this, and Arthur Moses scoring some hits during the two days of skirmishing, might have dimmed Justice Besanko's regard for our forthright witness.

If so, that was a pity. Later, Nicholas Owens acknowledged The Gunner's misfires, but judged him to be 'ultimately the most raw and honest witness of all'.

CHAPTER 75

NOT WALKING AWAY

Another big day. Another big witness.

Mid-week, mid-March and I am on the train, feeling a little pale. The rapid antigen test is negative. Nick McKenzie has also had an early start, having arrived from Melbourne. We meet at the court.

The Sergeant is waiting unsighted in the wings. He knows he will be asked whether he was interviewed for the *60 Minutes* report on Darwan. It puts all of us, but The Sergeant in particular, in an invidious position. Nick and I promised anonymity, but we also know rule number one: don't tell lies in the witness box. What to do?

The Sergeant—now a warrant officer—is sworn in. Dark hair and a dark suit. Suntanned, athletic. As he settles, he puts on reading glasses. There are maybe some nerves, but more prominent is a look that says, *I am ready for this.*

After The Sergeant provided his career background, his evidence in chief moved on to his professional opinion of The Redhead. The Sergeant thought him a 'good, steady soldier'. He remembered Ben Roberts-Smith offering a contrary opinion, calling The Redhead 'a coward' who 'lets the name of the unit down' and 'will let you down at some stage'.

The Sergeant was questioned about an incident from Afghanistan in 2010. At Deh Rafshan, he and another soldier were detaining an Afghan male. The Sergeant testified that 'this bloke was in serious fear', tensed in a foetal position, representing no threat, when Ben Roberts-Smith appeared. '[He] walked into the room . . . didn't say a word . . . got down on a knee' and, 'quickfire', while wearing Kevlar gloves, punched and kneed the man. The Sergeant said he protested and, wordlessly, Roberts-Smith walked away.

The next topic was pre-deployment training at Lancelin in 2012. The Sergeant described observing a PUC handling scenario; he watched from above while standing on a shipping container, as Ben Roberts-Smith took two new members of his patrol, The Mechanic and The Trooper, through the process. Another soldier (The Dog Handler), acting as the detainee, was nearby.

The witness said he heard Roberts-Smith order The Trooper to 'fucking kill him'; after some confusion, The Trooper had mouthed the word 'bang'. The Sergeant recalled Roberts-Smith putting his hand on the younger soldier's shoulder and saying, 'Are you good with that? Because that is the way it is going to be when we get over there.'

The Sergeant described his own reaction. Turning to a fellow soldier, he had said: 'What was that about? Geez, he's a fucking idiot.' Later, he had caught up with Roberts-Smith in the car park, and they'd argued. The Sergeant told the lofty VC to 'pull your head in', and then saw him walk off 'mumbling something . . . the only words I could decipher were "fucking war"'.

The ready room in Camp Russell in Afghanistan weeks later was the setting for the next encounter. Sergeant Blaine Diddams had been killed during the preceding 3 Squadron's last mission, and now 2 Squadron was about to head outside the wire on what some were calling a 'revenge job'. They were sorting equipment when Roberts-Smith told him, 'Hey mate, I'm going to talk the talk. I want you to make sure I walk the walk . . . Before this trip is over, I'm going to choke a man to death with my bare hands. I'm going to look him in the eye, and I'm going to watch the life drain out of his eyes.'

The Sergeant also remembered, from the pre-mission briefing, Roberts-Smith telling the assembled soldiers: 'So we're going to go back to the area. This is where Didds got killed, and, if those fuckers are up there, we're going to kill every last one of those fuckers.'

After Corporal Ben Roberts-Smith's first mission as a patrol commander ended ignominiously, with SAS patrols firing on one another, there was a debrief. When Roberts-Smith was asked to account for what had occurred, The Sergeant recalled, he 'straightaway started finger-pointing on the table and saying, referring to The Trooper, "That cunt, that cunt, I fucking gave him every opportunity, he's gone and let me down . . . His eyes rolled back in his head, and he started blazing away uncontrollably with his Minimi."' The Sergeant later spoke with The Trooper, who told him about being assaulted by Roberts-Smith and, once back in Australia, being subjected to a further threat.

To another mission in 2012. All patrols were involved in clearing a series of compounds near the Helmand–Uruzgan border. The Sergeant told the court he saw Roberts-Smith holding an Afghan male by the shirt against a wall and punching him. He also saw a little girl, three to four years old, crying as she looked to the man Roberts-Smith had against the wall. When Roberts-Smith let the man go, the little girl ran to him.

The witness said he asked: 'What's going on here, RS?' and RS replied, 'He's a fucking bad cunt . . . when I was questioning him, I asked him if that was his daughter. He said, "Yes," and I asked him what her name was, and he hesitated . . . I've got two daughters and I know what their names are.'

The Sergeant suggested that, given RS had 'ragged on [harassed] the bloke', there could well be another explanation for the hesitation. 'I looked at him, shook my head and walked off,' he testified.

To Darwan. As a troop sergeant for Rotation XVIII in 2012, The Sergeant was located at the Troop Headquarters, back from the village, with no direct eyes on Roberts-Smith's patrol. Just before extraction, he heard Roberts-Smith on the radio: 'Alpha, this is 2-1. That's one EKIA. We've just engaged a spotter.'

As they departed by helicopter, The Sergeant looked down and 'saw what I believed was the body of the man that RS had just engaged'.

Early in 2013, at the SAS home barracks, The Sergeant caught up with his friend The SSE, who told him, 'Ben Roberts-Smith kicked a man off a cliff.' He said he could not at first believe what he was told, and asked how The SSE knew this.

'Well, if you don't believe me,' The SSE had replied, 'go and ask The Gunsmith.'

Either that day or the next, he did so: '"Hey mate, I've got a question . . . Did RS kick a bloke off a cliff?" And he said, "Yeah, bro."'

Nicholas Owens asked The Sergeant to detail what he was told, and how he responded.

The Sergeant said The Gunsmith had described the kick, the man with his hands bound behind his back, his head hitting a rock and a tooth flying out; a 'wave of panic' had overcome The Gunsmith, as well as a recognition 'that he had to get out of that patrol'. The Sergeant said he reported the allegation to three other sergeants, and the matter was then taken to The RSM.

All four sergeants, he said, met with The RSM around mid-2013 to discuss Ben Roberts-Smith, raising not only serious war crimes allegations from 2009 and 2012, but 'issues with the Victoria Cross' and 'bullying'. The Sergeant reported that The RSM had asked, 'What are you hoping to get out of this?' To which The Sergeant had replied, 'It's not what I want to get out of this, it's what needs to be done.'

The Sergeant told also of a meeting with a different regimental sergeant major in 2014, this time to assist The Trooper. Because Ben Roberts-Smith had been instrumental in The Trooper's lost career, his name came up and inquiries were reactivated. The Sergeant did not know the outcome of further meetings.

Nicholas Owens SC took The Sergeant to the next topic, which happened to be me.

Owens: 'Have you met Chris Masters? And just reflect on whether you are willing to answer that question.'

The Sergeant: 'Your Honour, I object to that question on the grounds of self-incrimination.'

The witness withdrew and the routine played out. Glenn Cridland, The Sergeant's barrister, set out a case for an immunity certificate, given his client's exposure to a penalty for being in prospective breach of ADF media rules. His Honour determined that reasonable grounds for granting the certificate applied. The witness returned and was asked whether, in this circumstance, he was willing to give evidence.

The Sergeant assented. He told of being contacted by me to be interviewed for *No Front Line* in 2015. He sought approval to do so and was told the interview could go ahead, as long as he did not talk about 'any classified stuff'.

He told the court how he'd met up with my brother, Roy Masters, in Melbourne, where he also came into contact with Nick McKenzie. Owens probed further and The Sergeant acknowledged that he had ultimately agreed to be interviewed for *60 Minutes*. He had at first refused, but an accumulation of concern about lives 'adversely affected' and an 'aggressive intimidation and threatening campaign' swung him. 'That's why I decided to speak with Mr McKenzie and appear in *60 Minutes*, to be a voice from within.'

What happened next caused me acute discomfort. The first draft notes, produced in confidence by Nick and me, were introduced into evidence, and so became available to the other side.

Arthur Moses SC began his cross-examination of The Sergeant after lunch: 'Were you jealous of Mr Roberts-Smith?'

The Sergeant: 'I've never been jealous of Mr Roberts-Smith.'

Moses: 'Were you bitter and twisted?'

The Sergeant: 'I've never been bitter and twisted, no.'

Moses moved swiftly to Tizak. 'You've told people within the SASR that Mr Roberts-Smith did not deserve to be awarded the VC in respect of the Battle of Tizak, correct?'

The Sergeant: 'Yes.'

Moses: 'And that's something that has been burning within you, hasn't it . . .?'

The Sergeant: 'That's incorrect, Mr Moses. I would say I've put that to bed probably back in 2013, when I found out about the allegation that he kicked an innocent man off a cliff.'

All through the afternoon, Arthur Moses berated one of his client's prime accusers. Sections from my notes, in which Roberts-Smith was criticised, were read to the court, with The Sergeant asked to account for words—sometimes his and sometimes mine. He was asked about participating in the *60 Minutes* program, unidentified and disguised.

Moses: 'Is there a reason you did not want your face shown on national TV making allegations against the Victoria Cross winner, that he was a war criminal?'

The Sergeant: 'Because I was a serving member at the time.'

Moses: 'Is it because that you didn't have the courage to put your name to the allegations?'

The Sergeant: '. . . [Y]ou could say, yes, probably I didn't have the courage to do that, yes.'

Excerpts from the *60 Minutes* report, featuring the now outed soldier, were shown again. Arthur Moses laboured his apology regarding yet another screening. '[I]t's part of life's burden to watch . . . *60 Minutes* once, but to watch it five times—'

His Honour: 'It's not a matter of apology.'

Moses: '—is a matter of punishment.'

The video was again shown. It was stopped and restarted as Arthur Moses challenged content.

Moses: 'Was that you saying that the individual that kicked the detainee off the cliff was Ben Roberts-Smith?'

The Sergeant: 'That was me, yes.'

Moses: 'Did you see him kick somebody off a cliff?'

The Sergeant: 'No, I didn't.'

The Sergeant said he had heard it from a direct witness. He said he understood the difference between an allegation and proof, and again denied that his stance against Roberts-Smith stemmed from jealousy or hatred.

And then, in the seconds before the adjournment for the day, there came a witness statement that underscored why all this painful national introspection was worth it.

After Arthur Moses had flung yet another accusation—that The Sergeant was hunting for dirt—the witness responded: 'Mr Moses, if I'm told that a war crime has possibly been committed of a man being kicked off a cliff . . . who has his hands bound behind his back . . . was dragged under a tree, was left to wait there in agony and was then executed—my responsibility is to make sure that allegation is heard.'

The words should be etched in stone at Campbell Barracks.

Cross-examination resumed the following morning. Arthur Moses SC pursued the prospect that The Sergeant had become obsessed by Roberts-Smith's VC. He was accused of rumour-mongering and character assassination when interviewed by me.

Moses trawled through my 22 pages of notes. 'Now, what about this comment: why did you tell Mr Masters that Mr Roberts-Smith isn't a bright bloke?'

In reply, The Sergeant cited Roberts-Smith twice failing to gain certification as a medic.

Moses pointed to my notes, referring to a comment that Roberts-Smith was flat out writing a report. 'Do you recall saying that?'

The Sergeant: 'That is correct, I did.'

Moses: 'And did you say to him: "Now he is supposed to be running Channel 7 in Queensland. Can't imagine him writing an annual report." Why did you need to say that to Mr Masters?'

The Sergeant: 'That was an opinion that I had—he has gone from [being] a corporal in the unit who was flat out writing a report on one of his soldiers.'

Moses: 'Do you have a Master of Business Administration?'

The Sergeant: 'I don't have anything . . . I left school in Year 10, Mr Moses.'

The witness rejected repeated assertions he was nasty and jealous. He defended his view that Roberts-Smith was a bully from his school days, saying Roberts-Smith had admitted that, when in 3RAR, he had acted as an enforcer upon instructions from his company sergeant major.

He was challenged also about what he told Nick McKenzie and about whether his motivation for speaking out was to influence the IGADF inquiry. The Sergeant said his concern was the opposite: that intimidatory pressure was being applied to prospective IGADF witnesses.

His interaction with The Gunsmith was examined next. The Sergeant said another motivation for speaking out was the psychological impact on The Gunsmith from the cliff kick. 'I think it is fair to say [it] destroyed his life,' he testified.

Moses countered, recalling The Gunsmith's evidence of being 'manipulated' by The Sergeant: 'You destroyed his life, didn't you?'

The Sergeant: 'No, I don't think I did at all.' He accepted that The Gunsmith had disengaged in 2014, and had said he did not want to be involved. But subsequently he had been 'happy to talk with me'.

The Sergeant acknowledged he felt some regret about participating in the *60 Minutes* program, but did not believe he had been used. Moses reached deeper into my notes, asking about a reference to Roberts-Smith having used cocaine and steroids. Again, The Sergeant said this was told to him by Roberts-Smith. The barrister found plenty more gossipy references. The Sergeant defended his commentary in the main, as reasonable responses to informed questions.

Back to the alleged bullying of The Redhead, whom The Sergeant saw as a 'poster boy for resilience' after 'eight years of being called a coward'. He recalled being nearby in 2012 when Roberts-Smith allegedly pushed The Redhead in the chest, growling, 'Get out of the way or I will fucking kill you.' He told the court he had not heard this directly; it had been passed on to him by another soldier.

Arthur Moses returned to the comment of Roberts-Smith being not particularly bright: 'You were saying that to Mr Masters just to stick the knife into Mr Roberts-Smith?'

The Sergeant: 'No, not at all.'

Moses: 'What about the next comment: "Like a frill-necked lizard, when he is threatened, it all comes forward, and when you put something on him, he backs right off." Is that a reference to Mr Roberts-Smith?'

The Sergeant: 'That was an analogy I used, yes.'

The cross-examination careened like a pinball across a platform of multiple issues: complaints about Roberts-Smith's CDS; his performance on Rotation XVIII; The Trooper blamed for the blue-on-blue; and matters already covered, such as the legitimacy of the Victoria Cross. My 22 pages provided plenty of fodder.

Friday morning at 10.15 and they go at one another again. Arthur Moses has made a strong case that The Sergeant is less than dispassionate about Ben Roberts-Smith.

But, equally, the witness has countered with plausible, even professional, explanations for why he'd raised the red flag on a comrade. In response to charges of amplifying gossip, he fired back, stressing the seriousness of the Darwan cliff kick allegation. He again made the point that, as a senior NCO, he was 'not walking away from that'.

Armed with my 'off-the-record' notes, Moses put it to The Sergeant that many references to Roberts-Smith were never going to make it into *No Front Line*. The Sergeant conceded some comments were 'petty gossip', and that, unsurprisingly, given Roberts-Smith's high profile, I had asked many questions about him. This was true. Knowledge of the Koran Ghar controversy had heightened my curiosity.

He was asked whether he attended the book launch, and said no. He was asked whether he had been given approval to speak with Nick McKenzie. Again, no. He accepted there had been 'unauthorised engagement'.

The Sergeant was queried about the hostility within his own ranks to 'blokes speaking to the media'. He did not remember accusations of them being 'media whores', but did recall pejoratives such as 'snitches', 'dogs' and 'rats'.

Asked whether he understood that unauthorised engagement constituted a prospective criminal offence, he replied, 'I've known that for the last 28 years, Mr Moses.'

Questioned about the meeting in Melbourne in 2018 with Nick McKenzie and my brother Roy, a former rugby league coach, he said the majority of the conversation was 'talking rugby league'.

Friday's interrogation focused in the main on these unauthorised contacts with media and what was revealed in our notes. Roberts-Smith's legal team appeared to think they were onto something, because nowhere in my notes was there any reference to allegations of war crimes, such as the Darwan cliff kick.

Being held over for a weekend, isolated in the sterile setting of a hotel room, was hardly on The Sergeant's wish list. It can feel like punishment. Thankfully, and perhaps in anticipation of a marathon grilling, he had packed a second suit.

It's 10.15 am on Monday, 21 March, day 56. Solicitor Monica Allen is sitting with her client. Roberts-Smith is examining notes. Before cross-examination resumes, she takes her place a few rows from the front.

Arthur Moses SC swept in. He seemed angry.

Moses: 'I want to suggest to you that your evidence that you told The RSM that there had been an allegation of a war crime was false. What do you say to that?'

The Sergeant: 'Well, I say that is false, Mr Moses.'

Moses contended the meeting was instead about bullying allegations and the Victoria Cross action. He pointed out that Roberts-Smith had not nominated himself for the VC, and that it had been approved via a thorough external process.

The Sergeant's own performance at the Battle of Tizak came under attack. 'You declined to take the initiative to neutralise enemy machine guns, correct?'

The Sergeant said he had taken the initiative to 'stay alive' and had no regrets about his personal performance.

Moses contended that he was jealous of the admiration Roberts-Smith had received.

The Sergeant rejected this, reminding the barrister that he'd accompanied Roberts-Smith on the VC promotional tour in 2011.

Moses: 'You haven't been able to stop thinking about Mr Roberts-Smith since he got the VC?'

The Sergeant: 'Mr Moses, RS left the unit . . . early 2013 . . . I have got on with my life . . . I don't sit in a dark corner at home thinking and dwelling on RS . . .'

Moses: 'But you did sit in the shadow of dark on the *60 Minutes* program?'

The Sergeant: 'Yes, I did.'

Old ground was traversed again and again. About my notes. About the newspaper reporting. About how and when Nick McKenzie and I learned of the Darwan allegation.

Moses asked whether The Sergeant had read through my notes. He had.

Moses: 'There is no reference to this in his notes, is there?'

The Sergeant: 'No, not that I read.'

The senior counsel made the same point about the pre-deployment mock execution from 2012, which was also absent from my notes.

Moses: 'What I want to suggest to you is that you fabricated that allegation in order to throw mud at Mr Roberts-Smith. What do you say to that?'

The Sergeant: 'That allegation is again 100 per cent true and I stand by it, Mr Moses.'

Arthur Moses leaned in, asking why he had not reported the mock execution incident to superiors. The Sergeant said he dealt with it himself, by telling Roberts-Smith to 'wake up to yourself, grow up and pull your head in'.

Moses: 'This is part of your narrative of wanting to be a hero, isn't it? You've never challenged Mr Roberts-Smith, have you?'

In opposite corners, the length of a cricket pitch apart, The Sergeant looked towards Ben Roberts-Smith and said, 'I have challenged him . . . on a number of occasions.'

There was suddenly a familiar flurry. Post-it notes going forward. Ben Roberts-Smith shaking his head. Him and Monica Allen in whispered exchanges. Back and forth between Ben, Monica and the bar table.

The reference in my notes to 'lies and embellishments' in Roberts-Smith's VC citation came under the microscope, with Arthur Moses asking for evidence. The Sergeant, glasses on, was taken through the citation paragraph by paragraph. The Sergeant said the reference in the citation to Roberts-Smith exposing himself to enemy fire was when he threw a grenade but failed to pull out the pin. Some of what he learned about the VC action, he said, had come from Roberts-Smith himself.

A closed court session finished the day.

The Sergeant was back in open court the following morning. Nick McKenzie and I were both in court, and Arthur Moses SC was again in a fiery mood.

The Sergeant's complaints about Roberts-Smith's alleged poor performance as a patrol commander during Rotation XVIII were disputed. The then troop sergeant defended his professional opinion that Roberts-Smith was undeserving of his CDS.

The morning wore on and the repeated challenges wore thin—as, it appeared, did Arthur Moses' temper.

Moses: 'It never was part of your role as a senior NCO to push allegations in the media against one of your former colleagues. Do you accept that?'

The Sergeant: 'Mr Moses, I will accept—'

His Honour: 'Just pause, Mr Moses. I won't tolerate raising the voice to the extent that you did in this court.'

Moses: 'Yes, Your Honour.'

A closed court session followed. The day wound down. The Sergeant was finally released.

According to reporting in *The Australian*: 'One of Ben Roberts-Smith's chief critics spent hours leaking to journalists about the elite soldier's personal life, marriage and "f..k-ups" in Afghanistan but a shocking war crime allegation didn't seem to warrant a mention, a court has heard.'[1]

It was often frustrating for Nick and me, sitting up the back and obliged to hold our tongues. Arthur Moses had implied, when levelling attack after attack on The Sergeant, that we had used him. He was now having to answer for our reporting. Because we had pleaded truth in our defence, the focus in the case was more on what was reported than on how it was reported. As a result, to our mixed feelings, we were not going to be called as witnesses.

It was hard on occasions not to rise to my feet and offer an explanation. My notes for the book from 2015 and 2016 made no mention of the cliff kick because not until 2017 was it divulged. To me, at least, it was not surprising that in those earlier years these men had chosen not to reveal to me, an outsider, these war crimes that would ultimately heap scandal on them and their regiment.

The spectre of summary executions and the like did not begin to loom large until after the IGADF inquiry kicked off in mid-2016. After I heard the first serious allegation, I began to ask follow-up questions. In court, Nicholas Owens SC pointed to correspondence that demonstrated my knowledge of the cliff kick: I had raised it with Roberts-Smith in July 2017, well before the reporting under challenge began.

I came away thinking that maybe journalists should never make notes.

CHAPTER 76

'SIMULTANEOUSLY IN LOVE AND AFRAID'

The afternoon session on Tuesday, 22 March 2022. Yet another person is conveyed with great reluctance to the witness box—Person 17. Ben Roberts-Smith's former lover was designated with this descriptor by the court, and I'll use it here. It's anodyne, for sure, but less loaded than 'The Girlfriend' or 'The Mistress'.

Petite, well-groomed, articulate and nervous, she was asked by Nicholas Owens SC how she met Ben Roberts-Smith. A lunchtime function in October 2017, she said, had blurred into the afternoon and evening, with them both flirting and confessing to problems in their marriages.

That evening turned into many. Person 17 felt herself falling for Roberts-Smith, but he warned her, 'You don't want to fall in love with me, I'm not the greatest guy.' Nonetheless, after a series of trysts, she said, they began to plan a life together. Ben wanted to move to the United States, but Kerry Stokes 'had said to him that it would look like he was running away'.

It was a painful experience for yet another witness who did not want to be there. Nicholas Owens SC was as gentle as possible in leading evidence but even so tears flowed, with Person 17 asking, 'Can we have a small break, please?'

His Honour: 'Yes, certainly.'

Person 17 was in the box for two days, the majority under cross-examination from Bruce McClintock SC. It was harrowing. McClintock held nothing back. And the witness held to her story. The central allegation, that she had been punched by Roberts-Smith in a Canberra hotel room, was persistently challenged. Person 17, with a legal background of her own, through further tears, insisted she was telling the truth.

The allegation of the assault in the hotel room was always going to be one of the most testing components of the trial. Difficult for everyone: Person 17, Ben Roberts-Smith, Nick McKenzie, David Wroe and me—and now Justice Anthony Besanko. After a mountain of deliberation, the fact remained: there were only two people in that room.

CHAPTER 77

'TERRIBLE FOR OUR COUNTRY'

The day was almost spent when Andrew Hastie took his seat in the witness box. The presence of the assistant minister for defence caused the watching media pack to expand. The former SAS captain, now a junior minister, was not only newsworthy. Here at last was a secret soldier with a name.

Nicholas Owens SC asked about The Redhead. Hastie considered him 'a bright person, confident and very competent . . . well regarded by his peers'. He said talk of the bullying of The Redhead by Ben Roberts-Smith was widespread through the regiment.

Owens asked for an example, and Andrew Hastie recalled an incident at the Bindoon Training Area, when soldiers were gathered at breakfast and the Channel Seven *Sunrise* program was playing on a television in the background.

'Mr Roberts-Smith appeared . . . in his service dress, full of medals, and he was talking about mental health charities that he was supporting,' he said. '[A soldier] stopped for a second and said loudly, so that everyone could hear, "RS gave The Redhead depression. Now he is going to help him fight it," and everyone laughed.'

Turning to Afghanistan, Owens asked about Hastie encountering Roberts-Smith on a brief familiarisation mission undertaken in October 2012. Hastie recounted sitting with Roberts-Smith in the mess and being told that officers should be kept back from the action because they 'just get in the way'.

That same week, Captain Hastie joined 2 Squadron and Ben Roberts-Smith for a mission to Syachow. So too did another SAS operator, who at the time, like Hastie, was not attached to 2 Squadron. Designated by the court as Person 66, we will call him The Ring-In. Hastie and The Ring-In, having both lived in Campbell Barracks' 'married patch', knew one another.

Hastie was in the second flight of Blackhawks arriving at Syachow, after Ben Roberts-Smith and The Ring-In. He saw PUCs being tactically questioned. He saw a dead Afghan and his former 'married patch' neighbour. 'He stood out because he was standing slightly off from the rest of the patrol, looking nervous. And I just met his eyes briefly, and I just thought: *That's not the person I know—happy-go-lucky, kind of country Aussie*.'

Hastie departed the scene. He was a few compounds away when he heard a radio call of shots fired, but 'I did not hear a shot'. Soon after, Ben Roberts-Smith walked past him, 'and he looked me in the eye and said, "Just a couple more dead cunts."'

Owens took the witness to the post-action debrief, where he heard Roberts-Smith's account of the engagement: he said one of the insurgents was gunned down by his patrol after reaching for a grenade.

Andrew Hastie was back in court the following morning, Friday, 25 March. His examination in chief recommenced and Nicholas Owens SC asked what was discussed when Hastie met The Sergeant in 2014.

The witness remembered The Sergeant being 'greatly vexed about his concerns around certain incidents overseas that had not been dealt with by chain of command . . . he was frustrated that . . . Mr Roberts-Smith was Father of the Year and enjoying a high profile in the community . . . he also expressed concern about the Victoria Cross citation.'

Owens: 'And you mentioned . . . you had also heard things about the PUC being kicked off a cliff . . . Do you have any recollection of who you heard that from?'

Hastie: 'No, I don't . . . I heard it from multiple people . . . You know, soldiers are oral historians: things get passed around by word of mouth, and that's how you pick up what's going on.'

Owens: 'No further questions, Your Honour.'

Bruce McClintock SC had vacated the first chair, which meant it was Arthur Moses SC's turn to cross-examine. An enthralling battle of wits would ensue between the wily barrister and the lucid politician.

Moses' opening gambit was to cast the relationship between Hastie, Nick McKenzie and me as base and transactional. Cooperation, he argued, meant we got stories, while Hastie was rewarded with favourable treatment.

Andrew Hastie conceded that a journo/politico symbiosis existed, but thought (as I do) that generally the media got the better of the deal.

Bullying was next; Moses asked for its definition.

Hastie: 'Well, it's a bit like pornography: you know it when you see it. And I have been at the end of bullying myself.'

Hastie accepted that he had never seen Roberts-Smith bully The Redhead. He also accepted that the mocking of someone could constitute bullying.

The two then went at it over Hastie laughing at the comment made by one of his soldiers that Roberts-Smith had given The Redhead depression and was now helping him fight it. Hastie held his ground and argued that funny jokes 'have a bit of truth in them'. He said that, on a scale of seriousness, this was not of a high order, and he was not ashamed of his conduct.

His relationship with Ben's presumed detractors was pursued. He recalled speaking to The Veteran and another soldier after Rotation XVIII in 2012. 'I can still remember [The Veteran's] exact words: "People are doing stupid shit overseas. Don't do it. Don't be that guy. Don't ruin your life."'

Moses turned to The Sergeant. Andrew Hastie said that when the *60 Minutes* program had aired, he had no idea of the identities of the featured SAS operators. Regarding The Scout, he told Arthur Moses: 'He's a very good man.' Hastie said The Scout, 'along with Mr Roberts-Smith', had originally inspired him to undertake SAS selection.

Questioned as to whether he knew if any of these men were sources for McKenzie and me, he said he did not know and had not asked, adding, 'I was blown away by how well-sourced they were.'

When asked for it, Andrew Hastie's word picture of The SSE was, for me, perfection: 'He has a thousand-yard stare. Doesn't say a whole lot. He just gets on with the job.' His words took me back to the taciturn revelations from the same witness box three weeks earlier.

Moses came to the point: 'You dislike Mr Roberts-Smith, don't you?'

Hastie: 'I don't dislike Mr Roberts-Smith . . . I pity Mr Roberts-Smith, Mr Moses.'

Moses: 'You pity him, okay?'

Andrew Hastie's emotion surfaced. His voice breaking, he said: 'I pity the whole process. I don't want to be here . . . I was subpoenaed for this and yesterday, before I appeared in court, I rang my father . . . and I asked him, "Pray with me," and he prayed for Mr Roberts-Smith as well. That's how I feel about this, because this is terrible for our country. It's terrible for the SAS. It's terrible for the Army. It has touched a lot of lives. No one wants to see this. But until we deal with it, we can't move forward.'

The topic turned to pride. Andrew Hastie said his initial high regard for Roberts-Smith had changed. The barrister wanted to know how it was that, given his limited dealings with Ben Roberts-Smith, he could consider himself an authoritative commentator.

Hastie: 'I've made numerous comments, that's correct. But generally speaking, they've been in support of the IGADF and the process, and I've talked about the importance of rule of law and accountability.'

Moses: 'Have you previously suggested that Mr Roberts-Smith is a hypocrite?'

Hastie: 'I might have. I just don't have a recollection of it.'

Moses: 'Have you heard others suggest that Mr Roberts-Smith is a hypocrite?'

Hastie: 'Yes, I have.'

Arthur Moses wanted detail. Andrew Hastie said in his time at the regiment he often heard Roberts-Smith's name connected to 'bad stuff that happened in Afghanistan'. Pressed for examples and forced to search his memory, Hastie perhaps came up with more than Moses bargained for. He identified over a dozen soldiers who had made such comments.

The senior counsel persisted in his efforts to turn the junior minister's words against him. Having captured the witness's agreement that in general it was wrong for an officer to pass to a journalist 'rumours and gossip', Hastie was challenged about expressing disquiet to me about 'members taking the law into their own hands'. Andrew Hastie said I was not the only journalist to ask such questions, and he had raised the same concern with his superiors.

Regarding his responsibility as an officer to go further and report notifiable incidents, such as extrajudicial killings, Andrew Hastie said that, to do so, he would have needed a 'pretty strong case'.

He admitted his anxiety was fuelled by 'rumours, but also a gut feeling that something wasn't right'. He had chosen to exert influence ahead of the rotation by talking to his squadron commander, 'and then talk[ing] to my NCOs and set[ting] the parameters for our troop'. Hastie told the court he would never forget his troop sergeant's response: 'I'm not going to Afghanistan to put dirt farmers on their knees and shoot them in the back of the head.'

Arthur Moses turned back to Andrew Hastie's relationship with Nick and me, and the alleged advantage received. The politician accepted that Nick and I were 'friends of a kind', and denied that he'd simply told us what we wanted to hear. Hastie defended his engagement with us as a quest for accountability motivated by his belief in public interest journalism.

Then, for political junkies, there was a faint frisson. As it happened, the Liberal member for Canning was going toe to toe with a political ally. Arthur Moses SC had flirted with Liberal Party preselection, telling *The Sydney Morning Herald* in 2006 that in the long term he would 'like to consider a career in either federal or state politics'.[1] And, at this very moment, Moses was known for something stronger than a flirtation—as the love interest of former NSW Liberal premier Gladys Berejiklian.

In parrying the claim that he had appeared on *60 Minutes* to support his media mates, Andrew Hastie saw an opportunity to deflect his accuser's words: 'Mr Moses . . . I must say, I'm very sympathetic to your speech that you gave to the National Press Club in 2019, where you argued that public interest journalism is critical to a healthy democracy . . . I think we share a strong view on this.'

There was a break for lunch. The afternoon session focused on a series of articles by Nick McKenzie and me, with Arthur Moses SC intent on positioning Hastie as a source. There was a lot of fishing. When the barrister sought to tie unattributed quotes to Hastie, the witness responded varyingly: 'That was not something I would say' . . . 'No' . . . 'I can't rule it out'.

For the rest of the day, Hastie was hammered about further Nine reporting and an alleged allegiance to our side. It was revealed he had been joined as a co-defendant with Nine in a separate defamation action, with the broadcaster covering the costs. He accepted that this represented a benefit to him, but said he was not 'beholden to the respondents'.

Moses took Hastie to his own writings about Afghanistan and the Brereton inquiry. The politician was this time obliged to answer for his own words. He told the court his shame for what occurred on the battlefield was not sourced to Roberts-Smith, but on Brereton's collective findings of credible information of unlawful killings by '25 Australian Special Forces soldiers'.

At the end of the Friday, Andrew Hastie was handed the short straw of a weekend of exclusion. His cross-examination had not concluded.

Hastie reappeared on Monday, 28 March, day 61. From the corridor outside 21A I spotted Ben Roberts-Smith looming large near the public entrance and Andrew Hastie a short distance away. Suits and ties and masks. I nodded to Hastie, and we all moved inside.

It was on again. The indemnification by Nine was revisited. Andrew Hastie rejected Moses' contention that he had tailored evidence in the Roberts-Smith case to assist the respondents in return for this 'gift'.

The next subject was dreams. A familiar chill ran through me: I realised my notes were again about to be hurled in someone's face. My research for *No Front Line* was brandished.

The last quote on the last page of my Andrew Hastie interview was about a dream in which Roberts-Smith figured:

> We have killed one of our own guys and we have covered it up and this is the deep truth that I carry, and I wake up fearful and my whole day is ruined . . . It is not what I have seen but what I have heard and the calling to account that will ultimately come to some people.

It was a dream, not reality. Roberts-Smith had not killed a fellow member. There was no incident to cover up. Andrew Hastie saw it as a 'metaphor for what we had done to ourselves'.

In answer to follow-up questions, Hastie said he had experienced Afghanistan-related nightmares, but no night tremors. He was not seeing a psychiatrist or psychologist.

Another reference in the notes was to the practising Christian, Hastie, speaking to the avowed atheist, The Sergeant. The former SAS captain recalled how they had engaged in 'deep and meaningfuls'—in his words, 'pastoral care'. They had 'talked about cosmic justice, and all the rest of it. You know, took a bit of a theological bent because . . . that's the way we sometimes chatted.' This led to questions about The Sergeant's alleged 'obsession' with Roberts-Smith's Victoria Cross.

Hastie: 'I wouldn't say obsession. I've met some obsessive people in politics, and he does not strike me as obsessive . . . focused certainly, but not obsessive.'

Arthur Moses SC moved on, as he had done before, to what was not in my notes—there was no mention of serious war crimes. 'What I want to say to you is you fabricated your evidence about what you say

Mr Roberts-Smith told you at Syachow, that is, these words: "Just a couple more dead cunts." What do you say to that?'

Hastie: 'I say that's false. It's clear in my mind.'

Queried about bullying, Hastie recalled getting some 'special treatment' during selection. Ben Roberts-Smith, a menacing instructor—the 'Corporal Punishment' figure, as it was termed in the SAS—was not accused of singling him out. Hastie saw varying definitions: 'Sometimes there's personal bullying, sometimes there's institutional bullying.'

Nick McKenzie's notes were also thrown at the witness. Arthur Moses again highlighted the absence of the Syachow 'dead cunts' quote.

Hastie: 'I have been very careful about what I've said.'

Arthur Moses also asked about Captain Hastie's evidence of the encounter in the Camp Russell mess, with Corporal Roberts-Smith declaring that 'officers should be kept away from the action'. The barrister wanted to know what Hastie said in response.

Hastie: 'Look, I probably would have . . . kept the peace. Mr Roberts-Smith was at the apex of the SASR power structure at the time.'

Moses: 'Are you saying that to suggest that somehow Mr Roberts-Smith had influence over what the SAS did as a corporal?'

Hastie: 'I'm saying he was a very public figure with growing celebrity, and he . . . had a lot of ceremonial duties, and by virtue of that, he had a lot of influence. Absolutely.'

He went on to say that he interpreted Roberts-Smith's comment as a 'discreet message . . . to get out of the way and let us do what we need to do'.

Moses: 'And were you meaning to imply there was something sinister about that?'

Hastie: 'I do now, yes.'

Cross-examination reached into the afternoon, through a closed court session and back to open court. All the way, Arthur Moses held to a central premise: that Andrew Hastie was engaged in the tawdry trade of shopping rumour in return for flattering words from a pair of scandal-mongers. Soft targets, you might think, given the poor public regard for politicians and journalists.

Moses: 'You were expressing views to them off the record, correct?'

Hastie: 'No, they were putting propositions to me.'

Moses: 'Yes, you need to say that, because the truth is too awful for you to admit that you have been a constant leaker concerning Mr Roberts-Smith, haven't you, to Mr McKenzie and Mr Masters—correct?'

Hastie: 'No, I have not.'

Moses: 'And you've been using those allegations to gain with Mr Masters and Mr McKenzie favour so that they can praise you as a politician—correct?'

Hastie: 'No, I have not. And I can tell you, Mr Moses, there's not a great political dividend from being involved in these proceedings.'

I make no secret of feeling indebted to the departing witness. His contribution to our reporting was immense. Andrew Hastie gifted our work with intelligence, insight and moral clarity.

Arthur Moses punished him for stretching truth when he had done no such thing. As with many of the witnesses, Hastie was wary of inflaming controversy, of invoking war crimes when he was uncertain of the evidence.

Moses scorned him for responding to intuition, to gut feeling. But, from another perspective, those very spidery senses were exactly what was needed—and what went missing—in Afghanistan. If the officer corps was completely unaware of 'bad stuff', there is no escaping a finding of suspended curiosity. Sensible soldiers will tell you they want officers who are leaders and not one of the boys. They respect, sometimes grudgingly, those who are less 'good on the tools' as the 'perceptive bastards' who see through the bullshit.

Public life is hard. I admire Andrew Hastie for putting principle before politics, and for sticking his neck out.

CHAPTER 78

'YOUR HONOUR, I'M UNWILLING'

In the last half-hour of proceedings on Monday, 28 March, The Ring-In took the stand. Forlorn witnesses, shuffling reluctantly into the dock, had become the norm. But in this case, the feet dragged more slowly and the furrows were deeper. For months, The Ring-In, through his legal representative, had sought a mental health dispensation. As for our lawyers, he refused all interview requests.

His determination to keep his distance came as no surprise. Nick McKenzie and I had picked up his story on the special forces grapevine, second-hand and blurry, for sure. We had heard that, in October 2012 at Syachow, Ben Roberts-Smith had pulled The Ring-In aside, taken two PUC'd Afghans into a cornfield and instructed The Ring-In, as well as another soldier, to shoot them. After the men were gunned down, Roberts-Smith was alleged to have lobbed a hand grenade at the corpses.

This is the alleged incident Captain Andrew Hastie had witnessed only in its aftermath, when he heard the EKIA radio call, saw his formerly happy-go-lucky neighbour, The Ring-In, looking ashen and heard Roberts-Smith boast, 'Just a couple more dead cunts.'

After the blooding, and upon his return to Australia, The Ring-In was said to have entered a downward psychological spiral. We were told that the once-buoyant, married soldier had become a cheerless bachelor, alone and despondent in a sterile apartment. When the IGADF's inquirers came knocking, his friends encouraged him to tell the truth and help clear his conscience. That was as much as we knew. Nick and I presumed he had done so, but we had not heard it from the primary source.

His mental health exemption request having been denied, The Ring-In, stocky and bearded, with his hair tousled and his nerves clearly frayed, all wrapped up in a blue business suit, faced up to Nicholas Owens SC.

His evidence in chief was barely underway, with The Ring-In acknowledging that Ben Roberts-Smith was his patrol commander in October 2012, when his barrister, Jack Tracey, was forced to rise. As we had seen multiple times before, the witness sought a certificate against self-incrimination. He departed the court.

There was legal debate and, when the witness was recalled, His Honour explained that he would grant a certificate. Justice Besanko then asked The Ring-In whether he was 'willing or unwilling to give evidence'.

The Ring-In replied, 'Your Honour, I'm unwilling to give the evidence.'

Crunch time. Justice Besanko asked Nicholas Owens SC whether he was requesting the witness be required to give evidence.

Owens: 'I am, Your Honour. Yes.'

His Honour: 'Yes, well it might be convenient to deal with that in the morning, I think.'

At 4.24 pm, The Ring-In withdrew.

The following morning was consumed by legal argument, which shuttled between open and closed court. Jack Tracey, for The Ring-In, put to the court that, if his client was compelled, the evidence given 'would involve self-incrimination of the gravest nature'.

Nicholas Owens, soon after, gave more than a clue as to what offence they were talking about: 'Now, at the end of the day, I can concede frankly that it is possible for me to win this case without succeeding in proving the murder at Syachow, and it won't shock Your Honour to learn that I hope to do so. But it is equally possible that I could win this case by only proving the murder at Syachow . . . It's our submission that the central importance of the evidence can't be denied.'

Justice Anthony Besanko adjourned the trial in the early afternoon, notifying the parties that he would reserve his decision.

We crowded into our small adjoining interview room. The chocolate box was again plundered.

This was another watershed moment. As Owens had pointed out, The Ring-In's evidence could prospectively win us the case. We were hopeful, but not particularly optimistic.

All through the trial's legal argument, it became clear that a fundamental principle guiding Besanko's decision-making was to ensure witnesses did not suffer prejudice to their own legal rights. Owens' reading was that the judge was unlikely to allow this witness, The Ring-In, to become collateral damage in the Ben Roberts-Smith fight.

I called Dean Levitan the following morning, and learned that the ruling was expected later that day. So, on the train and back into town.

At 2.15 pm we took our seats. Ben Roberts-Smith, in his usual corner eyrie, could well have been as nervous as the rest of us. After assurances were given that all parties had returned negative rapid antigen tests, Justice Besanko spoke: 'I have decided that the court will not require The Ring-In to give the evidence under section 128(4) of the *Evidence Act 1995*.' He was not satisfied that this would be '[in] the interests of justice'.

The demeanour of The Ring-In, just metres from our barristers, showed palpable relief. Nicholas Owens thought the fact that the witness had claimed privilege and the relief he had exhibited were nevertheless important in the overall mood of the trial.

Owens was allowed to put two key questions to the witness. First: 'On a mission in October 2012, when you were a member of Mr Roberts-Smith's patrol, did you shoot a PUC?' And second: 'On a mission in October 2012, when you were a member of Mr Roberts-Smith's patrol, did Mr Roberts-Smith direct you to shoot a PUC?'

The Ring-In twice objected.

His Honour asked Owens whether he would press the court to require the evidence be given.

Owens said, 'I do, Your Honour. But I accept Your Honour will not.'

And he was right.

Arthur Moses SC had no questions for the witness.

We were disappointed, depressed even, as we wound our way out of the labyrinth of the court. As ever, there was no easy path to winning. But who could miss the ear-splitting reverberation to The Ring-In's silence about what happened at Syachow?

The question for us now was less what was true as whether we could prove it.

CHAPTER 79

ROADKILL

We were nearing the end of our witness list. The Trooper was another exhibiting acute reluctance.

When we first spoke with him, he made plain his deep desire to put all things Ben Roberts-Smith VC, MG behind him. But I also thought I detected in The Trooper a burning sense of injustice at having ended up as collateral damage along his former patrol commander's path to glory. At Campbell Barracks, some of the Roberts-Smith disbelievers took to nicknaming such victims 'roadkill'.

The Trooper was not able to escape his subpoena. Although not a witness to war crimes, he had important evidence from pre-deployment and in theatre, and this fitted a few more pieces of the jumbled jigsaw into the big picture.

The Trooper joined the SASR from the same Army unit as Ben Roberts-Smith, 3RAR. He recalled for Nicholas Owens the training episode at Lancelin before the 2012 deployment, when a fellow soldier, The Dog Handler, was on his knees, playing the role of a PUC, and The Trooper was standing over him. The Trooper heard Roberts-Smith's order: 'Shoot him.' He expressed confusion, but, after catching on, as he put it: 'I went,

"Bang, bang."' His patrol commander then said: 'That's how it's going to be on the day.'

The Trooper said he later spoke to The Dog Handler, who advised him: 'Don't get involved in that shit—it's not good.'

Owens moved straight on to the Chora Valley mission of 14 and 15 July 2012. The Trooper described it as 'SR', a special reconnaissance mission to flush out insurgents believed to be responsible for the death of Sergeant Blaine Diddams two weeks earlier. The Trooper was a machine gunner in a foot patrol led by Roberts-Smith that would set up a blocking position. The enemy was to be squeezed in their direction by an aerial assault team. As a qualified JTAC (joint terminal attack controller), The Trooper would also act as a signaller.

The Trooper told the court of immediate difficulties with comms (communications). He said that, as he was busy changing the codes and frequencies for his main radio, he asked Roberts-Smith to change the battery, explaining that this process, once started, had to be completed within 30 seconds or else internal codes would be cleared and communication lost. Because Roberts-Smith said they did not have time, The Trooper said critical MBITR (multiband inter/intra team radio) communication was lost.

At the moment he assumed the blocking position, he heard simultaneously the approach of helicopters and 'three shots fired in quick succession'. He saw three rounds splash near the head of The Rifleman. The Trooper said Ben Roberts-Smith made a 'quick action plan' to merge his patrol with another blocking patrol, and his team set off moving across open ground in tactical bounds, that is advancing in stages, mutually providing cover for one another.

The Trooper: 'Out of my right-hand peripheral vision I saw movement . . . which I perceived to be a threat . . . conducive to someone holding a medium-calibre machine gun . . . and started shooting in that direction.' He told the court he experienced 'a few stoppages', so he changed the ammunition belt. In all, he said, he fired 'no more than five bursts' before his patrol commander shouted, 'Cease fire! Cease fire! Cease fire!'

Then, 50 metres away from the position just fired on, he saw blue smoke. This indicated the presence of a friendly force—the other blocking patrol. And in the same area, he saw a woman and a child emerging from a wadi, the woman holding a birdcage.

The mission was abandoned. As they waited for helicopter extraction, he said Roberts-Smith came to him and asked, 'I want you to tell me who were you shooting at—a woman and child, or the Taliban . . . You don't have to tell me now.' Then he walked away.

In his usual position in the rear corner of the court, near the window, Ben Roberts-Smith had listened intently, hunched over his phone when The Trooper spoke of perceiving a threat.

The narrative continued, with The Trooper moving on to the patrol room at Camp Russell upon their return. He said he was with his team-mates when Ben Roberts-Smith marched in. 'Stand up,' he recalled being ordered.

Owens: 'And what happened after he told you to stand up?'

The Trooper: 'After I stood up, he punched me . . . on the left jaw, left of my jaw.'

Owens: 'And did you suffer any after-effects of the punch?'

The Trooper: 'It rattled me . . . I did not expect to be punched.' He said Roberts-Smith then shouted at him. The tirade ended with the words, 'As far as I'm concerned, that's it' and 'Nothing leaves this room.'

But it was far from over. A day later, the squadron's sergeant major told him the shooting incident was regarded as a 'blue-on-blue'—that is, friendly forces being fired upon by their mates—and he 'would be going home'.

The Trooper thought he was moved to another patrol and not sent home because 'other patrol commanders raised concerns surrounding what actually happened on the ground'.

It's worth remembering that The Trooper was not the first to fire. He had responded to fire that he perceived as a threat. Indeed, a member of the other blocking patrol accepted responsibility for discharging the first rounds.

The Trooper was asked to prepare a statement. He told the court that Ben Roberts-Smith had instructed him not to mention firing on civilians. 'He said I would go to The Hague [home of the International Criminal Court] if I put it that I was firing at a woman and child.'

The witness declared to the court that, following his removal from Roberts-Smith's patrol, he suffered a professional decline. 'Yes, Your Honour . . . my performance started slipping. I noticed I was withdrawing a lot from my teammates. And essentially, I started getting into depression, anxiety . . . I just couldn't operate. Couldn't think clearly. Couldn't sleep.'

Back in Australia, The Trooper was given a notice to show cause as to why he should not be removed from the regiment. Then in February 2013, he said, Ben Roberts-Smith had telephoned, telling him, 'If you threaten myself or my family, I will fuck you up.' He took this to mean there would be consequences if, in defending his position, he revealed that Roberts-Smith had punched him.

Owens: 'Did you respond to what was said?'

The Trooper: 'Yes . . . I said, "I'm not a cunt."'

Owens: 'Did he say anything in response to that?'

The Trooper: '"I'm not a cunt either."'

As it transpired, The Trooper was removed from the regiment and, at his exit interview, he made a complaint to The RSM about the assault.

Owens: 'Are you aware whether the complaint was pursued?'

The Trooper: 'As far as I'm aware, it wasn't.'

Cross-examination began late morning. Arthur Moses SC seized on The Trooper's discomfort at being here, emphasising his having been dragged into this by other soldiers who'd spoken to the media. The witness agreed this was so. The barrister also extracted an admission that The Trooper was embarrassed at the time of his termination from the SASR.

Moses: 'And one of the reasons why you don't want to be here is you don't want there to be the potential disclosure of matters that occurred in Afghanistan—correct?'

The Trooper: 'No.'

Whatever his performance issues in the SAS, in the witness box The Trooper demonstrated courage under fire. Moses went in hard, but the witness was succinct, unhurried and considered in rebuttal.

Taken to the blue-on-blue, he repeated his evidence of seeing the 'splash' above The Rifleman's head. He explained the difficulty created by the battery issue, which meant a loss of inter-troop communication. He repeated his evidence about sighting a perceived threat and, fearing that Ben Roberts-Smith was being targeted, he'd opened fire in the direction of the threat.

Moses: 'Do you recall Mr Roberts-Smith telling you to stop firing?'

The Trooper: 'Yes.'

Moses: 'And do you recall Mr Roberts-Smith asking you what you were firing at?'

The Trooper: 'Yes.'

Moses: 'And do you recall Mr Roberts-Smith yelling out for a target indication?'

The Trooper: 'Yes.'

Moses: 'And you didn't reply, did you?'

The Trooper: 'I replied.'

Moses: 'Well, what I'm suggesting [is] you didn't.'

The Trooper: 'That's incorrect.'

The witness recalled Roberts-Smith asking him for a target indication as he was firing and rectifying a stoppage. He said he identified two enemy at no more than 100 metres. He rejected Moses' contention that the woman and child had emerged as he was firing. He insisted they appeared only after he'd ceased firing. He further rejected being unwilling to take responsibility for his bad judgement.

Moving on to the punch, Moses asked whether he remembered Roberts-Smith's first words as he entered the patrol room, which he said were effectively: 'What were you doing?'

The Trooper: 'That did not happen.'

Moses: 'I want to suggest to you it did, and that you giggled at him and chuckled and he told you to stand up. Do you recall that?'

The Trooper: 'That did not happen.'

Moses: 'And that's when he punched you in the face. Do you recall that?'

The Trooper: 'The version of events: he came to the door, shut the door, told me to stand up and punched me. That's what happened.'

There was more argument. Arthur Moses put to him the Roberts-Smith version: that, after the punch, The Trooper was castigated for firing his weapon 'uncontrollably' and alerted to 'how devastating it could have been to you and the unit had the woman and the child been killed'.

The Trooper said he did not recall events after he was punched, apart from being told by his patrol commander as he left the room: 'As far as I'm concerned, that's it.'

The Trooper said he did not lodge a complaint or raise the issue of the assault with any of his superiors until his exit interview.

Moses: 'Were you seeking to justify the poor performance and behaviour of yourself that led to the termination of you by the SASR?'

The Trooper: 'Getting punched? I knew that raising this allegation would have no bearing or effect on my performance.'

Arthur Moses called for Nick McKenzie's and my notes of interviews with The Trooper. Given his unwillingness to cooperate, there were none.

In the afternoon an argument was mounted that The Trooper had lied in his evidence that he wanted to put all this behind him. Arthur Moses contended that he became depressed, suffering from stress and anxiety, because of the shooting incident involving the woman and child.

The Trooper admitted embarrassment at being removed from the patrol, but denied Moses' proposition that he considered seeking redress by going to the media. He disagreed that at Chora he had panicked and 'sprayed bullets'.

He was questioned about his contact with Andrew Hastie and The Sergeant, telling Moses he had discussed with The Mechanic 'trying to get out of this proceeding'. And he confirmed having told him about the punch.

Ben Roberts-Smith's counsel turned back to The Trooper's exit interview with The RSM, securing an admission that The Trooper had not told him about the mock execution at Lancelin.

Moses: 'The reason you didn't mention it . . . is that's something that you have made up, haven't you, with The Sergeant?'

The Trooper: 'Your Honour, I vehemently deny that allegation.'

Moses pressed further, the focus this time on bullying: 'You've never suggested, have you, that Mr Roberts-Smith bullied you? Correct?'

The Trooper: 'No, I have not.'

Moses: 'No, you accept, don't you, that Mr Roberts-Smith has not bullied you? Do you accept that?'

The Trooper: 'Depends what your definition of bullying is, Mr Moses.'

Moses: 'Well, I'm asking you. Do you accept that Mr Roberts-Smith has not bullied you?'

The Trooper: 'I would say, Mr Moses, that punching somebody in the face [and] berating them in front of the patrol could be considered a form of bullying.'

More withering words from Moses. The Trooper counterpunched, accusing Roberts-Smith of further intimidation: 'I believe if someone says, "If you come for me or my family, I will fuck you up," that is considered a form of intimidation. Yes.'

Moses: 'Do you blame Mr Roberts-Smith for your removal from Gothic 2 [his patrol]?'

The Trooper: 'I do not . . . Your Honour, I hold nothing against Mr Roberts-Smith, and I hold nothing against Fairfax for bringing me here. I've been compelled to be here, and I don't want to be here. I'm just answering these questions honestly. And honestly, no, I don't.'

The questioning moved to closed court, and soon after another day was spent, with The Trooper due to return to open court on Friday. When open court resumed late morning, we discovered that the Roberts-Smith dirt file had been dusted off.

The Trooper was hit with a fusillade of criticism about his performance in the SAS. Alcohol consumption figured heavily. He confessed to drinking, but not to excess, 'like others'.

Moses: 'Do you recall an incident in 2012 when you were so drunk in Kabul that you took a phone from a female liaison officer and took photos of your penis?'

The Trooper: 'I do, yes.' The witness, by now clearly weary, acknowledged this was stupid, and the action of someone lacking maturity. Arthur Moses proposed it was also the conduct of someone who denies responsibility.

There was stern disagreement: 'I took responsibility for that action, Mr Moses.'

The barrister was on a roll. He claimed The Trooper had failed to accept responsibility for the shooting incident at Chora.

The witness remained unbowed: 'I do take responsibility for my failures, Mr Moses, and I do not believe that was a failure. I acted in accordance with being in "troops in contact", firing to protect my mates moving across open ground.'

By the lunch break, his evidence was completed. The Trooper had endured a welter of punishment, conceding embarrassment about performance issues and foolish drunkenness. But he had held firm on cornerstone evidence. The Trooper supported The Sergeant's and The Mechanic's accounts of the mock execution at Lancelin. He was unwavering in his belief that he had been scapegoated over the blue-on-blue incident at Chora. And for this he was less inclined to blame Ben Roberts-Smith than 'the organisation as a whole'.

CHAPTER 80

WHERE NOBODY WANTS TO BE

Monday, 4 April 2022, day 66. I have stayed overnight at my daughter's home in the inner suburbs. We have visited her sister, who has just given birth to Astrid Alice, my fourth, spellbinding grandchild. I am sent off in the morning with packed sandwiches. A septuagenarian feeling like a schoolboy. As I enter the MinterEllison bunker clutching my school lunch, Tess McGuire is amused.

Dean Levitan, having managed a weekend's respite in Melbourne, has just flown in. Peter Bartlett appears and gives us a briefing. He is wary of talking up our chances, but seems positive, letting on that so far it has gone better than expected.

With Jeremy Forbes and trolley loads of files, we walk the four blocks to the Federal Court. In Phillip Street we fall into step with the barristers, who have also been busy in chambers.

At the screening gate, I indicate to the security staff my titanium knees, which unfailingly trigger the alarm. The guards nod their familiarity and wave me through. Upstairs on the 21st floor I show off photos of tiny Astrid Alice. Smiles all around, before the game face is assumed and we take our seats.

The Mentor is next; to the court he is Person 31. We know each other a little. When I was researching my book, he had come keenly recommended as one of the 'two o'clock in the morning courage' types. In other words, not flashy or showy, but always there. Lots of experience, lots of trauma to work through, but remaining professional and decent all the way.

He had fought at Tizak in 2010, in The Sergeant's patrol. His 'mentor' tag comes from a role he took on in Afghanistan in 2012, helping instruct the Afghan partner force. Again, unsexy, and unselfish; not something the thrusters wanted to take on, but important.

Nicholas Owens SC asked about 'blooding'. To the best of his knowledge, The Mentor recollected, The Sergeant had told him of The Gunsmith being blooded on a job.

He was asked about The Redhead. Having picked up on negative scuttlebutt about the former reservist, The Mentor said that, when they'd deployed together, he had watched closely. 'Throughout that deployment The Redhead proved to be a very valuable team member. I don't recall ever having to question what he was doing . . . It was a unique operation, yet it did have the possibility of extreme danger if things went wrong . . . I never once saw that he showed any sign of not being capable to handle himself and look after the team if required.'

Owens turned to the pre-deployment training at Lancelin in 2012. He recalled the PUC handling scenario involving Roberts-Smith, The Mechanic, The Trooper and The Dog Handler. He remembered being with The Sergeant, watching on from atop a shipping container. He recalled, either there or soon after, The Sergeant exclaiming: 'For fuck's sake, Mr Roberts-Smith has had The Trooper do a scenario of executing a PUC.'

The Mentor thought this 'somewhat concerning', telling His Honour: 'I recall walking past Mr Roberts-Smith outside the mess accommodation and stopped, and we had a quick chat, [using] words to the effect: "Fuck, you need to pull your head in. You know, you can't be doing that shit." I recall Roberts-Smith looking down, grunting, nodding and then walking off.'

Owens moved to the topic of The Lieutenant, and the issue of whether he was the Wakunish partner force officer removed from the squadron in

2012 over the shooting of a dog, when a ricochet fragment had wounded an SAS operator.

As we had learned from the applicant's outlines of evidence, five witnesses uniformly asserted that this was so. It was contentious, given our allegation that Roberts-Smith pressured The Lieutenant to have a PUC executed at Chinartu on 12 October 2012. If he had been removed from the squadron, and could not have been at Chinartu, our allegation was dead in the water.

In his instructor's role, The Mentor had worked closely with the Wakunish partner force. His clear recollection was The Lieutenant was not removed; it was a different soldier.

The next topic was The Trooper and the blue-on-blue. Again, there was familiarity, as The Mentor took The Trooper in after he was ejected from Roberts-Smith's patrol. He remembered Roberts-Smith being 'notably angry' about his new patrol member's performance.

Darwan was the last topic within The Mentor's evidence in chief. His recollection was more what he'd learned on his return to Australia—of The Sergeant telling him that he'd heard from The Gunsmith that 'Mr Roberts-Smith . . . kicked a PUC off the cliff'.

There was an adjournment to closed court, where, for an hour, a tense exchange took place. When open court resumed at 12.16 pm, Ben Roberts-Smith could be seen standing in the corner, staring at The Mentor as they took their seats. There was clearly some history there. Seated in the courtroom somewhere between the two of them, I felt I had some personal insight into that.

While researching *No Front Line*, I had noted and somewhat admired The Mentor's balanced neutrality on Roberts-Smith. In response to pointed questions about Roberts-Smith, he was always fair. In all the inter-unit wrangling, he had chosen to tread the cautious path of the honest broker. I remember telling him that that was also the way I wanted to play it.

But Ben Roberts-Smith knew The Mentor had spoken with me, and he appeared to presume the worst. Some time later, I was able to hear a telephone conversation between the two men that Roberts-Smith had recorded. (This is referred to in Chapter 13.) He then wrote a letter to a member of The Mentor's family, complaining of the contact and causing The Mentor some heartache.

In the January 2018 phone call to The Mentor, with paranoia pulsing down the line, Roberts-Smith bemoaned: 'You've got to understand my position, mate, and how many people got together and deliberately targeted me by fucking colluding about a lot of shit . . . I find it pretty fucking hard to take.'

Ben Roberts-Smith did not know The Mentor was never a party to any such alleged collusion.

Arthur Moses SC was again cross-examining. Moses set about establishing what was an admittedly close relationship between The Mentor and The Veteran. The Mentor said he knew of The Veteran's letter of complaint regarding Roberts-Smith's CDS, but told the court he 'chose not to sign it'.

The Mentor confessed to a friendship also with The Sergeant, Roberts-Smith's other nemesis—and, for that matter, with The Scout. He knew The Scout had given evidence in this case. He acknowledged they had discussed Roberts-Smith, but '[The Scout] hasn't said whether he likes him or dislikes [Roberts-Smith] to me'.

Arthur Moses drew The Gunner, too, into the circle of friends proposed as enemies. 'During your time within the SASR,' he asked The Mentor, 'is it fair to say that there was a pro–Ben Roberts-Smith camp and an anti–Ben Roberts-Smith camp?'

The Mentor: 'I would say people had different opinions of Mr Roberts-Smith.'

A little further on, Moses: 'Did you have negative views of Mr Roberts-Smith?'

The Mentor: 'I didn't while I was in the regiment, no.'

Moses: 'But later you did?'

The Mentor: 'I didn't dislike him, but I felt the system let down the members of his patrol, and Mr Roberts-Smith himself, in the sense that those accusations that were brought out in the patrol should have been dealt with within the command and it wasn't, from what I understand due to weak leadership, and hence we're now dealing with this in court, where nobody wants to be.'

The witness said his view of Ben Roberts-Smith did change, and conceded that this was largely based on what others had told him and in the face of his regiment failing to act. He'd heard about Darwan and Whiskey 108, and the alleged bloodings, such as on the Syachow job involving The Ring-In. Arthur Moses pressed hard for the who, what, when, where and why. The witness was generally unsure of specifics.

There was a break for lunch. The walls were closing in. I showed the pics of Astrid Alice one more time and walked down to Dymocks to buy a book. A bookshop can be like a forest of leaves—therapeutic, like bushland. I returned with Patrick Radden Keefe's *Say Nothing*, recommended by Nick. The rattle of a fire alarm delayed the restart.

—

At 2.27 pm, Arthur Moses was back on his feet. The Mentor was back in his chair, being questioned about his contact with me. He acknowledged that we had spoken, and that he had attended the *No Front Line* launch. The last time we communicated, he said, was when I revealed to him that his telephone conversation with Roberts-Smith in 2018 had been recorded.

The Mentor disclosed that, in earlier conversations, I had asked him about allegations concerning the applicant. He told the court: 'And I said, "The best thing that you can do is go and talk to Mr Roberts-Smith yourself."' He knew who Nick McKenzie was, he said, but they had never spoken.

Moses swung back to The Trooper, who, after the 2012 blue-on-blue, was transferred into The Mentor's patrol (in exchange for The Replacement).

The Mentor had witnessed a slide in The Trooper's performance, but 'I wouldn't say he let down the regiment. He has let himself down.' He said they had spoken in the last weeks, in what was described as a 'welfare call'.

Midafternoon there was an adjournment, to allow the witness time to review documents regarding Defence Instructions (General) that outlined the mandatory reporting of notifiable incidents, when reasonable suspicion existed of a criminal offence having occurred. Arthur Moses returned to all that gossip about bloodings, Whiskey 108 and Darwan that had not been reported. And, more to the point, there was knowledge closer to home about the mock execution at pre-deployment training, after which The Mentor said he had admonished his decorated comrade.

Ben Roberts-Smith VC, MG's barrister was a laser-guided missile, homing in on every skerrick of detail. The Mentor said the verbal exchange took place at the training establishment, 'between the hangar and the mess', with no one else present, either 'that night or the next day'.

Moses: 'You're just making this up, aren't you?'

The Mentor: 'No, Mr Moses.'

Moses, soon after: 'Did you report it to anybody?'

The Mentor: 'No . . . Looking back, I should have.'

It was a full-on day. The Mentor withdrew at 4.15 pm to sweat it out overnight.

The Mentor was not a headline witness. He had no direct evidence of any alleged war crimes, but Arthur Moses SC was unrelenting. I felt for the witness. He was a close fit to the classic portrait of the SAS operator—understated, at home in the shadows—and yet, at 10.16 on the Tuesday morning, he was back under the spotlight.

On one hand, you have to give credit to an advocate for pulling out all stops for his client. On the other, it can look like a cruel twisting of the knife.

Moses: 'It's correct to say, isn't it, that you've had a number of traumatic experiences while serving as a member of the ADF?'

A flurry of interjections, with the answer redacted. Nicholas Owens SC objected on relevance. His Honour asked the witness to step outside.

Special forces operators do not have normal jobs. Exposed during his long career to routine savagery, The Mentor had seen the unseeable. I had heard that psychological support had proved critical to him in getting on with his life.

He was represented at these proceedings by his own lawyer, a former Royal Marines Commando, John Dalzell, who rose, determined to head off Moses at the pass. Dalzell argued that his client should not be taken in detail through 'the most traumatic episodes in his life' if no causal link could be established between those events and 'any memory problem'.

Moses persisted. His Honour told him to 'please sit down', and ruled that the questions would be allowed, but in a closed court.

When the parties trooped back to open court twenty minutes later, cross-examination returned to the flashbang incident involving The Gunner. The Mentor admitted he had lied when he took the blame in order to cover up for a mate, telling the court: 'I did it because I didn't have faith in the hierarchy at the time . . . I was a patrol commander, and I took responsibility for it.'

Moses stepped back through other topics already covered: bloodings, the performance of The Trooper, The Mentor's opinion turning against Roberts-Smith, and in another in favour of The Redhead. Moses revived The Redhead's failure to bring gun oil on the 2006 Koran Ghar mission, and asked about another blot in The Redhead's copybook, when he failed a sniper's course.

Moses: 'In terms of your experience in the position that you held within the SASR, the failure of a specialist course is a relevant matter to take into account as to whether a soldier is suitable to have a command position in a patrol?'

The Mentor: 'I would say it's relevant if you're going to be a sniper.' The witness dismissed the proposition that it disqualified The Redhead from holding a command position.

As was now routine, Arthur Moses called for the notes of an interview I'd conducted with The Mentor for *No Front Line*. After they were received, I noted Ben Roberts-Smith hunched in concentration over the four typed pages.

He was probably disappointed, in that, as was consistent with The Mentor's evidence, he rated barely a mention. But never mind—Arthur Moses did his best to turn the absence of commentary to his client's advantage.

The Mentor was taken back to evidence he had given in court about his knowledge of The Ring-In being allegedly blooded by Ben Roberts-Smith, the alleged executions at Whiskey 108 and the cliff kick at Darwan. Asked whether he had revealed any of this to me, he answered: 'No.'

Consistent with others, when first interviewed (in his case, in April 2016), The Mentor had shown no eagerness to link Ben Roberts-Smith to war crimes. And now that 2022 had rolled around, with Nick and I having dug deeper, and with the IGADF reporting credible evidence of multiple war crimes, we knew much more. The fact that, in the earlier stages of our research, The Mentor had not readily revealed allegations of bloodings and executions to us was held against him—and against us.

I came to wonder at times whether the attacks on our witnesses were as much about punishing all who dared speak against Roberts-Smith as about proving his innocence.

CHAPTER 81

DEAL OR NO DEAL

Monday, 11 April 2022, day 68. For a change, sunglasses, buried somewhere in the bottom of the bag, needed to be found. Sydney shop windows glared and distracted as we trudged to court. At 10.15 am, the witness, with a number-one haircut, broad shoulders in a constricting suit and tie, took his seat and was affirmed.

There had been intense backroom wrangling for more than a year before The Replacement entered the box. Before that, the bush telegraph had been active, communicating to Nick McKenzie and me fragments of a story that he had been another 'rookie' blooded by Ben Roberts-Smith.

In April 2021, two months before the trial commenced, Justice Besanko had refused our application to issue The Replacement a subpoena. That decision was no grand surprise, given we had insufficient information, the prospective witness was patently unwilling to provide it, and we'd had no direct contact with him.

But Dean Levitan, under Peter Bartlett's guidance, was persistent, making numerous calls to The Replacement's counsel, Sean Richter. Meanwhile, the other side, Mark O'Brien Legal, was just as eager to clutch him into their fold.

As the trial progressed, and particularly after evidence from Ben Roberts-Smith and the Afghan witnesses, the case for having The Replacement testify was strengthened. He was, after all, a member of Roberts-Smith's patrol at Darwan, and therefore prospectively in possession of illuminating detail.

In September 2021, we inched in front in the tug-of-war for this important witness's cooperation. The Replacement and his lawyer agreed to two video conferences; one month later, he provided a statement. Justice Besanko thereafter allowed the subpoena: The Replacement could be called to give evidence in the trial.

The Replacement confirmed to Nicholas Owens SC that he had been transferred into Ben Roberts-Smith's patrol from The Mentor's patrol on Rotation XVIII in 2012. Owens moved straight to the Darwan mission. The Replacement remembered being tasked with clearing compounds; as he did so, he saw some fighting-age males (FAMs).

The Replacement told Owens that he had been inside the final compound at Darwan with Ben Roberts-Smith, The Gunsmith and The Sniper. When shown a photograph, The Replacement had identified the compound. His sighting of Afghans from the local area was consistent with the evidence of Mangul Rahmi and Mohammed Hanifa. In contrast, Ben Roberts-Smith's evidence was that there were no Afghans in this final compound, where we alleged Ali Jan had been detained.

The Replacement thought he was there for about half an hour, before he was sent back to the helicopter extraction site with The Terp, where he waited for a further half hour. During that time, he heard no engagements. The Blackhawk helicopter arrived, settling in a dust cloud before the rest of his team appeared. They then returned to Camp Russell.

Half an hour into The Replacement's evidence in chief and another big moment. We knew The Replacement had not been at the scene of the alleged cliff kick, but we understood he had some knowledge of what we alleged had occurred. While in their ready room, unpacking and storing their gear, either The Gunsmith or The Sniper had spoken to him.

Owens: 'What words did they say to you, as best you can recall?'

The Replacement: 'That an individual had been kicked off a cliff and subsequently shot.'

Intakes of breath. Heads down, furiously jotting. I am grateful for Peter and Dean's persistence, and of course for the compelling presence of the once-elusive final member of Ben Roberts-Smith's patrol. The Replacement went on to tell Owens that he had not discussed the incident with Roberts-Smith.

Minutes later, another hot topic. The alleged blooding of The Replacement had occurred, we understood, at Fasil, on the last mission of Rotation XVIII, on 5 November 2012, almost eight weeks after Darwan. This was the mission The Medic had referred to in his evidence, when he recalled Ben Roberts-Smith exulting that the killing of the Afghan teenager was the most beautiful thing he had ever seen.

Owens asked The Replacement whether he had participated in the mission. He responded: 'I wish to object on the . . . grounds it may incriminate myself.'

He withdrew while his barrister, Sean Richter, identified a number of reasons why his client should not be required to answer questions about Fasil. He would be incriminating himself in an offence 'of a most serious nature'. It was not in the interests of justice. And there was 'no written outline dealing with this', the Fasil mission.

A session in closed court followed. Back in open court, His Honour offered to provide a certificate guarding against self-incrimination. The witness said that, even so, he was unwilling to give evidence. Owens, familiar with Justice Besanko's position that he would not compel the witness in these circumstances, moved on.

Owens: 'Have you ever heard the term "throwdown"?'

The Replacement: 'Yes.' He went on to explain it was likely to be 'a weapon. Other military equipment, for example a magazine, grenade.'

Questioning then proceeded down the same cul-de-sac. When asked whether such items were carried by members of Roberts-Smith's patrol in 2012, he requested a certificate and was ultimately excused a reply.

The Replacement's cross-examination by Arthur Moses SC commenced at 11.35 am. Moses' immediate focus was not on anything from Afghanistan, but on communications in Australia between our lawyers, the witness and Sean Richter.

In this high-stakes contest, both sides played tough.

Moses: 'It's fair to say, isn't it, that you've been apprehensive about giving evidence before this court?'

The Replacement: 'Correct.'

Moses then took him through three years of concerted resistance to being here in the dreaded witness box. The Replacement revealed that he and his wife were in treatment for mental health conditions—in his case, severe post-traumatic stress disorder. His wife was also 'dying of cancer'. He said he had repeatedly told our lawyers that he hadn't witnessed the alleged murder of Ali Jan. He had no wish to incriminate himself and 'no interest in helping the respondents'.

The Replacement said he believed he would not be subpoenaed, but was subjected to renewed approaches after Ben Roberts-Smith gave evidence that only he could contradict. Moses asked whether a deal had been proposed, whereby The Replacement could be asked about Darwan but 'steer clear of Fasil'.

The Replacement: 'Yes.'

Arthur Moses then trod a fine line, querying whether the witness felt he was being painted into a corner—if he didn't give evidence about Darwan, the respondents would make an allegation that he had murdered someone at Fasil. Moses said he was not asking The Replacement 'to make a statement about what happened at Fasil', but about whether he felt pressured.

The witness again objected, based on self-incrimination. We were back in the cul-de-sac. After more legal argument and an adjournment, open court resumed soon after midday.

The Replacement was again unwilling to give evidence. Moses pressed, and the witness again withdrew. Moses argued that, given the witness's acknowledged mental health struggle and the alleged pressure from our lawyers, 'Your Honour will take into account the likelihood that the witness's evidence may be unreliable'.

His Honour again ruled that The Replacement was not required 'to give evidence in relation to the last question'.

Moses shifted tack, asking whether The Replacement believed that, if he did not assent to our request to cooperate, he would be subpoenaed as a hostile witness and asked questions about Fasil. He replied, 'Yes.'

Moses: 'And you considered that to be a threat?'

The Replacement: 'Yes.'

The witness further agreed that he had suffered from anxiety when he provided a statement.

Moses: 'And is it fair to say that you signed the statement because you wanted to get the respondents off your back?'

The Replacement: 'Yes.'

Moses, soon after: 'It's correct, isn't it, that in September 2021 you agreed to give your evidence in relation to Darwan as part of a deal with the respondents, so they didn't ask you questions about Fasil, correct?'

The Replacement: 'Yes.'

Moses: 'Had they not approached you to say that they would [not] ask you questions about Fasil if you gave evidence in relation to Darwan, you would not have met with the respondents' lawyers?'

His Honour: 'Well, I don't understand the question, Mr Moses. I didn't understand it the first time you asked it and I don't understand it again.'

In clarifying, Arthur Moses stepped through the process: that the witness understood he would not be asked about Fasil, and that this was why he had agreed to meet, on the understanding that he would give evidence about Darwan. The Replacement concurred.

The morning session concluded.

At 2.15 pm we filed in again, Ben Roberts-Smith carrying two large files and The Replacement toting a water bottle as he took his seat.

Arthur Moses SC picked up on the misery that had befallen The Replacement, driven by the reporting of alleged war crimes in Afghanistan and the spectre of the IGADF inquiry.

Moses: 'I think you told your psychologist—and please correct me if I am wrong—that you felt like you were being blamed for things, whilst others were getting off scot-free, without being blamed for things?'

The Replacement: 'Correct.' He also agreed that, as a result, his mental health had deteriorated, as had his capacity for recall.

Moses: 'Do you accept that your recollection of specific details of the mission at Darwan may be wrong?'

The Replacement: 'Yes.'

Taken through the events of that day, and in light of the confusing static generated by rumour and reporting on what had or had not occurred, the witness was asked whether he might be wrong on detail. The Replacement conceded this was possible.

Moses: 'And do you accept that you may have been wrong, and the last compound you cleared with Mr Roberts-Smith's patrol was further to the north than you gave evidence about earlier today?'

The Replacement: 'I don't personally believe so, no. I believe we reached the limit of the compounds.' Pushed further, he stuck to his position.

But his interrogator persisted: 'Do you accept your recollection may be wrong?'

'It's possible.'

It was a torrid day, at the end of some traumatic years for the beleaguered former soldier. At midafternoon came those precious words: 'No further questions.'

'I was told to testify or else: SAS soldier', *The Australian* headlined its coverage of the day in court.[1] In the propaganda war, Arthur Moses SC might have won some ground in prosecuting the 'deal'. It could be argued the witness's credibility was compromised in a trade-off to talk about Darwan and not about Fasil. On another reading, the charge of a 'deal' was irrelevant, in that Justice Besanko had already ruled the witness give evidence. And I wondered whether Ben Roberts-Smith's team might genuinely have wanted to hear what The Replacement had to say about that latter mission.

Regarding Darwan, some further important pieces now fitted into the puzzle. The Replacement was strong on what he had seen in the last compound, conceding only a 'possibility' that he was wrong. And there was his stunning recollection of what he'd heard later in the ready room—that Ben Roberts-Smith had indeed kicked an Afghan off a cliff.

CHAPTER 82

A WITCH-HUNT

Easter week and a gear change as we motor forward, now approaching the twelfth week of a trial that was initially thought would run for half that time.

Following the evidence of The Replacement, The Gunner is recalled. He faces further questions in closed court, about alleged disparities in his testimony before Justice Besanko and the IGADF. After this, it is the other side's turn to present evidence in support of Ben Roberts-Smith. I am tasked with providing as much background as I can muster about witnesses on the Roberts-Smith list. On the Sunday, Ben is photographed relaxing with his girlfriend at a pub in Paddington.

Easter Tuesday was 19 April 2022. When the applicant's team assembled, they were fused, upbeat, as if loading a bullet—and the metaphor did not end there. When the next witness was sighted, he was projectile-like. The crown of his head was spherical, and his hair was close-cropped. Below the neckline, he was all muscle and energy in a tightly buttoned black suit. The Scot was their big gun.

Arthur Moses SC began by unwrapping a bejewelled CV. The former Royal Marine deployed to Northern Ireland, Iraq, Africa, the Balkans,

South America and more. After service with the Special Boat Service in East Timor, he transferred to Australia's SASR. Following six trips to Afghanistan he secured a coveted exchange with America's famed SEAL Team Six. And now, at the age of 50, after 28 years as a soldier, The Scot was based in Nashville, Tennessee, where he was the senior vice president and part owner of a security business.

Moses took his time in revealing to the court this substantial experience, and The Scot's specialist skills as a patrol commander and water operator. He met Ben Roberts-Smith in 2002,[1] when he joined the SASR. They first served in the same patrol in 2009, and their relationship was 'very good'.

Perhaps to help disarm any suggestion of collusion, The Scot said he was also close to, and in regular communication with, The Hunter, The Freefaller and The Bodyguard. Regarding the latter, he said they were also 'business associates'.

The Scot's decision to appoint Ben Roberts-Smith as his second-in-command was 'an easy one'. He explained: 'I had seen how capable he was from the moment he left selection all the way through.'

Asked about the rules of engagement, The Scot said that, as patrol commander, he 'enforced them'. 'I would make sure [patrol members] all understood them to begin with, and I wouldn't let anything happen that went against the rules of engagement.'

Asked about blooding, he acknowledged that he knew the term.

Moses: 'During the 2009 deployment . . . did you ever say to anyone, "We're going to blood the rookie?"'

The Scot: 'Never.'

It was closing on midday when Moses took The Scot inside the compound at Whiskey 108, to the heart of the trial. The Scot remembered a tunnel being found; it was first detected in his presence, as he recalled, by one of two Afghan National Army soldiers accompanying the troop.

The Hunter, being small of stature, ventured down the tunnel brandishing his pistol. After a couple of minutes, The Scot said, 'he stuck his head up and said it was clear'.

During the compound clearance, a 'rummage' produced a large cache of weapons. The Scot said the find was being discussed when he heard gunshots coming from outside. He ran towards the noise, sighting Roberts-Smith and The Gunsmith and shouting to them. Roberts-Smith said 'they were all right', and he had engaged the enemy. The Scot said he then reported over the radio 'two KIA', or killed in action.

The clock wound past midday as the witness described a plan to destroy the weapons cache, and the luncheon adjournment was then called.

As we retired to the small interview room, I listened as our barristers pondered aloud whether The Scot's account of Whiskey 108 corresponded with their case theory.

After the lunch break, legal argument ensued. At issue was a common legal principle known as the *Browne v. Dunn* rule. It would be invoked many times. It means that when a witness testifies and counsel intends to introduce contradictory evidence, the substance of that challenge should be put to the witness, allowing them fair opportunity to comment.

Numerous matters in The Scot's testimony, Nicholas Owens QC now argued, had not been put to the respondents' witnesses. One glaring example was his claim that an Afghan National Army member had discovered the tunnel. As Owens put it: 'The evidence that has been given [by The Scot] about what happened at Whiskey 108 departed so far from the case that was put to any of our witnesses in cross-examination that there would be no fair ability to conclude the trial unless those witnesses were recalled.'

That was not going to happen. After some toing and froing, Justice Besanko said he would 'consider the arguments' but would 'like to proceed'.

The Scot was recalled. He resumed his account of moving from Whiskey 108 to reconnoitre Whiskey 109, and of sighting the body with the prosthetic limb. He removed and checked the limb for explosive componentry and found nothing, he said. The Scot marked on a map his movements in relation to the body and the compound.

Arthur Moses asked his witness whether ISR was in use. (ISR, or intelligence surveillance reconnaissance, is sometimes used as a shorthand descriptor for the presence of unmanned aerial surveillance—a drone.)

The Scot said it was. ScanEagle (or 'ScanBudgie', as it was jovially referred to, given Australia's tiny inventory in comparison to that of the United States) was on station. He recalled moving away from the compound and clearing it of all local nationals, so an air strike could be called to destroy the cache of weaponry.

The Scot was asked about the prosthetic leg—and did not miss, so to speak, the opportunity to put the boot in. As the patrol members were lined up to go, he said, he had asked Ben Roberts-Smith where the leg was.

Moses: 'And did Mr Roberts-Smith say something to it?'

The Scot: 'Yes, he did.'

Moses: 'What did he say?'

The Scot: 'He said, "Dickhead's got it" . . . Excuse my language, Your Honour.'

He was referring to Ben's nemesis, the patrol commander we call The Veteran. The Scot said he saw the prosthetic leg again at the Camp Russell drinking hole, the Fat Lady's Arms.

Moses: 'Did you drink from it?'

The Scot: 'Yes . . . It was a culture thing. Some of the more junior members of the patrol were doing it, and never ask your men to do something you're not willing to do yourself. So I did. I drank out of it once.'

The Scot's evidence in chief moved on to the Battle of Tizak, beginning with the planning process. Now he sunk the boot in again, but this time to a different fellow patrol commander, The Reader. 'As usual, he handed it off,' he commented. 'He didn't want any part of it . . . pretty much just dropped the bundle.' The Scot claimed that he and The Freefaller then took charge and worked up a battle plan.

The witness was led through a vivid account of 'basically landing in a hornet's nest' of 'over 100 Taliban'. The culmination was his patrol's assault on an elevated compound. 'They had three machine guns on us,' he noted. Roberts-Smith, The Gunsmith and The Corporal, on the left flank, were receiving most of the fire. 'We made a decision that we were going to take the guns out. I pulled out a frag. For us, we say "frag out", [that] means grenade going out. If we say "grenade", it means incoming. I called "frag out", put it in. One of the machine guns stopped firing and RS ran at the wall . . . [and] killed the remaining machine gunners.'

The fighting continued late into the day. There was more criticism of The Reader, who The Scot said 'nearly fragged some of his own friendly troops'.

'RS, even though they didn't like one another, he still volunteered to go with [The Reader] in pursuit of an insurgent sighted among some rocks,' he continued. 'That guy brought his gun to bear and started engaging him, and The Reader engaged and killed that . . . last guy.'

Perilously low on ammunition and anticipating a counterattack that did not eventuate, they waited through the night for evacuation, arriving back at Camp Russell at 3.30 am. 'Everyone was pretty spent, so we sent everyone to bed. Well, we let them have a couple of beers first and then sent them to bed.'

The Scot's account of the famous battle rounded out the day. But his evidence in chief was not completed, and when he returned to the witness box on Thursday, 21 April, Moses asked him about the process of writing up the reports that led to the Australian Army announcing that Ben Roberts-Smith would be awarded the Victoria Cross. The Scot said he read the citation and saw no inaccuracy. He did, however, read a media article soon after that linked the VC award to allegations of bullying.

After the Victoria Cross, Australia's next highest honour is the Star of Gallantry. The Scot was asked how other members of the patrol reacted when they learned that this was to be awarded to him. The Scot alleged that The SSE 'felt he should have been awarded something'. (This had earlier been refuted by The SSE, who told the court that, although he'd fought shoulder to shoulder with The Scot, he was not upset about missing out on a medal.)

The Scot further recalled The Gunsmith's wife approaching him at a barbecue, wanting to know 'where her husband's medal was'. The Scot said he told her 'to wind her neck in—which means mind her own business, Your Honour'. He said that The Gunsmith later put it to him that the first enemy machine gunner, who was presumed to have been killed by

The Scot's grenade, could in fact have been killed by The Gunsmith's gunfire. The Scot said he agreed.

Moses: 'Now, can I ask you this: has any member of the SASR raised with you that Mr Roberts-Smith did not deserve the Victoria Cross for his action at Tizak?'

The Scot: 'No.'

Later in the morning, Moses addressed the IGADF inquiry. The Scot said he was interviewed in May 2018, and that at that time he'd seen The SSE in the waiting area.

Moses: 'Following your interview, did you tell anyone that you had been in to see the IGADF?'

The Scot: 'Yes.'

Moses: 'And who was that?'

The Scot: 'Ben Roberts-Smith.'

Moses: 'What did you say to him?'

The Scot: 'I told him to prepare himself. It was a witch-hunt.'

The Scot further admitted telling Roberts-Smith that The SSE had been 'dragged in as well'. Arthur Moses, presumably pre-empting cross-examination, asked about the document The Scot had prepared for Roberts-Smith following his IGADF interview.

The witness objected on the basis of self-incrimination. The turnstile again spun, with The Scot leaving the court, His Honour granting a certificate and the witness agreeing to give evidence.

Moses asked what The Scot had done with the document he prepared. The Scot said he'd emailed it to Roberts-Smith. He had done this, he said, because he was without legal representation, he'd moved to the United States and he 'wanted to complain about the treatment'. He said Addisons Lawyers came to represent him, with the fees covered by the Seven Network.

There was the odd open mouth, at least at our bar table, when The Scot then announced that he'd only found out Seven was footing his legal bill two days earlier, when he'd started giving evidence.

A closed court session followed, with open court and legal argument resuming after lunch. Around midafternoon, Nicholas Owens SC began his cross-examination.

In law as in journalism, sometimes it's best to start with a big question—and this one was a doozy: 'How many allegations of murder are you aware of being made against a patrol of which you were the patrol commander and Ben Roberts-Smith was your 2IC?'

The Scot: 'Three.'

Whiskey 108 accounted for only two of them, Owens continued, so what was the third?

The Scot answered: '2010.'

This referred to an alleged incident of three murders from 14 May 2010 at West Dorafshan. The Scot admitted knowledge of this allegation, which was not a part of our case.

Our senior counsel went to the point. If war crimes were proved, notably from Whiskey 108, The Scot could go to prison. 'What I want to put to you is that you've in fact come here to give a deliberately false account of events at Whiskey 108, because you think it would be to your advantage in deterring prosecuting authorities from pursuing you in relation to those charges?'

The Scot: 'That is not true.'

Owens turned back to the West Dorafshan allegation, in which another soldier, designated by the court as Person 8, had allegedly been blooded by The Scot and Roberts-Smith.

The Scot: 'We don't blood people. I thought I made that clear.'

They went toe to toe. Earlier, through his evidence in chief, The Scot had appeared relaxed, confident. He had even yawned at times. But now Owens—tall, his head bowed, slightly rocking back and forth, polite, never shouting—remained relentless. A thick folder at his elbow, he sometimes briefly consulted with Lyndelle Barnett and Chris Mitchell; but he did not let up.

The Scot was no longer yawning as he parried. He had no reason to lie, he said. There was no risk of jail, because there had been no murders. He was angry with the news reporting and disappointed with the liars who had spoken to the media. He said he did not give much thought to the incriminating evidence given by The Gunsmith and The SSE, his former comrades.

Owens: 'Well, you give The Reader a lot of thought—do you agree with that?'

The Scot: 'Yes.'

Owens: 'You know, don't you, that The Reader has given evidence that people came out of the tunnel at Whiskey 108?'

The Scot: 'I don't know that, but I'm not surprised that The Reader came here talking crap about myself and RS.'

Wound up, The Scot now let fly. He didn't just intensely dislike The Reader, he hated him. He agreed that he had deliberately offered gratuitous negative commentary about The Reader through his evidence in chief. The Scot admitted he had called The Reader a coward to his face.

Owens: 'It's the worst insult you can offer a soldier . . . to call him a coward?'

The Scot: 'And that's how seriously I take it. In 28 years, he's the only man I've ever called a coward.'

If any of the soldiers who fought at Tizak were tuned in to the Federal Court's YouTube channel at this moment, they might have been on the edge of their seats, some perhaps gritting their teeth. The Reader was a widely respected soldier. In fact, if he hadn't been at Tizak that day, Ben Roberts-Smith would in all probability not have been perched in rapt attention in the opposite corner.

Owens: 'Well, in fact, you know, don't you, that [The Reader] saved Mr Roberts-Smith's life at the very last contact of the day at Tizak, when he shot the insurgent hiding behind the rock—correct?'

The Scot: 'No, he did, I will give you that. He shot one person that day.'

Owens turned to further incriminating testimony, this time from The Scout and The Gunner. 'It's correct, isn't it, that you're angry with them for giving evidence for the respondents?'

The Scot: 'No, I just don't like them.' He said he thought people who had spoken to the media 'should be sacked'.

Owens next queried The Scot's surprising contention he had only found out the Seven Network was paying his legal bills this very week, in April 2022, although his dealings with the appointed lawyer had commenced in May 2020. The Scot said he presumed he would pay his own legal bills, and had kept $100,000 in a bank account for that purpose. He had never asked how much Addisons would charge and never queried why he was not sent bills.

Owens revealed to the witness that, so far, bills totalling around $170,000 had been submitted to Seven Network (Operations) Limited on behalf of him, The Sniper and The Hunter.

Owens: 'It's not honest evidence, is it, to say that you haven't raised the topic of fees with your lawyer in nearly two years?'

The Scot: 'I haven't.' He rejected being beholden to Ben Roberts-Smith.

Owens returned to The Scot's IGADF interview, and his knowledge of a legal requirement to not disclose to anyone what was said. He was shown the text message from Emma Roberts revealing his phone call to Ben Roberts-Smith, which described 'being drilled for hours . . . lots of questions about Ben, even the VC action . . . obvious someone has said a hell of a lot'.

Owens: 'Now, you accept, don't you, that you breached an order by making that call to Ben Roberts-Smith?'

The Scot: 'No.'

Owens: 'Why do you not accept that?'

The Scot: 'Because I never told him any of the details of the interview. I told him it was a witch-hunt. That's not details.'

It was a testing day for both Owens and The Scot. As the clock swept past 4 pm, the witness was queried about his use of prepaid phones and apps such as Signal to maintain contact with Roberts-Smith.

Owens: 'You and Mr Roberts-Smith have discussed over many years how to tell the story of what happened at Whiskey 108 to explain away war crimes—correct?'

The Scot: 'There has been no collusion, not from our side . . . Your witnesses have been colluding for the last twelve years.' It was understandable that he would be talking to his friends, he contended. 'It's hard not to when you see lies in a newspaper.'

At 4.15 pm Justice Besanko gave The Scot the usual instruction not to speak to anyone about his evidence while under cross-examination.

'I understand, Your Honour,' The Scot replied.

That evening, a spokesman for Seven West Media's executive chairman, Kerry Stokes, said Seven shareholders were not underwriting the legal costs of Ben Roberts-Smith's witnesses, which were being 're-charged' to Stokes' private company, Australian Capital Equity.

When we reassembled the following morning, Ben Roberts-Smith and I converged at the door. It happened a few times. I thought I saw worry lines. We knew to be polite.

Cross-examination worked through more devilish detail of the Whiskey 108 mission. Nicholas Owens reprised evidence that Roberts-Smith had borrowed a suppressor from The Cyclist, prior to the older Afghan being shot by The Gunsmith in an alleged blooding. The Scot countered: 'He wouldn't have had to borrow anyone's suppressor. We all carried suppressors. I don't know why he would have to borrow one.'

In journalism, we say there is nothing like a killer document. A signed property deed or a telling photograph can constitute incontrovertible proof. Equally, in a courtroom, forensic evidence tends to trump interminable debate. And in this respect we claimed a secret weapon.

Our barrister Chris Mitchell, a former war crimes investigator, had pored over thousands of photographs, the bulk coming via subpoena from the ADF. Lots also from Roberts-Smith's lunch box stash, and others from our own sources.

The Cyclist's evidence about being asked for a suppressor was odd, but odd in a way that hinted at veracity. Why would this curious snippet be invented? When Chris Mitchell searched the photos from Whiskey 108 supplied by the ADF, he noted that The Gunsmith's weapon was not fitted with a suppressor. It was no smoking gun, but revealing all the same.

Nicholas Owens questioned The Scot about the use of suppressors. He acknowledged they were more often fitted for night use. So there was a likelihood The Gunsmith had carried his suppressor, but in his pack, meaning it was not so readily accessed.

The next detail explored, by virtue of the vast photo library, was more punishing. Owens asked about the expressions 'rookie' and 'rookie fuck'. In his evidence, Ben Roberts-Smith had been adamant the terms were not used—and The Scot agreed.

Nicholas Owens SC put it to The Scot he was denying using the term 'rookie' in order to dismiss any proposition that the phrase 'blooding the rookie' was ever used.

The Scot: 'That's not correct.'

Chris Mitchell had not just glanced through the trove of photos; he had zoomed in and picked up pertinent details, including what was scrawled on the walls of the Fat Lady's Arms and the accommodation facilities.

Owens asked about 2 Squadron's 2010 rotation, when The Scot's patrol had embraced a new member. That meant the new boy was no longer The Gunsmith, but a soldier known to the court as Person 8. And in one telling image, six names could be seen inscribed on the patrol room door, of which the last was clearly visible as 'Rookie Fuck'. (As we saw earlier, a nod to the movie *Super Troopers*.)

Owens: 'Do you agree with me that there was the name of each patrol member but, instead of Person 8's name, the words "rookie fuck" appeared?'

The Scot: 'I don't remember that.'

There was an adjournment to closed court. In his old regiment, The Scot had a mixed reputation. Nicknamed 'the Tartan Tannoy' (and worse), he positively bellowed confidence and candour, but there was also admiration and respect for his aggression and bravery in the field. Now, in his third day in a space that tested a different aspect of character, The Scot was faltering.

Upon return to open court, The Scot was probed about his contact with fellow friends and supporters of Ben Roberts-Smith over the IGADF interviews, the sharing of USBs, their reaction to newspaper reporting and the like. Owens asked about Roberts-Smith meeting The Scot at Beaver Creek, in the United States, in 2019, after he had visited The Hunter in New Zealand. The Scot acknowledged there had been conversation.

Owens: 'Did you discuss the killing of two PUCs at Whiskey 108?'

The Scot: 'There were no PUCs killed at 108.'

The witness was shown photographs, some retrieved from the buried lunch box.

Owens: 'Do you see there's a photograph of an SAS soldier dressed in a Ku Klux Klan costume?'

The Scot: 'Yes.'

Owens: 'Who is that?'

The Scot: 'I wasn't there at the time, but I believe it's The Hunter.'

The court adjourned at 12.45 pm. Dean Levitan, Tess McGuire and I couldn't face another sterile sandwich, so we made our way to the David Jones food hall. In transit, we noticed The Scot pacing outside, puffing on a cigarette. The media scrum, camped nearby, were oblivious to his presence.

After the break, Nicholas Owens SC put to the witness that glaring comment, 'I'm going to blood a rookie', overheard by members of The Veteran's patrol outside their room before the Whiskey 108 mission. This was denied. Owens followed up. 'And you stood in the doorway of his room and were dancing a jig?'

The Scot: 'A jig . . . absolutely not . . . are you stereotyping me because I'm Scottish, Mr Owens?'

Owens: 'No, I'm suggesting that you stood in The Veteran's doorway in a jovial mood, dancing a jig.'

The Scot: 'If I was ever in The Veteran's doorway in their room, I was never in a jovial mood because I didn't like any of them.'

The rest of the afternoon was spent with The Scot struggling to explain his account of Whiskey 108. He repeatedly insisted no men were hauled from the tunnel. He stuck to his guns on two insurgents legitimately engaged outside. He could not account for why at first he saw only one of the bodies. He did not think it odd that two armed insurgents would suddenly materialise at the very moment he sent Ben Roberts-Smith and The Gunsmith outside.

Owens: 'It was a detail you added into your story to attempt to conceal the fact that you knew two people were pulled out of the tunnel and executed.'

The Scot: 'That's not correct.'

Evidence concluded at 4.15 pm on a Friday on the verge of Anzac Day. It would be a lonely long weekend for The Scot.

On Anzac Day, Ben Roberts-Smith had been spotted drinking alone in Redfern. Court and cross-examination resumed on Tuesday, 26 April 2022. Roberts-Smith would catch up with his chief witness at the end of this day—day 73.

Chris Mitchell had again been examining photos. Nick McKenzie joined me on the approach to court.

At 10.32 am, The Scot: 'Good morning, Your Honour.'

His Honour: 'Yes, thank you . . . Yes, Mr Owens.'

Our barrister obtained from the witness an assurance he had not discussed his evidence with anyone since the preceding Friday, and it was on again.

Nicholas Owens SC returned to Whiskey 108. The Scot said that, after the two insurgents were shot, he reconnoitred a neighbouring compound and, upon his return, sighted 'another dead insurgent' just metres from the prosthetic leg victim.

Owens: 'You didn't wonder how the body had appeared in that location, where it hadn't been before?'

The Scot: 'No.'

He was visibly squirming. Pleading eyes across the room. The Scot was now increasingly hesitant.

Owens: 'You would agree, wouldn't you, that you keep changing your story as you discover flaws in it?'

The Scot: 'No, not at all.'

He was shown a photograph of the old man, the alleged victim of the blooding.

Owens: 'You would agree, wouldn't you, that there is a significant quantity of blood and brain matter on the ground right next to him?'

The Scot: 'Yes.'

Owens: 'And you would agree, wouldn't you, that there is no way that that body had this photograph taken at least ten minutes after it was shot in another location—correct?'

The Scot: 'I can't answer that.'

Owens: 'Well, it's clear, isn't it, that the body is lying exactly where it was in fact shot?'

The Scot: 'I don't know.'

Our senior counsel pointed to cut grass and cooking ovens near the old man that were not visible in the photo of the man with the prosthetic leg. The Scot rejected the proposition that this indicated the old man's body was photographed inside the compound. The photograph also showed an SSE bag on the corpse with words 'NW corner tunnel'.

Owens: 'He was shot right next to the tunnel in the north-west corner of the compound—correct?'

The Scot: 'No.'

A tactical site exploitation report was shown; it identified the old man as having been found in 'northeast corner Whiskey 108, in courtyard containing tunnel complex'.[2]

Owens: 'Do you see that?'

The Scot: 'Yes.'

Owens: 'And that, again, is an accurate description of where the body was found—correct?'

The Scot: 'It's not where I saw the body.'

The cross-examination now turned to the conversation, overheard by The SSE, between Roberts-Smith and The Scot after the alleged blooding.

Owens: 'You said words to the effect of, "You've just done this while the ISR [overhead surveillance] is still flying above and might have recorded you"?'

The Scot: 'No, I don't agree with that.'

The witness acknowledged he had made a radio call to the JTAC inquiring about the presence of the ISR 'at some point'.

Owens: 'You needed to know whether two war crimes had been filmed?'

The Scot: 'No.'

Owens: 'Now, I put it to you your denials are false?'

The Scot: 'No, I don't agree with that.'

There was more denial when Owens took him to another alleged comment, upon return to base, that he had 'finally blooded the rookie'.

Another closed court session, with The Scot returning to open court after the lunch break.

Owens again asked about the Channel Seven cost agreement. The witness understood he could have accessed legal support funded by the ADF, but considered that 'useless'.

Owens: 'Are you aware that, after that fact was disclosed in court last week . . . Channel Seven requested that a company called Australian Capital Equity repay any amounts that Channel Seven had paid in relation to your legal fees?'

The Scot: 'I did not know that.'

He further submitted that he did not know Kerry Stokes had approved the payments.

Owens: 'It's the case, isn't it, that you've come to court to lie about what happened at Whiskey 108, to ensure that Mr Roberts-Smith continues to intercede with Mr Stokes to ensure that your legal fees are paid going into the future—correct?'

The Scot: 'No that's not correct.'

When Nicholas Owens SC had concluded, there was re-examination by Arthur Moses SC. He took The Scot back through Whiskey 108, advancing defensible explanations for discordant evidence. He took him back to the Beaver Creek meeting in 2019, which The Scot maintained was a family holiday.

In this final session, The Scot was invited to put the boot in once more—this time to the man who had initiated the accursed IGADF inquiry.

The Scot was asked why he decided to leave the Australian Defence Force. He said it was because of a comment made when he was tasked with a hostage rescue mission to Afghanistan. The hostage was half-Australian, half-British. The alleged comment that rankled him was: 'Well she's not a real Australian anyway.'

Moses: 'And who made that comment?'

The Scot: 'It was SOCAUST.'

Moses: 'Major General Sengelman?'

The Scot: 'Yes.'

I doubt Jeff Sengelman would have been pleased. His name was being gratuitously invoked; and, as I understood it, he refuted the allegation strenuously. Senior command was in no position to comment, considering the mission was classified—and had been something of a non-event, in that the British had not requested Australian assistance.

It was not a good day for The Scot. Having been released, he was able to catch up with Roberts-Smith for drinks.

At the fag end of a taxing day, he was making his way to a lift in his hotel, when he was stopped by two detectives from the Office of the Special Investigator. He swore at the men and, according to later evidence, rudely resisted handing over his phone. The Scot was arrested.

Ten months later, The Scot pleaded guilty to the charge of hindering a Commonwealth official. A second charge of causing harm was dismissed. Magistrate Miranda Moody said, on her reading of the police facts, The Scot 'behaved like a drunken fool.'[3]

CHAPTER 83

RATS AND SNITCHES

It is an Anzac alliance of sorts. The Hunter (Person 35) has flown from New Zealand to support his mate. Bantam-like, he struts to the box, cocksure and unkempt, for the final session of the day. The seat would still have been warm following the departure of another Commonwealth cousin and mate, The Scot.

The Hunter provided background to Arthur Moses SC of transferring from the New Zealand SAS to Australia in 2008, because the pay and conditions were 'way better'. He had already met Ben Roberts-Smith when they earlier participated in joint counter-terrorism training.

After taking him through a range of deployments, Moses asked about working with the Afghan National Directorate of Security (NDS) partner force soldiers, commonly known as Wakunish. The Hunter knew of their leader, The Lieutenant, because of one memorable incident.

He said he was in a compound with an interpreter and The Lieutenant in 2012. They were questioning locals when a large Afghan hound on a chain nearby began barking. He said The Lieutenant took it upon himself to shoot the animal. The bullet went through the dog, then 'ricocheted up and hit another team member as he had come through a doorway'. As a result, The Lieutenant was removed.

After 30 minutes, evidence in chief that day concluded. As The Hunter headed for the rear private exit, Ben Roberts-Smith walked the length of the courtroom to shake his good mate's hand.

There was confusion the following morning when the lawyer Rob Ranken, counsel for both The Hunter and The Scot, could not be found. An explanation soon emerged. Mr Ranken was some blocks away, at the Sydney local court, helping bail out the preceding witness, who had spent an ignominious evening in a cell.

When the delayed Rob Ranken communicated to the court that matters should proceed, Arthur Moses SC rose and turned again to The Hunter. Having rounded off his story of the curious incident of the dog and the stray bullet, he turned to Rotation IX, in 2009. The Hunter had never heard The Scot speak of 'blooding', or The Gunsmith referred to as the 'rookie fuck'.

They stepped through the Whiskey 108 mission. The Hunter was a member of The Freefaller's patrol, on the right flank. He marked on photographs the comparative manoeuvres of the respective patrols. Over the radio, he heard that a tunnel had been found near an animal pen, under 'a piece of Hesco mesh' with 'chopped feed on top of it to hide it'. He could not recall the presence of Afghan partner force members, but The Freefaller was there, along with Ben Roberts-Smith.

So who would go down the tunnel? The Hunter, of jockey dimensions, laughed when his horse-sized mate volunteered. 'Ben wasn't going to fit. I was.'

He told the court there was no call-out, and no grenade lobbed in. He removed his body armour, fixed his night-vision goggles and entered, pistol first.

Moses: 'Did you locate or observe any individuals in the tunnel?'

The Hunter: 'No.'

He instead found a mat covered with AK magazines, ammunition, documents and communications devices. He came out to report the find and ventured back to recover the equipment. Photos of the cache were shown to the court.

Moses: 'When was the first time that you heard a suggestion that two local nationals had come out of the tunnel at Whiskey 108?'

He replied that the first time he heard this was in media reporting. And it was also in the media that he first heard the story of Ben Roberts-Smith allegedly executing an Afghan at the compound. The Hunter added that he first heard the allegation of The Gunsmith being blooded 'from these proceedings'. He knew the prosthetic leg was cleaned out and used as a novelty drinking vessel, and yes, he did drink from it.

The next subject was Tizak from Rotation XII in 2010, where The Hunter also fought in a patrol commanded by The Freefaller. While his team advanced through an orchard under intense fire, he said, he did see The Scot's team, including Ben Roberts-Smith, assaulting the machine-gun nests on higher ground.

Arthur Moses was beginning to ask The Hunter whether he later heard from some within the SASR that Ben Roberts-Smith had not deserved his Victoria Cross when the court adjourned for lunch. Upon return, The Hunter said this had occurred with The Sergeant, in the presence of The Gunsmith, at a mission readiness exercise at Cultana, South Australia. At that point, The Gunsmith had not received his Medal for Gallantry and was 'upset that he hadn't been recognised'. The Sergeant, he alleged, went through a 'blow by blow' account of why Ben Roberts-Smith did not deserve the VC. The Hunter said he made a note of the conversation and alerted Roberts-Smith via email.

Darwan followed. The Hunter was on the first helicopter flight. Upon disembarkation, his team moved at a 'quick pace' and came across fighting-age males in two large compounds. At the first compound, he said, he and The Corporal engaged two insurgents.

On the move to meet up with the troop, he encountered Roberts-Smith, noting he was soaking wet. 'He showed me the weapon and explained to me he had an engagement on the other side of the river and swam the river . . . to do an SSE . . . and see if it was our objective.'

The Hunter said that the first he heard of an allegation of a breach of the rules of engagement at Darwan was in the media in 2018. He knew from the reporting that 'Leonidas' was Roberts-Smith, and claimed he had heard The Veteran call him by this name.

This was news to me. I understood a nickname had attached itself to Roberts-Smith, but that it was 'Achilles'.

Arthur Moses turned to Chinartu. The Hunter said he did not recall seeing The Lieutenant there.

Another closed court interlude consumed the rest of the day. Classified material, and there was a lot of it, could not be ventilated in open court. Legal argument and more closed-court-dominated proceedings until The Hunter's evidence in chief restarted at 10.33 am on Thursday, 28 April 2022.

Moses had some final questions. The Hunter had never seen 'throw-downs' in use. He had retained imagery from Afghanistan and had mailed it to Roberts-Smith. Then to the party at the Fat Lady's Arms, colourfully illustrated on *60 Minutes*.

Moses: 'Did you wear a costume at that party?'

The Hunter: 'I did.'

Moses: 'What costume did you wear?'

The Hunter: 'I came as a Klansman.' He told His Honour that he thought it funny to do so, as another soldier 'was coming in blackface'. The witness sanitised his embrace of vigilante violence and hatred as a 'parody', in that 'they're pretty pathetic and I was making a joke of it'.

Moses: 'Thank you. And were you reprimanded by anyone in the chain of command for dressing up in that fashion at that party?'

The Hunter: 'No, I was not. I actually won the fancy dress competition that night.'

The witness acknowledged seeing a kill board on Ben Roberts-Smith's patrol room door, but said they were common in Afghanistan. He admitted drawing winged penises—his trademark, a caricature of the SASR's winged dagger—but said he never drew one kicking a PUC off a cliff.

Nicholas Owens' cross-examination of The Hunter began with a quote: '"When some fuckwit in a suit starts questioning your integrity and using his fucktard snake logic, he learnt getting his tonsils bruised by some lecturer's spotty dick at their non-binary law school, remember one thing: that this cunt will be one of the first to be held down and drowned in a muddy puddle for his fancy jacket when society crumbles."'

It was posted on social media the previous morning, and had been 'liked' by The Hunter. One of Tess McGuire's many roles was to monitor such posts. For some time, she had tracked The Hunter's unabashed free speech.

This quote was accompanied by a doctored photograph of a man with a 'Fairfax Media' label. The Hunter retreated to a familiar defensive perimeter: 'That's a bit of dark humour, and I don't think it really should be taken seriously. It's made in jest . . . it's meant to agitate, and it seems to have worked.'

In the celebrated 1992 film *A Few Good Men*, based on Aaron Sorkin's stage play, Colonel Nathan Jessup (played by Jack Nicholson) is disinclined to explain himself to people who 'sleep under the blanket of freedom'. He tells the military lawyer Daniel Kaffee (Tom Cruise) that there is an unsanctioned truth about men and war—a convenient public blindness to the reality that rough men are an essential and unheralded social safeguard. This sentiment is frequently, if less eloquently, invoked when the subject of war crimes is debated, particularly on social media.

In this other courtroom, Nicholas Owens SC, like a considerably taller Tom Cruise, took The Hunter along a similar path: 'Do you agree that you think that the safety and security of our society is underpinned by the actions of people like Mr Roberts-Smith in Afghanistan—correct?'

The Hunter: 'And you draw that conclusion from a tick or a heart . . . I don't really follow your argument, but any society needs a decent and well-trained military to protect them, then yes.'

Owens: 'Do you agree it's destructive to question the conduct of individual members of the military in what they did overseas?'

The Hunter: 'I think it is, yes.'

The witness was steady in his defence, unwilling to fulminate like Jessup—at least not in a courtroom.

Owens: 'I put it to you that in fact you were outraged that the conduct of Mr Roberts-Smith in Afghanistan is being scrutinised in this court?'

The Hunter: 'I find it upsetting his conduct is being scrutinised, yes.'

Owens: 'And you will say anything in this courtroom to help Mr Roberts-Smith win this case—correct?'

The Hunter: 'I'm here to tell the truth, Mr Owens.'

Owens put to the witness that, in anticipation of the trial, he had recently 'unliked' a series of posts he had formerly 'liked'. The Hunter denied doing so.

Tess McGuire had been assiduous in tracking his social media. There were more memes, one of Afghan women during the evacuation of Kabul holding a sign saying, 'Help us Soldier C'. Soldier C referred to SAS Trooper Oliver Schulz, seen on *Four Corners* shooting an unarmed Afghan in a field. Another sign parroted a line from the same soldier: 'Drop these cunts.'

The Hunter could not remember those posts, but admitted to liking others that disparaged our witnesses as 'rats and snitches'. He said: 'I consider your client's witnesses to be lying, yes.'

Our senior counsel moved to Darwan. The Hunter further dug his heels in, fighting off repeated questions, insisting he did not go to the final compound.

Owens: 'And the reason you've been resisting accepting that obvious proposition for the last few minutes is because you know that is the compound where it is alleged Mr Roberts-Smith kicked Ali Jan off the cliff—correct?'

The Hunter: 'That's incorrect . . . he didn't kick someone off the cliff.'

Owens: 'How do you know?'

The Hunter: 'Because I know my friend Ben, and I know he wouldn't do that.'

The Hunter further contended The Terp was with him at all times at Darwan, in contradiction of our case theory that he attended and interrogated Afghans in the final compound.

Back to the 'rats and snitches'. Owens pressed him on how he could know they were liars, and how he justified his persistently offensive commentary. The Hunter claimed that The Redhead's conduct at Chora in 2006 was 'hardly something to be proud of', while conceding he had not been on that mission. Asked for further examples of 'poor conduct' by The Redhead, he replied: 'Give me a minute, I will think of something, he was a pretty poor soldier. The list is long.'

Owens: 'Did you ever work with him in a patrol?'

The Hunter: 'No, I didn't.'

Owens ticked off a list of subpoenaed witnesses, who with general reluctance had spoken against Ben Roberts-Smith and had thus attracted The Hunter's keyboard disdain.

'They're not good soldiers, Mr Owens, it's true.'

Again, The Hunter was forced to concede that, in the main, he was in no position to know whether or not their evidence was truthful.

Owens: 'Do you remember liking a post that said: "Fun fact: Ali Jan and the gentleman that Soldier C met in the field were both Taliban and by default were terrorist paedos"?'

The Hunter: 'I would have liked that.'

Under a barrage of challenges, The Hunter's support for Ben Roberts-Smith was unwavering. Questioned about the 'rookie fuck' sign on The Scot and Roberts-Smith's patrol room door in 2010, he denied ever having seen it.

More photographic evidence emerged from Chris Mitchell's research, as The Hunter was taken back to his account of The Lieutenant being removed after the dog-shooting incident. Following hours and hours of scrutiny, images of The Lieutenant on operations were located, time-stamped after the date The Hunter insisted he had departed. Further documentation from the International Security Assistance Force (ISAF) confirmed that The Lieutenant was not the soldier stood down.

Just before noon, the trial moved to closed court to examine classified operational detail. It was not until after 4 pm that open court was again in session, and the spring seemed to have gone from The Hunter's step. Having seen the evidence, he finally conceded, 'I must have remembered incorrectly.'

Owens: 'What I want to put to you very clearly is that you have never had a memory failure, and you deliberately came up with a lie that The Lieutenant had been removed from the NDS at the end of July in order to help Mr Roberts-Smith?'

The Hunter: 'That's 100 per cent incorrect, Mr Owens. That was my memory of it, Your Honour.'

Proceedings adjourned for another day. And the next morning, at 10.36 am, Nicholas Owens SC returned to the now disproven tale of The Lieutenant and the shot dog. The Hunter maintained his position that he was honestly mistaken about The Lieutenant. He had not cooked up the story to help his mate, nor discussed the issue with other pro–Roberts-Smith witnesses, The Freefaller, The Scientist, The Bodyguard, The Corporal and The XO. He did not know The Corporal, The Scientist and The XO all had the same story.

Asked whether he had sought independent legal support because he feared a war crime allegation might be levelled at him, The Hunter turned the question on the questioner: 'Are you alleging that I've done anything wrong, Mr Owens?'

The barrister reminded the witness that he was here to answer questions, and took him to the ABC's report of the two Afghans engaged by The Hunter and The Corporal at Darwan. Locals had claimed the victims were unarmed.

His Honour advised The Hunter that, before answering, he had a right to seek a certificate against self-incrimination. But he was having none of it: 'I have been advised, Your Honour . . . if I may speak, that report is a lie. Those two insurgents that were engaged in that compound were legally engaged, under our RoE [rules of engagement]. They were armed. So I don't need a certificate for that.'

The Hunter said he was aware the incident was under review by the Office of the Special Investigator. And further, yes, he wanted independent legal support to cover costs he could not personally afford.

Owens had the witness shown a loan agreement from Seven to Ben Roberts-Smith to meet the costs of these defamation proceedings and the IGADF inquiry. He put it to The Hunter: 'You did know that Mr Roberts-Smith had agreed to be responsible for your legal fees?'

The Hunter: 'That's incorrect, Mr Owens.'

Owens, soon after: 'And you are prepared to come to this court to lie to ensure that that arrangement continues—correct?'

The Hunter: 'That's incorrect, Mr Owens.'

There were more questions about multiple meetings with Roberts-Smith and fellow supportive witnesses, eliciting repeated assurances from The Hunter that allegations of war crimes at Whiskey 108, Chinartu and Darwan were not discussed.

Repeated questions about the tunnel at Whiskey 108—with Owens putting to The Hunter the contrary versions from fellow soldiers of two Afghan men emerging—failed to budge the witness. 'That's incorrect, Mr Owens' and 'No one came out of the tunnel, Mr Owens' were on a constant loop.

A luncheon adjournment was called at 12.44 pm. The Hunter had been bowled middle stump on The Lieutenant, but had otherwise maintained a stubborn defence, albeit without the aggressive irreverence that marked his opening flourishes.

At 2.15 pm he was back in the box. After being shown photos of the bodies at Whiskey 108 and challenged about evidence revealing no drag marks, which seemed to indicate strongly that the older man had been killed inside the compound, The Hunter remained unmoved.

The Hunter had been one of the soldiers present at pre-deployment training when Roberts-Smith was alleged to have instructed patrol members to mock-execute PUCs, so he was further questioned on that.

Owens: 'I put it to you that Mr Roberts-Smith said words to the effect of, "If someone had been shot, you would put your weapon that you've carried into target down and photograph them so that they would be deemed an enemy combatant."'

The Hunter: 'That's incorrect, Mr Owens.'

More questions about Darwan and Chinartu. Although The Hunter now acknowledged The Lieutenant was present for the latter mission, he did not remember him being there. His memory was equally frail on how the targeted individual, Objective Stolen Idea, was killed.

Closed court rounded out the day, and the week. The Hunter had drawn the short straw, set to endure a weekend in isolation, in cross-examination limbo.

One development from the Friday that would have ongoing repercussions was the outing of protected-identity witnesses. It happened often enough in court, through slip-ups from the witnesses themselves and sometimes the barristers. When mistakes like this occurred, the record was redacted.

But this time there was no mistake. A protected witness or witnesses had been deliberately named by an idiot or idiots abroad. According to the court, 'unidentified foreign individuals' had committed a flagrant breach. Up to this point, the court had allowed public access to coverage of the trial by YouTube, but that arrangement was now terminated.

Monday, 2 May 2022 was day 77. Early morning, inside the MinterEllison bunker, I renew my stash of N95 masks and rapid antigen tests from a large but depleting box in the corner. We continue to regularly test and, as before, this one comes up negative. The Hunter is to be re-examined by Arthur Moses SC. Again, we bounce between open and closed court.

He was taken back to Chinartu and the allegation that a member of the Afghan partner force had executed a PUC in his presence. The Hunter made clear this was not so; if it had occurred, he would have 'raised that up the chain of command'.

Social media was also back on the agenda—and a touch of tit-for-tat.

Moses: 'Has there been social media about this case that you have not liked?'

The Hunter: 'Yes . . . They are in the form of tweets from Mr McKenzie.'

Nick McKenzie had regularly tweeted about the case. His most recent post followed the drama of The Scot the previous Tuesday evening:

> BREAKING: big news linked to ongoing war crimes investigations run by federal agencies. First arrest made. Former SAS soldier arrested in Sydney. Charged with obstructing/hindering/intimidating Commonwealth official and causing harm to law officer. More to come . . .

The Hunter finished his testimony in time for lunch. On his way out, he nodded to his friend Ben Roberts-Smith. I can't know what was in their minds, but it was unlikely to be rapture. Yes, The Hunter had been resolute in support of Ben at Whiskey 108, insisting that no Afghans were pulled from the tunnel and no one was executed. More witnesses with the same song sheet were no doubt waiting in the wings. But a trial like this is more than a numbers game. Credibility also counts.

After the applicant's first witness ended his week of evidence in handcuffs and a cell, the next was shown cavorting in a Ku Klux Klan outfit. Hardly the big start you might expect in validation of Australia's most decorated living soldier.

CHAPTER 84

RICOCHET

In *Roberts-Smith v. Fairfax Media Publications Pty Limited*,[1] there is tight competition for the prize of most reluctant witness. My vote goes to the next to front up. After lunch on Monday, 2 May 2022, it is The Scientist. Tall, tanned, gym-fit and with prematurely greying hair, he settles in acute discomfort.

Behind the usual reasons for the heel-dragging, there is something else. The Scientist has friends on both sides. He is close to both The Redhead and Ben Roberts-Smith.

The Scientist, known for his scholarly background, gained selection to the SASR in 2004. Arthur Moses SC swiftly established a series of subsequent deployments. In 2010 he was 2IC to The Sergeant but missed the Battle of Tizak after he contracted malaria. When he was redeployed to Afghanistan in 2012, he was a corporal.

The witness knew Ben Roberts-Smith from his selection year and regarded him as 'a good friend'. He usually spoke to him 'between once a week and once a month'.

Moses asked about his relationship with The Sergeant. The Scientist said: 'We have a professional relationship, because he is my superior, and there is no angst between us.' Equally, he was on good terms with The Scout, The Scot, The Freefaller, The Hunter and The Bodyguard.

The Scientist told His Honour he had not discussed his evidence with fellow witnesses. Then came the key question, regarding an Afghan Wakunish ('Waka') soldier shooting a dog. The Scientist said he had not discussed this with The Scot, but had raised it with Roberts-Smith. This occurred, he said, when he was preparing his outline of evidence. Because he was not a witness to the incident, he told the court, he had contacted the soldier who had been wounded (Person 57), asking, 'Who was the Waka that shot the dog that ricocheted and hit you in the arse?'

Moses: 'And what did he say?'

The Scientist recalled the response: 'It's not the bloke that everyone thinks it is. It's the pudgy Waka.'

Regarding Whiskey 108 in 2009, he described an uneventful patrol. He did not see a tunnel nor any fighting-age males. The first time he heard an allegation that two Afghans had been found in a tunnel was eight years later, in 2017. He did learn of a prosthetic leg being recovered upon return to Camp Russell, and he did drink from it. 'It seemed to be the thing that was done,' he said.

Asked about Ben Roberts-Smith's Victoria Cross, he nominated The Sergeant and The Veteran as being critical of the honour and considering it undeserved.

Moses asked about the mission to Chinartu in 2012, in pursuit of Objective Stolen Idea. While an earlier witness, The Scout, had given detailed evidence that The Scientist had patrolled alongside him, he said he did not recall the mission.

There was an adjournment to closed court and, upon resumption in open court, a return to the dog and ricocheting bullet. The Scientist was asked to read his outline of evidence, specifically the following paragraph:

> I recall that early in our deployment, in about late July/early August 2012, the Commander of the NDS, The Lieutenant, was removed from participating in missions with the SASR after he shot a dog and the bullet ricocheted, hitting another patrol commander in the leg.

Moses: 'Are there any corrections you wish to make to that paragraph?'

The Scientist: 'The identity of the person was never known to me because I wasn't there . . .'

Moses: 'When did you realise there was an error in that paragraph?'

The Scientist: 'After I submitted it and asked Person 57 for clarity on it.'

The next topic was 'blooding the rookie'. The Scientist said he was familiar with the term, but only from 2017, when it had been canvassed in the media and discussed by some of his peers.

Nicholas Owens SC began his cross-examination later in the afternoon. There was an immediate tussle over Whiskey 108.

Owens: 'Before 2017, did anyone tell you that two people behind a trapdoor or in a tunnel at Whiskey 108 were shot?'

The Scientist: 'I don't remember . . . I had heard the rumour. I do not know who told it to me. It was a rumour that was going around.' Pressed for further detail, The Scientist constantly cited his 'very poor recollection'. He was certain, however, that he had not discussed 'step by step' what occurred at Whiskey 108 with The Scot.

There was more frailty of memory when The Scientist was asked about The Gunsmith being referred to as a 'rookie fuck' in 2009 and those very words adorning a 2010 patrol room door.

At 4.10 pm the witness was relieved by the screech of a fire alarm. My knees wobbled as I stumbled down 21 flights. Justice Besanko was sighted, becalmed at street level. Roberts-Smith's entourage milled nearby and then drifted away, the proceedings having been adjourned. I was forced to wait for the all-clear before I ascended and recovered my briefcase. Someone coughed noisily on the long train ride home.

As usual, the next morning I took a rapid antigen test and, as usual, was negative.

At 10.36 am Nicholas Owens SC returned to the subject of The Scot's patrol room door in 2010. The Scientist did not recall seeing the sign, nor hearing anyone referred to as a 'rookie fuck'.

The next topic was how The Scientist came to help Roberts-Smith both as a witness and by supplying him with photos. The Scientist said he was in Toowoomba in 2018 when, by coincidence, he ran into his former comrade. 'G'day, how [are] you going, how's things?' he inquired, recalling to the court that Roberts-Smith was 'in a pretty bad mental state at the time . . . being hit up in the media.'

He said he ended up driving back to Brisbane with Roberts-Smith and visiting Channel Seven. He told his friend he had photographs and video from 2009, which he shared with him.

The Scientist, having already told the court he had no memory of the Chinartu mission in 2012, was true to form. He could not recall Roberts-Smith saying at that time, 'We're going straight for the VRI', nor checking bypassed compounds with The Scout, nor PUC'ing Afghan males.

There was little joy as well in pinning down the time The Scientist first heard a rumour of executions at Whiskey 108, although he was certain he did not hear it when the mission went down.

Owens: 'I want to put to you that you also understood at that point in time that men had been found in the tunnel and shot?'

The Scientist: 'No, that's not true.'

After an adjournment to await the judge's ruling on a waiver of privilege matter, Owens proceeded. It was back to the dog and a burning question. Given it was now understood that The Lieutenant was not the errant Wakunish soldier, and that The Scientist had long known this, having checked with the victim, somehow the assertion had stubbornly remained in his outline of evidence.

Owens: 'When is the first time that you can recall anybody telling you that The Lieutenant was the person who shot the dog . . .?'

The Scientist: 'When I met with—'

Moses: 'Objection.'

The Scientist: '—Ben's lawyers.'

The objection was pursued, with Moses pointing out that The Scientist's testimony had strayed 'into conversations with the applicant's solicitor', which were privileged.

After some debate, His Honour held that privilege was waived.

Owens: 'Who is the first person that used the name of The Lieutenant?'

The Scientist: 'Ben's lawyers.'

Arthur Moses SC, who was earlier spotted yawning, now had a Cheshire cat's grin. I could not fathom why. His witness fumbled in his explanation of how this error had occurred; he said he did not have a lawyer at that time and had been 'fairly naive in thinking that [an] outline of evidence was just an outline, and that prior to the trial I would go and redo it'.

We broke early for lunch. Dean Levitan, Tess McGuire and I stretched our legs, heading for Circular Quay to queue for a fresh sandwich. There was eager discussion. The applicant's allegation that The Lieutenant was not present at Chinartu, originally touted as a killer blow, had boomeranged—or, if you like, ricocheted.

In the afternoon, Nicholas Owens SC trawled through a long email chain between The Scientist and Roberts-Smith's solicitor Monica Allen. Despite the witness knowing the dog story was false, it survived a range of iterations.

Owens: 'What I want to put to you is the reason you were willing to allow [the relevant paragraph] to be included in your outline of evidence is because you were prepared to give false evidence to that extent to help Mr Roberts-Smith.'

The Scientist: 'That's not true.'

It was a miserable time in the box for The Scientist, and it was not over. Justice Besanko told him he might be required to return. As had occurred with The Gunner, a request was put to the Commonwealth to compare the testimony he'd given in the defamation trial with that given to the IGADF.

The Scientist left looking weary. A popular and respected soldier, he had been intent on having the back of his mate Ben Roberts-Smith. But he had probably been of more help to our side.

CHAPTER 85

A PATROL DIVIDED

Reaching the front door of my home after The Scientist's evidence and a long train ride, I relegate myself to the spare room. Getting off to sleep is harder these days, and I am not at my best. When I wake on Wednesday, 4 May 2022 and take a rapid antigen test, I am not surprised to see two red lines. The lawyers are notified and, after Panadol and some befuddled idleness, I log in to watch the proceedings from home.

The next witness was The Freefaller. He is godfather to one of Roberts-Smith's daughters and, within the regiment, an outspoken ally. Unlike some others—The Scot, for example—he is not so clearly tied to Roberts-Smith by war crimes allegations. Peers regard The Freefaller as a serious and skilful soldier, immersed, as they put it, in 'green'.

To Arthur Moses SC he revealed that, months earlier in 2022, he had been posted out of the SASR to a training warrant officer position. In his 32 years as a soldier, there were numerous deployments and a break between 2003 and 2006, when he worked as a security contractor in the Middle East. He had also deployed to Afghanistan on exchange with the US Special Forces.

Moses took his time establishing rock-hard credentials, before moving to Rotation IX in 2009. The Freefaller was, you will recall, a patrol commander at Whiskey 108, and his team were now split down the middle by this court case. On The Freefaller and Roberts-Smith's side were The Hunter and

The Bodyguard. Subpoenaed by Nine/Fairfax were The Cyclist, The Driver and The 2IC.

The 2IC was first on The Freefaller's chopping block: he told Moses that later in the rotation he had The 2IC removed for 'performance issues'.

On the subject of 'blooding the rookie': he had not heard the expression until it was later mentioned in the press. Nor had he heard the term 'rookie fuck'.

The Freefaller's patrol was the next to enter Whiskey 108 after The Scot's patrol, both tasked with the 'fight-through'. He recalled seeing Afghan women, but no fighting-age males. Then the find—this time, his.

The Freefaller: 'During the process of that back-clearance, I was rummaging along . . . the eastern wall of the courtyard . . . I was clearing hay and grass . . . and . . . came across basically a steel mesh grate that was covering . . . a tunnel.' He said he took an offensive stance, covering the tunnel with his weapon, and made a call on the radio. 'The only two people I distinctly recall being in that area when I was pulling cover on that tunnel [were] The Hunter and Ben Roberts-Smith.' He did remember 'an interpreter or an ANA [Afghan National Army] partner force soldier shouting something in Pashtun'.

Consistent with The Hunter's evidence, he said Roberts-Smith volunteered to go down the tunnel and so too The Hunter, who, because of his smaller size, was chosen. The Hunter crawled in headfirst and about a minute later called out the tunnel was clear, but that 'there was a lot of shit in there'.

Moses: 'Did any fighting-aged males come out of that tunnel?'

The Freefaller: 'No.'

He recalled the patrol commanders rendezvousing in the vicinity of the tunnel, and an order being given to clear the neighbouring Whiskey 109 compound. In court, maps and photographs were marked to indicate the route taken.

It was now 12.44 pm, with a luncheon adjournment called. While my colleagues took the common path to our interview room, within my quarantine station I made my way to a cup of tea, and at 2.15 pm logged in once more.

The Freefaller continued his account. As he left Whiskey 108, he noticed The SSE 'kneeling in the vicinity of an EKIA.' He said he spotted two bodies outside the compound.

Later, back at base, he saw the prosthetic leg repurposed as a drinking vessel. He told His Honour, 'There were elements of the troop that had a heavy drinking culture, which caused friction throughout the rotation, and to . . . ease that friction I drank out of the vessel as patrol commander.'

He was not aware of the allegation of two Afghan males extracted from the tunnel in 2009 until reading about it 'around the 2017/2018 time frame.'

Arthur Moses moved on to 2010 and the Battle of Tizak. In recounting the fighting that day, The Freefaller was back in the air and on the ground. You could hear it in his voice. The helicopters took withering fire on insertion from dominant enemy positions. In recounting the life-saving gallantry of comrades under fire, the hardened soldier was soon in tears.

The Scot's, The Sergeant's and his own patrol were pinned down and unable to manoeuvre. He credited a call by The Scot—to effect a breakout by attacking the right flank—with turning the tide. It took the weight of fire off his patrol, giving him the opportunity to regain the initiative.

His composure was not completely lost. In his tension-packed account, he found a moment to complain of communication problems and 'trepidation' by The Reader's patrol about reaching higher ground and providing fire support.

The Freefaller went on to explain that, after the battle, all patrol commanders participated in a debrief and later wrote after-action reports. He did not become aware of the award of a Victoria Cross to Ben Roberts-Smith until December 2010.

Moses: 'Has any member of the SASR said to you that Mr Roberts-Smith did not deserve his VC for his actions at Tizak—that is, said to you directly?'

The Freefaller: 'No.'

An adjournment to closed court consumed the rest of the afternoon, with The Freefaller's evidence in chief proceeding on Thursday, 5 May.

Moses returned to the 'performance issues' concerning The 2IC in 2009. The Freefaller criticised an 'inability to understudy', his failure to bring correct equipment and his weakness 'during the close-quarter battle phases of compound clearance'. This led, he said, to a lack of trust and The 2IC's removal.

The Freefaller acknowledged emailing Ben Roberts-Smith imagery of Whiskey 108 after he had been interviewed by the IGADF, but insisted he had not discussed his evidence with his friend.

Moses concluded with questions about throwdowns. In the ten-year span of his service in Afghanistan, The Freefaller had never heard the term. Nor was the placing of a weapon on a dead insurgent to legitimise a killing something he had ever observed.

Nicholas Owens SC began his cross-examination in the late morning. He first asked about the two bodies sighted by The Freefaller outside Whiskey 108. Repeated questions about what he remembered failed to produce details. The Freefaller did not recall seeing the prosthetic leg there, and he could not comment on the age of the victims.

Owens questioned him about his communication with Roberts-Smith and The Scot before the outlines of evidence were prepared. Our senior counsel asked whether markings on photographs by Roberts-Smith were to indicate where 'he was going to say he was standing when he engaged an insurgent outside Whiskey 108'. The Freefaller said that was not his recollection.

Asked about a visit to Roberts-Smith's Queensland home on 7 July 2019, four days after The Scot provided imagery of Whiskey 108, The Freefaller acknowledged he had sat with Roberts-Smith in his study. He did not recall whether they looked at the imagery on the computer, but he denied that they worked together on their respective outlines of evidence.

Showing him his outline, Owens pointed out a reference to The Freefaller seeing the prosthetic leg. Yet in court he had just given evidence to the contrary.

Owens: 'What I want to put to you is that, in fact, you have deliberately lied when you came to this court and said you don't have a recollection that it was the man with the prosthetic leg, because you were trying to create the impression that it could have been the old man—correct?'

The Freefaller: 'No . . . that's not correct.'

Owens applied a laser focus to the shifting stories of where the bodies were located. Ben Roberts-Smith was committed to an account that the old man was shot outside. The Owens case was that Roberts-Smith's witnesses came to recognise this meant there would have been three bodies outside, considering the earlier engagement by The Scout. The Freefaller appeared troubled in acknowledging, 'I can't tell you where the third body is.'

Owens: 'And what I want to put to you is that you've changed your account, as given under oath to His Honour, from the account on your outline because you were trying to help Mr Roberts-Smith—correct?'

The Freefaller: 'That is not correct, Your Honour.' But he did say his recollection was not 'robust', and the outline had been composed ten years after the event.

Owens tightened his grip. He referred to the evidence indicating that the body of the old man was inside the compound, such as the cooking implements seen nearby, and the SSE bag labelled 'NW corner tunnel'. 'What I want to put to you is that the body of the old man was in fact in the courtyard where the tunnel was found.'

The Freefaller was equally resolute in pushing back: 'No, that's incorrect, Mr Owens.'

There was further argument about inconsistencies between The Freefaller's written statement and his oral evidence. The witness professed a weakness in proofreading.

To the location of the tunnel itself. He could not recall whether it was Afghan women who first indicated its presence or whether he was the one who cleared the hay and grass covering the entrance. He could not deny The Cyclist's or The 2IC's presence, but was certain The Reader was not there. He categorically denied evidence from members of his own patrol that, first, the old man came out and, second, the man in white emerged, lifting his trousers to indicate his prosthetic leg.

The Freefaller: 'That didn't occur, Mr Owens.'

The arm wrestle persisted up to the luncheon adjournment. After repeated denials, The Freefaller appeared to be dry of throat, and sounding wearier. For me, watching on at home, he was not always convincing.

Upon resumption at 2.15 pm, Nicholas Owens SC was no less polite and no less relentless. The Freefaller, if awkward at times, remained focused, articulate and no less resolute. The two skirmished over just how thorough he had been in responding to subpoena demands that he provide imagery to the court.

Owens charged the witness with dissembling and being reluctant to pinpoint where he was when the alleged two engagements occurred. He had falsely claimed he could not recall hearing shots, because he knew they were executions, Owens suggested. The Freefaller ultimately conceded that he must have heard Roberts-Smith's noisy and unsuppressed Minimi machine gun.

Owens: 'What I want to put to you is that you are avoiding committing to a particular period of time that you heard the engagement because you are worried that whatever you say will be inconsistent with the account that Mr Roberts-Smith has given.'

The Freefaller: 'That's incorrect . . . that's your opinion, Mr Owens . . . that's not my opinion of why I can and can't recall exactly what happened.'

They continued to wrestle.

Owens: 'And I want to put to you my case for any comment you are able to make—that not only did people come out of the tunnel, but the old man, being one of them, was shot by The Gunsmith at the direction of The Scot, with Mr Roberts-Smith standing by and saying, "Shoot him." What do you say to that?'

The Freefaller: 'I've got no comment on that, because it didn't happen.'

Owens, soon after: 'And I want to put to you that the other man who came out of the tunnel, the man with the prosthetic leg, was shot by Mr Roberts-Smith outside the compound. Do you accept that?'

The Freefaller: 'No, I don't accept that.'

The Freefaller had told Arthur Moses during his evidence in chief that the first he had heard of 'blooding the rookie' was years later in the media. Owens had the court attendant show the witness the 2010 photograph of the 'rookie fuck' sign on the patrol room door.

The Freefaller: 'I can't recall seeing that sign in 2010, Mr Owens. But if it is on . . . the outside of their door, I would have walked past it.'

The subject of emotion was next. As we had seen, there was an alpha male cohort within the SAS, who were notorious for concealing their feelings, but who were often rubbed raw by the adversarial grindstone of the court.

Was The Freefaller angered by our reporting? 'Angry, frustrated, dismayed, disappointed, all those emotions, yes.' But he denied he felt particularly betrayed by fellow patrol members The 2IC, The Cyclist and The Driver.

Challenged about his approach to The 2IC, to allegedly dissuade him from giving evidence against Ben Roberts-Smith, The Freefaller invoked emotion in framing his response. He argued that he wasn't trying to stop a witness from turning up, but rather fulfilling his responsibility as a leader to offer pastoral care.

Despite his low opinion of The 2IC, he said he was 'looking out for his emotional wellbeing'. He had said to The 2IC: 'Hey, we understand that this would be highly emotive . . . bringing up past experiences.'

The Freefaller explained: 'As you saw yesterday . . . I was quite emotional on the stand, because this is what happens when you recall significant events in your life.' He claimed he was merely making The 2IC aware of 'processes and means that . . . you don't have to attend'.

Watching on from home, I saw the witness stretching a very long bow.

The Freefaller regarded his connecting Ben Roberts-Smith with The Scout in Canberra in 2018 as having nothing to do with the court action; rather, it was about 'catching up with old comrades, so to speak'.

Owens: 'I put to you that that answer is false, and you knew full well that Mr Roberts-Smith wanted to speak to The Scout after he had learnt that he would be giving evidence in this case?'

The Freefaller: 'No. That is not correct.' Queried about the numerous contacts he had with Roberts-Smith and fellow witnesses, The Freefaller denied it was for the purpose of harmonising accounts. Owens raised evidence of encrypted phone calls and meetings, a holiday on Hamilton Island, and finally a dinner with Roberts-Smith and his solicitor Monica Allen.

Owens: 'And it's correct, isn't it, that during that dinner, Mr Roberts-Smith gave you a copy of the notes from the IGADF interview?'

The Freefaller: 'No. That is not correct.'

Court wound up for the day with The Freefaller's evidence not quite complete. On Friday, 6 May 2022, Nicholas Owens SC had a few more questions about information passed to Roberts-Smith via USB in 2019. Again, the witness could not recall.

Arthur Moses SC briefly re-examined. The Freefaller said that, although he knew there was a Taliban leader with a prosthetic leg being targeted in 2009, he could not recall whether this was specific to the Whiskey 108 mission.

He further assured the court that he had addressed subpoena requirements with the 'utmost of seriousness'. The fact that the video sent to Roberts-Smith was not included in the material he had provided following the subpoena was not because he had not looked for it, but because he had not responded to the subpoena 'as thoroughly as maybe what I should of'.

There was more closed court before Ben Roberts-Smith's close friend and ally was free to go.

Later, Arthur Moses SC would speak highly of his performance in the witness box. From my perspective, he was their best witness so far, in that he applied his mind without the cavalier bravado of some of his predecessors. He also appeared far better prepared than the applicant's earlier witnesses. But I also wondered whether, for all that, he was still located in their same parallel universe.

The objective of the trial was to test the veracity of evidence of competing witnesses on whether our reporting was truthful. But for some of the witnesses, The Freefaller included, the contest often seemed more about who were the tough guys and who were the pretenders.

CHAPTER 86

SOMETHING THAT WOULD ATTRACT SCANDAL

Day 82. Monday, 9 May 2022, and for me it is day six of quarantine. My nose is clear. My throat was never sore, but I still have a slight cough. I'm way better off than my fellow citizens crowding intensive care. At 10 am I tune in. It will be a short but important session for today's witness, The RSM, known to the court as Person 100.

No matter the outcome of this trial, a scorching question will long endure: where did the system fail? It is true that the ADF got out in front of the war crimes scandal after Major General Jeff Sengelman bit the bullet, and the IGADF inquiry was initiated. It is also true this could only have occurred because some SAS members spoke up. But, as the evidence had so far revealed, the wellspring of rumour and dissent about something rotten in the state of the SAS could be traced back years earlier, to at least 2009.

The Brereton inquiry did not begin until 2016. And this was three years after rumour fomented into something closer to evidence, when a number of allegations—the bullying of The Redhead and the assault on The Trooper—and concerns by a group of non-commissioned officers about the Victoria Cross award and alleged war crimes, all washed up at the door of this witness, Person 100, the SASR's regimental sergeant major.

So what went wrong? By the end of day 82, it would be clear that The RSM vehemently rejected the proposition that a systemic failure had anything to do with him.

Arthur Moses SC immediately established the witness's position as the SASR's then senior soldier. As such, he was obliged to report allegations of misconduct up through the chain of command.

The RSM remembered meeting a group of sergeants in his office in 2013. He recalled The Sergeant announcing that 'we as a collective . . . [are] here to raise some allegations' pertaining to Mr Roberts-Smith. He said their complaint was about the VC and bullying. The RSM recalled 'the collective' as not being all that cohesive; one member had said he was there more to observe.

The Reader was remembered for telling The RSM that, at the 2010 Battle of Tizak, 'I shot an enemy combatant that Mr Roberts-Smith has later claimed'. And The Sergeant had returned to Tizak in 2012, pacing the ground to determine that 'the awarding of the Victoria Cross wasn't in accordance with the citation'.

The RSM also recalled the 2006 Koran Ghar action being raised as the moment when a 'belittling' campaign of The Redhead by Ben Roberts-Smith began.

His response to the group, he said, was that the awards process was very thorough, passing through 'multiple layers of assessment boards', and an honour such as the VC was not something readily rescinded. As to the bullying, he said those claims would be followed up.

Moses: 'Did any of the sergeants at that meeting raise any concerns with you that Mr Roberts-Smith had broken the rules of engagement whilst serving in Afghanistan?'

The RSM: 'There was no mention of that, and there was no hint that that was mentioned either.'

Following the meeting, he reported the conversation to his commanding officer, in person and on the same day. The RSM said it was agreed that the bullying issue would be followed up, but 'he did not think that the unit could do anything about the awarding of the Victoria Cross, and that was something that wasn't in his capacity as the commanding officer to manage'.

The witness told Arthur Moses he could not find the file note of the sergeants' meeting and did not have access to the 'secret network' (the Defence Secret Network) 'because it related to instances of operations overseas'. Neither could he find the file note of his meeting with the commanding officer.

A similar gathering followed within two days, this time with four corporals. He recalled three of them as The Gunsmith, The Scout and The SSE. Like the earlier meeting, it was an unarranged 'walk-in'. The purpose replicated that of the first meeting. He remembered complaints that 'Roberts-Smith was not a fit and proper person to be awarded the Victoria Cross; that they had been bullied . . . and [Roberts-Smith] claimed to have committed acts on the battlefield that were attributed to them'. He nominated this as The Gunsmith's main issue.

Again, The RSM said no one in this group raised concerns about breaches of the rules of engagement. Again, he told the group he could do nothing about the Victoria Cross, but he would follow up the bullying allegations. Once more, he had not been able to locate any file note for that meeting, or for his follow-up with the commanding officer.

He told the court a quick assessment of the bullying complaint regarding The Redhead ensued, and later a mediation.

Arthur Moses SC next took The RSM to a different complaint, by The Trooper. The RSM remembered him declaring, 'I was assaulted by Mr Roberts-Smith whilst in operations in Afghanistan, sir.' The RSM said that, in response, he had requested The Trooper provide a statement and list of witnesses. He asked whether he would front a trial. 'And The Trooper said, "I will not."' So, according to The RSM, 'there was very little that I could do'.

At this point, his evidence in chief moved to closed court. When the public hearing resumed, just before noon, Moses asked The RSM about a further meeting he'd had with The Trooper when the latter left the SASR.

Moses: 'At that exit interview, did The Trooper raise with you any issues concerning Mr Roberts-Smith that he wanted you to deal with?'

The RSM: 'No, I specifically said . . . "Is there anything that you wish raised . . . as a result of your service as SASR?" to which he replied, "No."'

Nicholas Owens SC rose. 'You don't dispute, do you, that The Trooper told you he was punched by Mr Roberts-Smith?'

The RSM: 'No, that's what The Trooper said.'

The witness accepted that the punch, acknowledged now by Ben Roberts-Smith, constituted a criminal offence under the *Defence Force Discipline Act*.

Owens: 'Because it's very serious, isn't it, for a senior member of the Defence Force to assault a more junior member of the Defence Force?'

The RSM: 'Yes, it is, sir.'

Owens: 'And you accept, do you not, that, upon a notifiable incident coming to your attention, you had an obligation to report it—correct?'

The RSM: 'That would be correct, sir.'

Owens: 'But you did not report it—correct?'

His Honour paused proceedings to query whether the witness sought a certificate against self-incrimination. There was another adjournment. Upon resumption, The RSM's counsel told His Honour there would be no application for a certificate. When the question was again posed, The RSM denied failing to report the assault.

Owens: 'To whom do you say you reported it?'

The RSM: 'I reported that to the commanding officer.' He said the commanding officer told him to investigate the allegation.

Owens then queried The RSM about what allegations had been disclosed. He said he did not recall The Gunsmith telling him he witnessed the assault on The Trooper. He agreed that The Redhead had told him of an assault and a death threat. And he agreed that, as with The Trooper, he had requested The Redhead gather witness statements.

Owens wondered about The RSM's fearlessness in pursuit of the truth. He noted that the quick assessment of The Redhead's bullying accusation had occurred only after Ben Roberts-Smith VC, MG asked for it to be investigated.

Owens: 'What I want to put to you is that your response was different when The Redhead made a complaint and when Roberts-Smith made a complaint. Do you agree that the response was different?'

The RSM: 'No.'

Owens, later: 'And I want to put to you that the reason you did not wish to instigate an investigation against Mr Roberts-Smith is because you thought it would be a controversial thing—correct?'

The RSM: 'That is incorrect, sir.'

Owens: 'And you thought it would be something that would attract scandal within the SAS—correct?'

The RSM: 'That is incorrect, sir.'

Nicholas Owens returned to The RSM's first meeting, the one with the sergeants. 'Now, it's correct, isn't it, that at that meeting, The Sergeant said to you words to the effect of "I've just been told of an allegation here of a war crime"—correct?'

The RSM: 'Incorrect, sir.'

Owens: 'And he told you that that is what he had been told by The Gunsmith—correct?'

The RSM: 'Incorrect, sir.'

There were repeated challenges. The RSM refused to concede knowledge of the alleged Darwan cliff kick before it was reported in the media. When it was put to him that the four corporals attending the second meeting were not as he had nominated, and that The Scout was not present, he said that was not his recollection. The RSM dismissed the proposition that he had also been told of the Whiskey 108 allegations.

Owens: 'And it's correct, isn't it, that The Sergeant responded to you, "It's not what I want to get out of this, it's what needs to be done"—correct?'

The RSM: 'That's incorrect, sir.'

———

It was all over before lunch.

Owens' final question: 'It's correct, isn't it, that you did not want to have allegations of serious misconduct against Mr Roberts-Smith investigated in 2013, because you thought it would reflect poorly on the reputation of the regiment?'

The RSM maintained a committed defence: 'That is incorrect, sir.'

As I watched on, via videolink, it occurred to me that, unlike most of the witnesses, who appeared on sufferance, this witness might have been more willing than the others, even though he was in fact subpoenaed. He had a strong motive to defend a reputation—in this case, his own.

It also struck me as very odd that no records of a series of meetings, with two groups of soldiers and with his commanding officer, could be found. Despite a mass of bureaucratic oversight, a precise account of where the system had failed remained missing in action.

CHAPTER 87

FRIENDS

Another key witness, The Sniper, is next. He is a further victim of mental trauma following service in Afghanistan, and another to have resisted being dragged into this reviled defamation action. But, for all that, he stuck true to Team BRS. One explanation might be plain and simple loyalty. Another, the choking entanglement of their fortunes in the shooting of Ali Jan, at Darwan, on 11 September 2012.

On Tuesday, 10 May 2022, Arthur Moses SC commenced evidence in chief. The Sniper hailed from Roberts-Smith's 3RAR, and was selected into the SASR in 2009. He described Roberts-Smith as 'a good friend and has been for a long time'. In 2020, The Sniper was medically discharged from the Australian Army.

He told Arthur Moses he well understood the rules of engagement. If a combatant surrendered and did not pose a threat, they were to be detained. And if a breach of the rules was observed, it would be reported.

Watching on, I saw a composed and articulate witness who seemed well prepared, if a little dry of throat. Arthur Moses suggested he drink some water before they commenced a long trawl through common battlefield methodology.

The first incident traversed was the Chora Valley mission at the beginning of Rotation XVIII, which had culminated in a blue-on-blue and the removal of The Trooper from Roberts-Smith's patrol. As a fellow patrol member, he remembered Roberts-Smith yelling at The Trooper to cease fire.

Upon return to Camp Russell there was a discussion. 'Ben was pressing The Trooper as to what he was actually shooting at,' he testified. 'The Trooper was unable to come up with an answer. At one point, he did say all he could see was some civilians—women and children—and that was concerning . . . [A]t that point, The Trooper . . . did not seem to understand . . . [W]hat I observed shortly after was Ben hit The Trooper.'

The 11 September 2012 Darwan mission was approached down the long road. The Sniper named the three Australians—Stjepan Milosevic, James Martin and Robert Poate—who had been shot and killed two weeks earlier by Afghan National Army sergeant Hekmatullah. 'Since that day, our mission had been to hunt that person down,' he said. Darwan pinged on the radar when it was thought locals were 'harbouring him in the area'.

Arthur Moses showed The Sniper photos of Darwan, asking him to indicate the movements of his patrol after their insertion by helicopter. He described the sighting of an armed 'squirter' on the other side of the Helmand River. Both he and his patrol commander, Roberts-Smith, engaged the insurgent, to unseen effect. Roberts-Smith then removed his body armour and waded the river. The Sniper later saw him dragging a body and holding up a recovered weapon. The Sniper remembered Ben positioning the body 'for identification purposes'.

Roberts-Smith then waded back across the river, recovered his body armour and showed The Sniper the captured AK-47, which had been damaged, he presumed, by their earlier gunfire. Also recovered were 'half a dozen detonators, which appeared military grade, which was very odd'.

They soon after commenced the clearance of the village. He said local nationals were present and an interpreter was needed, in that 'my Pashto was not flash'. He could not recall taking anyone into detention during a clearance process over 'multiple hours'.

When his patrol reached 'our limit of exploitation to the south', the interpreter was released. Under Roberts-Smith's orders, he was escorted by The Replacement to meet a requirement 'in a different location'. This left The Sniper with Ben Roberts-Smith and The Gunsmith in an area now cleared. He saw no fighting-age males and could not recall the presence of women or children. With the help of the court attendant, he marked the location on a diagram.

They awaited orders for extraction. Once received, he led the way, navigating a dry creek bed. As was standard operating procedure, the vicinity was to be cleared 'of any potential threats to our LZ [landing zone]'.

Moses: 'And what happened next?'

The Sniper: 'Shortly after coming out of the dry creek bed, I identified an individual in amongst the corn. This individual was moving . . . in a very suspicious manner . . . The person was carrying a radio, which led me to make the assessment that this was a spotter [trying to] report on our disposition and movements.'

The Sniper said the spotter 'appeared to be trying to remain concealed, noting that our helicopters were on approach, and I assessed the person posed a threat to our extraction and our friendly forces, and so I engaged'.

He said he could not see Ben Roberts-Smith at this point, but he heard another weapon, which he soon learned was his comrade's as he 'closed up on me'. He could not see The Gunsmith. He estimated the spotter was shot at 'a distance of about fifteen metres'. He thought he fired 'three to five rounds'.

With the helicopters fast approaching, a hasty SSE was conducted by The Sniper and The Gunsmith. An Icom radio was recovered. The Gunsmith took photos and marked the evidence bag.

At 12.44 pm, the court adjourned. Half a day in, and The Sniper's evidence aligned for the most part with the account of his patrol commander, Ben Roberts-Smith. What could not be missed, however, was a clear contradiction with the evidence of the second-in-command—and his former best friend—The Gunsmith.

At 2.15 pm, Arthur Moses SC resumed evidence in chief. His witness was shown more photographs.

Moses: 'Do you see blood on the person's face?'

The Sniper: 'I see blood on the person's face, yes.'

Moses: 'Do you know what the cause of that was?'

The Sniper: 'I do not know what the cause of that is.'

Moses: 'And it's alleged by the respondents in this case that the wounds on the person's mouth were caused by his head hitting a rock after he was kicked off a slope by Mr Roberts-Smith. What do you say about that allegation?'

The Sniper: 'I reject that allegation.'

The Chinartu mission of October 2012 was canvassed. The Sniper recalled little of the hit-out. Asked whether he later heard a rumour of an unlawful killing having occurred, he said, 'No, I did not.' Asked whether he had 'any concerns about the leadership of your patrol by Ben Roberts-Smith', he replied, 'Never.'

He could not recall the Syachow mission. The Sniper was sure Ben Roberts-Smith had not directed The Ring-In to execute a PUC. He could not recall the launch on Fasil in November 2012 (where The Medic gave evidence of the alleged execution of a male teenager).

Closed court consumed most of an hour.

Back in open court, the evidence in chief took the witness to pre-deployment training at Lancelin earlier in 2012. Moses asked whether he had heard any talk of the use of 'throwdowns' and the execution of PUCs. 'No, I did not,' The Sniper replied.

Perhaps pre-empting a challenge to the witness's objectivity, Moses asked if he knew who was paying his legal fees. The Sniper said he did not know. In explaining how he had come to be represented by the law firm Addisons, he said he became 'very upset' after appearing unrepresented before the IGADF in 2017, and 'as a result I reached out to my friend Ben, who was a very good friend'. He said Roberts-Smith told him he was 'happy to make inquiries as to some legal representation on my behalf. I agreed to that, and little more was said.'

Questioned about the kill board on the back of his patrol door at Camp Russell, he admitted having seen it, but said they were common through history on 'aircraft and ships'. As to the etching of the 'winged penis', he knew the artwork was a specialty of The Hunter, but he had never seen such an image kicking a PUC off a cliff.

The court adjourned at 4.18 pm.

The following morning, Ben Roberts-Smith was hunched in his usual position in the corner. There were only a few questions remaining in The Sniper's evidence in chief. Roberts-Smith's friend resumed his seat.

Arthur Moses SC probed an emotional pressure point, asking how long The Sniper had known The Gunsmith.

This produced an impassive reply: 'I first met The Gunsmith in 2010.'

From then on, he explained, the two had become more than brothers-in-arms. In 2014, The Gunsmith acted as best man at The Sniper's wedding. And their conflicting accounts of what happened at Darwan had severed more than a friendship. They had not spoken in four years.

The Sniper: 'In 2018 I was made aware . . . again of allegations that had been put to me. I was aware in 2018 that The Gunsmith had said . . . certain things which have given rise to these allegations, and I felt incredibly hurt by that, that someone who was so close for a number of years, who has been a mentor and a good friend, not just professionally but personally, would have said such things that . . . caused me so much grief and heartache. So, once I was made aware of his involvement, I wrestled with it for quite a while, to the point of even speaking to counsellors about the best way to proceed. Eventually, I made a decision to reach out and call him, and it was brief. But I laid it out that I was hurt deeply. I was disappointed . . . and that from this time forward . . . our personal relationship was over.'

Moses, soon after: 'Were you ever directed by Mr Roberts-Smith to execute a PUC?'

The Sniper: 'No, I was not.'

Moses: 'Were you ever directed by Mr Roberts-Smith to breach the rules of engagement while serving in Afghanistan?'

The Sniper: 'No, I was not.'

Moses: 'Did you ever execute a PUC during a deployment to Afghanistan?'

The Sniper: 'No, I did not.'

Nicholas Owens SC's cross-examination followed. He began by tracing The Sniper's footsteps at Darwan to the moment of the encounter with the spotter.

The Sniper repeated his evidence that he sighted a radio in the Afghan's hand. He could not remember which hand. He believed this occurred after he crossed into the field from the dry creek bed. Asked how far into the field he had moved, he believed maybe a bit more than 'one or two metres'.

Considering the cornfield was thickly vegetated, Owens asked how high it had grown. The Sniper considered and then replied: 'potentially' between five and seven feet.

Owens then queried his ability to sight an insurgent in 'thickly planted crops', fifteen metres away. The Sniper said it was 'because I could', the movement having caught his eye. Someone, by his crouching manner, was 'trying to maintain concealment'.

The Sniper's outline of evidence had not mentioned the sighting of an Icom radio in this fleeting movement; he had identified it as being found later, during the SSE process. Owens asked why the sighting was not mentioned in his outline.

'Well, the radio was recovered from the body during the SSE. It was not . . . the first time that it was seen.'

Owens: 'Look at two sentences on. You say: "The presence of the radio confirmed he was a spotter and therefore a legitimate target." Do you see that?'

The Sniper: 'I do.'

Owens pressed, arguing that The Sniper's oral evidence about seeing the radio in the spotter's hand was false.

'I disagree with that, Mr Owens.'

Owens returned to The Sniper's contention that he had seen no PUCs in the final compound. While The Sniper agreed that PUCs had been detained, he could recall no detail about where or when.

For months, in the background, our legal team had worked hard to plot minute-by-minute movements. Sametime chat radio transmission logs subpoenaed from the ADF were matched with grid references on the photos. By identifying where and when Afghans were detained, and the required movements of The Terp and others, an accurate portrait was able to be drawn that comprehensively challenged Ben Roberts-Smith's version of events.

Owens pointed to a call at 9.30 am identifying 'clearances nearing LOE [limit of exploitation]'. A further call at 11.09 am reported 'an additional EKIA [enemy killed in action]'. This referred to The Sniper's engagement in the cornfield.

The witness became defensive when Owens highlighted the wide discrepancy between the time he said they waited at the compound (around ten minutes) to that indicated by the log (around an hour and a half). This was important, given our case theory that the kicking incident, the execution and the SSE process took longer than ten minutes.

The timing and movement of the interpreter was also important, given that, if he was required, that was a strong indicator of the presence of detainees such as Ali Jan. The Sniper not only resisted admitting the longer lag time, but also that the interpreter had stayed with them.

To our team, the proposition that The Replacement would go missing for nearly two hours made no sense. Besides, a month earlier, The Replacement had confirmed that he had been in the final compound with the interpreter until he was tasked with escorting him to the helicopter landing zone half an hour before extraction.

Owens: 'What I want to put to you is that one reason why you have knowingly given false evidence about when and where The Replacement was sent back is because you know it is the respondents' case that

The Replacement and the interpreter were in that last compound for a period of about an hour?'

The Sniper: 'Mr Owens, with respect, I reject the assertion that I am knowingly giving false evidence. I've come here in good faith to tell the truth.'

He continued to dispute the proposition that fighting-age males were found in the last compound. He also denied, in contradiction of Afghan witnesses' evidence, the presence of a military working dog and its handler, another member of his patrol. To the Afghan witnesses, the dog was particularly well remembered as it had bitten one of them.

Owens: 'So you're saying now you have a positive recollection there were no dogs in that last compound?'

The Sniper: 'Correct.'

From beginning to end, the Darwan mission ran five and a half hours. A large taskforce, including Commandos, surrounded the village. There was an overwatch position, with a clear line of sight to the point The Sniper said the spotter was engaged. There was aerial surveillance by a Heron drone and Apache helicopters with body-heat sensors. The respondents contended that, under these circumstances, a spotter could not have remained undetected, but this contention was again rejected by the witness.

Owens: 'You and Mr Roberts-Smith have concocted a false story to say that there was a spotter in the cornfield to cover up the fact that Mr Roberts-Smith kicked a PUC off a cliff and that you shot him in that field—correct?'

The Sniper: 'That's not correct.'

The location of the shooting was the next issue under challenge. The Sniper had marked on a photograph where the spotter was engaged. Owens put it to the witness that the true location was within a line of trees adjoining the cornfield. Owens further identified the grid reference on the SSE bag as being inconsistent with where The Sniper said the engagement had occurred.

Using more photographs, Nicholas Owens SC swung his cross-examination to focus on the SSE search of the body. He noted the victim's legs were folded, which he argued was incompatible with a head-to-toe search. The witness said there was 'no right or wrong way to roll a dead body'.

One stark detail, which had been noted by many, was the blood pattern on the victim's left wrist. The witness was shown a photograph of this area, enlarged. It showed a straight line with blood on one side and not the other.

Owens: 'What I want to put to you is that this man was wearing flexi cuffs at around the time he was bleeding—correct?'

The Sniper: 'I disagree with that, Mr Owens.'

In the clinical confines of the courtroom, the gruesome inquisition continued. Another photographic enlargement was shown of what Nicholas Owens contended were 'four bullet holes right in the area around that man's heart'. The Sniper 'could not confirm if these are bullet holes'. He did not know where his own and Roberts-Smith's rounds landed. He believed the victim had been static and 'more front-on' when he was shot.

Senior counsel went in for the kill, so to speak, pointing out how unlikely it was for a neat four-round cluster of bullets to the heart to strike down a victim 'moving laterally' at fifteen metres.

Owens: 'It's correct, isn't it, that when you shot this man, he was standing only a metre or two away from you with his hands handcuffed behind his back?'

The Sniper: 'That's incorrect, Mr Owens.'

More blood. More close-ups, this time of the victim's left arm and torso. The witness was asked to focus on the ripped tunic alongside a 'significant flesh wound'.

Owens: 'That is clearly not a bullet entry wound—correct?'

The Sniper: 'I can't comment on that, Mr Owens.'

Owens: 'What I want to put to you is that if that man had been shot four times in the heart while his hands were handcuffed behind his back, that is the sort of wound you would expect to see by reason of the bullets exiting his body—correct?'

The Sniper: 'That's not correct, and that did not happen, Mr Owens.'

Then to the mouth and face. The witness again disagreed that the 'ragged wound' did not look like it was caused by a bullet.

Owens: 'It is the case, isn't it, that that wound was sustained by this man as he hit his mouth as he fell down a cliff—correct?'

The Sniper: 'That's incorrect. That didn't happen.'

Through the long morning, I began to wonder whether The Sniper's fealty to his former patrol commander might, if only internally, be wavering a touch. Owens' softly spoken queries were landing hard, with the answers increasingly barren. The Sniper was likely relieved when the luncheon adjournment was called.

For the afternoon session, Nicholas Owens SC methodically stepped through the evidence of what we believed occurred at Darwan. He told of men being PUC'ed in the final compound. Of two taken outside and the interpreter sent away. One man had been punched by Roberts-Smith. The other was made to stand. Roberts-Smith spoke to him, and the man laughed. The tall Australian soldier then stepped back and launched a kick, sending him over the cliff. The Sniper moved down to the creek bed, shot the Afghan and placed an Icom radio on his body.

To every accusation, The Sniper responded, 'That did not happen,' or 'That is not correct.'

Owens moved on to the communication The Sniper had maintained with Ben Roberts-Smith since the beginning of the IGADF inquiry. Noting the dates of each of the Sniper's scheduled interviews, Owens paralleled his communications with the applicant. For example, when he was interviewed on 21 September 2017, he'd had a telephone conversation with Roberts-Smith the day before. He denied anticipating that he would be asked about the cliff kick allegation and discussing this with his friend.

Owens wanted to know what they had talked about. An aggrieved witness responded, 'More about the personal impact that the experience has had on me.'

When The Sniper was further summonsed to be interviewed by the IGADF in June 2018, there was another phone call to Roberts-Smith.

Again, The Sniper said it was not to discuss evidence but because 'he's a good friend and because . . . he's someone who has my welfare at heart, and I just needed someone to talk to'.

When the arrangement was struck for Mark O'Brien Legal and Arthur Moses SC to act for him, he said he did not ask how much they charged or whether he would have to pay because he 'had other important matters to deal with at the time as well'.

This legal representation extended to The Sniper's appearances before the IGADF inquiry and his dealings with the AFP. Via his barrister, The Sniper had declined an AFP interview request. Subpoenaed records showed that, to this point, around $125,000 in legal fees had been charged on his behalf.

Owens: 'You understood, didn't you, that if you were going to continue receiving free legal representation, you needed to make sure that the evidence that you would give in any legal proceedings was evidence that would support Mr Roberts-Smith—correct?'

The Sniper: 'That's not my understanding at all, Mr Owens.'

The Sniper had also communicated with Roberts-Smith shortly after the first reporting, on 8 June 2018, of the alleged Darwan execution. On 9 June 2018, Ben Roberts-Smith flew to Perth, where the two men caught up. The Sniper said the Darwan cliff kick was 'not a topic of conversation'.

Owens: 'That is not honest evidence, is it? It is the fact, is it not, that you did talk about the fact that you thought the allegations that had just been published in this newspaper would be discussed at your upcoming [IGADF] interview?'

This was denied, with a faint qualifier: 'We made mention that stuff . . . had come up in the paper.'

The meeting was a few days out from The Sniper's second scheduled IGADF interview. He told the court that he and Roberts-Smith did not discuss topics to be canvassed by the inquiry. 'Our discussion, Your Honour, mostly centred around my wellbeing. [Roberts-Smith] understood . . . it had been a stressful time for me and my family, and that was his chief concern.'

Yes, there was stress, his interrogator posed, because he feared what one friend, The Gunsmith, might have told the IGADF inquiry, and that the story cooked up with his other friend, Ben Roberts-Smith, might not be believed.

On 12 June 2018, one day before his interview was scheduled, The Sniper flew to Sydney. As it happened, Roberts-Smith was also in Sydney. Owens put to him that they met in his hotel room before the IGADF interview. This he could not recall, but the dinner afterwards was remembered.

The Freefaller joined them, as did The Sniper's wife who had accompanied him to Sydney for support. After his first IGADF interview in 2017, The Sniper said he had suffered a 'near mental breakdown': 'She thought it would be a good idea to get some good friends together, just to, I guess, unwind.'

In January 2020, a further IGADF interview was scheduled back in Perth, which again coincided with a visit from his friend Ben Roberts-Smith, who a month earlier had also been before the Inspector-General. Ultimately, on mental health grounds, the Sniper was excused from appearing.

Owens asked The Sniper about the anger that boiled within him—against the IGADF interrogators, and against those friends who had betrayed him. The Sniper thought disappointment was a more accurate description. With regard to his former best friend, The Gunsmith, he said: 'I am not angry with him. To be honest, I pity him. I feel for him. He was a great friend, a great man, and I know that he struggles, and I really feel for him. I do.'

The Sniper had also described Roberts-Smith as 'a very good friend'. Owens posed another motive for enduring loyalty: 'What I want to put to you is that you are aware that the standard or the burden of proof in these proceedings is lower than in a criminal case.'

The Sniper: 'I am aware.'

Owens followed up, pointing out that if Roberts-Smith succeeded in the defamation action, the prospect of criminal charges for both of them lessened. 'You agree, don't you, that you and Mr Roberts-Smith share a common interest in relation to the defence of the allegations at Darwan?'

The Sniper: 'If by "common interest" you mean that there's allegations of him as a war criminal and me as a war criminal, then yes. But each of us have our own paths to tread in trying to clear our names.'

———

Wednesday's proceedings drew to a close, with another hearing scheduled for Thursday, 12 May 2022. Nicholas Owens SC had more questions about Chinartu next.

Again matching Sametime chat communication and grid references, the barrister charted manoeuvres. The Sniper's memory was not improving. He had no knowledge of a weapons cache being discovered by The Scout; nor of the mood changing, of hearts hardening, with the Afghan occupant's life suddenly in the balance.

Asked about Roberts-Smith allegedly ordering The Lieutenant's soldiers to 'shoot him, or I will', The Sniper responded: 'I did not observe any of this, Mr Owens.'

The Sniper was also present at Fasil for the squadron's last mission in 2012. He told His Honour he had almost no recollection of it. He did not remember the interception of the Hilux vehicle and the detention of its four occupants. But, as he had told Arthur Moses, he did recall the kill board on his patrol room door.

Owens: 'And you remember, before the last mission, that kill board had a tally of eighteen?'

The Sniper: 'I don't recall the tally that we had.'

Owens: 'And it's correct, isn't it, that Mr Roberts-Smith had said words to the effect of, "Only two to go to get to twenty"?'

The Sniper: 'He did not say that.'

He was shown the SSE photograph of the deceased Afghan male we alleged was the youth removed, trembling, from the Hilux. The Sniper did not recognise the person in the photo.

Owens was not finished; more photos and documentation were shuffled. Forensic analysis undertaken by Chris Mitchell had focused not only on what could be found in the imagery, the maps and the radio logs, but also on what was *not* recorded. While photos could be found of three men PUC'ed from the Hilux, there was no record of the final occupant. The barrister, having scoured hundreds of reports, noted this as unusual.

Owens: 'It's correct, isn't it, that the fourth PUC that was handed to you, in addition to the three that I've just shown you photos of, was the person deceased in the photo I showed you a moment ago?'

The Sniper: 'No, I reject that, Mr Owens.'

The Sniper, alongside Ben Roberts-Smith for all of his 2012 tour, was also present for pre-deployment training. He denied all assertions of planned execution of PUCs; of ensuring there were no prying eyes in the sky; of officers kept to the rear; and of 'throwdowns' on hand. Owens presented specifics: of The Gunsmith carrying an 'AK-47 with a folding stock', of The Replacement 'sometimes carrying webbing or a Russian grenade'. To The Sniper, this was 'ridiculous'. Firstly, because it was 'illegal'. Secondly, because no operator, burdened with at least 40 kilograms of equipment, would take on more.

Then to the punch. The Sniper was present in their patrol room when Roberts-Smith swung a fist at The Trooper. After The Trooper complained, Roberts-Smith requested a statement from The Sniper, which he provided. Owens noted that in this account 'there is no mention of Mr Roberts-Smith punching The Trooper'. In penning his supportive statement, The Sniper preferred to use the words 'sternly counselled'.

Repeatedly challenged about having downplayed an assault, The Sniper refused to budge. 'Sternly counselled' was, for him, the whole truth, and in no way was he 'trying to protect Mr Roberts-Smith'.

Closed court rounded out most of the remaining morning session. Just before lunch, Arthur Moses SC briefly re-examined The Sniper. His witness clarified evidence on the procedure for processing PUCs at Darwan. He explained how the drones and Apache helicopters were used to detect threats. And he restated his position of not knowing where his rounds landed when engaging the spotter.

As the expression goes, and as I saw it, The Sniper had stuck to his friend like shit to a blanket—without managing to dispel the stink.

At Darwan, he shot a spotter, four rounds to the heart at fifteen metres. Ben Roberts-Smith had said he was shot at a distance of two to five metres. Roberts-Smith claimed he joined the action after hauling his way up an embankment that did not prominently feature in other testimony. The Sniper said that, through thick foliage, he saw a radio in the hand of the spotter, something he failed to describe in his outline of evidence. A tonne of further detail, about PUCs in the final compound and the return of the interpreter, cast further doubt not only on his credibility, but also on his capacity to get his story straight.

Throughout his testimony The Sniper exhibited a great deal of pity for himself, and none for the slain Afghan. But, then, this was to be expected if the line was to be held, and if the court was to be convinced that Ali Jan was a threat who had been lawfully killed.

CHAPTER 88

'THAT'S NOT TRUE, SIR'

Friday, 13 May 2022 was a lucky day for the hardworking lawyers turning up at Courtroom 21A. They would get an early mark.

It was over and done with before morning tea. The applicant's lawyers called Terry Nichols, a former Army officer who was present at the Veterans' Employment Program awards function at Parliament House in March 2018.

At around 9.30 pm, as the function closed, Nichols said he was approached by Ben Roberts-Smith's partner for the evening. Person 17, as she was known to the court, was 'unsteady and . . . quite slurred in her speech'. At her request, he tried to reconnect her with Roberts-Smith after she fell down a flight of stairs.

Nichols said she had a 'very large haematoma on the left side of her forehead above the eye, which I gather was a direct result of landing head-first on either the bottom of the stairs or the landing itself'.

He was concerned, but she said she was 'okay' and needed to see Ben. The witness said they were soon reunited. Roberts-Smith said, 'Thanks, mate,' and walked off.

It was clear, convincing evidence about the fall, which had been acknowledged by Person 17.

Nicholas Owens SC had no questions.

Monday, 16 May 2022 is day 87, and The Corporal is Ben Roberts-Smith's next witness. They fought together at the Battle of Tizak in 2010, The Corporal on the left flank alongside Roberts-Smith and The Gunsmith. Undoubtedly brave, he was not included in the glow of battle honours that ensued.

In the immediate aftermath of the battle, some comrades thought The Corporal harboured misgivings about the awards. This was rejected, with The Corporal now positioned assuredly in the pro-BRS camp.

Earlier in 2022 he had been medically discharged from the Army (at the rank of sergeant). A former Commando, he was selected into the SASR in 2007, meeting Ben Roberts-Smith during the follow-up reinforcement cycle, and found he 'enjoyed working . . . under him'.

In 2010, having joined The Scot's team, with Ben Roberts-Smith as the 2IC, The Corporal could not recall hearing the terms 'rookie' or 'rookie fuck'. Nor was he told he needed to be 'blooded'.

Taken to the Tizak battle in June, he described how he, Roberts-Smith and The Gunsmith were pinned down, while the other three members of their patrol, to the right, started engaging the enemy from a small compound.

'That's when Ben managed to bound up closer to the enemy, behind some cover.' Over on the right flank, he saw The Scot throw a grenade into the enemy position. This enabled his team to break into the open courtyard, where they saw 'multiple dead insurgents'.

The Corporal said he was the first man into the compound. 'And we started clearing into the room. Engaged. Got a stoppage. I peeled out. The Gunsmith, same thing. Got a stoppage. And then Ben went through and made entry, and we backed him up.' He said the rest of the patrol then joined them, and 'that was the initial break in . . . the action that Ben was awarded the Victoria Cross for'.

He recalled later involvement in troop debriefs, and in September 2010 preparing a statement in support of Ben Roberts-Smith's citation. Arthur Moses SC asked, 'Did you have any issues with Mr Roberts-Smith being awarded the Victoria Cross?' To which he replied, 'No.'

The Corporal provided support for the now discredited case of The Lieutenant being stood down after shooting a dog. However, he had not seen the incident and could not recall how he was told about it.

Moses asked about Darwan. 'It was a troop hit, the witness recalled, a full-blooded mission in pursuit of the rogue Afghan soldier Hekmatullah. The Corporal and The Hunter had 'engaged [and killed] two fighting-aged males' who were 'armed and posed a threat to us'. He told Moses that, from all his Afghanistan deployments, he estimated seeing 'closer to a hundred' dead Afghan males.

For the Darwan mission, the interpreter accompanied his patrol. He recalled encountering PUCs during the initial stage of compound clearance, but not later. He was not certain the interpreter stayed with his patrol for the duration, but could not recall him leaving at any time. He did not see Ben Roberts-Smith on the day.

Upon return to Camp Russell, The Corporal heard nothing about Roberts-Smith allegedly kicking a PUC off a cliff. Similarly, he did not hear of the allegation that Roberts-Smith ordered Wakunish partner force soldiers to execute an unarmed Afghan at Chinartu until years after.

He did remember The Scout being on the Chinartu mission. He did not see him discover a weapons cache, nor Roberts-Smith order an execution.

After 40 minutes in closed court, the public hearing resumed. Arthur Moses moved on to pre-deployment training. The witness heard no talk of throwdowns being used to falsely legitimise unlawful killings. Asked about drawings of a 'winged penis', he remembered this as the work of The Hunter, but he had never seen any depiction of such a figure kicking a PUC off a cliff.

The 2013 meeting with The RSM was next. He could not recall being in attendance. He had never seen Ben Roberts-Smith breach the rules of engagement, nor did Roberts-Smith ever direct him to do so.

Nicholas Owens SC's questions began just before lunch. The first subject was The Lieutenant. Owens asked whether The Corporal had a clear recollection of the man he believed was stood down. The witness asserted that he was able to distinguish physical differences between The Lieutenant and Person 123, the commander he understood to have replaced The Lieutenant.

The luncheon adjournment provided 90 minutes' respite. Upon return, The Corporal clung to his account and denied discussing the identity of the dog shooter with Roberts-Smith, The Hunter and The XO.

Owens requested that proceedings move back to closed court. When the parties reassembled in open court an hour later, Owens referred the witness to his original outline of evidence. The Corporal disagreed that his claim of The Lieutenant being stood down was designed to assist Roberts-Smith's case.

Owens was punishing. He repeatedly accused The Corporal of knowingly giving false evidence. In the face of the highly credible and contrary account, he was equally persistent in responding: 'That's not true, sir. I've always had the assumption for the last ten years that The Lieutenant was the one who was involved in the shooting.' The Corporal further denied colluding with The Hunter to give false evidence.

They turned to Darwan. The Corporal reprised his account of engaging two insurgents with The Hunter. He remembered PUCs being tactically questioned to determine who should be returned to Tarin Kowt. He accepted that the interpreter was needed for tactical questioning and was unlikely to have stayed with The Hunter and himself for the entirety of the mission.

At 4.13 pm, evidence concluded for the day.

When The Corporal resumed his seat on Tuesday, 17 May 2022, Nicholas Owens SC asked him when he first heard the story of a PUC being kicked off a cliff. The Corporal said he knew nothing of this until the IGADF hearings in 2017.

Owens: 'I want to put to you that the first time you heard that a PUC had been kicked off a cliff at Darwan was in a period of a matter of days after the mission itself, in the lines at Camp Russell. Do you agree with that?'

The Corporal: 'No, I do not.'

He also denied seeing a picture of a winged penis kicking a PUC off a cliff. And he again disputed being present at a meeting with The RSM in 2013. Owens went into the detail of what was allegedly discussed, citing the subjects of bullying, the Battle of Tizak and Whiskey 108. All this was rejected, as well the proposition that he had attended a further meeting with a different RSM in 2014. According to Owens, at the latter meeting, The Gunsmith 'broke down in tears' as the cliff kick and the blooding were raised. The Corporal maintained his position that he was not there.

There were many more single-word negative responses to allegations that The Corporal was aware during pre-deployment training of plans to use 'throwdowns'.

The 'rookie fuck' sign on his own patrol room door in 2010 was raised. He was shown the photograph. He admitted he must have seen it 'multiple' times, and conceded he must have known it referred to a fellow patrol member, but he had no recollection of the term.

The final round of questioning in open court went back to Chinartu and the alleged execution of the Afghan detainee after the discovery of a weapons cache.

Owens: 'Now, I want to put to you that you do, in fact, have a recollection of the event I've just put to you.'

The Corporal: 'Not at all, sir.'

Owens: 'And I want to put to you that the reason you are falsely denying that you have a recollection is because you are trying to assist Mr Roberts-Smith in this case—correct?'

The Corporal: 'No, that's not true.'

A further half-hour in closed court brought Owens' cross-examination to an end. It would be up to Justice Anthony Besanko to determine whether the witness regarded his first duty as being to the court or to his friend, Ben Roberts-Smith.

CHAPTER 89

AN ORCHARD TOO FAR?

I am still in isolation. While I'm now testing negative, close contacts have extended my quarantine. I continue following the case via videolink, which is the next best thing to being there. It's frustrating all the same.

The next witness to front, on Wednesday, 18 May, was The Bodyguard. Even from the distance of my quarantine station, his nervousness was apparent. His voice faltered a touch as Arthur Moses SC stepped him through the basics.

The Bodyguard was in an infantry security detachment at Australia's embassy in Baghdad, Iraq, in 2005, when he first met Ben Roberts-Smith, then deployed for a prospective hostage rescue mission. (Ultimately, the mission did not proceed; Australian citizen Douglas Wood was later rescued by Iraqi soldiers.)

Two years later, The Bodyguard passed selection and was posted to 2 Squadron SASR. His first deployment to Afghanistan was in 2009, when his patrol commander was The Freefaller. In 2010 and 2012 he deployed again, this time assigned to The Sergeant's patrol.

By 2017 he was a father; he had discharged from the Army after having, as he put it, 'reassessed my priorities'. He maintained a friendship with Ben Roberts-Smith and also with The Scot. Upon leaving the SASR, he formed his own security company, which on occasion worked with The Scot's company.

Having established The Bodyguard's background, Arthur Moses asked for his understanding of lawful conduct. The Bodyguard said he was well briefed on the rules of engagement and had no knowledge of any members being engaged in unlawful killings and related misconduct.

He remembered the walk into Whiskey 108 in 2009. He recalled The Scot's team entering first; his patrol, led by The Freefaller, followed soon after. He saw no males, 'just some women and children' close to where the patrol made entry. The two patrols searched the compound. This was made more difficult for The Bodyguard because of the weapon he was carrying, a belt-fed 7.62mm machine gun.

When the tunnel was discovered, he saw The Freefaller, The Scot, Roberts-Smith and The Hunter standing nearby. He said The Hunter 'pushed the point' about entering the tunnel, and did so with The Freefaller standing guard behind him. Soon after, The Bodyguard saw The Hunter's head pop up.

Moses: 'Did you hear him say something?'

The Bodyguard: 'He said, "Clear" . . . he informed The Freefaller and anyone else in the vicinity that he had found a bunch of equipment in the tunnel.'

By now we had heard the tunnel story many times. However, with respect to the discovery of fighting-age males, there were two polar-opposite versions. Along with Roberts-Smith and The Scot, The Bodyguard, The Freefaller and The Hunter all said no one had emerged. The other three members of The Freefaller's patrol—The 2IC, The Cyclist and The Driver—had given contrary evidence.

Next came something completely new—at least to our side of the courtroom.

Moses: 'And what did you do after that?'

The Bodyguard: 'I pushed forward from that compound . . . There was an orchard area and I asked The 2IC to assist me with that clearance.

He declined because he stated his rifle was too long. He had a SR-25 sniper rifle [the same length as The Bodyguard's 7.62mm gun]. And then The Cyclist joined me and we cleared the orchard area.'

Stunning. This new orchard-clearing story had twin barbs. First, it skewered The 2IC as a shirker, and second, it took The Cyclist out of the compound, discrediting his evidence that he had witnessed two executions.

Nicholas Owens SC rose to formally object 'on *Browne v. Dunn* grounds'—that is, on the basis that this alleged orchard expedition had not been put to either The 2IC or The Cyclist during their cross-examination by the applicant's team.

The Bodyguard was allowed to proceed. He said that, because of his bulky machine gun and the thick foliage, he had to crawl on his hands and knees. He was grateful for The Cyclist's assistance.

He remembered seeing, between Whiskey 108 and Whiskey 109, the body of a dead fighting-age male. Shown photos, he could not identify the person depicted as the dead man he had seen, but he confirmed the location of this dead man had been 'outside the compound'.

He had not heard about the alleged execution of two PUCs until this appeared in media reporting in 2018. He did see the prosthetic leg on the walk out, strapped to the back of The Veteran. He saw it later at the Fat Lady's Arms, and 'at some point I drank out of it'.

Arthur Moses was able to establish that his witness had not killed an enemy combatant in action prior to his 2009 deployment. Despite this, he was never known as a 'rookie' or a 'rookie fuck'.

They moved on to 2010. As with The Scientist, The Bodyguard had not fought at Tizak, as both men had contracted malaria.

Then to 2012 and Darwan, where The Bodyguard was present as a member of The Sergeant's patrol. He said he encountered Ben Roberts-Smith, who was 'wet, and the reason the memory is clear is that he had detonators . . . that were unusual, and . . . really valuable to the Taliban . . . And the enemy rifle he was carrying had, I believe, a 5.56[mm] round lodged in the breach, which disabled the weapon . . . I thought that has probably been a reason that Ben Roberts-Smith is alive.'

Arthur Moses asked about the post-operation debrief, and whether he had heard a rumour about a PUC being kicked off a cliff. The Bodyguard replied, 'No, I did not.'

Moses: 'When did you first hear about that allegation?'

The Bodyguard: 'The media reports back in 2018.'

There was an adjournment to closed court, with open court resuming just before lunch. Arthur Moses had two more questions.

Moses: 'Did you see any fighting-aged males come out of the tunnel from Whiskey 108?'

The Bodyguard: 'I did not.'

Moses: 'Have you been interviewed by the IGADF?'

The Bodyguard: 'I have not.'

The *Browne v. Dunn* objection to the orchard evidence was debated in the absence of the witness. Nicholas Owens made the point that his coming cross-examination of The Bodyguard would 'look quite different' depending on whether 'the new evidence about the orchard' was or was not excluded.

Justice Anthony Besanko explained that he was yet to rule on a similar objection raised regarding The Scot's evidence. He said there was some work to do before his rulings and reasons could be published. By mid-afternoon, it was decided that cross-examination would proceed.

Owens: 'You accept, of course, that you are very good friends with Mr Roberts-Smith?'

The Bodyguard: 'That's correct.' He said that, before proceedings commenced, the two of them had spoken every few weeks.

He was asked about his contact with Roberts-Smith's lawyers since the proceedings began. They had met 'possibly once or twice more. Once in person, where I met with Monica.' In July 2019, when The Bodyguard's outline of evidence was composed, he said, 'I read through the final draft and approved it.'

Owens: 'It's correct, isn't it, that nowhere in that outline of evidence is it mentioned that you cleared the orchard outside Whiskey 108 with The Cyclist?'

The Bodyguard: 'Yes, he's not in that outline of evidence.'

Queried about why such an important detail would be omitted, The Bodyguard explained: 'It's not a secret that I've kept hidden . . . It was a part of the day . . . as was the rain, which may not be in the outline of evidence.'

The Bodyguard told the court he had not spoken with The Scot, The Hunter or The Freefaller since they gave evidence. While he had spoken with Ben Roberts-Smith, they had not discussed Whiskey 108. He told the court he was unaware of The Cyclist's evidence of The Gunsmith borrowing a suppressor and shooting a man in the tunnel courtyard, and of Roberts-Smith machine-gunning another man outside.

Owens: 'I want to put to you that you have only invented this story about clearing an orchard with The Cyclist after you came to learn that The Cyclist saw Mr Roberts-Smith and The Gunsmith shoot PUCs.'

The Bodyguard: 'That is incorrect. I cleared that orchard with The Cyclist.'

Asked whether he knew about The Cyclist's evidence from media reporting of the trial, The Bodyguard said this was not so. 'I don't have a lot of time. I've got three little kids and an international business. I don't read the news every day.'

Owens raised the heat. Pressed on how it could possibly be that such pivotal testimony had been left out of his outline, The Bodyguard appeared stung and pushed back. 'The story is fact . . . It was as frivolous as what I cooked for breakfast that morning . . . I didn't see it as a pivotal element of the clearance. It was a non-event, except for the fact that The 2IC, due to a lack of courage, did not clear it with me.'

Owens pressed on. If he was positioned inside the compound, how did The Bodyguard know there was an orchard? Why did he believe it needed to be cleared?

He said he went looking for work, because 'that's what we do.'

The witness did remember hearing gunfire, but was unclear about where he was at the time. He had no recollection of hearing the burst of a Minimi machine gun.

Throughout his evidence, the witness referred to having a 'liminal memory' of some events. When Owens asked for an explanation, he said some incidents stood out and some did not. For example, The 2IC's refusal to clear the orchard was a 'liminal memory'. Further, The Bodyguard had a liminal memory of seeing one body, but was less clear about seeing further bodies.

Back in court the following morning, Nicholas Owens returned to the orchard. Why would it be cleared after the compound was declared secure, and not before? The Bodyguard said he did not believe the compound was declared secure until after he and The Cyclist had investigated the orchard.

Owens suggested that clearing the orchard would have been the subject of planned battle orders, and would have been undertaken by an entire patrol rather than two soldiers. Also, 'the most junior member of a patrol would never be telling the second-in-charge of his patrol to come with him to do that—correct?'

Clinging to his account, The Bodyguard insisted, 'Incorrect.'

At 2.17 pm on Thursday, 19 May 2022 his Honour informed The Bodyguard, 'There are no further questions for you, and you are released and are free to go.'

Watching on from home, I felt there was a touch of desperation in the orchard story; for the other side, it could well backfire. On our side, a ruling on whether or not The Bodyguard's thorny tale would be admissible was keenly awaited.

CHAPTER 90

TOUGH ENOUGH

There was room to squeeze a further witness in on the afternoon of Thursday, 19 May 2022. He was another soldier from Roberts-Smith's alma mater, 3RAR.

The man I am calling The Specialist, and who was known to the court as Person 36, joined the ADF in 1997. He undertook SASR selection in 2001 and, like many from this cohort, had multiple deployments to Afghanistan. As a vehicle gunner, he was tasked with carrying 'specialist' equipment. He was discharged from the Army in 2019. His evidence in chief was taken by Ben Roberts-Smith's third top silk, Matthew Richardson SC.

The Specialist first met Roberts-Smith when they deployed together to Butterworth, Malaysia, with 3RAR in 1999; from then on, they had maintained a friendship. His relevance to this case took us back to 2006. Although he had not participated in the Koran Ghar mission, The Specialist was a member of Roberts-Smith's patrol at that time. Richardson asked whether he'd had an opportunity to observe the performance of The Redhead.

The Specialist: 'Yes, I did.' The Redhead was 'questionably and potentially below the standard required. He appeared to need extra supervision over what you would expect from a qualified SAS soldier.'

Asked for specific examples, The Specialist referred to evidence canvassed earlier in the trial. While in an overwatch position, his patrol observed several rockets being fired from a distant compound. The Redhead was directed to respond, using an 84mm anti-tank weapon. He was eating his lunch at the time and, according to The Specialist, needed to be ordered three times before discarding his food and taking action.

The Specialist described a protracted and intense engagement, with The Redhead continuing to underperform. In the end, he said, another member of the patrol had taken over the weapon.

As the second-in-command, The Specialist 'put forward a recommendation based on my observations that he potentially be reviewed for his suitability to be an SASR operator'. Asked why he prepared the report, he explained that, in a small high-performance unit, there was no room for weakness.

And it was for The Redhead's own benefit: 'I had observed on several times him waking up screaming at our accommodation when we were back in the safety of the camp. For me, there was a duty of care for his safety as well, both on the impact of the stress of combat and the risk that, if we were engaged in close-quarter battle, that he may go into freeze behaviour and put his own life at risk.'

Questioned as to whether he'd ever observed Roberts-Smith threatening, bullying, assaulting or spreading rumours, The Specialist said, 'No.' Not until 2013 did The Specialist become aware of any bullying allegation against Roberts-Smith.

Cross-examination began in the midafternoon. Nicholas Owens referred the witness to a string of later appraisal reports on The Redhead that were complimentary.

Owens: 'Overall, would you agree that The Redhead was a young soldier who needed mentoring?'

The Specialist: 'No, I wouldn't agree. Not on basic skills.'

Owens, soon after: 'You would agree, wouldn't you, that you were not, in 2006, a particularly effective mentor of The Redhead?'

The Specialist: 'No, I disagree with that.'

Moving to the allegation that The Redhead was slow with the 84mm anti-tank weapon, Owens asked whether The Specialist had been equally slow to provide a target indicator. This was denied.

Owens: 'Well, it's correct, isn't it, that The Redhead kept shouting, "Where do you want me to fire it? Give me a target indication"?'

The Specialist: 'No, that's not correct.'

Owens asked the witness whether the relentless criticism of The Redhead might have contributed to his underperformance. The Specialist disagreed.

Owens: 'And what I want to put to you is that, once he was removed from an environment where he was relentlessly criticised, The Redhead has gone on to have a very successful career in the SAS?'

The Specialist: 'No, I don't believe that to be true.'

Owens: 'Now, whether or not you observed anything, you would agree, wouldn't you, that in all circumstances, making a death threat to another soldier is unacceptable?'

The Specialist: 'Well, to be honest, early in my training career, there were things said in debriefs that I would have probably perceived as death threats. So, I guess it just depends on the individual and how they perceive that feedback.'

Owens: 'So is this right? Your view is that people ought to be tough enough to take a death threat?'

There was an objection from Matthew Richardson and some further wrangling, before the line of questioning was allowed.

Owens: 'It would never be acceptable to say to someone that you are going to put a bullet in the back of their head, would it?'

The Specialist: 'No, it would be unlikely . . . that it would be acceptable.'

At 4 pm The Specialist was released, following a few more grudging concessions that threatening and punching was not on. In old-school 3RAR style, the witness's condemnation of bullying was notably unenthusiastic.

CHAPTER 91

HOT WASH

We had considered calling The Rifleman as a witness, but the other side beat us to it. At 10.18 am on Friday, 20 May 2022 he was affirmed. The court was still masked up, with Ben Roberts-Smith in his usual opposite corner, hunched over his phone. Arthur Moses SC was back in the lead.

The Rifleman deployed to Afghanistan with 3 Squadron SASR in 2011 and 2012. The latter deployment overlapped with Rotation XVIII, meaning he had a short attachment to the incoming 2 Squadron. This put him in Ben Roberts-Smith's patrol for that initial hit-out to the Chora Valley in July, alongside The Gunsmith, The Sniper and The Trooper.

As prior evidence had revealed, the purpose of the mission was to clear a compound of interest known to have harboured insurgents who were believed responsible for the death of Sergeant Blaine Diddams two weeks earlier. Roberts-Smith's patrol and another, led by an operator designated by the court as Person 55, were tasked with walking in and setting up a blocking position. This would trap any enemy flushed into the open after the rest of the troop inserted via helicopter.

The witness related how his patrol had arrived early and set up on the eastern side of the compound, while the other patrol settled to the south-west.

As he picked up the sound of approaching helicopters, The Rifleman felt a round impact close to his head. It came from the general direction of the patrol that was to the south-west. A single shot, he thought, from a suppressed weapon.

Ben Roberts-Smith issued quick orders and they moved in extended file, The Trooper with a Minimi machine gun on the far right, The Rifleman in the middle and Roberts-Smith on the left. 'We were pretty much in line with each other towards that patrol,' The Rifleman explained, 'when The Trooper started to engage with his light machine gun.'

The Rifleman, seeing no threat, yelled to The Trooper, asking what he was firing at. Ben Roberts-Smith shouted the same query. The Trooper did not respond. After seven rounds were fired, the Minimi experienced a stoppage. The Trooper rectified it and, still not responding to their queries, continued firing. Then there was a pause and Roberts-Smith ordered a 'peel back'. The Trooper and The Rifleman joined Roberts-Smith.

'What were you firing at? What were you firing at?' The Rifleman recalled the patrol commander asking, but The Trooper was still 'unable to respond'. The Rifleman told Arthur Moses they then saw blue smoke from the location of the second patrol, which signified the presence of friendly forces. At the same time, 'a small group of women and children carrying various items—one was a birdcage, which was quite odd—appeared from that general direction as well'.

The Rifleman said The Trooper now responded, telling his team-mates: 'No, I wasn't shooting at that patrol. I was shooting in that general direction, where the women and children appeared.'

The apparent blue-on-blue and the absence of an enemy meant the mission was aborted.

Upon their return to Camp Russell, there was the usual troop debrief. The witness described this, in military terminology, as a 'hot wash', where different perspectives are merged for the sake of lessons learned. He recalled 'a bit of confusion [about] what was happening on the ground'.

The meeting then divided, with The Rifleman and other junior operators leaving, while Ben Roberts-Smith and other patrol commanders stayed on. Along with The Gunsmith, The Sniper and The Trooper, The Rifleman waited in their room for Ben Roberts-Smith to return.

He recalled them being sombre and a bit shocked, except for The Trooper, who was 'jovial'.

When Ben Roberts-Smith returned, The Rifleman recalled, he ordered The Trooper to 'stand up'. 'I can't remember [the] time frame,' he continued, 'but [Roberts-Smith] then struck The Trooper.'

Nicholas Owens SC began his cross-examination, and the topic swung back to the start of the Chora Valley mission. Owens asked The Rifleman whether he heard Roberts-Smith telling his patrol they were going back to 'where Didds [Sergeant Blaine Diddams] got killed', and that 'if those fuckers are up there, we're going to kill every last one of those fuckers'.

The Rifleman: 'No, that's not correct.'

Owens asked about the shouted requests to The Trooper for target indicators, putting it to The Rifleman that, far from not responding, The Trooper had replied, 'Two enemy,' and provided a distance and direction.

The Rifleman: 'Incorrect.'

The witness was challenged about how many rounds had impacted near him. If he thought he had received fire from a suppressed weapon, did that not immediately indicate to him that it had come from an Australian soldier? The Rifleman said that was not correct, but acknowledged 'confusion'.

Owens now turned to the post-mission troop debrief, or 'hot wash'. 'It's correct, isn't it, that there was no suggestion during the troop debrief that there had been a blue-on-blue initiated by Person 55's patrol?'

The witness responded: 'That was when the confusion started happening, and a bit of argument . . .' He said it had got 'messy', and all but the patrol commanders had left the room.

Owens: 'I want to put it to you that the only suggestion of a blue-on-blue mentioned in the troop debrief was a blue-on-blue initiated by The Trooper—correct?'

The Rifleman: 'No.'

The witness resisted the proposition that a junior soldier, The Trooper, had ended up bearing the brunt of blame for what had been a bungled mission.

Owens: 'I put it to you very clearly that the talk of the blue-on-blue, initiated by Person 55, did not emerge until several days after the troop and patrol debrief.'

The Rifleman: 'That's not correct.'

Owens: 'And it's correct, isn't it, that you had heard Mr Roberts-Smith say that the blue-on-blue had been initiated by The Trooper?'

The Rifleman: 'No.'

Owens wanted detail about the supposedly buoyant demeanour of The Trooper before he was punched.

The Rifleman: 'He was not laughing . . . It was more of a jovial attitude towards the whole thing.'

Owens wound up his cross-examination, but The Rifleman's time in the witness box was not quite over. Arthur Moses rose with a final question about the location of the Chora Valley mission: 'Why did you know that was the area where the late Blaine Diddams was murdered by the Taliban?'

The witness responded: 'I was on that patrol.'

The Rifleman was released before lunch, and Justice Anthony Besanko asked for an update on future witnesses. It was the Friday of the trial's thirteenth week, and the list was almost expired.

The game of numbers had not gone so well for Ben Roberts-Smith. Twenty-six witnesses had turned up for the respondents; thirteen so far for the applicant. His counsel now announced a series of late withdrawals.

CHAPTER 92

HOLDING FIRM

Day 92. Monday, 23 May 2022. Australia has a new government, led by Anthony Albanese, and I am at last out of quarantine. As the various teams merge at the court entrance, Arthur Moses SC asks after my health.

Although we are determined opponents, I am trying not to take all this too personally. Moses and I occasionally exchange pleasantries—and besides, with a shared allegiance to the Parramatta Eels rugby league team, we have something in common that eclipses the defamation trial of the century.

The XO looked more like a suburban bank manager than an old-hand special forces operator. Thickset, grey hair, glasses and a ruddy complexion; the British accent fills in another corner of the profile.

He had a similar CV to The Scot's, having moved from the Royal Marines to the Special Boat Service and on to Australia's SASR. A 35-year career encompassed deployments to Northern Ireland, Iraq, the Balkans, East Timor and Afghanistan. In 2020, he retired with the rank of major.

This day's evidence focused on Rotation XVIII in 2012, when he had acted as squadron executive officer, or XO. As he explained to Arthur Moses, one of his responsibilities was oversight of helicopter load plans.

Since a fatal helicopter crash in 2010, knowing who was on which aircraft had become paramount.

Another of The XO's tasks was supervision of partner ratios. A sore point for many personnel at the fag end of Australia's longest war was the assignment of increased numbers of Afghan forces. The plan for Afghans to assume responsibility for the security of their country meant better trained foreign soldiers were left behind. As The XO explained, the dictate was strict. If the required ratio of Afghan soldiers was not available, the mission would be cancelled.

This meant The XO had visibility of the issue of The Lieutenant and the shot dog. He said he had not spoken with this particular NDS partner force member, but he was familiar with the incident, having been informed of it by The Veteran at a meeting in July 2012. And he told Arthur Moses that, subsequently, he did not see The Lieutenant's name on load plans.

This evidence placed The XO in the 'gang of five'. If the initial evidence of The XO, Ben Roberts-Smith, The Hunter, The Corporal and The Scientist was to be believed, The Lieutenant could not have been at Chinartu when Roberts-Smith allegedly ordered the execution of a PUC. Any notion of a conspiracy, however, was dismissed. The XO made clear to Arthur Moses that he had not spoken to any of the other four about this evidence.

The XO's relationship with Roberts-Smith was the next topic. He recalled a first meeting in Iraq in 2005. As with The Bodyguard, he came into contact with Roberts-Smith during the planned mission to rescue the Australian hostage Douglas Wood.

When The XO transferred to the SASR two years later, as a maritime water operations specialist, he became Roberts-Smith's supervisor. A mentor-like friendship ensued.

By 11.48 am, after an hour of closed court, it was the turn of Nicholas Owens SC to ask questions. He pressed for detail on what The Veteran told The XO at the meeting in July 2012. The XO remembered being told that an Australian soldier had been wounded by a ricochet when the dog was shot. At that stage he did not know whether The Lieutenant had pulled the trigger or ordered the shooting. But the consequence, in any case, was his removal from command.

Owens wondered how, if The XO had never met The Lieutenant, he remembered his name when compiling his outline of evidence in June 2019. And he followed up: 'Could you in June 2019 recall the name of any other NDS partner force member?'

The XO: 'No.'

After further probing, The XO conceded that The Mentor may have been the source of the dog story, rather than The Veteran.

The XO was more confident that he had not seen The Lieutenant's name listed on the load plan for the latter part of the rotation.

As he had done with the other witnesses committed to this account, Owens put it to The XO that he was back to front on The Lieutenant: that another soldier was responsible for the shooting, and it was The Lieutenant who had been brought in as a replacement. By our reckoning, the dog shooting incident had occurred on 31 July. Given that The Lieutenant had not assumed command until 21 September, he was clearly in theatre for the Chinartu operation on 12 October.

But The XO could not be budged, insisting we were the ones who were 'incorrect'.

Owens: 'And I want to put to you that the reason The Lieutenant's name wasn't on a helicopter manifest in August 2012 was because he didn't take over as a commander of the NDS until September—correct?'

The XO: 'No, The Lieutenant wouldn't have been there because he was removed from command at the end of July.'

Nicholas Owens sought an adjournment to closed court. Given the proximity to the lunch break, the restricted session would wait until 2 pm. Since a non-publication order applied, I can't say whether the witness's position on The Lieutenant was in any way altered by contrary evidence.

The rest of the week was quiet, at least in Courtroom 21A. A recall of The Scientist to closed court was scheduled. A few more witnesses fell away, and some background work was required to clear the way for the 40th and final witness.

CHAPTER 93

LEADERSHIP IN THE STAND

Day 97. Wednesday, 1 June 2022. I had heard good things about The Captain (Person 81) when I worked on *No Front Line*.

In the early months of 2009, soldiers from the 7th Battalion of the Royal Australian Regiment (7RAR) were caught in protracted skirmishes along the Dorafshan River at Kakarak. On 16 March, Corporal Matthew Hopkins was killed by a gunshot to the head.

On 12 April, 7RAR was still under fire, with 2 Squadron SASR watching on from above. Corporal Dave Farrell MG described a 'good display of leadership' on that day by their young troop captain, who ordered a daring daylight assault on key 'compounds of interest'.

Additional sensitivities applied to the presence of the trial's final witness. The officer, since promoted, continued to serve in Special Operations Command. This elevated status was perhaps reflected in his choice of counsel. The Captain would be represented by Greg Melick AO SC, a major general in the Australian Army Reserve (retired), and national president of the Returned Services League.

Subpoenaed by the applicant, this was another case of a witness appearing 'cold', with no opportunity for counsel to test the evidence before The Captain was affirmed.

He told Arthur Moses SC he did not see any engagements on 12 April, but he was aware of some gunfire on approach. As was standard operating procedure, for the early phase, his Troop Headquarters element stayed to the rear. And when Whiskey 108 was declared secure, he moved forward.

The troop captain picked through the rubble of 'significant destruction' from the earlier bomb strike. He said he did 'see people in Whiskey 108', specifying an Afghan woman: 'Yes, one of the memories I do have is a lady sweeping.' He also saw 'body parts' and 'rocket paraphernalia'. He observed no 'individuals within the compound being PUC'ed', nor, once on site, did he hear any engagements.

The Captain was aware that a tunnel had been discovered. He told Arthur Moses he did not remember whether he observed it or learned about it later. He also said he was not told anything about fighting-age males being found, but was aware that 'items' had been recovered.

The issue of the rendezvous (RV) between patrol commanders and Troop Headquarters was raised. The Captain confirmed that standard operating procedure was for it to occur after the compound was declared cleared. And the point of doing so was to consolidate forces before ordering the move to Whiskey 109. He could not recall who was present at the RV or what was said.

When he moved to Whiskey 109, he noted a dead body, but could not recall specific detail, such as a prosthetic leg. The Captain told Moses that the allegation of two men being taken from the tunnel and executed was known to him—but he had heard this only recently, after the IGADF inquiry began.

Asked what he would have done if this had been raised, he said: 'I would have reported it.' As to the prosthetic leg, he saw it 'either in the Fat Lady's Arms . . . or back at work [in Australia]'.

At 3.12 pm proceedings moved to a closed hearing, before court adjourned for the day.

When court resumed the following morning, Nicholas Owens SC cross-examined. The Captain could not say when he was informed that two enemies were killed at Whiskey 108. He accepted that he only knew what he had been told. The witness was shown photographs.

Owens: '[Are you] unable to say one way or the other whether the old man was executed by The Gunsmith, encouraged by Mr Roberts-Smith and The Scot . . .?'

The Captain: 'I couldn't say, no.'

Owens: 'And does it also follow you are unable to say one way or another whether the man with the prosthetic leg was executed by Mr Roberts-Smith?'

The Captain: 'I couldn't say.'

Returning to the tunnel, The Captain now said, 'I have a recollection of the tunnel. You know, this story has been told so many times now, I do find it seems to adjust regularly, but from my recollection, yes, I remember seeing the tunnel.' He was unsure whether that was before or after the commanders' RV.

As troop captain, he explained, he had a set of all-consuming responsibilities. He was concerned to ensure that his flanking units were not exposed to 'friendly fire'. The unmanned aerial vehicle above had to be coordinated. His electronic warfare specialist and interpreter were monitoring Icom radio chatter for prospective threats. He needed to stay on top of that, as well as to ensure medical support was on hand and that soldiers back at the vehicle drop-off were kept updated.

Owens: 'Is it certainly the case that, during the RV, you don't recall there being any engagement just outside the walls of the compound?'

The Captain: 'That is correct.'

Owens: 'And is it certainly the case that none of the patrol commanders, during the RV, left the RV to go and investigate any engagement?'

The Captain: 'I don't recall.'

Close observers would have noted that this testimony was at odds with that given earlier in the trial by one of the patrol commanders also present. The Scot had given evidence that he heard shots fired outside the compound when he was at the RV.

Owens summarised: 'Our case is that the old man and the man with the prosthetic leg were found in the tunnel, were PUC'ed, and then were murdered by one or more of The Gunsmith, The Scot and Mr Roberts-Smith, without your knowledge or authorisation. Are you able to say anything about that proposition?'

The witness hesitated, ultimately responding: 'I couldn't speculate on that.'

Proceedings moved back to closed court. Half an hour later, at 11.25 am, when the parties reassembled in open court, Arthur Moses asked for a brief re-examination.

Moses: 'On 12 April 2009, did you observe any conduct by The Gunsmith, The Scot or Mr Roberts-Smith that caused you to have a suspicion that they PUC'ed and murdered anybody?'

The Captain: 'No, I didn't.'

Readers of *The Australian* on 2 June 2022 would have regarded The Captain's evidence as helpful to the applicant. 'Roberts-Smith's claims bolstered by SAS officer' was the headline on a report by Perry Duffin after his first day of evidence.

That was not the way I saw it. For me, his evidence was of no clear benefit to either side. If anything, it was more illuminating of the big question shadowing this trial: of command accountability.

If brazen war crimes had occurred at Whiskey 108, why was leadership in no position to know what had happened, or to do anything about them?

CHAPTER 94

A STARK CHOICE

Day 103, 18 July 2022. A Sydney Monday, cold and unforgiving. Each side has been granted four days to present their closing submissions.

Arthur Moses SC led off, with a sting of anger in his voice: 'Regrettably, neither Mr Masters nor Mr McKenzie chose to give evidence in this case.' Our work, he alleged, 'arose out of years of character assassination by disgruntled members of the Special Air Service Regiment, who fed Mr Masters and Mr McKenzie information for their own purposes.' The result, according to Moses, was that we then gullibly wrote 'sensationalist' accounts, 'presumably to obtain accolades'.

The alleged murder at Syachow by The Ring-In—no longer relied upon, after Justice Besanko ruled he would not be compelled to answer questions—was a prime example of our 'carelessness'. The seriousness of all fourteen defamatory imputations was such that it would not be good enough for us to say 'we nearly got there'. Moses argued that we had fallen short.

Bruce McClintock SC was not in court. Moses' tag-team partner was instead Matthew Richardson SC. He rose to address the court on reputational damage and economic loss, his robe at one point slipping from his shoulders.

Richardson pointed to coverage that referenced the positive, such as Roberts-Smith being awarded the Victoria Cross and the Medal for

Gallantry, and being nominated as Father of the Year, as well as being chair of the Australia Day Council. 'Those things are mentioned to make it worse, to show what the respondents allege is the enormous gap between the public and the sordid truth known by the insiders,' Richardson argued.

While it was acknowledged that Ben Roberts-Smith was a polarising figure and plainly disliked by some of our witnesses, this did not reflect the big picture. Richardson cited evidence from other witnesses of Roberts-Smith's 'good reputation in the SAS'.

The accusation that Roberts-Smith murdered teenagers for medals was contemptible, he went on. Richardson reprised his client's words in response to the charge: 'I've explained to Your Honour what happened at Tizak in 2010, and in the course of my duty, trying to protect my friends and fight what was a large battle, I had to kill a young man who was holding a machine gun. From that moment on, I have lived with that every day, and I struggle with it. So I have the respondents question me about shooting and murdering a teenage boy. It's just shameful; shameful. Because not only did it not happen, but they know it didn't happen, so they changed their story again to fit what they needed to fit and it still didn't work, so they know it's false. They know it and they still say it. They still ask the question, because they have to. It's disgraceful.'

Roberts-Smith's distress over the reporting of his dead friend Matt Locke's involvement in the shooting of a young Afghan male at Koran Ghar was next. The highly paid barrister quoted his highly paid client's disgust: 'I find it utterly reprehensible. No basis to do that at all. It's even more damaging to me, particularly the respondent or Mr Masters who has profited off what we have done in Afghanistan through his many books.'

Meanwhile, while I was rolling in the royalties from two books, as Richardson recounted, Ben Roberts-Smith's returns from his public-speaking business were in decline. The barrister told the court that in 2015 his client had made half a million dollars; after the defamatory stories were published in 2018, his public-speaking income had fallen to $300,000.

A libel of the utmost seriousness called for extreme compensation. A cap on defamation awards, a reform the besieged news industry hoped might lessen the volume of 'hurt feelings' litigation, was currently set at $443,000. But it applied only to non-economic loss. Richardson argued that, considering three separate proceedings against three mastheads, his client could be awarded 'up to three times' the capped figure. And on top of that, Roberts-Smith deserved special damages for economic loss and, we presumed, an eye-watering figure for 'aggravated damages'.

To conclude his opening, Richardson reached for another impassioned Roberts-Smith quote: 'I have so much respect for the Victoria Cross and what it stands for, for the Australian Defence Force, people that I have worked with. I love my family, my children, and that's what keeps me going, to set the record straight. And that's why I'm here.'

It was early afternoon when Nicholas Owens SC began to headline the truth defence. He recalled the opening of the respondents' case 'over a year ago', when he had outlined His Honour's 'stark choice between effectively irreconcilable accounts'. As he put it, 'someone is lying here'.

Roberts-Smith's lawyers alleged that only two of our witnesses, The Gunsmith and The Gunner, were 'deliberately dishonest'. That meant a lot of the respondents' SAS witnesses were inaccurate or mistaken. To the proposition that, thirteen years on, the frailty of memory and exposure to rumour explained a gruel of slip-ups by the applicant's witnesses, Owens went to the significance of events—such as the Afghans being dragged from a tunnel and a man being kicked off a cliff—as 'not like the question of whether one had toast or cereal for breakfast'.

The lofty senior counsel devoted the remainder of the afternoon to Whiskey 108. In my imagining, it was as if a human drone hovered over the compound. Not needing to rely on notes, Owens was omniscient as he recounted myriad details with calm precision. He cited The SSE, The 2IC, The Cyclist, The Driver and The Reader as giving unchallenged evidence of what they saw in the tunnel courtyard. Exposure to rumour was 'very low and infrequent'. The telling details they gave about what they saw had not been provided by media reports.

Owens wondered how, in the absence of evidence of alleged collusion (unlike in the tale of The Lieutenant and the shot dog), five witnesses could have the same false memory of Afghan men emerging from a tunnel. 'It's not said that they've got together and cooked up a story,' he argued. 'It's not even suggested that they've spoken to each other about their evidence.' These witnesses were not linked by friendship; the majority of them were 'not knocking down our door . . . they were subpoenaed, and each of them came along, and each of them gave, it is accepted, honest evidence.'

While The Bodyguard had presented a challenge to the respondents' tunnel courtyard evidence, this, according to Owens, was 'designed to provide some prayer to Mr Roberts-Smith's case'. He dismissed The Bodyguard's evidence as a 'deliberate recent invention'. As to The Scot's support for Roberts-Smith, Owens pointed out that he had 'the additional motive to lie—of himself standing accused of involvement in the murder of one of the PUCs'.

Owens further argued that the location of the bodies—that of the old man in particular—presented 'an intractable problem for Mr Roberts-Smith's case'. Roberts-Smith's first account was that both men had been shot outside and then dragged closer to the compound. But the next day Roberts-Smith had recanted his evidence, saying he had made a mistake. As Owens pointed out, The Scot was the only other witness to give evidence about moving a body, and 'no other witness has said they saw that body out there'.

The court adjourned at 4.14 pm. We settled in the interview room for a quick confab. Our team was making out a strong case, but was it strong enough? Not only were Nine/Fairfax and McKenzie/Masters in a fight against Ben Roberts-Smith VC, MG, we were also struggling under the burden of proof. And, tellingly, as was observed over an empty box of Cadbury's Favourites, the other side had shifted ground. The strident proclamations that Roberts-Smith was completely innocent had given way to a new charge: that his accusers were well short of proving guilt.

CHAPTER 95

UNWRITTEN RULES

There is drizzle as Peter Bartlett and I make our way to court. Along the way we spot Ben Roberts-Smith and Monica Allen treading the same path. As before, when they near the media scrum, with photographers craning like meerkats, Monica drops back.

Proceedings resumed at 10.15 am on Tuesday, 19 July, with Nicholas Owens SC back in hover pattern over Whiskey 108. He highlighted the evidence of The SSE as compelling, not just in his recollection but in 'the accuracy of the contemporaneous post-mission reporting', such as the SSE bag marked 'NW corner tunnel' and time-stamped photographs.

Owens also pointed out that The Cyclist had not only cogent evidence of two shootings, but also testimony that was consistent with the location of the bodies. Roberts-Smith's 'strange' request to borrow The Cyclist's suppressor was a 'more, not less plausible' account, because 'this is a detail that someone would have not created if they were making up a lie'.

Grappling with the accusation that The Cyclist could not credibly explain why he did not report what he said he saw, Owens was less confounded: 'He understood the unwritten rule to be that you toed the line and you did not make waves. There was, we submit, Your Honour, clearly a culture of silence within the SAS.'

Another witness to give direct evidence of an execution was The Scout. When he was cross-examined, much was made of a discrepancy between his evidence and my note-taking. I had recorded 'RS had an M14 and The Gunsmith a Minimi', when in fact The Gunsmith had carried an M4 and Roberts-Smith a Minimi. In his evidence, The Scout revealed that he did not know who the soldier was who he saw firing the Minimi.

Owens: 'The response we make to that is: that is exactly what The Scout said he thought on the day.'

The Scout had been caught out in a lie—not in court, and not about war crimes, but rather about his contact with the media. There was ground to make up. Owens: 'Although Your Honour would approach The Scout's evidence with caution, in light of the fact that he was dishonest on a topic, at the end of the day, Your Honour would accept that he was honest, and Your Honour would approach his evidence on its own terms.'

The Gunner also gave direct evidence of an execution. Positioned near The Scout at Whiskey 108, he corroborated the account of the machine-gunning of the man with the prosthetic leg. As it happened, his veracity was also under challenge after a disparity was revealed between his testimony and what he had told the IGADF.

Owens: 'The Gunner came along to the court to tell the truth, even though it pained him to do so in relation to Mr Roberts-Smith, and even though he felt no sympathy and no qualms for the two men who had been killed. He gave truthful evidence about what he saw outside Whiskey 108.'

By late morning, Owens was repositioned over the village of Darwan, with his helicopter view of the matrix of evidence. He summarised the Roberts-Smith account: that there were no fighting-age males in the final compound; that The Replacement was sent back with the interpreter; and that he and The Sniper engaged a spotter in a cornfield on the way to the helicopter landing zone.

In obstinate contrast, the evidence, according to Owens, clearly placed Afghan males and the interpreter in the last compound. The Gunsmith, The Replacement, Mohammed Hanifa and Mangul Rahmi all said so. And if Ben Roberts-Smith's account of The Replacement taking the interpreter back was correct, they would have been separated from his patrol for an hour and a half, despite it being a ten-minute round trip.

Regarding the shooting of the spotter, Roberts-Smith said that, before engaging, he had to climb an embankment at least one and a half metres high on his hands and knees. Addressing this, the Afghan witnesses said the rise was either non-existent or below knee height. The Replacement remembered no embankment; even The Sniper recalled 'walking, not climbing'.

As Owens' junior, Chris Mitchell, came to see it, there was generally a purpose to Roberts-Smith's lies. He needed to account for why a spotter would suddenly appear on the periphery of a hive of armed soldiers. In Roberts-Smith's version, his sight picture was initially obscured. As Owens explained, 'The embankment was there to explain what we would say is an otherwise implausible account, which is that this spotter, so called, was right on the edge of the cornfield, in full view.'

The Sniper's evidence was also designed to address 'the implausibility of a spotter simply being on the edge of a cornfield'. His account of shooting at him from fifteen metres away through a thick cornfield and seeing an Icom radio in his hand was inconsistent with the evidence of every other witness, and with the GPS coordinates on the SSE bag.

The key witnesses at Darwan, The Gunsmith and the Afghans, had all been accused of dishonesty by the applicant's lawyers.

Owens: 'The submission has to grapple with how it is that three illiterate Afghan villagers on the other side of the world, with no connection whatsoever to The Gunsmith, have given evidence which, in all material respects, corresponds with what The Gunsmith says happened. They all spoke of being in the final compound, seeing a tall soldier wet from the waist down, seeing someone kicked off a cliff, all at the exact same time, the exact same date and the exact same location as The Gunsmith described.'

The Replacement also gave unchallenged evidence of the cliff kick, having heard it from The Gunsmith and The Sniper on their return to Camp Russell.

At the lunch break there was still light rain. We put the phone on speaker and gave Melbourne-based Nick McKenzie a quick update. When Dean Levitan and I ducked out for a coffee, we spotted Len and Sue Roberts-Smith at a cafe table under shelter. Ben's parents had been dutiful in providing aid and comfort to their elder son. There were strained looks. It must have been hard for them.

In the afternoon session, the question was addressed as to how it was that a brazen cliff kick in the open, within line of sight of the overwatch position and a great many other prying eyes, was not seen by others.

Owens said he did not have a clear answer: 'Perhaps [Roberts-Smith] assessed the situation and determined that people were engaged in other tasks and weren't looking . . . Perhaps he could see them looking in the other direction. Maybe he just didn't care that there were eyewitnesses.'

It was a good question, bereft of a good answer. As Owens pointed out, there were also witnesses to the Whiskey 108 killings; one of them described the shooting of the man with the prosthetic leg as 'an exhibition execution'. After the Darwan mission, there was allegedly at Camp Russell a picture drawn of a winged penis kicking a man off a cliff, and rumination among some about what had occurred. And there was always that SAS culture of silence, either knowingly or unknowingly, expertly and surreptitiously compartmentalising corporate knowledge.

The following morning, Wednesday, 20 July, we lined up again. I nodded to Ben Roberts-Smith but he did not respond. As the trial wound to a close, he seemed a little less chummy with his barristers.

Then the call to order, and Nicholas Owens SC was back in the skies over Darwan. He would have another long day on his feet.

The Apache helicopters and Heron drones were cited: how was it that their scanners did not pick up the presence of a spotter prior to their departure? Was not the tight cluster of wounds at Ali Jan's heart consistent with the execution of a stationary target at close range? And wasn't this also true of the exit wounds and the neat line of blood on Ali Jan's wrist that indicated his hands had been bound? The Afghan witnesses had no trouble identifying Ali Jan. 'They knew him from their lives in Darwan, and what they are saying is that they recognise that man that they know in the photographs.'

Owens moved to Chinartu. The allegation of the murder of a detained Afghan man, following the discovery of a weapons cache, would be harder to sustain. It was not built on as large a bed of evidence as there was at Darwan. However, though The Scout was our sole witness, his account was substantially corroborated by a detailed study of the records of the 12 October 2012 mission.

The operational summary, we contended, had been falsified to account for the murder. With close examination of the timings and documentary evidence, this could be demonstrated. Further, we argued, in contradiction of Roberts-Smith's claim, that The Lieutenant was present for the mission.

Owens: 'We say that the lie about The Lieutenant was a deliberate lie told by Mr Roberts-Smith, which evidences a consciousness of guilt.' Indeed, as Owens put it, 'the accuracy and reliability of The Scout's evidence, is . . . astonishing when compared against the objective evidentiary record'.

The notes I made four years earlier were shown to accord with the Sametime chat logs; according to Owens, they matched 'the objective timing perfectly'. The Sametime chat recording an enemy killed in action just before extraction was exactly as The Scout said.

Chris Mitchell had also noted an important detail in a photograph of the weapon supposedly carried by the PUC whom we alleged had been shot—its barrel was wrapped in cloth. This indicated it was recovered from a cache, as we asserted, and it would hardly have been so clad if it had been wielded in anger. The timings on the photos also fitted our story.

The next topic was the five witnesses who all falsely claimed The Lieutenant could not have been at Chinartu following the dog-shooting incident. Owens reinforced the credibility of The Scout by pointing out that, despite a welter of evidence that asserted otherwise, he was correct about The Lieutenant being present at Chinartu.

Owens: 'What's the significance of the fact that people tried to lie in addition to the fact that we say their evidence is wrong . . . [and] knowingly false? [It is why] we say Your Honour might infer a consciousness of guilt on the part of Mr Roberts-Smith.'

The case for collusion was powerful. The evidence of The Scientist, for example, was described as 'startling'. 'He agreed that he had never known who it was who shot the dog,' Owens said, 'never known who it was that got removed. He didn't know The Lieutenant. He didn't know any of those matters. He wasn't present at the incident. When he was asked, in effect, "Well, how did it come to be that this outline of evidence came to be prepared containing this positive recollection?", he said that the first time he had ever heard The Lieutenant's name was when it was mentioned to him by one of Mr Roberts-Smith's lawyers.'

Glancing to my left through the morning, I began to discern what I thought was distress in the demeanour of the man who had launched this case. If so, perhaps by late morning it had become too much. Ben Roberts-Smith rose to his feet and walked out of the court. His parents followed, his father soon after returning alone. And at 12.02 pm Ben was back, as was his mother. I might have been mistaken, but to me it looked like they had been weeping.

With his back to these movements, Owens proceeded uninterrupted. He argued that the lie had not originated in court, but well before—indeed, at the point when Roberts-Smith met with The Scout at the East Hotel in Canberra in October 2018, and came to recognise a need to neutralise an opponent.

At 12.43 pm, everyone took a break. Owens was the one on his feet, but all of us felt the mental fatigue. The atmosphere must have been thick in the other camp's interview room too, down the hall directly outside Courtroom 21A.

Upon return, there was a little more on Chinartu. While I might have been deficient with some of my note-taking, Owens was more generous on this occasion. He contended that my notes got the timing right. The execution had occurred after the PUC count was transmitted, as evidenced by the radio log. This, of course, created a problem for the record-keeping, given that one from that number had just been shot.

Owens dealt with the criticism that we had not called The Lieutenant. His response was that The Lieutenant could have equally been called by the other side. 'He is a witness who, in relation to the incident at Chinartu, we say was part of the conduit between the order given by Mr Roberts-Smith and the execution of the PUC by one of the men under his command.' There was no basis, according to Owens, for an expectation that The Lieutenant would be in our camp.

The Fasil allegation of the murder of an adolescent male on 5 November 2012 was another where we needed to make our strongest case. Again, our only witness was a single soldier, and this time it was not a shooting observed firsthand. The Medic had told the court it was days later that Ben Roberts-Smith had boasted to him about having 'shot the cunt in the head'.

Again, we sought support for The Medic's evidence in documentary records and radio logs. There was no argument that a Hilux vehicle containing bomb-making equipment had been interdicted and four occupants detained. And there was no issue that three of them had returned to Tarin Kowt; but Nicholas Owens SC queried the fate of the fourth, the adolescent.

We had pored over material subpoenaed from Defence and found photos of three men detained on that day. Markings on tape on the back of their clothing identified them as GB1, GB3 and GB4. GB referred to the call sign 'Gothic Bravo'. There was no argument that the men came from the Hilux. But Mitchell's search for the missing GB2 had ended in a question rather than an answer.

Owens: 'So we say the overwhelming inference is that no photograph was taken of the adolescent, GB2, and the question is: why?' Roberts-Smith's explanation was either the adolescent had been released or GB2 was someone else. The latter proposition made no sense. GB2 was removed from the Hilux. And the release of a PUC, particularly after weapons were found, was contrary to standard practice. Mitchell could find no other examples of this having occurred.

Owens: 'So, after excluding those two possibilities, it seems to us that really it is only [possible that] he was murdered, or some inexplicable mistake was made.'

As Owens observed, there was no challenge to the honesty of The Medic, but more to the reliability of his memory. The fact that Fasil was the last mission of Rotation XVIII was one good reason it would be remembered. The Hilux interdiction was also vivid in the mind of The Medic, who had seen a teenager 'shaking like a leaf'.

The Medic had exhibited sensitivity when describing the horrors he observed. But this, according to our senior counsel, did not make him unreliable. 'He was, it is my submission, a witness who had a unique level of insight into the effect that his experiences in Afghanistan had on him and his mental health.'

The memory of the later encounter with Roberts-Smith was equally intense. As Owens argued, how would you easily forget someone saying 'I pulled out my 9-mill, shot the cunt in the side of the head, blew his brains out, and it was the most beautiful thing I've ever seen'?

Roberts-Smith's barristers had ridiculed this as a 'lurid' account that painted their client as an 'ostentatious psychopath'. But they had not explained away the allegation in terms other than it being the product of a false memory. As Owens pointed out, a more credible explanation might have been that it was a joke—that Roberts-Smith was 'trying to wind The Medic up'. But nothing of the kind was asserted. Instead, absolute denial.

In written submissions, we had accepted not being able to make out the case of another murder and blooding at Syachow by The Ring-In. It was lost, we recognised, as a result of the legal ruling that The Ring-In was not required to give evidence. Nicholas Owens SC explained, though, that this allegation was not formally withdrawn, in the absence of 'a reasoned decision rejecting our case'. And we in turn rejected the proposition that there was never a basis for bringing the claim, in that we did have a strong idea of the evidence The Ring-In would have given.

Moving on to the mock execution at Lancelin, Owens proposed a strong case, with The Trooper, The Sergeant and The Mechanic corroborating one another's accounts, and The Mentor providing further support. Owens highlighted The Mechanic's evidence as honest and candid.

The episode also addressed a challenge made against our case: that the applicant had no motive to murder detainees. Lancelin alone shot holes through this, unmasking Roberts-Smith's adherence to an informal code that called for the elimination of any suspected enemy combatants found in Afghanistan's badlands.

At 4.15 pm, His Honour adjourned. For over 100 days, the 68-year-old Justice Anthony Besanko had remained fully attentive. I never once saw him flag, nor give anything away.

CHAPTER 96

ZERO DAMAGES

Thursday, 21 July, and it is still raining. I can feel my wet socks as I take my seat. Nicholas Owens SC rises at 10.16 am. The matter that kicked this whole saga off—the Koran Ghar mission that led to the bullying of The Redhead—is next.

The young soldier, who had joined the Army in 2000 as a reservist, had subsequently risen, despite adversity, through the SASR to the rank of sergeant. Owens described him as 'one of the most impressive witnesses to be called on the case on either side'.

In contrast, The Redhead's arch nemesis was described as 'a witness who lacks credit'. The 2006 Koran Ghar mission itself was a prime example. Ben Roberts-Smith had given 'multiple versions of that engagement, which are now conceded to be, at a minimum, wrong'.

Two of Roberts-Smith's comrades at Koran Ghar, originally listed as witnesses, were not called. The UK patrol commander (Person 33) and the American radio operator (Person 23) were not able to explain why a false report was sent from the observation post, nor could they corroborate Roberts-Smith's assertions of The Redhead as a failure.

Owens stated that we had never characterised the killing of the young man at Koran Ghar as a war crime. It was more that 'going loud' had compromised the fundamental objective of a covert intelligence-gathering operation.

Roberts-Smith's repeated lies about the action that garnered him a Medal for Gallantry, and the fact The Redhead knew the official record was false, were, according to Owens, 'why Mr Roberts-Smith developed what we would describe as an enduring obsession with The Redhead. And it provides an explanation for what we say was a relentless escalation in the bullying of The Redhead after the Koran Ghar mission.'

The novice trooper's deficiencies on the mission were candidly acknowledged by The Redhead himself. And subsequent performance reviews demonstrated his growth as a soldier. However, Roberts-Smith had carried on undermining The Redhead's career with 'spiteful vindictiveness'.

The next subject was more bullying, this time of The Trooper. Roberts-Smith's contention was that he had no reason to deflect blame for the bungled mission at Chora in 2012, because he had no responsibility for the blue-on-blue. Owens thought otherwise. He said that laying the blame at the feet of The Trooper meant the incident was not investigated. Had there been an inquiry, it 'had the potential to reflect poorly on Mr Roberts-Smith, because he was the lead planner for the blocking phase of the mission'.

The Person 17 allegation of domestic violence was probably our most difficult to sustain. Ben Roberts-Smith's companion on 28 March 2018 had fallen on steps, bruising her face. She alleged he had later struck her, which was difficult to prove, given the intractable fact that there was no witness other than Roberts-Smith himself. And Roberts-Smith forcefully denied that he would ever hit a woman.

Owens noted that two further witnesses, Neil Mooney and Jed Wheeler, poised to support his separation claim, had not been called.

Owens then went to conduct that further reduced Roberts-Smith's credit. He had concealed and destroyed evidence. He had threatened witnesses—every sign of a man aware of his guilt. There were also those constant flurries of good mates catching up, welfare checks and the like at the time of the IGADF interviews.

Owens: 'The timing, the sequence and what is known about the content of the conversations, we say, points inexorably to a conclusion that what was being discussed was the content of the key missions that were at the time understood to be the subject of the Inspector-General's inquiry.'

Court adjourned for the lunch break.

In the afternoon session, Nicholas Owens SC identified spikes in data usage on burner phones at key stages as the war crimes inquiry unfolded. He pointed to the intimidation of Ben Roberts-Smith's professed enemy, The Veteran, whose home was raided by police after media reporting of alleged gun smuggling.

Roberts-Smith's denials of orchestrating the campaign did not sit comfortably with the evidence of the private inquiry agent John McLeod, who sent the emails that initiated the coverage and the raid. Nor that of his former wife, Emma Roberts, who recalled Ben telling her, 'What happened to The Veteran will scare the others.'

Owens: 'Can I just pause to note this? Of course, Mr Roberts-Smith has trenchantly criticised contact with media by many of our witnesses, but those criticisms, we say, should be viewed with deep scepticism, given his anonymous campaign waged through the media against The Veteran. His criticisms, we say, are driven by self-interest, not principle.'

Another letter, this time sent by Roberts-Smith under his own name to the commanding officer of the SASR in mid-2018, complained of my approaches to members who were allegedly leaking. Owens said Roberts-Smith, unhappy with the response, then penned the threatening letters, two of which notoriously arrived in the postbox of The SSE.

Again, persuasive evidence had been given by John McLeod and Emma Roberts about a red-handed Ben Roberts-Smith. His own evidence to the court attempted to reverse-spin a story that this paperwork, some of it in his own handwriting, was not evidence of blackmail, but an innocent attempt to obtain home addresses so some suspected individuals could be placed under surveillance. Owens, 'with respect', described the explanation as bizarre and implausible.

Owens, with his tall-timber sway, always engaged and eloquent, rarely referring to notes, had been at this all week. He must have been exhausted. In the late afternoon, Lyndelle Barnett took over to address damages—that is, financial compensation.

She argued that, all through the trial and before, Ben Roberts-Smith's litter of false evidence meant 'there would be no injustice in awarding zero damages'.

His Honour, in a brief exchange, noted the expressions 'nominal damages' and 'no damages' in our written submissions, querying whether we saw a difference. Barnett replied: 'No, Your Honour. Historically, courts would award nominal damages as a sign, in a sense, of contempt—that the plaintiff didn't deserve any more. In some cases, it is referred to as the smallest currency in the realm.'[1]

Was this a portent? Probably not.

CHAPTER 97

A NONSENSE CASE

Closed court consumes most of the morning of the last day of the second-last week of the trial. For me, Nicholas Owens SC's summation has been steady and unremitting. Waves of logic crashing on arguments of sand. When he rises, Arthur Moses SC is more flamboyant. He is generous with zinger quotes for the attendant media—and he is in rescue mode.

His client, Ben Roberts-Smith, has appeared increasingly worried. Constantly at Ben's side, father Len Roberts-Smith, a Queen's Counsel and judge in his own right, would have a good handle on prospects.

'How often have I said to you that, when you've eliminated the impossible, whatever remains, however improbable, must be the truth.' Arthur Moses began his address with a quote from the fictional detective Sherlock Holmes, proposing fiction as our stock in trade. 'The respondents refer to themselves in many ways, such as investigative journalists, but they are not war crimes investigators. They want the court to accept a fanciful and salacious case theory based on conjecture, speculation and imprecise testimony.'

There was an impossible contradiction, Moses proposed, between the true-life distinguished citizen war hero and the mirror-cracked media image of a rancorous psychopath. 'The case, with all due respect, is a nonsense and, quite frankly, embarrassing. It is more like a Walter Mitty production than an attempt to mimic Sherlock Holmes.'

According to Moses, the respondents' case theory had been 'chopped and changed'. Originally, The Lieutenant was said to be present at the alleged Darwan execution, and so too the interpreter. Neither was called and the allegation was reconstructed, proposing that The Sniper was the killer and The Gunsmith a witness. The 'shifting sands' accusations demonstrated the journalists' inadequacy: 'They are not police. They don't have access to all the evidence. They don't have the powers of law enforcement, nor do they have access to all Defence Force material to present a case such as this. Yet that's what they walked into court and boldly sought to do on Day 1 of this matter.'

Moses cited Roberts-Smith's assault on The Trooper as proof of a glaring contradiction. How could a man, angry at one of his soldiers for almost killing a woman and child, be guilty of wanton breaches of the rules of engagement: 'Seriously, that's the proposition.'

And to Tizak, where he saved lives and earned the Commonwealth's highest gallantry award: 'The case evolves from him allegedly trying to cover up murder in 2009 . . . and then in 2012, after receiving the Victoria Cross, he is involved in four murders, not conducted in a clandestine fashion, but out in the open, and apparently, in one instance, bragging about it to a man he barely knew. Seriously? To use the words of one of the respondents, of course that's extraordinary. If something sounds too good to be true, then it usually is not true.'

Through the day, Moses used the word 'seriously' seven times, an adverb reloaded as a noun and projected with scorn. The murder accusation was not proved. According to Moses: 'What they have proven is why responsible journalists and media outlets should never say that someone is a murderer who has not been charged, let alone convicted . . . I mean, what did they think they were doing?'

The respondents had proposed the mock execution training allegation as proof of motive. Moses, 'with respect', said this 'confused issues of intent' and was plainly ridiculous. There was plenty of evidence to show

Roberts-Smith returned suspected enemy combatants alive, and plenty of testimony that he was never observed breaching the rules of engagement. The alleged murder of Ali Jan Faqir, because he smiled twice at Roberts-Smith, did not gel with an allegation that he was driven by a compulsion to eliminate suspected Taliban.

While previously characterising the third respondent—meaning me—as 'credulous', Moses now called me 'esteemed' and 'serious' when he cited my notes as proof of the dishonesty of The Sergeant and The Scout. Both witnesses had denied some draft text that we contended may have been incorrectly recorded or embellished.

The Sergeant was singled out as a liar and a hater: 'He did not sit there for any noble reason . . . he is a-gossiping around the place about Mr Roberts-Smith, and he would make Mrs Mangel from *Neighbours* blush, in respect of his amount of gossiping concerning Mr Roberts-Smith.'

The Gunner was also in his crosshairs: 'That man is a liar. He has given inconsistent versions about what occurred at Whiskey 108 . . . that witness subscribed to the unjudicial dictum of "It's not a lie if you believe it", with apologies to George Costanza from *Seinfeld*.'

Arthur Moses SC was giving his all, and so too were those behind him. Throughout the day, a scurry of lawyers were reaching for lever-arch files and identifying transcript references. Justice Besanko was engaged. Head down, taking notes. Watching on, from up the back, I had previously wondered how they would deal with our five-card trump: the compelling correlation at Darwan, of two Australian soldiers and three Afghan witnesses telling the same story.

Moses soon provided an answer. He was far from convinced, arguing that to call this consistency was 'a rather generous reading of their evidence'. And the Afghans' third-party contact with the middleman who arranged their interviews meant their evidence could not be regarded as 'uncontaminated': 'Now, Your Honour should also note these witnesses are hardly neutral. They describe Australian soldiers as infidels. I mean, they're not neutral.'

The notion that an SAS culture of silence explained why nothing was complained of or reported until many years later was also dismissed.

Arthur Moses said only one witness, The Cyclist, used this as an excuse: 'There is not one jot of evidence that anybody reported any allegations of criminality of the kind now levelled at Mr Roberts-Smith in alleged murders in 2009 and 2012.' Moses wondered how this could be reconciled when witnesses such as The Veteran, whom he accused of hating Roberts-Smith, could not wait to 'throw him under the bus'.

The luncheon adjournment was called at 12.44 pm.

When we resumed at 2.15 pm, I was taken back to my interview with Ben Roberts-Smith in April 2017. At that time, I was urged by Roberts-Smith to prefer the official records—that is, contemporaneous reporting from the battlefield—rather than warped revisionism from sullen opponents.

Arthur Moses picked up the baton. '[W]hen documents don't suit the case theory of the respondents,' he said, 'they apparently contend that Your Honour should not pay any regards to them because they are fabricated, without explaining how that could possibly be so and who was in on the fabrication.'

In ascertaining the truth through a fog of rumour so many years on, Moses reached for a case from my personal archive. The Street Royal Commission was precipitated by the 1983 *Four Corners* report 'Big League', which investigated alleged collusion in committal proceedings against a former New South Wales Rugby League boss Kevin Humphreys. In his judgment, Justice Laurence Street, while noting the presumed credibility of witnesses such as stipendiary magistrates, had cautioned against the reliability of memory.

Arthur Moses proffered some quotes from Street's findings, including the following: 'In the intervening five or six years, rumours waxed and waned . . . The sheer frailty of human memory of necessity required a most anxious and critical appraisal of the evidence of the witnesses, no matter how credit-worthy they might be.'

Much of the afternoon was devoted to the tall order confronting Arthur Moses' opponents. Roberts-Smith was owed a presumption of innocence. The case was not about money, but vindication. The grave charge of murder was not only levelled at his client but at other witnesses, such as The Gunsmith and The Sniper.

The last topic for the day was Whiskey 108. Moses emphasised the imprecision of a range of memories: 'Different witnesses gave different versions of events in relation to how many people came out of the tunnel, who discovered it, who the detainees were handed to.'

He went to The Cyclist's evidence of Roberts-Smith borrowing his suppressor, to minimise the sound of an execution, but then: 'Minutes later Mr Roberts-Smith, according to the respondents' case, elected to use the loudest weapon that was available to the troop on the mission to execute the man with the prosthetic leg.'

And then the people who occupied the same ten-by-fifteen-metre courtyard, which became 'a hive of activity', did not see two Afghans executed. He listed witnesses from both sides: Ben Roberts-Smith, The Scot, The Freefaller, The Hunter, The Bodyguard, The 2IC, The Reader or The Captain.

Moses further noted that the body of the old man was not *seen* in the courtyard by Roberts-Smith, The Scot, The Freefaller, The Hunter, The Bodyguard or The Captain.

The courtroom clock nudged 4.15 pm but, as it happened, we weren't quite finished.

His Honour had a question: 'You've mentioned The Bodyguard now twice in the course of your submissions, and he's mentioned, I think, five or six times in your written submissions. You haven't addressed his evidence about clearing the orchard.'

Moses: 'Yes, of course, I will be coming to that. Yes, thank you, Your Honour.'

Ben Roberts-Smith's lead counsel, Arthur Moses SC, impassioned and committed through a taxing five hours on his feet, might not have been pleased with the way the day ended. The media offered their assessment of the day's play; *The Australian* chose the headline 'Roberts-Smith's barrister tears strips off Nine'. Its reporter, Perry Duffin, wrote that Nine, Nick McKenzie and I had been depicted as 'pseudo war crimes investigators'. We were 'less like the forensic Sherlock Holmes and more like the daydreaming Walter Mitty'.[1]

Nonetheless, that last question by Justice Anthony Besanko hinted that Team BRS needed something more than rhetorical flourish.

CHAPTER 98
LOOKING TRUTH IN THE EYE

Monday, 25 July 2022. Day 108. I am limping, feeling my age, having fallen on steps at home. This has been a long haul and we are nearly there. I am surprised to see Ben Roberts-Smith is not present. His parents settle, leaving vacant their son's usual seat.

—

When the hearing resumed at 10.15 am, Arthur Moses SC responded to His Honour's question about The Bodyguard's orchard clearance evidence with a concession. Nicholas Owens SC's *Browne v. Dunn* challenge won the day. The 2IC and The Cyclist, placed by The Bodyguard outside the compound rather than at the scene of the alleged crime, had not been questioned about the last-gasp alleged orchard clearance.

Moses: 'That evidence, Your Honour, for reasons of fairness in relation to the witnesses of the respondents, will not be relied upon by the applicant.'

But Roberts-Smith's senior counsel was quick to return serve. He swung the spotlight to the allegedly irreconcilable accounts of The Cyclist and The SSE at Whiskey 108. The SSE heard a burst of gunfire at a time when The Cyclist overheard a single suppressed gunshot.

Moses returned to the site of the tunnel, where The 2IC, The Driver, The Reader and The SSE saw no execution, pointing out to the Adelaide-based judge that 'it was busier than the Rundle Street Mall on a Saturday afternoon, but nobody saw this, nobody heard it'—apart from The Cyclist.

Moses was not accusing The Cyclist of lying, but rather querying why he would say nothing for eleven years, until his IGADF interview. And not, it seemed, at his first interview, in 2019, but at the second, in 2020. He implied that the slow reveal might have been influenced by stress and the reading of media reports.

Arthur Moses identified further discrepancies in the accounts of The 2IC and The Reader of how the call-out occurred and the manner in which the Afghans were removed. He accused our side of 'cherry-picking' details that suited our case theory, and regarded them as not good enough to meet the court's Briginshaw standard, requiring serious scrutiny of serious allegations.

Moses noted that The Cyclist gave no evidence about searching, handcuffing and blindfolding the PUCs; nor was this listed in contemporaneous records.

The alleged borrowing of The Cyclist's suppressor was not revealed until 2020. Moses considered this 'peculiar' and 'improbable'. The Scot proposed it would have been just as easy to retrieve it from The Gunsmith's pack. The Freefaller also had doubts.

Moses: 'And I just stop there to make this observation about The Freefaller. He was a most impressive witness, this man. A distinguished soldier who came here and gave his evidence politely, in a considered fashion, had allegations of a heinous nature put to him, which had to be withdrawn, in respect of his conduct. But this is, on any view, an experienced Australian soldier, a man of the highest level of training.'

Arthur Moses recounted The Freefaller's view that it was the operator's responsibility to access a suppressor, because if it was needed, 'you would have to be able to put it on yourself'.

The reason why the Whiskey 108 allegations of executions generated rumour but were never reported was because they 'didn't happen',

Moses said. The fact that members would drink from a dead man's leg further indicated that the story was false.

And back to The Bodyguard. While his evidence about the orchard clearance would not be relied upon, Arthur Moses argued he was nevertheless a witness of credit. 'We say [we] rely on his evidence in respect of other issues, such as blooding the rookie and whether the tunnel was discovered before the tunnel was declared secure, and we say he was an impressive witness.' Addressing His Honour's question about The Bodyguard's 'other evidence', 'we respectfully submit, Your Honour, it has no effect'. Moses referenced case law advising against any adverse inference.

Then the high-calibre assault on our case. The Gunsmith was another powerful witness for the respondents; but for the Darwan allegation, rather than Whiskey 108, where he was allegedly blooded. Yet, as Moses pointed out, 'this court is asked to make a finding that The Gunsmith is a murderer, but that was never put to him, and he was never given an opportunity to deal with that issue'. Moses said that, as with other witnesses, he could have been questioned and 'he could simply have objected on the grounds of section 128 [privilege in respect of self-incrimination]'.

Moses: 'It is pretty clear that the reason why the respondents steered away from putting this critical allegation against The Gunsmith in their examination in chief is because they wanted to keep him onside as part of the deal they brokered with him about what topics he would not give evidence about.' According to Moses, the respondents should not be allowed to 'go soft' on Whiskey 108, so as to achieve the findings sought regarding the alleged cliff kick.

Another key witness to alleged executions, The Scout, was dismissed as an outright liar and perjurer—'not about contact with journalists but about making an allegation that a colleague of his committed murder'. The lies, according to Moses, were swallowed 'hook, line and sinker' by Nick McKenzie and me.

The witness standing nearby at Whiskey 108 who corroborated The Scout's account was given similar treatment. The Gunner, 'another star witness for the respondents, is also a liar and a perjurer'. The 'exhibition execution', as alleged by The Gunner, had 'more holes in it than Swiss cheese'. While Moses contended that The Cyclist's account of the same murder was down to a contaminated memory, The Scout's and The Gunner's testimonies resulted from fraudulent collusion.

Arthur Moses awarded the last word on Whiskey 108 to The Captain, who had observed nothing that gave him cause for suspicion.

The mock execution prior to Rotation XVIII was next, decried as another fraud. Moses believed it was introduced for the sake of 'building a motive against Mr Roberts-Smith for the alleged murders that are pleaded in relation to Rotation XVIII'. 'Ridiculous' and 'hopeless' was the proposition that a newly minted VC would instruct junior members to break the law.

Nine/Fairfax produced four witnesses to the scenario training episode. Arthur Moses attacked two of them. The Trooper, who was allegedly given the instruction, 'had an axe to grind against Mr Roberts-Smith because of his ultimate removal from the regiment'.

The Sergeant, who said he observed and later admonished Roberts-Smith, according to Moses had two reasons to lie. The first was his 'obsession' about the Victoria Cross, and the second an eagerness to 'throw mud'.

A witness called by the applicant to contest the account was The Dog Handler. He had not given evidence because of his location abroad; the proposed videolink testimony could not meet closed court requirements. But at this point the evidence of The Mechanic and The Mentor, also present at the scenario training, was not challenged.

To Darwan again, in greater detail. Arthur Moses SC reminded His Honour that our original allegation, now withdrawn, had The Lieutenant involved in the alleged execution of Ali Jan Faqir. And then our revised account 'landed on The Sniper'.

The applicant's team had also been busy studying photographs and maps, and poring over records. A significant feature in the media reporting had been a prominent geographical feature—the cliff.

Moses: 'With all due respect, Your Honour, there is no cliff. It's more like a sandy knoll. I mean, there are bigger knolls here in Sydney or Henley Beach in Adelaide.'

Moses reprised his argument that our position on motive was paradoxical. We said Roberts-Smith wanted to rid the battlefield of Taliban, yet this man, Ali Jan, was killed for laughing, twice.

Moses: 'That is, of course, highly improbable, that an experienced Australian soldier, trained in tactical questioning and dealing with individuals, would lose his control and kick someone because they laughed at him.'

Doubt was cast on whether the Icom radio found with Ali Jan was the one recovered from the shooting at the river. The Gunsmith had noticed its screen was fogged, presumably after contact with water. But, as Moses pointed out, that Icom had been taken away by the troop sergeant.

The presence of the interpreter in the final compound, up until half an hour before the helicopter extraction, was disputed.

Moses: 'The relevance of the interpreter being in the southernmost compound is that our friends need that finding to be made in order to corroborate the evidence of the Afghan witnesses.'

In a case to be decided on the balance of probabilities, it was no surprise that the words improbable and implausible were liberally sprinkled through Arthur Moses' final submission. He pointed out the demand for the sole interpreter on a busy mission, 'controlling a large number of PUCs', was such that this was simply 'improbable'.

What was also improbable was for Roberts-Smith and others to 'go through an elaborate process to cover up the alleged unlawful killing', and then soon after to tell people about it back at Camp Russell.

Moses also had doubts about disclosure of the cliff kick allegation well after 2 Squadron returned to Australia. There were inconsistencies in accounts by The Gunsmith, The SSE and The Sergeant about when the incident was first revealed; in his estimation, The Sergeant was out by three years, and The SSE by seven years. Moses believed that 'no credible motive can be attributed to [The SSE] for not reporting a matter if it had been disclosed to him'.

At 12.44 pm, everyone broke for lunch.

—

We were back in court at 2.15 pm. Upon return, the iniquity of the deal was revisited. Arthur Moses SC described The Gunsmith as a hero for his actions at Tizak, and 'not a murderer', as we had alleged for his actions at Whiskey 108. The issue regarding Darwan was whether The Gunsmith had been incentivised to give answers favourable to the respondents 'so that he was not asked questions about Whiskey 108'.

The Replacement, our other SAS witness at Darwan, was folded into the same argument. Moses described him as another soldier 'who had served his country with distinction'. And he said this distinguished soldier also felt threatened about being accused of 'the murder of a PUC at Fasil', which was why he answered the subpoena and gave evidence about Darwan.

The Afghan witnesses, who we asserted had corroborated the evidence of The Gunsmith and The Replacement, were hardly 'pristine', Moses asserted. They were not subpoenaed and they were supported—money for food, rent and medical expenses for over a year.

As already submitted, the Afghans' regard for foreigners as infidels counted against their neutrality. And their cooperation had been brokered through a paid middleman. Further, Moses argued that the positive impact they had made was to be discounted because cultural differences, translation difficulties and the less-than-ideal means of communication, via videolink, prevented any nuanced assessment of their testimony.

Arthur Moses continually referenced the Briginshaw standard: the seriousness of the charge calling for the closest scrutiny of evidence. With regard to the demeanour of the Afghan witnesses, Moses had doubts that a remote camera was up to the task of looking truth in the eye.

Arthur Moses also identified glitches in their testimony. He noted that the interpreter for the Australians was accused of waving a pistol around—but interpreters were not allowed to have weapons. He noted that the witness, Shahzada Aka, said Roberts-Smith had communicated in Pashto: 'Now, Mr Roberts-Smith has a lot of talents, as we know, but he doesn't speak Pashto.'

Evidence of observable wounds by virtue of supplied photographs was, Moses submitted, not good enough. The respondents' proposition that the imagery indicated Ali Jan had been shot when bound was based on conjecture and not scientific proof.

The allegation of a murder at Chinartu was also rejected. The Scout, according to Arthur Moses, had no credit, and another central witness, The Lieutenant, had not been called.

The allegation of another murder at Syachow should be equally rejected, as The Ring-In had not given evidence and there was no eyewitness.

As for the alleged murder at Fasil, it had no evidentiary support: the theory advanced by the respondents was 'wildly improbable', Moses argued. 'On the one hand, the respondents allege that Mr Roberts-Smith, through his report at the debrief, must have lied, and that the documents were falsified to cover up a murder, and on the other hand, they have him boasting about the murder in florid terms within days to a medic he doesn't know particularly well.'

At the conclusion of Day 108, Arthur Moses SC said the marathon public hearing was nearing an end, although time would be required in closed court to traverse more sensitive detail.

We gathered for a quick debrief. Much of what was asserted about conflicting evidence from our witnesses was not a bother. While Moses saw contradictions, we saw differences, readily explained by the passage of time.

But I was worried about the allegedly heinous deal. Testimony from The Gunsmith and The Replacement was critical to a truthful resolution. But there was no hiding from a nagging concern that Justice Besanko might be persuaded by Arthur Moses' dim view of the arrangement that brought forth their evidence.

CHAPTER 99

IMPROBABILITIES

The morning of Tuesday, 26 July was mostly spent in closed court. No notebooks or recording devices allowed, and evidence that was often more complex and technical. It was also harder to hear up the back. Our lawyers claimed that, at one soporific moment, I had been spotted nodding off; I assured them I was just closing my eyes.

At 12.36 pm, the public hearing resumed. Arthur Moses SC returned to Fasil, having rushed the topic when proceedings were concluding the day before. There was no eyewitness to the alleged murder, he contended, and, as records demonstrated, the adolescent male detainee was not photographed because he had been released.

Moses then dealt with allegations made by The Sergeant of Ben Roberts-Smith assaulting Afghans. This witness was to be regarded as 'discredited because of his obsession with Mr Roberts-Smith and the gossiping about Mr Roberts-Smith because of the Victoria Cross'. Arthur Moses also pointed out that The Sergeant's story was not corroborated by other witnesses.

Further challenges would wait until after the luncheon adjournment.

At 2.15 pm, Arthur Moses resumed. He reaffirmed earlier arguments that The Sergeant's accusation had not appeared in the extensive notes

I had prepared for *No Front Line*. And our proposition that The Sergeant's appearance on the *60 Minutes* program was 'noble and appropriate' attracted little but scorn.

Moses: 'His explanation for going on the program was rubbish.' The senior counsel's silver tongue occasionally had an edge to it, which sometimes triggered a polite reprimand, with Justice Besanko standing guard over the prevailing ethic that counsel should refrain from personal comment.

His Honour: 'You mean it was incorrect.'

Moses: 'Yes, Your Honour, it was incorrect.'

Moses continued, arguing that public commentary by The Sergeant could not have been about confronting a 'cover-up', given that the IGADF inquiry was then well underway. 'It wasn't noble, Your Honour, not at all. It was the antithesis of being noble.'

The 'friendly fire' episode featured next. The argument that Ben Roberts-Smith had scapegoated The Trooper made no sense, in that it was not Roberts-Smith's patrol that had initiated the blue-on-blue. The Trooper's response was as a result of being 'overwhelmed by the situation'. Punching The Trooper was regrettable—but, considering The Trooper might have killed a woman and child, his patrol commander Roberts-Smith was understandably 'mightily upset'.

The indefatigable advocate at this point gave himself a rest and His Honour thanked him. His fellow senior counsel Matthew Richardson rose to deal with Koran Ghar and the bullying of The Redhead.

Richardson began by establishing that the shooting of the young male by Lance Corporal Ben Roberts-Smith and Sergeant Matthew Locke was a legitimate engagement 'furiously agreed by everyone'. The Redhead accepted the Afghan was a likely spotter. The pursuit of him was, Richardson asserted, authorised by the patrol commander. Our case—that the action compromised a mission meant to stay quiet—was something that 'cannot be known'.

While both The Redhead and The Sig believed the Afghan had not seen them, Ben Roberts-Smith gave evidence that 'his sharp turn-off was very deliberate and very noticeable'. The fact that the battle that followed was 'about nine hours later' supported the argument that the patrol was not compromised. And, further, Roberts-Smith 'was in this case following orders'.

Richardson quoted the official patrol report, which went to this pivotal moment, stating that 'a decision was made to pursue and neutralise the threat'. Its author, the British patrol commander designated as Person 33, was well placed to explain all this, but regrettably he did not give evidence. (Nor did the last living member, the American radio operator designated as Person 23.)

Richardson referred to the former patrol commander's non-appearance: 'I just wanted to point out to Your Honour . . . that Person 33 suddenly refused to give evidence after military lawyers in his country became involved.'

So, as with The Trooper and the blue-on-blue in the Chora Valley six years later, there was no reason for Ben Roberts-Smith to deflect blame to anyone. Despite accusations that the Medal for Gallantry awarded to Roberts-Smith was besmirched, 'there is nothing before the court to suggest a material error in the citation or anything that suggests or affects the conduct of and the bravery of my client that it records'.

Richardson moved on to the claimed bullying of The Redhead by Ben Roberts-Smith. The first alleged incident, of being slapped on the back of the head while vehicle training in Australia, was not supported by eyewitnesses or contemporaneous records. Nor was the alleged threat to put a bullet in the back of his head, or the door slamming, spitting and pushing.

Richardson argued that concerns expressed about The Redhead's skill levels and competence, principally from Matt Locke, did not constitute bullying. The Redhead had failed a sniper course. A campaign of bullying suggested 'sustained conduct over a long period', which had not been demonstrated.

Matthew Richardson SC presented his case with little of the flamboyance of his colleague to his left. He was lucid and logical—and at times, for me, unnerving.

The analogue clock on the wall had now wound past 4 pm. Monica Allen had moved back to sit next to Ben Roberts-Smith. They conferred in whispers. Richardson returned to his seat and Arthur Moses SC took over.

Intimidation was again the subject. Moses moved to the allegation that his client was behind the threatening letters intended for The Redhead and The SSE. Ben Roberts-Smith had worked at Campbell Barracks for ten years, so it was improbable he would need to ask his then wife for the postal address.

Moses: 'There is simply no plausible explanation for why Mr Roberts-Smith would write the names and other information of The Redhead and The SSE on scraps of paper and not include the readily attainable PO Box address.'

When the proceedings concluded for the day, I noticed Len and Sue Roberts-Smith, shoulder to shoulder, staring impassively ahead. I sometimes saw them at St James Station as we made our way home. I would have liked to nod a pacifying 'no hard feelings', but I could not reasonably have expected reciprocated goodwill.

The following morning, we were back in court and Arthur Moses SC picked up where he'd left off. The alleged intimidation by Ben Roberts-Smith of The SSE because he knew the truth about Whiskey 108 made no sense, Moses argued, because The SSE acknowledged 'that he did not observe Mr Roberts-Smith breach the rules of engagement'. It followed that there was no cause for alarm when The Scot sighted The SSE when they both attended IGADF interviews.

Sending a letter to The Redhead was equally illogical. Moses proposed that 'favourable' coverage of him in *No Front Line* made it clear The Redhead had spoken with me. (He hadn't.) Roberts-Smith's lawyers had already written to The Redhead to put him on notice—so why a further anonymous letter?

Moses said of John McLeod, who admitted his involvement: 'One cannot, of course, foreclose the possibility that Mr McLeod, who was of course exposed as a fantasist, could off his own bat have sent the letters.'

As to the police raid on the home of The Veteran, Moses said that while his client did give McLeod information about his nemesis fellow soldier, he did not know McLeod would contact a politician and a journalist. In consideration of The Veteran's complaint about the CDS award, Moses contended: 'The only person that has been doing the attacking is The Veteran towards Mr Roberts-Smith.'

Of Roberts-Smith's meeting with The Scout at Canberra's East Hotel in 2018, Arthur Moses believed the respondents got it grievously wrong with a 'tortured construction' of the conversation between the two men. Roberts-Smith was innocently seeking a realistic understanding of what allegations were being made against him. 'On no reasonable view could this be construed as an attempt to suborn a witness,' Moses said.

And there was no evidence that Roberts-Smith had asked his friend The Freefaller to speak to another prospective witness for the respondents, The 2IC. The Freefaller told the court he had spoken to The 2IC 'out of concern for his welfare', and not at the instigation of Ben Roberts-Smith.

Arthur Moses next dealt with 'a narrative of collusion', referring to successive trips his client made that accommodated meetings with supporters. Perth was where Ben Roberts-Smith grew up and where his parents lived, and his wife and children regularly accompanied him when he headed west. When he met with The Hunter in New Zealand it was to attend his 40th birthday party, and again his wife and children came along.

Equally, the visit to the United States that included a catch-up with The Scot was long planned and a family holiday. At that stage, both The Scot and Roberts-Smith had completed their evidence at the IGADF and filed outlines of evidence for the defamation action, so 'there was nothing to collude about'.

Moses further argued there was no collusion between five of his witnesses over the hairy tale of the shot dog and The Lieutenant, who was allegedly punted. For Roberts-Smith, The Hunter, The Corporal, The Scientist and The XO to all have deliberately lied presumed that 'they must have known their recollections were false . . . That proposition, we say, Your Honour, is misconceived and should not be accepted.'

On the fourth day of his closing submissions, Moses appeared wearied, but no less infuriated by the injustice visited on Ben Roberts-Smith VC, MG. A national hero had been brought to his knees by jealousy and cowardice, and by journalists swallowing rumours 'like salmon jumping on a hook'. 'They've urged upon the court a case which is one of mere suspicion, surmise and guesswork,' he argued, 'to condemn a man, who served his nation with great distinction, as a war criminal.'

After further brief submissions from Matthew Richardson SC, the applicant's case closed soon after 11.30 am on Day 110.

Ben Roberts-Smith's legal team could be satisfied they had given the media plenty of good copy. They were buoyant when leaving the court, apparently confident that they had also presented a convincing argument to Justice Anthony Besanko.

CHAPTER 100

MISSING TREASURE

As with the opening addresses, Nicholas Owens SC was allowed a brief reply. It was approaching noon on Wednesday, 27 July 2022, when he weighed in, neither strident in attack nor apologetic in defence. A story like this is reported on the facts and defended on the facts.

For example, we accepted as a fact that men were in the tunnel at Whiskey 108. 'A chain of reasoning' linked proof of murder to another fact: that, at the time these men were killed, they were under the control of Australian forces. There was motive for the murder from 'the fact that The Scot wanted to blood the rookie'.

The pre-deployment training mock execution episode back in Australia went to both intent and motive, in that it provided an explanation for killing unarmed detainees 'regardless of the lawfulness of doing so'.

Regarding Darwan: 'How could the evidence of two SAS witnesses correspond so precisely with the evidence of three Afghan witnesses, when there is no evidence of collusion or contamination between them?'

In the hour and a quarter of Owens' final statement, the word 'lacuna' regularly surfaced. In legal terminology, this refers to a gap where no applicable law applies. In a case to be decided on the balance of probabilities, evidence contained in that missing space might be important. According to Roberts-Smith's lawyers, this, for example, could well apply to the reporters' source notes.

Much had been made of the records of interviews with The Sergeant and The Scout, originally denied to the applicant until Justice Besanko reversed his privilege ruling. What else was out there? It was argued that a further 'treasure trove' of evidence from other witnesses might have fallen into such a gap.

In truth, Owens countered, differences between the written notes and oral testimony of The Scout were minor, and the fact that The Sergeant withheld information about war crimes in earlier interviews was no proof that they did not occur.

Further: 'The overwhelming majority of our witnesses were not sources. The SSE, notably, was never a source; The Redhead, never a source; and the court knows that The Gunner, The 2IC, The Cyclist and The Reader were never sources, because they only came to [the respondents'] attention as part of circumstances connected to the PAP [potentially affected persons] notices. Mr Roberts-Smith has repeatedly pointed out that we didn't have any direct contact with The Gunsmith; he was clearly not a source. The same applies to The Replacement. So the complaint that there is a . . . potential trove of undisclosed source material out there, we say, is not established.'

Next he turned to The Lieutenant, whose alleged absence from the Chinartu mission was originally trumpeted as a winning card for Ben Roberts-Smith. When this was disproved and The Lieutenant was shown to have been present at Chinartu, Team BRS was obliged to climb down—but they disavowed any proposition that five witnesses making the same mistake amounted to conspiracy.

The Roberts-Smith defence adjusted, proposing that the absence of The Lieutenant from our witness list represented another lacuna. What might he have said? Owens pointed out that The Lieutenant was just one of 'a large number of eyewitnesses' at Chinartu. We had already argued that our opponents could equally have subpoenaed him.

Owens: 'The fact that there was a concerted effort to give false evidence that The Lieutenant had been removed from the troop and was not present on 12 October is powerful evidence in itself, we say, that the evidence of The Lieutenant was feared by Mr Roberts-Smith to be seriously adverse to his case.'

Another lacuna 'hinted at' concerned our three Afghan witnesses. According to Owens, the applicant had made 'the suggestion that there was somehow some unexplained gap or vacuum in relation to how my clients had found the Afghan witnesses'. But our senior counsel could see no facts of 'contact of an inappropriate kind by a middleman, third party or collusion between the witnesses or other contamination which might [have harmonised] their accounts with that of The Gunsmith and The Replacement'.

Next he moved to The Bodyguard and his Whiskey 108 'orchard too far' evidence. Counsel for Roberts-Smith, having surrendered this part of The Bodyguard's testimony, maintained their reliance on his other evidence—for example, as to when the tunnel was found and the compound secured. Owens maintained that this evidence could not be 'disentangled' from The Bodyguard's claim that the compound could not be declared secure until the orchard had been cleared.

Owens also addressed the 'hive of activity' argument. Arthur Moses had seen The Cyclist's evidence as unreliable in light of contrary accounts from The SSE, The 2IC, The Driver and The Reader. If the execution alleged by The Cyclist occurred, according to Moses, it would have been witnessed by the others.

Owens reasoned otherwise: 'We say if you take into account the whole of the evidence of The SSE, The 2IC, The Driver and The Reader, in fact there is an entirely coherent picture which is presented with their evidence and The Cyclist's. Namely, a tunnel was found; The Cyclist stepped away; men came out of the tunnel; men were PUC'ed; people dispersed; then The Cyclist stepped out and saw what he said he saw. All of those witnesses' accounts, we say, fit neatly together and there is no incoherence.'

That thorny 'deal'—by which The Gunsmith was allegedly given favourable treatment regarding his alleged execution of a PUC at Whiskey 108 in exchange for dishing the dirt on Ben Roberts-Smith at Darwan—was also covered. Moses had asserted The Gunsmith was denied procedural fairness, 'not having been told that Your Honour is being invited to find that he's a murderer'.

With the help of the team behind him, Owens wheeled back through the transcripts to a series of questions put to The Gunsmith by the applicant about the alleged Whiskey 108 execution. From Moses himself: 'I want to put it to you that Mr Roberts-Smith did not order you to kill an unarmed PUC at Whiskey 108.'

The answer: 'I object, Your Honour, on the grounds of self-incrimination.'

Regarding the alleged SAS 'code of silence', and the proposition that The Cyclist was the only witness compelled to remain tight-lipped, Owens reached further into the transcript files, to the evidence of The Medic, who said: 'There was a code of silence within the regiment as to these things occurring. The fear of retribution. Would have been a career-ending move. I would have been ostracised.'

Our senior counsel concluded with further references to evidence of collusion between Ben Roberts-Smith's witnesses. And as to the proposition that John McLeod might have sent the threatening letters off his own bat: 'That was not put to him, and we say that is comprehensively undermined by the fact that the letter contained details that Mr McLeod could never have himself known. [It contained] only detail that could have been known to Mr Roberts-Smith.'

It was nudging 12.45 pm when Justice Anthony Besanko thanked all parties and announced that he would reserve his judgment. 'Parties will be advised when I'm in a position to hand it down.'

The following evening, the team got together for some good Italian food and wine. It was not a Bacchanalian, Fat Lady's Arms affair. In defamation actions, it is hard to feel you have ever won, and in this case that was certainly so. But it had been a long, stressful and exhausting road that called for respite.

We stumbled into the street afterwards at about 11 pm. I didn't quite say it, but I loved them all. Journalists can feel very lonely when they are sued. A loss means everything to us: self-respect, integrity, employability. Everything is on the line. While there will be no comfort in loss for the lawyers, they do not have the same investment. Well, not usually. But in this case I felt they were every bit as committed.

There would be anxious months ahead. Peter Bartlett thought we had done better than he originally anticipated. Nicholas Owens was mostly confident. On the big ones, Darwan and Whiskey 108, we ran strong. Chinartu and Fasil were more difficult, given our dependence on single witnesses—but for all that, thanks largely to Chris Mitchell, we were in the hunt.

Syachow was already lost, and any reality check would tell us we could not be confident of success with all fourteen imputations. The allegation of assault at the Realm Hotel, well-founded in our view, was always going to be tough to sustain.

Over the years, I have noted with keen interest the coalescing of great teams. You see it in sport. I saw it at *Four Corners*. Complementary talent would come and go. There was some design to it, but mostly it felt like serendipity. This was a great team.

CHAPTER 101
TRUTH WINS

On 25 May 2023, ten months on from the end of the 110-day trial and in hospital for a cataract operation, I saw a message flash on my phone: 'Judgment next Thursday at 2.15 pm.' A nurse was about to take my blood pressure. I told her it was likely elevated.

There was not much sleep through the passing nights. As ever, I was frightened not only for Nick, myself and Nine, but also for my industry and our country. This case had tested truth, character and the nation's courage.

The war crimes saga had had a lonely trajectory: so many people—respected friends among them—had advised that this was all better left alone. But this was not for me. The healthiest relationship a journalist has with the public is one that tests and challenges; the worst and easiest path is to deny and flatter. We should argue, respectfully, when discomforting facts are in play.

From the start, the 'war hero as a war criminal' story resisted fine-tuning. I felt we had never found the frequency that connected to a receptive public. So, on the day of judgement, 1 June, it was heartening to arrive outside the Federal Court, with Nick McKenzie at my side, and see public interest writ large.

The press pack was the biggest we had ever seen. Many of them had fought us—but, for all that, they probably understood that a loss for us was also a loss for them. We learned the court had a record number of viewers watching its video coverage. The public, too, was engaged and invested.

We also learned that Ben Roberts-Smith had ducked the big day. He was holidaying in Bali and had been photographed sunning by a pool. Back in 2021 and 2022, his attendance was regular. His absence now felt cowardly; I wondered whether it signalled a lack of confidence.

As we moved through the massed media, Nick expressed discomfort at being 'papped'. Thinking out loud, I responded: 'Aren't we supposed to be the storytellers rather than the story?'

We moved to Courtroom One, which offered a larger space. Anticipation was like static electricity. The Commonwealth lawyers motioned Nick and me to two empty seats at the rear bar table. Nicholas Owens SC and his team were in front. Owens said he had not been so nervous since the day The Gunsmith appeared to give evidence.

Arthur Moses SC and Matthew Richardson SC were, as usual, to the left of our team, this time looking grim. Bruce McClintock SC, we learned, was unable to attend as he was undergoing surgery.

The bang on the door. The court rises as Justice Anthony Besanko appears. His Honour explains that his 700-page ruling will be summarised. This will be brief. Intakes of breath.

He starts by identifying the reports complained of, and the imputations conveyed, regarding the alleged murders at Whiskey 108, Darwan, Chinartu, Syachow and Fasil. And, further, regarding broken rules of engagement, blooding, assault, bullying and domestic violence.

The first clue it is going our way comes when Justice Besanko outlines our truth defence: 'With respect to the justification of substantial truth, the respondents' Particulars of Truth are very substantial.'

We are on the edge of our seats. He proceeds, wading through a page of legalese, and then: 'The applicant's conduct and actions on the mission to W108 as found means that the respondents have established the substantial truth of imputations two, three, four, five, six and nine.' We have succeeded also with Darwan and Chinartu—truthful reporting of four murders.

Next, the Syachow and Fasil allegations, with which we have not succeeded. His Honour rules that we have not established the Particulars of Truth here. He is also not satisfied that we made our case regarding the domestic violence allegation. 'However, I consider that the respondents have made out the defence of contextual truth.'

So, another win, of sorts. Justice Besanko determines that the gravity of the murder findings has overwhelmed the gravity of these unproven allegations, which have thereby inflicted no further damage to Ben Roberts-Smith's reputation.

Spoken coolly, yet somehow generating more heat, Justice Besanko's final words: 'In light of my conclusions, each proceeding must be dismissed.'

It was an emphatic victory. Hugs. Nine's managing director of publishing, James Chessell, was the first to face the media. The words prepared in the event of a loss were not necessary. He spoke of vindication.

I followed, thanking James and Fairfax for the brave call to publish in 2018, and Nine for backing us all the way. I wanted most of all to recognise the soldiers who stayed the course—to pay tribute to their physical and moral courage in speaking what had been a punishing truth. Detractors wanted to characterise our work as denigrating soldiering. Really, it was the opposite: it was about preserving their integrity.

Nick's words to the press pack took us to the barren fields of Darwan and the heartache for a family brought down by cruelty and indifference. I hope this resonated. He spoke of brave soldiers who had called out inhumanity and, on the other side of the world, fellow citizens enduring pain and suffering that couldn't be ignored.

We did not relish the win. Investigative journalism inflicts its own suffering—and that also should not be ignored. Our mood was equal measures of exhaustion and relief.

Soon after came the customary disappointment at how the matter was spun on social media and in the tabloids. The none-so-blind brigade were back with a central talking point: *Ben has not been found guilty . . . This was a civil defamation trial, not a criminal case . . . The standard applied was balance of probabilities rather than beyond reasonable doubt.*

They were continuing to ignore potent evidence. They were continuing to pretend it was all about heat-of-battle, fog-of-war miscalculations, when for years our reporting and the Brereton findings had made clear this was not so. They were continuing to ignore the fact that the critical testimony came from twenty of Ben Roberts-Smith's fellow soldiers.

The nay-sayers are wrong, just as Ben was wrong. I have come to the view that Roberts-Smith and many of his backers believe that what matters above all else is power. Dominance is their guiding light. Ben thought the omnipotence of his presence, of Stokes' money, of his top-shelf legal team was what counted. In contrast, we saw the guiding light as truth.

The following day, *The Sydney Morning Herald*'s headline said it well: 'Truth Wins'.

CHAPTER 102

LEST WE FORGET

Improbabilities galore. Yes, it was improbable that a Victoria Cross recipient would deploy to Afghanistan and instruct junior soldiers to shoot prisoners. It is hard to understand why he would boast to someone he barely knew about blowing a teenager's brains out. And how can it make sense that an experienced special forces professional would kick someone off a cliff because they laughed, and do so in the open for all to see?

Yes, on the surface, it didn't add up. But investigative journalism—and, for that matter, the machinations of life—is not about what is on the surface.

When Ben Roberts-Smith VC, MG deployed to Afghanistan in 2012, he should have had nothing to prove, but that was not the case. Public regard for the war hero was not matched by private respect. The nickname 'Achilles' identified perceived weaknesses, particularly of character. There was no doubt Roberts-Smith was a brave soldier—but, up close, he was not always considered a good soldier. There was too much evidence of medal-hunting, bullying, scapegoating, ego and entitlement.

When veterans sit together on Anzac Day and make eye contact across the room, they want to see respect, expressed in a simple nod, a knowing look. Soldiers mostly fight for one another. That is the sacred bond, and it can't be confected. They must return from war with their self-worth intact. It is an essential component of the next, often more challenging chapter: getting on with life.

And this is where it went monstrously wrong. Craving identity, Ben Roberts-Smith found the shape of who he wanted to be in the persona of the killing machine. The special forces operative, amped in popular media to superhero veneration, became a poster boy. We could not help ourselves. The seven-foot-tall and bulletproof Anzac avatar assumed the pedestal.

Due diligence was not done, neither on Ben Roberts-Smith nor on the SAS. When he was awarded his Victoria Cross in 2011, too many of the special forces warrior caste, other ranks and officers alike, came to believe their own bullshit. Worse, the cult status the special forces warriors awarded themselves became a barrier to sanction. One of the Army chaplains equated the SASR's default cover-up of misconduct with the Catholic Church's record of concealing child sexual abuse.

In the year following the awarding of the VC to Ben Roberts-Smith, the lie culminated in national disgrace. A harmless dirt farmer was callously murdered—and we offered three cheers.

That part is shameful. The next part is not. There are soldiers in Australia's Special Air Service Regiment who have moral as well as physical courage. While those who spoke endured condemnation from many of their brothers, it is hoped that some glancing consideration might be given to the probability that they saved their regiment. Had these revelations erupted as a scandal that was unforeseen and not self-reported, the SASR would have been lucky to escape disbandment.

Australian soldiers weren't alone in committing war crimes in Afghanistan. An impossible blood trail somehow invited it. Against the clamour to look the other way, Australia sought truth.

While the ADF leadership bears responsibility for catastrophic command failure, it can't be said they did not act. Major General Jeff Sengelman, with the support of Lieutenant General Angus Campbell, initiated the IGADF inquiry. And Major General Paul Brereton, fearless and thorough against imposing odds, upturned the discomforting truths. A maxim impressed on ADF recruits to always 'do the right thing' has itself been tested. As one person blighted by a wearying, obstruction-filled process of reform put it to me, 'Why should it be so difficult?'

And it's strange too that Australia's principal public reckoning on war crimes would occur not at the behest of the government but via civil, privately funded litigation. It should not have happened. In the end, we estimate that this de facto war crimes trial cost the competing parties around $25 million.

And why did it happen? Essentially, because Ben Roberts-Smith sued, and his mentor, Kerry Stokes, had the funds to back him. The war hero cum Seven executive probably felt he had no choice. The allegations against him were too serious to ignore. Yes, it would have been more sensible to keep his powder dry for any criminal trial, but back in 2018, when the statement of claim was filed, he had cause to believe he would win.

Looking back, I would say that when the trial was meant to start, in June 2020, Roberts-Smith was in a stronger position. We had good witnesses, but probably not a solid enough case to overcome our bigger enemy: the burden of proof. But as chance had it, the delays imposed by the Covid-19 pandemic allowed us to strengthen our witness list and evidentiary base.

Most helpful were the PAPs. Access to the IGADF's potentially affected persons notices in December 2020 brought critical evidence to bear, which was probably the difference between winning or losing on the Whiskey 108 allegations.

I make no bones about it—the case was not won on journalism alone. The work of our lawyers in accessing further witnesses and finessing evidence made an aeon of difference.

And here is an important point. Let's say we had been denied those temporal advantages—the additional witnesses, the PAPs, the finessing—and we had lost. The journalism would have been declared not good enough. Yet we were not wrong.

A big reason journalists hate the defamation system is the base prejudice it inflicts. A newsroom has little similarity to a courtroom. The news industry is more about being first and fast rather than thorough and accurate. A source of unease for any journalist approaching a defamation trial is the prospect of being held to unrealistic standards.

There is a pervasive sense that those judging us have little idea of journalism's practical challenges. Of course, we should not have unlimited freedom to defame. But neither can high-pressure, resource-poor news gathering match the judicial standards of extravagant and time-consuming fact-checking.

The soldier's complaint that a decision taken in a split second should not be judged at leisure from afar has resonance. Months of judicial consideration is consistently applied to reporting that might be produced within a 24-hour news cycle.

It should also be acknowledged that the stern eye the judiciary applies to the news industry is also explained by some at times terrible reporting. Some of our competitors' coverage of this very matter is an example. To them I say, isn't the job speaking truth to power rather than the other way around?

Nick McKenzie and I constantly heard the refrain—and throughout the trial picked up on the prejudice—that journalists should stick to covering flower shows. Bruce McClintock SC said we were credulous. Arthur Moses SC said we were unqualified to undertake war crimes investigations. *60 Minutes* was regularly and sanctimoniously disparaged.

The most pernicious form of censorship, self-censorship, is commonplace in journalism. No wonder. Why would you even try something more challenging than the flower show?

So, a big thanks to Nine for backing us. Amazing and encouraging. And, by the way, we did have a war crimes investigator, Chris Mitchell, on our team.

Thanks also to those who turned up to give evidence. It is a brutal process. I have always hated it but, watching on, I gained a new perspective. However cruel and inhuman, it does get us closer to the truth. Many of the witnesses under subpoena exhibited apex credibility. They did not want to speak for us. They did not want to speak against Ben Roberts-Smith. Where else to go but the truth?

One motivation for cooperation, expressed by a few, was distress at the lot they saw visited on their fellows—as some put it, 'the BRS roadkill'.

That critical self-esteem mentioned earlier, which is far more sustaining than any medal, was robbed from those people of conscience who were cajoled into committing acts that ruined their self-worth.

Another alleged motivation—that they ratted on Ben out of medal envy—is far from reflective of multiple conversations. Soldiers have mixed regard for honours and awards; sometimes they even see them as a curse. However, there is substance in the argument that the first concerns raised were not so much about war crimes as the validity of the Victoria Cross.

But ruminations were not driven by envy. It was more about honours being bestowed on the undeserving, which thereby diminishes their overall currency. Work that professional soldiers saw as important—indeed, work that put their lives at risk—became a joke.

This is an awful story. But, like many an awful story, it is also useful, and it allows a reset on all things Anzac. The Ben Roberts-Smith VC, MG saga takes us beyond myth and theory, adding flesh to the bones of a century-old debate about Australian identity.

The occasion when Australians first fought as a nation—25 April 1915—became a foundational, national day. In a series of books that resonated through the decades, historian and Australian War Memorial pioneer Charles Bean characterised the digger as an exceptional fighter from a classless, largely rural society, who felt a deep devotion to his mates.

One hundred years later, as we began to come to terms with the truth in Afghanistan, Bean's embodiment of the Anzac looked a touch upside-down. Our most decorated soldier was an Albert Jacka–like killing machine, but on a mission devoted to restraining violence. Ben Roberts-Smith was a private-school boy, not from the bush but from Perth royalty. And his story should, at the least, remap the book of mates.

Killing defenceless Afghans was not only morally wrong, but also strategically counterproductive. It was peacekeeping's wooden spoon. In a war of choice, where there is no prospect of victory, the metric for success becomes professional conduct. How you play the game.

A story meant to be inspirational became a case study of failure. The hubris, the chest-beating, the rank romanticism that elevated a counterfeit exemplar did nobody, including Ben Roberts-Smith, any favours.

APPENDIX
GONG HUNTING

Does he deserve the medals?

The question was, to a degree, addressed through the court proceedings, but not in a way that required any ruling from the judge. The reporting that led to a defamation writ had taken no position on Ben Roberts-Smith's decorations. The process for determining honours and awards is no exact science. Nor is it territory in which outsiders should presume expertise, and I remain disinclined to do so. More qualified observers will make the call.

When they do, the court records from *Roberts-Smith v. Fairfax Media Publications Pty Limited* will be enlightening.

Roberts-Smith's first award, the Medal for Gallantry, was conferred following the Koran Ghar action of June 2006. In the Australian pantheon of bravery medals, the MG stands third behind the Victoria Cross and the Star of Gallantry.

Roberts-Smith was a member of a six-man patrol on a surveillance mission, tasked with providing intelligence on enemy movements in the Chora Valley, below their overwatch position on Koran Ghar. Three members of that patrol, Ben Roberts-Smith, The Redhead and The Sig, gave evidence at the trial. Two members, the patrol commander, Person 33, and the radio operator, Person 23, were listed as witnesses but did not give evidence. The final patrol member, Sergeant Matt Locke MG, was killed in action in 2007.

The Koran Ghar mission did not feature in Ben Roberts-Smith's statement of claim. The original reporting, while revealing discrepancies and generating controversy, had not contended that a war crime occurred. However, the bullying of The Redhead that flowed from the mission was included in the applicant's list of defamatory imputations.

What remains contentious about the award is the accuracy of the after-action report and supporting citation. As it happens, despite there being no allegation of a war crime, it was this contention that triggered the reporting that sparked the mammoth defamation action. And that emanated from Ben Roberts-Smith's own commentary on Koran Ghar.

In an Australian War Memorial interview, Roberts-Smith claimed that the first shots were fired after 'a couple of blokes just walked up . . . to the front of the OP [observation post] . . . all armed and wearing chest-rigs'. But to *The Australian*'s Brendan Nicholson, he said that a single 'armed insurgent walked to within 30 metres of their position'.

When I initially asked questions about this discrepancy, Roberts-Smith did not provide a direct response. Instead, I received a copy of a letter Roberts-Smith had written to the Australian War Memorial's director, Dr Brendan Nelson, via Roberts-Smith's solicitor, Mark O'Brien. It acknowledged 'inaccuracies' in his AWM interview.

The excuse offered was that:

> . . . at the time of the recording five years had passed since that day. I had conducted four more tours of Afghanistan and the interview itself was more than 2 hours and 40 minutes in duration. Without the benefit of the patrol report to guide me it would appear I have confused my many engagements and identified two insurgents initially locating our observation post as opposed to one. I also note I thought we cleared the insurgent bodies, but that again is not correct as identified in the patrol report.[1]

His correction was also flawed, failing to mention that this one 'insurgent' was unarmed, and the occupants of the observation post did not believe they had been 'located'.

While I accepted the imperfection of memory, it struck me as odd that such key errors could occur in Roberts-Smith's recall of the first major battle of his life, and which had earned him his first major medal. There was disagreement over the details. He claimed bullet strikes had triggered smoke from some kind of device in the insurgent's chest rig. Other soldiers told me they thought this unlikely. Neither The Redhead nor The Sig saw a chest rig or what was variously described as 'smoke' or a 'burn'. Was the smoke/chest-rig story meant to demonstrate the victim was a combatant?

Our argument was not that the shooting constituted a war crime, but that it had exposed and compromised a covert mission. And that The Redhead's and The Sig's knowledge of this had motivated Roberts-Smith to denigrate them in the aftermath.

Ben Roberts-Smith's counsel argued that the shooting and emission of smoke did not impair the mission, as the patrol was not attacked again until many hours later. And the disagreement was in any case irrelevant, as the patrol commander gave an order to 'go' in pursuit of the Afghan spotter.

That patrol commander (Person 33), a member of the British SAS, was expected to give evidence in the trial but ultimately withdrew. It would have helped to hear his account. In his after-action report, Person 33 did not specify that he gave the order, but rather that 'a decision was made' to pursue the Afghan. The Sig believed the pursuit had occurred on the initiative of Sergeant Locke and Lance Corporal Roberts-Smith.

It would also have helped to source the false radio report following the shooting, which stated an 'armed ACM [anti-Coalition militia] with AK variant weapon' was engaged after he was seen 'aggressively patrolling, both hands on weapon, ready to fire'. Ben Roberts-Smith believed this report had been prepared by the patrol commander.

The citation supporting the Medal for Gallantry references the opening encounter in this way:

> In one particular incident the Militia attempted to outflank the observation post. Lance Corporal Roberts-Smith was part of a two-man team tasked to move out of their relatively secure Observation Post in order to locate and neutralise the militia and regain the initiative.

An 'attempt' by 'militia' to 'outflank' the patrol is a poor description of a sole unarmed male twice walking in front of an observation post.

The citation also referred to the later battle, when Ben Roberts-Smith held off the enemy with his sniper rifle:

> Whilst isolated and in his precarious position, he observed a group of sixteen Anti-Coalition Militia advancing across open ground towards the Observation Post. Lance Corporal Roberts-Smith effectively employed his sniper rifle to stop their advance while receiving very accurate small arms fire from another group of Militia to his flank. Through his efforts, Lance Corporal Roberts-Smith maintained the initiative and ensured that his patrol remained secure by holding this position without support for twenty minutes. He was eventually reinforced by his original team member and together they continued to hold off the Militia advance for a further twenty minutes, until offensive air support arrived.

In his evidence in chief, Ben Roberts-Smith adjusted the absence of The Sig to 'roughly ten to twenty minutes'. The Sig had a different account. He believed the time it took to fix his weapon was 'no more than a minute'. While uncertain about the numbers they faced, The Sig thought the figure closer to eight rather than sixteen insurgents. And he did not believe that, at that stage, Roberts-Smith was receiving small-arms fire.

When cross-examined, Ben Roberts-Smith said the nominated period of twenty minutes did not refer specifically to The Sig's stripping the weapon, but the time it took for Roberts-Smith to push out front alone. In his closing address, Roberts-Smith's counsel Matthew Richardson SC summarised: 'It was put to him this was the twenty minutes during which there was a disputed period while The Sig was rectifying his weapon stoppage. But, no, in fact, it happened before that. So, there was no contest about the accuracy of that part of the citation.'

The Sig was not interviewed when the Medal for Gallantry citation was compiled.

The Battle of Tizak, for which Roberts-Smith was decorated with the Victoria Cross, occurred four years later, on 11 June 2010. Again, he was a member of a six-man patrol. Five of the six gave evidence in the defamation trial.

Roberts-Smith was positioned on the left flank with The Gunsmith and The Corporal. His patrol commander, The Scot, was on the right flank with The SSE and the patrol medic (designated Person 8). On The Scot's call, they undertook a full-frontal assault uphill through a fig orchard to overwhelm a heavily defended Taliban position.

Ben Roberts-Smith led the left flank attack, with The Corporal and The Gunsmith on either side. They moved towards the sound of the guns. At 60 to 80 metres out, as fire intensified, they crawled, each man firing to support the staggered forward movement of the others. According to Roberts-Smith in the trial, at twenty metres out, 'fire got to a point where we literally couldn't move forward anymore'. (In the VC citation, this distance is identified as 40 metres.)

He could see a low mudbrick wall above, and the muzzle flashes of 'multiple machine guns and small arms being fired at us'. Roberts-Smith could also see a small mudbrick outhouse with a 'big square window' to his right. It was a position with direct line of sight, and represented a serious threat. He said he yelled to The Gunsmith to cover him as he ran to the building, acknowledging the extreme bravery of his comrade, who stood upright before three angry machine guns to do so.

Once at the building, Roberts-Smith saw 'an insurgent grenadier with an RPG [rocket-propelled grenade] on his shoulder started to protrude the weapon through the window'. He engaged and killed the fighter. From this position, he could see The Gunsmith in the orchard, and The Corporal further out, his face in the dirt, with rounds splashing all around him.

In full view of The Gunsmith, Ben Roberts-Smith pulled the pin from a hand grenade, his comrade again rising to provide cover before the machine guns. The grenade was thrown. There was no explosion.

At this point, The Scot, on the right flank, threw a second grenade, which did detonate. In Roberts-Smith's reckoning, it took out the machine gun on the right—but two machine guns continued to rain fire on The Gunsmith and The Corporal, which is why he had to act.

To protect his comrades, Roberts-Smith ran to the mudbrick wall, engaged the first machine gunner 'and he went down'. Through a gap in the wall, he swung his M14 and killed the second machine gunner. The Gunsmith and The Corporal joined him, and together they crossed the courtyard to assault the main compound, later revealed as a mosque.

The Corporal took the lead, leaning around a corner to shoot at an insurgent. His rifle jammed. He peeled out of the way and Roberts-Smith made entry to engage the same insurgent, who dropped. Then, when Roberts-Smith sighted a second enemy, he swung his rifle but found his magazine was empty. Ben Roberts-Smith said The Gunsmith behind him engaged and killed the man, and 'by doing that, he saved my life'. Once the building was cleared, they were joined by the rest of the patrol.

The Gunsmith's evidence of this action was told to the court nine months later. Like Ben Roberts-Smith, he carried an M14 assault rifle. He remembered the decision to fight forward up the hill and seeing Ben Roberts-Smith beside him. He did not have 'eyes on' The Corporal, but learned later that, under fire, he was 'pinned down and unable to manoeuvre'.

The Gunsmith said he and Roberts-Smith provided mutual support as they fought forward. He said he spotted an insurgent with an RPG and alerted his comrade. And he pointed out the window in the building ahead on the right. Roberts-Smith responded: 'Cover me, I'm going to clear it.'

This was the point where The Gunsmith first stood up and took aim at the machine guns, covering Roberts-Smith as he reached the window. 'One dead enemy,' he recalled Roberts-Smith shouting above the gunfire.

The Gunsmith said that, using hand signals, he gave a target indicator of the location of two machine guns. Roberts-Smith showed him the grenade. 'I yelled at him, "Okay, on the count of three and we will throw it. One, two, three!"' He again stood upright and 'provided sustained accurate fire, as Ben rose to throw the grenade'. They both went to cover, but there was no explosion.

The Gunsmith then heard The Scot calling for target indicators, and also throwing a grenade, which exploded, prompting Roberts-Smith to leap forward. The Gunsmith did the same. By this stage, the fire coming their way was less effective. 'It became apparent that that individual was stunned from the grenade and was firing at . . . the tree line.'

Roberts-Smith attacked both machine gunners, and 'maybe two seconds later' The Gunsmith 'engaged the same individuals to make sure they were down'. Joined by The Corporal, they then approached the open door of the mosque, and The Corporal was first through 'the fatal funnel'. He engaged an insurgent and then peeled away to correct a weapon stoppage. Ben Roberts-Smith 'engaged the same individual and also had a stoppage'.

Being a large target, Roberts-Smith clung to the wall, manoeuvring to draw fire as The Gunsmith took on another insurgent 'with three rounds at point-blank range'. They then fought back and, when they were confident the compound was clear, married up with the rest of the patrol.

In undertaking the clearance, The Gunsmith came to a '100 per cent' belief that one of the machine gunners had been killed by him as he rose to provide cover for Ben Roberts-Smith to throw the grenade.

The Corporal's account was brief by comparison. He described the same uphill struggle under heavy fire. He thought most bullets were coming his and Roberts-Smith's way. He saw Roberts-Smith 'bound up closer to the enemy'. And he saw The Scot, off to the right, 'start readying a grenade'.

After his patrol commander threw the grenade, The Corporal was up and moving, as was Roberts-Smith, with The Gunsmith 'a few seconds behind'. They broke into the open courtyard, which was littered with dead.

They approached the mosque, 'and I was the first man in. And we started clearing into the room. Engaged. Got a stoppage. I peeled out.

The Gunsmith, same thing. Got a stoppage. And then Ben went through and made entry, and we backed him up.' Soon after, these intrepid three were joined by the rest of the patrol.

'I was sick of getting shot at' is how The Scot described his decision to order a full-frontal assault from an estimated '100 yards' out from the enemy positions. He said The SSE was the first to see a 'bad guy with a gun'. The SSE 'dropped' him, 'and that's when the world erupted. They basically knew we were there. There wasn't just one machine gun; there was three. He just lit us up.'

They had no choice but to fight. The six-man patrol inched forward to within 40 metres of the muzzle flashes, the leaves above them shredded by fire. Roberts-Smith, The Gunsmith and The Corporal, on the left, were receiving most attention. The two enemy machine guns on the right focused on those three, while the third machine gun swept towards The Scot, The SSE and Person 8.

The Scot said Roberts-Smith came to him and they decided to bomb the post. The Scot called 'frag out', tossed the grenade and 'one of the machine guns stopped firing, and RS ran to the wall'. The Scot said that within probably five seconds, The Gunsmith and The Corporal ran to join him.

As those three soldiers attacked through the door of the mosque, The Scot and The SSE traversed the side of the building, with Person 8 providing cover. As The Corporal entered the courtyard, he heard firing. 'A couple of them had stoppages. I can't remember who put the final shot in, but when they made entry, there was Taliban trying to protect one overweight guy inside the mosque who was obviously one of the guys we were after. So they were all killed. They came back out, and then I sent back to the rest of the troop—I was like, "Hey, we've got a break in. We're in the mosque."'

The SSE clearly remembered the machine-gun emplacements at the mosque, the enemy's main defensive position at Tizak. After The Scot gave quick battle orders, they moved to the edge of open ground and began the assault, immediately coming under fire.

Halfway across, The Scot, The SSE and Person 8, on the right flank, ceased fire as Roberts-Smith ran across to take cover behind a building, his movement restricting their angle of attack. Return fire was quickly resumed through a gap that opened between Roberts-Smith and The Gunsmith.

The Scot's team then made it to the cover of the right-hand side of the building. The SSE, while firing, could see Roberts-Smith on the left-hand corner of the building and The Gunsmith in open ground. He could not see The Corporal, who was further to the left.

At this stage, The Scot, stood up, pulled his grenade and threw it over the building. It went off. The SSE then moved with The Scot and Person 8; in doing so, he lost sight of Roberts-Smith's team to the left.

The SSE, shoulder to shoulder with The Scot, did not see the last desperate dash of Roberts-Smith, The Gunsmith and The Corporal. At that moment, his team came under fire from a different enemy position. They went to ground, retaliated and crawled to cover, from where he could then see his three comrades on the left 'move towards the doorway of the building'.

Of the six men who participated in this extraordinary feat of arms, three were formally honoured. Ben Roberts-Smith received the highest gallantry award, the Victoria Cross; The Scot received the second-highest award, the Star of Gallantry; and The Gunsmith received the third, the Medal for Gallantry.

The SSE was blunt in his appraisal of the Star of Gallantry award to his patrol commander, telling the court, it 'was written up to be the saviour of the day, and I said to him, "I don't believe it really was, mate. You didn't know where the grenade was going."' But he was equally forthright in his view that a leadership medal to The Scot was warranted: 'He became a legend, basically, as soon as he lined up the team and stepped off. One hundred per cent, absolutely he was deserved of an award.'

The SSE had misgivings as well about Roberts-Smith's actions, citing discussion within the team that 'the pin wasn't pulled correctly' on his grenade, and that 'Ben had entered the building directly behind the machine gun position . . . with a stoppage of his weapon'.

By contrast, The Corporal said in court he had no issues with the Victoria Cross being awarded to Ben Roberts-Smith.

The Gunsmith agreed that Roberts-Smith deserved the VC, and he himself did not deserve it, but noted that 'something as outstanding as what both Ben and myself did was politicised, and they could have, you know, accepted the fact that both of us did as much as each other on that day'.

It is a fair point. Ben Roberts-Smith credited The Gunsmith with twice standing upright to take on the enemy, and, once inside the compound, with saving his life. There is also credit in The Gunsmith's contention that he took out one of the machine gunners. And there is agreement that another machine gun was neutralised by The Scot's grenade.

But for all that, these observations do not invalidate the Victoria Cross citation, which states: 'Corporal Roberts-Smith, with a total disregard for his own safety, stormed the enemy position killing the two remaining machine gunners.'

We will never know the true combat effectiveness of the enemy at the point their position was overrun. And we can never discount the true bravery of all the soldiers who scaled the heights at Tizak.

The heart of the problem of honours and awards from Tizak is not in the battle itself, but in the bureaucratic machinations that followed. Initially, Ben Roberts-Smith was nominated for a Star of Gallantry. The Scot was to receive a different medal, and The Gunsmith nothing. The VC and SG were bumped up back in Australia, and the MG conferred two years later. All of which gave rise to a wellspring of discontent.

The Commendation for Distinguished Service is the third-ranking command and leadership award, after the Distinguished Service Cross and the Distinguished Service Medal. It is the only one of those three awards that is not postnominal (that is, the letters CDS do not follow the recipient's name).

While Roberts-Smith correctly asserts he did not ask for his medals, the CDS was a useful adornment when the retiring junior soldier, with scant leadership credentials, transitioned to a civilian career in senior management.

The CDS was specifically awarded for his 'leadership and courage as a patrol commander in 2012'. When it was announced on Australia Day 2014, that wellspring of discontent could not be contained.

A group of SAS sergeants signed a five-page letter of protest. Its last paragraph read:

> The men that were closest to operations and should have known about this, namely the patrol commanders, troop sergeant and troop commander had no awareness of this citation until the award was announced. We feel that the author of the citation should be made accountable. As SAS soldiers we are responsible for accurate reporting and honesty, in the field and in camp. This citation is a contradiction of those values and is an act of fraud.

Ben Roberts-Smith had been honoured with a CDS for his training and mentorship when his patrol imploded. His patrol was twice reconstituted after two members were removed. And, as we now know, one was assaulted by Roberts-Smith after the bungled Chora Valley blue-on-blue incident.

The peer assessment was scathing. The citation had stated that Roberts-Smith's 'performance in leading five special reconnaissance missions exemplified his professional approach and technical skill'. In response, the protest stated: 'Technical skill? Not one of these patrols had a positive outcome. These five patrols were the only missions that this patrol commander led, the lowest work rate of all the 2 Squadron patrol commanders in a four-month rotation.'

And all this before we learned of the bloodings, the throwdowns and the summary executions.

You don't have to be an insider to see that Ben Roberts-Smith's CDS should be removed, and its citation's author identified and queried. And you can't help noting that, while grumbling about medals is nothing new in the history of armed service, no award conferred on Ben Roberts-Smith has come without controversy.

Were they bestowed on merit alone, or because Ben was seen to be made of the right stuff?

ACKNOWLEDGEMENTS

My journalist mother pushed on me a fundamental principle of our trade: always try to finish what you start. We don't give up, she would say; we push on, and it is the pushing on that defines investigative journalism. When we are allowed persistence and manage to reach further, we enter uncharted territory and begin to probe the edge of originality.

The start of this story now feels lost in time. It is decades past when I first reported defence-related issues, became interested in balancing the concepts of peacekeeping and warfighting, and came to know a great many soldiers. That means this could be a very long chapter—considering there are so many to thank.

And I do owe them plenty. It is not easy for a civilian to write with authority about soldiering. Indeed, there are plenty of soldiers who will tell you it can't be done. While this book is not written from a soldier's perspective, the voices, thoughts, ethics and responsibilities of soldiering are all through the text.

The main reason this won't be such a long chapter is because of an unusual limit to the time-honoured news reporting principle of naming names. Many would not want their name here anyway, and as you have seen via a proliferation of pseudonyms, I am largely disallowed from identifying special forces personnel.

To all the unnamed I am indebted, as are all Australians to that band of brothers who demonstrated supreme moral courage in standing up for the true values of their regiment and the integrity of the Australian soldier. Andrew Hastie is one I can name, a soldier, citizen and now parliamentary representative who continues to put principle and moral intuition first. Another is former SAS Major Pete Winnall, who was punished for pressing on his men the importance of acting within the rules and personal conscience.

It was my firm intention to write this book with Nick McKenzie, and in doing so to honour a significant journalistic alliance. Nick and I worked well together as investigators, but regrettably could not coordinate the writing. We did try. I wish him well with his rival publication.

Michael Bachelard, James Chessell, Gail Hambly, Larina Alick and the indefatigable researchers at the Fairfax library were indispensable allies. And, somewhere above them, the silent heroes who made one of the great calls in the history of the news business. The initial decision to publish was made in the Fairfax offices before the Nine takeover. A course was then set, and unwillingness by Ben Roberts-Smith to settle was one reason it became hard to turn back. On our side, while concerns, commensurate with astronomic costs, mounted in the precincts of Nine management, the network was supportive all the way.

For me, the outcome of the case was a triumph as much, if not more, for the legal team as the journalists.

Nicholas Owens SC and Justice Anthony Besanko had more than a little in common. Both had graduated at the top of their Adelaide Law School classes as Stow scholars. They seemed also to share a courteous, firm and respectful courtroom sensibility. Owens' juniors, Lyndelle Barnett and Chris Mitchell, were more like equal partners: Lyndelle assured when stepping in as Covid sidelined Nic, and Chris with an astonishing command of detail that likely got us over the line on occasions when we might otherwise have failed.

In the solicitors' engine room, Dean Levitan was our nuclear power plant, ably complemented on the bridge by Peter Bartlett. Peter's experience and contacts across the nation were crucial to securing witnesses to our cause. The additional complexities of managing security provisions and liaising with Commonwealth stakeholders could not have been easy, but Jeremy Forbes made it seem so. And Tess McGuire, cheerful and engaging, was a tonic, not only for the journalists and lawyers, but also for the beleaguered, feet-dragging witnesses.

And a special mention to Sandy Dawson SC, who began this trial but was lost to us before the judgment was received. Sandy's work early on, securing access to the potentially affected persons (PAP) notices, may well have been the difference between winning and losing.

I have had plenty of fights with lawyers in my time. But overall we have much in common. The path to truth is testing, and the journey so much more productive when it is shared.

The race to the finish called for a great deal of editorial support. Richard Walsh frightened me into action. Julian Welch and Dannielle Viera, hunched at slips, made many a catch, and Angela Handley maintained a calming umpire's presence through testing times. I am grateful also for Elizabeth Weiss's insight and stewardship. Believe it or not, bringing a book to life can have its own battleground moments of foray, fury, panic, retreat and resolution.

Last of all, my family. I see journalism as a profession and a vocation. Responsibilities generate hardship to loved ones on the indispensable home front. I am grateful to my wife, Tanya, our children, sons-in-law and siblings. Indeed, I offer sheepish thanks to my rugby league–credentialled brother, Roy, who advanced me undeserved credit among the sport-mad Digger Diaspora.

For an investigative journalist, that objective of finishing what we start has dragged on into the realm of grandparenthood. Mindfulness is often cited as an antidote to stress. In the last years, my time has been divided largely between the court, this book and babysitting. There is no better relief than a received hug from Aidan and Callum when I pick them up. Taking Grace to ballet became my week's highlight, on par with jiving to Jackson Browne with her little sister, Astrid.

I want a better world for them.

NOTES

A Rumour of War Crimes

1 Chris Masters, *Uncommon Soldier: Brave, compassionate and tough, the making of Australia's modern diggers*, Allen & Unwin, Sydney, 2012, p. 334.
2 Masters, *Uncommon Soldier*, p. 97.

Chapter 1: 2 June 2006

1 Interview with Chris Masters.
2 The June 2005 killing of three US Navy SEALs, and the survival of the fourth, Marcus Luttrell, is the subject of a 2013 motion picture, *Lone Survivor*.
3 Citation: 'Medal for Gallantry: Lance Corporal Ben Roberts-Smith, Special Air Service Regiment, Australian Army', <www.awm.gov.au/collection/C1270260>, 2006.

Chapter 2: 2 June 2015

1 Interview with Dr Peter Pedersen, Australian War Memorial, Canberra, 22 February 2011.
2 Brendan Nicholson, 'You think I'm brave? Meet my mates: Ben Roberts-Smith', *The Australian*, 23 April 2011.

Chapter 3: Lifting the Tin

1 Blenheim Partners, 'Character is the Foundation', *No Limitations* (podcast), Episode 61, December 2020.
2 Blenheim Partners, 'Character is the Foundation'.
3 Blenheim Partners, 'Character is the Foundation'.

Chapter 4: Achilles

1 Interview with Dr Peter Pedersen, Australian War Memorial, 22 February 2011.
2 Interview with Dr Peter Pedersen, Australian War Memorial, 22 February 2011.
3 Alex Mitchell, 'Soldiers in row over top-brass VC proposal', *The Age*, 26 December 2010.

4 Michael Ware, 'Behind closed doors', *Time*, 21 August 2000.
5 It is also interesting to note a parallel finding of the 3RAR Rough Justice inquiry and the later IGADF Afghanistan inquiry: of command turning a blind eye and failing to probe too deeply.
6 Ben Roberts-Smith, 'Australia Day Address 2015', Conservatorium of Music, Sydney, 23 January 2015.

Chapter 5: The Anzac Avatar

1 Australian obstetrician Dr William McBride became world famous in the 1960s when he discovered a link between thalidomide and birth abnormalities. In the 1980s he was struck from the medical register following findings of scientific fraud. One of his defence lawyers was a young Paul Brereton. There is a further link to this saga via William McBride's son, former Defence lawyer and proclaimed war crimes whistleblower David McBride (see Chapter 36).
2 Ben Roberts-Smith did receive an MBA, graduating from The University of Queensland in December 2016.
3 A book with this name, *Big Boys' Rules: The SAS and the secret struggle against the IRA*, by Mark Urban, was published by Faber & Faber in 1992.
4 Justice Paul Brereton, 'War Crimes in Australian History: From the Boer War to Vietnam', Military History Society of NSW, Anzac Memorial Hyde Park, Sydney, 4 June 2022.
5 Correspondence, Assistant Inspector-General of the Australian Defence Force, Major General P.L.G. Brereton AM, RFD to Inspector-General of the Australian Defence Force, Mr James Gaynor, CSC, 29 October 2020.

Chapter 7: The Rose Garden

1 Ben Roberts-Smith later claimed we spoke for only half an hour.

Chapter 9: Shooting Bambi

1 Email, Chris Masters to Ben Roberts-Smith, 5 July 2017.
2 Correspondence, Mark O'Brien Legal to Robert Gorman, CEO, Allen & Unwin, 11 July 2017.
3 Correspondence, Ben Roberts-Smith to Dr Brendan Nelson, 11 July 2017.
4 Correspondence, Mark O'Brien Legal to The Redhead (Person 1), 18 July 2017.
5 Correspondence, Mark O'Brien Legal to The Sig (Person 2), 19 July 2017.
6 Correspondence, Mark O'Brien Legal to The Sig (Person 2), 31 August 2017.

Chapter 10: Scoop

1 Correspondence (via LinkedIn), Nick McKenzie to Ben Roberts-Smith, 4 July 2017.
2 Correspondence, Mark O'Brien Legal to Nick McKenzie, 5 July 2017.

Chapter 11: Un-Australian

1 Chris Masters, *No Front Line: Australia's special forces at war in Afghanistan*, Allen & Unwin, Sydney, 2017, p. 106.
2 Unsourced letter 'from many loyal Australians' to Trent Dalton and Rory Callinan, November 2017.

3 Email, Rory Callinan to Chris Masters, 22 October 2017.

4 Nick Butterly and Sarah Martin, 'Victoria Cross recipient Ben Roberts-Smith hits out at a new SAS book *No Front Line*', *The West Australian*, 21 October 2017.

5 Amber Schultz, 'Ben Roberts-Smith's reputation fought in the media front line', *Crikey*, 12 November 2019.

6 Chris Masters, 'Should we really hear the truth about our war in Afghanistan?', *The Sydney Morning Herald*, 3 November 2017.

Chapter 13: Battlelines

1 Telephone conversation, Ben Roberts-Smith and The Mentor (Person 31), 28 January 2018.

2 Telephone conversation, Ben Roberts-Smith and The Mentor (Person 31), 28 January 2018.

3 Telephone conversation, Ben Roberts-Smith and The Mentor (Person 31), 28 January 2018.

4 Andrew Burrell, 'Inquiry into SAS "gun smuggling"', *The Australian*, 9 November 2017.

Chapter 18: Perth

1 Shane Wright and Grant Taylor, 'War memorial boss questions SAS book', *The West Australian*, 7 November 2017.

Chapter 21: The Great Hall and the Black Eye

1 Ben Roberts-Smith was chairman of the National Australia Day Council from 2014 to 2017.

Chapter 22: Stay Kind

1 Australian Army (Office of the Chief of Army minute), LTGEN A.J. Campbell, 'Use of Symbols in Army', 17 April 2018.

2 Mark Powell, 'Angus Campbell's Kumbaya Corps', *The Spectator Australia*, 23 April 2018.

3 Shane Wright, 'Not fair on SAS. SAS probe criticised', *The Weekend West*, 9 June 2018.

Chapter 23: The Terp

1 Transcript of ABC interviews, Sayed Jan, 11 December 2017.

2 Email, Nick McKenzie to Ben Roberts-Smith, 28 May 2018.

3 Email, Mark O'Brien Legal to Nick McKenzie, 30 May 2018.

Chapter 25: Leonidas

1 Chief of the Defence Force Order of the Day, Air Chief Marshal M.D. Binskin, 8 June 2018.

2 Shane Wright, 'Not fair on SAS. SAS probe criticised', *The West Australian*, 9 June 2018.

Chapter 26: 'You Weak Dog'

1 Australian Defence Force, media@defence.gov.au, statement, 14 June 2018.

2 Correspondence, Mark O'Brien Legal to IGADF, 28 June 2018.

3 IGADF, 'Reason for ruling of complaint concerning conduct of a lawyer said to be working for the Inspector-General of the Australian Defence Force Afghanistan Inquiry', 15 October 2018.

Chapter 27: Emissaries

1 Ross Coulthart, 'Spies, Lords and Predators', *60 Minutes*, 19 July 2015.
2 Paul Barry, *Media Watch*, ABC TV, 26 February 2018.
3 Cato & Clegg later became Cato & Clive.

Chapter 28: Seven vs Nine

1 Fergus Hunter and Dana McCauley, 'Roberts-Smith fails in move to stop publication of *Age*'s story', *The Age*, 11 August 2018.
2 'VC recipient denies allegations', *The West Australian*, 11 August 2018.

Chapter 29: Secrets, Lies and Newsprint

1 Jamie Walker, 'Nelson blasts "lowest" slur on hero soldier', *The Australian*, 13 August 2018.
2 Andrew Burrell, '"Jealousy" driving attacks on SAS hero: Vietnam War VC', *The Australian*, 15 August 2018.
3 'Lest we forget the SAS's bravery', *The Australian*, 18 August 2018.
4 Phoebe Wearne, 'Defence leaders under fire', *The West Australian*, 13 August 2018.
5 Tim Clarke, 'My reputation is ruined: VC hero', *The West Australian*, 18 August 2018.
6 Email, Tim Worner to Seven Network staff, 14 August 2018.

Chapter 30: History Wars

1 *Bean's Gallipoli: The diaries of Australia's official war correspondent*, Kevin Fewster (ed.), 3rd edn, Allen & Unwin, Sydney, 2007, p. 206.
2 Charles Bean, *The Official History of the War in France 1914–1918*, Volume IV, 1941, Angus & Robertson, p. 772, n. 115.
3 Dr Brendan Nelson, interview with Alan Jones, 2GB, 15 August 2018.
4 Michael Bachelard, 'Historians call out War Memorial chief', *The Age*, 18 August 2018.
5 Bachelard, 'Historians call out War Memorial chief', *The Age*, 18 August 2018.
6 Bachelard, 'Historians call out War Memorial chief', *The Age*, 18 August 2018.
7 Bachelard, 'Historians call out War Memorial chief', *The Age*, 18 August 2018.
8 Dr Brendan Nelson, National Press Club of Australia address, Canberra, 19 September 2018.

Chapter 32: Showdown at the East

1 Sky News, 19 October 2018.
2 Deborah Cornwall, 'Roberts-Smith pursuit "malicious"', *The Australian*, 18 September 2018.

Chapter 33: Killer Angels

1 Rose Cunningham, 'Yarravel', *The Sydney Morning Herald*, 13 August 2018.
2 Frank Pulsford, 'Aspley', *The Australian*, 14 August 2018.

3 Australian War Memorial, *From the Shadows: Australia's Special Forces*, exhibition, 2017.
4 Tom McDermott and Stephen Hart, 'Armouring against atrocity: Developing ethical strength in small military units', in Peter H.J. Olsthoorn (ed.), *Military Ethics and Leadership*, Brill, Boston, 2017, pp. 16–55.

Chapter 34: A Game of Arithmetic

1 Katie Burgess, 'Australian War Memorial named Australia's number one landmark in Tripadvisor awards', *The Canberra Times*, 24 April 2018.
2 Staff reporter, 'From the Archives: 1941 War Memorial opened', *The Sydney Morning Herald*, 11 November 2021.
3 Lane Calcutt, 'Australian War Memorial overhaul gets go-ahead', Channel Nine News, 1 November 2018.
4 Calcutt, 'Australian War Memorial overhaul gets go-ahead', Channel Nine News, 1 November 2018.
5 Bevan Shields, 'Call to speed up Roberts-Smith probe slammed', *The Sydney Morning Herald*, 2 November 2018.
6 Richard Ferguson and Joe Kelly, 'Morrison slams war crimes claims', *The Australian*, 2 November 2018.
7 Paul Maley, 'Inquiry into ADF misses its deadline', *The Australian*, 26 October 2018.

Chapter 35: Protected Identity

1 Deborah Cornwall, 'Accuser of SAS hero "in danger" if named', *The Australian*, 20 November 2018.
2 Tim Clarke, 'War hero will be cleared', *The West Australian*, 24 November 2018.
3 'Suppression for "Person 17"', *The Age*, 25 January 2019.

Chapter 36: The Whistleblower

1 David McBride, Facebook, 16 November 2019.
2 David Wroe, 'What I've done makes sense to me: The complicated, colourful life of David McBride', *The Sydney Morning Herald*, 23 June 2019.
3 Wroe, 'What I've done makes sense to me . . .', *The Sydney Morning Herald*, 23 June 2019.

Chapter 37: Global Warriors

1 Paul Maley, 'March and a quiet beer in store for VC hero', *The Australian*, 24 April 2019.
2 'Gray Areas', Episode 2 of *The Line*, Apple TV, 2021.
3 'Rules of Engagement', Episode 4 of *The Line*, Apple TV, 2021.
4 'Rules of Engagement', Episode 4 of *The Line*, Apple TV, 2021.
5 Richard Spencer would later team up with former Australian ambassador to the United States Joe Hockey, Spencer taking the role of global chairman of the advisory firm Bondi Partners, with Hockey the president.
6 The UK war crimes inquiry was later re-established, modelled after Australia's IGADF inquiry.

Chapter 38: The Phoney War

1 Paul Maley, 'War crimes defamation case: "Witness wasn't there"', *The Australian*, 14 December 2019.

Chapter 39: *60 Minutes*

1 Paul Maley, 'VC hero denies execution claims', *The Australian*, 23 September 2019.

Chapter 40: Exodus

1 Paul Maley, 'Ben Roberts-Smith blasts Nine's "abuse of power"', *The Australian*, 6 October 2019.
2 Paul Maley, 'Fears of delay in war crime inquiry', *The Australian*, 17 September 2019; Lanai Scarr, 'SAS probe goes AWOL', *The West Australian*, 18 September 2019.
3 Paul Maley, 'Battle on the homefront', *The Australian*, 27 September 2019.
4 Maley, 'Battle on the homefront', *The Australian*, 27 September 2019.
5 Maley, 'Battle on the homefront', *The Australian*, 27 September 2019.
6 Carrie McDougall and Michael Bachelard, 'Shining the spotlight: Why we reported that Ben Roberts-Smith was under investigation', *The Sydney Morning Herald*, 27 September 2019.
7 Bianca Hall, 'Roberts-Smith applies to out news sources', *The Sydney Morning Herald*, 11 December 2019.
8 Paul Maley, 'ADF "ignored" VC winner Ben Roberts-Smith's anguish', *The Australian*, 15 November 2019.
9 Sharri Markson, 'War hero's advice: "Don't join the ADF"', *The Daily Telegraph*, 15 November 2019.
10 Paul Maley, 'War crimes defamation case: "Witness wasn't there"', *The Australian*, 14 December 2019.
11 Seven News, press release, 17 December 2019.
12 Paul Maley, 'They're calling me a murderer: War hero Ben Roberts-Smith', *The Australian*, 17 December 2019.
13 Seven News, press release, 17 December 2019.
14 Michael Bachelard, '*The Age* and *The Sydney Morning Herald* respond to Ben Roberts-Smith', *The Age*, 18 December 2019.
15 Bachelard, '*The Age* and *The Sydney Morning Herald* respond . . .', *The Age*, 18 December 2019.

Chapter 41: *Annus Horribilis*

1 Paul Maley, 'AFP grills war hero over killing', *The Australian*, 24 March 2020.

Chapter 42: The Killing Field

1 Mark Willacy, *Rogue Forces: An explosive insiders' account of Australian SAS war crimes in Afghanistan*, Simon & Schuster, Sydney, 2021, p. 59.

Chapter 43: The Lunch Box

1 Paul Maley, 'Open court "essential to war crimes rebuttal", says Ben Roberts-Smith', *The Australian*, 15 May 2020.

2 Maley, 'Open court "essential to war crimes rebuttal" . . .', *The Australian*, 15 May 2020.
3 Adam Cooper, 'Ben Roberts-Smith defamation trial delayed', *The Age*, 9 May 2020.
4 Lachlan Moffet Gray, 'War hero reveals taunts, anxiety and insomnia', *The Australian*, 9 May 2020.

Chapter 44: Entitled Pricks

1 Adam Cooper, 'Soldier involved in seven killings, statements allege', *The Age*, 3 June 2020.
2 Paul Maley, 'War hero accused in Afghan war "murders"', *The Australian*, 3 June 2020.
3 Maley, 'War hero accused in Afghan war "murders"', *The Australian*, 3 June 2020.
4 Paul Maley, 'War allegations are spurious: VC winner', *The Australian*, 6 June 2020.

Chapter 45: D&Ms

1 Karl Marlantes, *What It Is Like to Go to War*, Corvus, London, 2011, p. 247.

Chapter 46: Reverse Ferret

1 Ben Packham, 'Pawns in a deadly game', *The Australian*, 19 September 2020.
2 Packham, 'Pawns in a deadly game', *The Australian*, 19 September 2020.
3 Ben Packham, 'I will shoot you: SAS at war', *The Australian*, 10 October 2020.
4 'Lest we forget the SAS's bravery', *The Australian*, 18 August 2018.
5 'Lest we forget the SAS's bravery', *The Australian*, 18 August 2018.
6 'Lest we forget the SAS's bravery', *The Australian*, 18 August 2018.
7 'Lest we forget the SAS's bravery', *The Australian*, 18 August 2018.

Chapter 47: The PAPs

1 Adam Cooper, 'Ex-soldier's lawyers to fight release of papers', *The Age*, 9 October 2020.
2 'Investigator to test war crime allegations; PM on front foot before Afghanistan inquiry release next week', *The West Australian*, 13 November 2020.

Chapter 48: 'Possibly the Most Disgraceful Episode . . .'

1 Chief of the Defence Force, press conference, 19 November 2020; Inspector-General of the Australian Defence Force, *Afghanistan Inquiry Report*, Commonwealth of Australia, 2020, p. 33.
2 Inspector-General of the Australian Defence Force, *Afghanistan Inquiry Report*, p. 31.
3 'Roberts-Smith puts VC up as collateral in media brawl', *The Australian*, 20 November 2020.
4 Kieran Gair, 'War hero crucified by media', *The Australian*, 22 August 2020.
5 'Investigator to test war crime allegations; PM on front foot before Afghanistan inquiry release next week', *The West Australian*, 13 November 2020.
6 'Investigator to test war crime allegations . . .', *The West Australian*, 13 November 2020.

Chapter 49: Brereton Backlash

1 Nick McKenzie and Chris Masters, 'VC winner cheering in false leg picture', *The Age*, 21 December 2020.
2 Aaron Patrick, 'The defamation trial of the century', *Australian Financial Review*, 29 December 2020.

Chapter 51: Secrets of War

1 Ben Packham, '"Lewd crew" star now to fix SAS culture', *The Australian*, 13 April 2021.

2 'War hero fires back at "slurs": *60 Minutes* "totally false"', *The West Australian*, 15 April 2021.

3 Sophie Elsworth, 'Seven sticks by war hero after TV claim', *The Australian*, 13 April 2021.

Chapter 52: Feeling the Heat

1 Lane Sainty, 'Taliban fears in VC hero lawsuit', *The Australian*, 8 May 2021.

2 Ben Packham, 'Bryce declines VC hero's request', *The Australian*, 29 May 2021. Later, in court, Ben Roberts-Smith's counsel said Dame Quentin Bryce never withdrew her support but rather did not appear for personal reasons.

3 Michaela Whitbourn, 'Ben Roberts-Smith launches proceedings against ex-wife on eve of trial', *The Age*, 3 June 2021.

4 Whitbourn, 'Ben Roberts-Smith launches proceedings against ex-wife . . .', *The Age*, 3 June 2021.

Chapter 53: 'Credulous'

1 Daniel Piotrowski, 'Exclusive: SAS hero Ben Roberts-Smith looks fighting fit during a gruelling training session ahead of a battle to prove he is not a war criminal—as he breaks his silence on "the trial of the century"', *Daily Mail*, 6 June 2021.

2 Max Mason, 'Allegations "destroyed" him, Ben Roberts-Smith's parents say', *Australian Financial Review*, 6 June 2021.

Chapter 54: A Target on My Back

1 Myriam Robin, 'Ben Roberts-Smith's curious jogging route', *Australian Financial Review*, 7 June 2021.

2 Michaela Whitbourn, 'Lawyer, Roberts-Smith "not in a relationship"', *The Age*, 9 June 2021.

3 Kieran Gair, 'War hero romance rumour criticised', *The Australian*, 10 June 2021.

Chapter 60: Protection Racket

1 Anthony Galloway, 'Roberts-Smith wore Crusade badge', *The Age*, 27 July 2021.

2 Stephen Gibbs, report, *Daily Mail*, 8 August, updated 24 August 2021.

3 Matthew Benns and Clare Armstrong, 'SAS soldiers declare war on Brereton', *The Daily Telegraph*, 24 August 2021.

4 *The Ray Hadley Morning Show*, 2GB, 26 August 2021.

5 Nick McKenzie and Chris Masters, 'As Australia's war crimes investigations drag on, misinformation is catching up', *The Age*, 30 August 2021.

6 McKenzie and Masters, 'As Australia's war crimes investigations drag on . . .', *The Age*, 30 August 2021.

7 Andrew Hastie, 'A good day for the SAS', *Herald Sun*, 1 September 2021.

8 David Irvine AO, *Review of Special Operations Command Australian Army*, 15 June 2020, p. 23.

9 Ben Packham, 'SAS survives to fight another day in Dutton call', *The Australian*, 10 September 2021.

10 Audie Moldre, 'Cancel the flag folding ceremony—Restore 2 Squadron SASR', *Wandering Warriors*, 7 September 2021.

Chapter 61: 'I Know What I Saw'

1 'SAS trial hears witness is a liar who drank out of dead man's leg', *The West Australian*, 4 February 2022.

Chapter 63: 'The Most Beautiful Thing'

1 The Australian Army, 'Our values & contract', www.army.gov.au/our-people/our-values-contract>, 2023.

Chapter 75: Not Walking Away

1 Perry Duffin, 'BRS's accuser "left out the cliff kick"', *The Australian*, 19 March 2022.

Chapter 77: 'Terrible for Our Country'

1 Alex Mitchell, 'The battling Liberals who share a Labor exchange', *The Sydney Morning Herald*, 25 June 2006.

Chapter 81: Deal or No Deal

1 Perry Duffin, 'I was told to testify or else: SAS soldier', *The Australian*, 12 April 2022.

Chapter 82: A Witch-hunt

1 The Scot appears to be mistaken by one year. Roberts-Smith did not join the SASR until 2003.

2 There was a misunderstanding on the day of the mission about cardinal points. Upon clarification, the north-west corner was corrected to the north-east corner. The position of north is correctly shown on the diagram we have used on page 2 of the photo section.

3 Jamie McKinnell, 'Ben Roberts-Smith's witness pleads guilty to hindering Commonwealth official', *ABC News*, 6 February 2023.

Chapter 84: Ricochet

1 *Roberts-Smith v. Fairfax Media Publications Pty Limited* (No. 41) [2023] FCA 555.

Chapter 96: Zero Damages

1 This exchange recalls a famous British case that had notable parallels to our current proceedings. The 1964 *Dering v. Uris* libel suit in the United Kingdom was also born of war crimes allegations. Wladislaw Dering, a Polish doctor imprisoned in Auschwitz during World War II, was named as having undertaken medical experiments for the Nazis. The writ came about because there was a reference to him in a small footnote in Leon Uris's novel *Exodus*. Dering won the case, but was awarded damages of one half-penny, the smallest currency in the realm, plus liability for the other side's costs. In truth, this represented a shameful loss. Leon Uris fictionalised the trial in a later novel, *QB VII* (i.e. Queen's Bench, Court 7).

Chapter 97: A Nonsense Case

1 Perry Duffin, 'Roberts-Smith's barrister tears strips off Nine', *The Australian*, 23 July 2022.

Appendix: Gong Hunting

1 Correspondence, Ben Roberts-Smith to Dr Brendan Nelson, 11 July 2017.